Y0-ATD-184

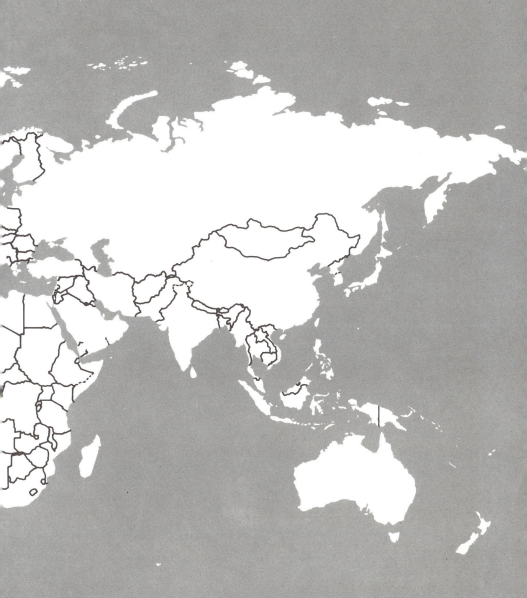

Iran
a country study

Federal Research Division
Library of Congress
Edited by Helen Chapin Metz
Research Completed
December 1987

On the cover: A fifth century B.C. drinking vessel in the shape of a winged lion, from Hamadan

Fourth Edition, 1989; First Printing, 1989.

Library of Congress Cataloging-in-Publication Data

Iran: a Country Study.

    Area handbook series, DA Pam.; 550-68
    Supt. of Docs. No.: D 101.22:550-68/987
    Research completed October 1987.
    Bibliography: p. 309.
    Includes index.
    1. Iran. I. Metz, Helen Chapin, 1928-   . II. Library of Congress. Federal Research Division. III. Series. IV. Series: DA Pam.; 550-68.
DS254.5.I742   1989   955   88-600484

Headquarters, Department of the Army
DA Pam 550-68

For sale by the Superintendent of Documents, U.S. Government Printing Office
Washington, D.C. 20402

Foreword

This volume is one in a continuing series of books now being prepared by the Federal Research Division of the Library of Congress under the Country Studies—Area Handbook Program. The last page of this book lists the other published studies.

Most books in the series deal with a particular foreign country, describing and analyzing its political, economic, social, and national security systems and institutions, and examining the interrelationships of those systems and the ways they are shaped by cultural factors. Each study is written by a multidisciplinary team of social scientists. The authors seek to provide a basic understanding of the observed society, striving for a dynamic rather than a static portrayal. Particular attention is devoted to the people who make up the society, their origins, dominant beliefs and values, their common interests and the issues on which they are divided, the nature and extent of their involvement with national institutions, and their attitudes toward each other and toward their social system and political order.

The books represent the analysis of the authors and should not be construed as an expression of an official United States government position, policy, or decision. The authors have sought to adhere to accepted standards of scholarly objectivity. Corrections, additions, and suggestions for changes from readers will be welcomed for use in future editions.

Louis R. Mortimer
Acting Chief
Federal Research Division
Library of Congress
Washington, D.C. 20540

Acknowledgments

The authors wish to acknowledge the contributions of the writers of the 1978 edition of *Iran: A Country Study,* edited by Richard F. Nyrop. Their work provided general background for the present volume.

The authors are grateful to individuals in various government agencies and private institutions who gave of their time, research materials, and expertise to the production of this book. The authors also wish to thank members of the Federal Research Division staff who contributed directly to the preparation of the manuscript. These people included Thomas Collelo, the substantive reviewer of all the graphic and textual material; Richard F. Nyrop, who reviewed all drafts and served as liaison with the sponsoring agency; Marilyn L. Majeska, who edited chapters; and Martha E. Hopkins, who edited chapters and managed editing and book production.

Also involved in preparing the text were editorial assistants Barbara Edgerton, Nerissa Dixon, Monica Shimmin, and Izella Watson; Vincent Ercolano and Ruth Nieland, who edited chapters; Carolyn Hinton, who performed the prepublication editorial review; and Shirley Kessell of Communicators Connection, who compiled the index.

Graphics were prepared by David P. Cabitto, assisted by Sandra K. Cotugno and Kimberly A. Lord. Harriett R. Blood prepared the physical features map. Carolina Forrester reviewed map drafts, and Greenhorne and O'Mara prepared the final maps. Special thanks are owed to Theresa E. Kamp, who designed the cover artwork and the illustrations on the title page of each chapter. Diann Johnson, of the Library of Congress Composing Unit, prepared the camera-ready copy under the supervision of Peggy Pixley.

The authors would like to thank several individuals who provided research and operational support. Afaf S. McGowan obtained photographs, Rhonda E. Boris assisted in editorial research, and Gwendolyn B. Batts performed word-processing.

Finally, the authors acknowledge the generosity of the many individuals and public and private agencies who allowed their photographs to be used in this study.

Contents

standard of living

List of Figures

Preface

Like its predecessor, this study is an attempt to treat in a concise and objective manner the dominant social, political, economic, and military aspects of contemporary Iranian society. Sources of information included scholarly journals and monographs, official reports of governments and international organizations, foreign and domestic newspapers, and numerous periodicals. Relatively up-to-date statistical data in the economic and social fields were unfortunately unavailable, even from the United Nations and the World Bank. Although the Introduction mentions events as late as June 1989, the cut-off date for research for this volume was December 31, 1987. It should be noted that Houman Sadri wrote the section on the Iran-Iraq War in chapter 5, and that Joseph A. Kechichian wrote the remainder of that chapter. Chapter bibliographies appear at the end of the book; brief comments on some of the more valuable sources suggested as possible further reading appear at the end of each chapter. Measurements are given in the metric system; a conversion table is provided to assist those readers who are unfamiliar with metric measurements (see table 1, Appendix).

The transliteration of Persian words and phrases posed a particular problem, and Dr. Eric Hooglund was most helpful in resolving these difficulties. For words that are of direct Arabic origin—such as Muhammad (the Prophet), Muslim, and Quran—the authors followed a modified version of the system for Arabic adopted by the United States Board on Geographic Names and the Permanent Committee on Geographic Names for British Official Use, known as the BGN/PCGN system. (The modification is a significant one, entailing the deletion of all diacritical marks and hyphens.) The BGN/PCGN system was also used to transliterate Persian words, again without the diacritics. In some instances, however, place-names were so well known by another spelling that to have used the BGN/PCGN system might have caused confusion. For example, the reader will find Basra for the city rather than Al Basrah.

An effort has been made to limit the use of foreign words and phrases. Those deemed essential to an understanding of the society have been briefly defined at the place where they first appear in a chapter or are explained in the Glossary.

Country Profile

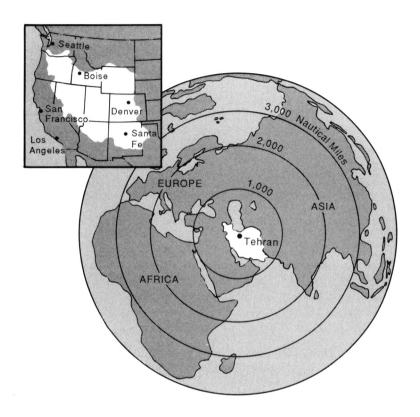

Country

Formal Name: Islamic Republic of Iran.

Short Form: Iran.

Term for Citizens: Iranian.

Capital: Tehran.

Geography

Size: Land area of about 1,648,000 square kilometers; sovereignty claimed over territorial waters up to 12 nautical miles.

Topography: Large Central Plateau surrounded on three sides by rugged mountain ranges. Highest peak Mount Damavand, approximately 5,600 meters; Caspian Sea about 27 meters below sea level.

Society

Population: Preliminary results of October 1986 census listed total population as 48,181,463, including approximately 2.6 million refugees from Afghanistan and Iraq. Population grew at rate of 3.6 percent per annum between 1976 and 1986. Government figures showed 50 percent of population under fifteen years of age in 1986.

Education: School system consists of five years of primary (begun at seven years of age), three years of middle school, and four years of high school education. High school has three cycles: academic, science and mathematics, and vocational technical. Government announced 11.5 million students in above school system in academic year 1986–87; percentage of school age population in school not published. Postrevolution decrease in university enrollments, particularly percentage of women students, which declined from 40 percent in prerevolutionary period to 10 percent in 1984. Number of students abroad also declined.

Health: Iranian Medical Association reported 12,300 doctors in 1986; 38,000 additional doctors needed to provide population with minimally adequate health care. Most medical personnel located in large cities. High infant mortality rate. Gastrointestinal, parasitic, and respiratory diseases other chief causes of mortality.

Languages: Persian official language and native tongue of over half the population. Spoken as a second language by majority of the remainder. Other Indo-European languages, such as Kirmanji (the collective term in Iran for the dialects spoken by Kurds), as well as Turkic languages and Arabic also important.

Religion: Shia Islam official religion with at least 90 percent adherence. Also approximately 8 percent Sunni Muslims and smaller numbers of Bahais, Armenian and Assyrian Christians, Jews, and Zoroastrians.

Economy

Gross Domestic Product: About US$168 billion in 1985, US$165 billion in 1986, and US$176 billion (estimated) in 1987 (figure given at official rate; unofficial rate as much as 10 times higher for United States dollar value of rial). Percentage of GDP growth 1.5 percent (real) in 1985 and 10 percent (estimated) in 1986. Inflation rate estimated at 20 percent in 1985, 30 percent in 1986, and 35 percent in 1987. Figures must be regarded with caution as official sources seriously underestimate rate of inflation and currency depreciation.

Gross National Product: 1986 estimate US$82.4 billion.

Industry: Oil major industry. In 1986 oil production averaged 1.9 million barrels per day; in January 1987 crude oil production averaged 2.2 million barrels per day, of which exports averaged between 1.5 million and 1.7 million barrels per day. Reported reserves of 48.5 billion barrels in 1986 ranked Iran fourth behind Saudi Arabia, Soviet Union, and Kuwait. Damage to Iranian oil installations during 1986–87 reduced oil production and exports substantially. Natural gas reserves claimed by government to be 13.8 trillion cubic meters in 1987. Oil and gas produced estimated 8 percent of GDP in FY 1986–87. Non-oil industry mainly agricultural products, carpets, textiles, and war-related manufacturing such as munitions. Industry employed approximately 31 percent of work force in 1987. Manufacturing and mining produced estimated 23 percent of GDP in FY 1986–87. Services produced estimated 48 percent of GDP in FY 1986–87.

Agriculture: Accounted for estimated 21 percent of GDP in FY 1986–87 and employed approximately 38 percent of work force. Despite regime efforts to promote self-sufficiency, Iran more dependent on agricultural imports in 1987 than in 1970s. Lack of progress resulted from unresolved land reform issues, government policies that did not provide incentives for farmers to invest, and migration to cities.

Imports: In 1983–84 about US$18.1 billion. Principal imports: road vehicles and machines (35 percent), manufactures and iron and steel (29 percent), and food and live animals (13 percent).

Exports: In 1985 about US$13.4 billion, of which all but about US$270 million from oil and gas. Oil exports in FY 1986–87 estimated between US$10.5 billion and US$11.5 billion; about US$900 million non-oil exports.

Major Trade Areas: In 1985 about 16 percent of imports from Federal Republic of Germany (West Germany), 13 percent from Japan, 7 percent from Britain, and 6 percent each from Italy and Turkey. In 1985 about 16 percent of exports to Japan and 9 percent each to Italy and Turkey.

Transportation and Communications

Roads: In 1984 a total of 136,381 kilometers of roads, of which 41 percent paved; of paved roads 16,551 kilometers of main roads and 34,838 kilometers of secondary roads.

Railroads: About 4,700 kilometers of railroads in 1987, including newly electrified track in north between Tabriz and Jolfa for Soviet imports; also rail connection with Turkey.

Pipelines: About 5,900 kilometers for crude oil; 3,900 kilometers for refined products; 3,300 kilometers for natural gas in 1987; some possibly inoperable as result of war damage.

Airports: In 1987 three international airports: Tehran, Abadan, and Esfahan. Other airports being expanded and construction for new ones planned.

Communications: In 1986 about 1.5 million telephones; 3,000 out of 70,000 rural communities had telephones in 1987 compared with 300 in 1979. Further telephone expansion planned. Additional microwave links opened between Tehran, Ankara, and Karachi in early 1980s.

Government and Politics

Government: Islamic Republic under Constitution of 1979, with Ayatollah Sayyid Ruhollah Musavi Khomeini as *faqih* (see Glossary) for life and ultimate decision maker. Executive branch included elected president, responsible for selecting prime minister and cabinet, which must be approved by parliament, or Majlis (see Glossary), elected legislative assembly. Judiciary independent of both executive and Majlis. Council of Guardians, consisting of six religious scholars appointed by *faqih* and six Muslim lawyers approved by Majlis, ensured conformity of legislation with Islamic law.

Politics: Islamic Republican Party, created in 1979, dissolved in 1987 because its factions made it unmanageable. Iran Freedom Movement, a nonreligious political party, existed in 1987 but had been intimidated into silence. Opposition political parties existed in exile abroad: monarchists, democrats, Kurds, Islamic groups, and Marxists. Regime stressed mass political participation through religious institutions, such as mosques, rather than political parties. Factories, schools, and offices had Islamic associations similar to mosque voluntary associations. Fervent religious zeal and support for the Revolution promoted by the Pasdaran (Pasdaran-e Enghelab-e Islami, or Islamic Revolutionary Guard Corps, or Revolutionary Guards).

Administrative Divisions: Country divided into twenty-four provinces (*ostans*), each under a governor general (*ostandar*); provinces subdivided into counties (*shahrestans*), each under a governor (*farmandar*). Most administrative officials appointive and answerable to central Ministry of Interior. In addition, each county had clerical *imam jomeh* chosen from among county senior clergy. *Imam jomeh* served as representative of *faqih.*

Foreign Affairs: Policy of Islamic revolutionary government based on export of Islamic revolution and liberation of Islamic and Third World countries generally. Other major policy was independence from both West and East, especially United States, the "Great Satan," and Soviet Union, the "Lesser Satan." War with Iraq, which began in 1980, had been very costly in men and matériel. War ended with Iran's acceptance of a cease-fire in July 1988.

National Security

Armed Forces: In 1986 army, 305,000; navy, 14,500; air force, 35,000. Two-thirds of army conscripted; majority of navy and air force volunteers. Pasdaran (Revolutionary Guards)—approximately 350,000.

Combat Units and Major Equipment: (Note: because of wartime losses, equipment estimates were highly tentative.) Army had three mechanized divisions, each with three brigades—each of which in turn had three armored and six mechanized battalions, seven infantry divisions, one airborne brigade, one Special Forces division composed of four brigades, one Air Support Command, some independent armored brigades including infantry and "coastal force," twelve surface-to-air missile (SAM) battalions with improved Hawk missiles, reserve Qods battalion of ex-servicemen, about 1,000 tanks, and about 320 combat helicopters. Navy had fifteen combat vessels and thirty naval aircraft in 1986; by late 1987 only some small patrol craft and a few Hovercraft believed operable; three marine battalions; naval air had about thirty aircraft, mainly helicopters. Air force consisted of eight fighter and fighter-bomber squadrons, one reconnaissance squadron, two joint tanker-transport squadrons, five light transport squadrons, and five SAM squadrons; about ninety operational aircraft in 1986. Pasdaran had possibly eight divisions loosely organized in eleven regional commands and numerous independent brigades.

Paramilitary: Basij "Popular Mobilization Army" volunteers— strength varied; in 1986 said to be 3 million.

Military Budget: (figures varied and unreliable) In 1985–86 military budget estimated at US$14.1 billion; total war-related expenses by 1987 estimated at US$100 billion.

Police and Internal Security Agencies: In 1986 Gendarmerie about 70,000, including border guard; National Police, approximately 200,000; SAVAMA secret police, number unknown.

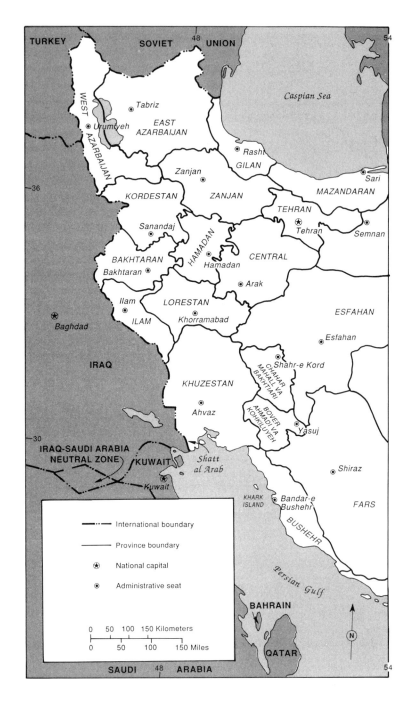

Figure 1. Administrative Divisions

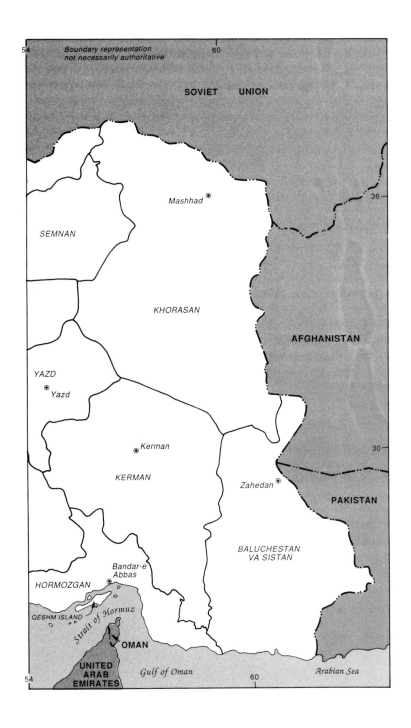

Introduction

DURING IRAN'S LONG HISTORY, the country has evolved its own great Persian civilization, in addition to forming a part of a number of world empires. Iran has created sophisticated institutions, many of which still influenced its Islamic regime in the 1980s. Despite the turmoil surrounding the establishment of its revolutionary government, Iran's development has shown continuity. Major trends affecting Iran throughout much of its history have been a tradition of monarchical government, represented in the twentieth century by Mohammad Reza Shah Pahlavi; the important political role of the Shia (see Glossary) Islamic clergy, seen most recently in Ayatollah Sayyid Ruhollah Musavi Khomeini; and, since the late nineteenth century, pressure for Westernization or modernization.

Iran has been distinguished for having regimes that not only conquered neighboring areas but also devised ingenious institutions. The Achaemenids (550–330 B.C.)—who ruled the first Iranian world empire, which stretched from the Aegean coast of Asia Minor to Afghanistan, as well as south to Egypt—created the magnificent structures at Persepolis, the remains of which still exist. The Achaemenids also inaugurated a vast network of roads, a legal code, a coinage system, and a comprehensive administrative system that allowed some local autonomy, and they engaged in wide-ranging commerce. Iran has also influenced its conquerors. Following its conquest of Iran, the Muslim Umayyad Empire (A.D. 661–750) adopted many Iranian institutions, such as Iran's administrative system and coinage. Moreover, Tamerlane (1381–1405), the famous Mongol ruler, made use of Iranian administrators in governing his far-flung territories.

Despite their primarily tribal origin, for most of the country's history the people of Iran have known only monarchical government, often of an absolutist type. For example, the Sassanids who ruled Iran for four centuries, beginning in A.D. 224, revived the Achaemenid term *shahanshah* (king of kings) for their ruler and considered him the "shadow of God on earth." This concept was again revived in the late eighteenth century by the Qajar monarchy, which remained in power until Reza Khan, a military commander, had himself crowned as Reza Shah Pahlavi in 1925. Many considered Reza Shah's son, Mohammad Reza Shah, to be an absolutist ruler in his later days, especially because of his use of the internal security force SAVAK (Sazman-e Ettelaat va Amniyat-e Keshvar) to repress domestic opposition.

After the Muslim conquest, Iran was strongly influenced by Islam and, specifically, the political role exercised by the Shia clergy. Such influence was established under the indigenous dynastic reign of the Safavids (1501–1722). The Safavids belonged to a Sufi religious order and made Shia Islam the official religion of Iran, undertaking a major conversion campaign of Iranian Muslims. The precedent was revived in 1979 in a much more thoroughgoing theocratic fashion by Ayatollah Khomeini.

In contrast to this traditional element in Iranian history has been the pressure toward Westernization that began in the late nineteenth century. Such pressures initially came from Britain, which sought to increase its commercial relations with Iran by promoting modernization of Iran's infrastructure and liberalization of its trade. British prodding had little effect, however, until Iranian domestic reaction to the growing corruption of the Qajar monarchy led to a constitutional revolution in 1905–1906. This revolution resulted in an elected parliament, or Majlis (see Glossary), a cabinet approved by the Majlis, and a constitution guaranteeing certain personal freedoms of citizens. Within less than twenty years, the program of Reza Shah stressed measures designed to reduce the powers of both tribal and religious leaders and to bring about economic development and legal and educational reforms along Western lines. Mohammad Reza Shah, like his father, promoted such Westernization and largely ignored the traditional role in Iranian society of conservative Shia religious leaders (see Shia Islam in Iran, ch. 2).

Mohammad Reza Shah also strengthened the military by considerably expanding its role in internal security matters to counteract the domestic opposition that arose after Mohammad Mossadeq's prime ministership (see Mossadeq and Oil Nationalization, ch. 1). In addition, the shah stressed defense against external enemies because he felt threatened by the Soviet Union, which had occupied Iranian territory during and after World War II. To counter such a threat, the shah sought United States military assistance in the form of advisory personnel and sophisticated weaponry. He also harshly repressed the communist Tudeh Party and other dissident groups such as the Islamic extremist Mojahedin (Mojahedin-e Khalq, or People's Struggle) and Fadayan (Cherikha-ye Fadayan-e Khalq, or People's Guerrillas) organizations.

Meanwhile, the shah promoted Iran's economic development by implementing a series of seven- and five-year economic development plans, of which the first was launched in 1949. The programs emphasized the creation of the necessary infrastructure and the establishment of capital-intensive industry, initially making use of Iran's enormous oil revenues but seeking ultimately to diversify the country's economy by expanding heavy industry. In the 1960s, the shah also paid attention to land reform, but the redistribution of land to peasants was slow, and in many instances the amount of land allocated to individual farmers was inadequate for economically viable agricultural production. Moreover, Iran experienced high inflation as a result of the shah's huge foreign arms purchases and his unduly rapid attempts at industrial development and modernization. Members of the bazaar, or small merchant class, benefited unevenly from the modernization and gained less proportionately than the shah's Westernizing elite (see Urban Society, ch. 2). This lack of benefit from reforms was also true of the inhabitants of most small villages, who remained without electricity, running water, or paved roads (see Oil Revenues and Acceleration of Modernization, 1960–79, ch. 3).

Many factors contributed to the fall of the shah (see The Coming of the Revolution, ch. 1). Observers most often cited such factors as concern over growing Western influences and secularization, the ignoring of the religious leaders, the repression of potential dissidents and of the Tudeh Party, and the failure of the bazaar class to achieve significant benefits from the shah's economic development programs. Following a brief secular provisional government after the shah was overthrown in 1979, clerical forces loyal to Ayatollah Khomeini took control and launched a far-reaching Islamic revolution.

In Khomeini's revolutionary regime, the Ayatollah himself acted as policy guide and ultimate decision maker in his role as the pious jurist, or *faqih* (see Glossary), in accordance with the doctrine of *velayat-e faqih* (see Glossary), under which religious scholars guided the community of believers. Iran, officially renamed the Islamic Republic of Iran, became a theocratic state with the rulers representing God in governing a Muslim people, something not attempted previously even by the twelve Shia Imams (see Glossary).

The Constitution of 1979 designates Khomeini as the *faqih* for life. The Assembly of Experts in 1985 designated Hojjatoleslam Hosain Ali Montazeri as the deputy to Khomeini and thus in line as successor. In 1988 it was not clear, however, whether the country would accept the choice of the experts when Khomeini died.

Other than appointing Khomeini *faqih* for life, the revolutionary Constitution provides for political institutions to implement the legislative aspects of the government. An elected legislative assembly, the Majlis, charged with approving legislation devised by the executive, was dominated by Muslim religious leaders. The Constitution also created the Council of Guardians to ensure that laws passed by the Majlis conformed with Islam. In practice, the Council of Guardians has been conservative about economic legislation, blocking Majlis measures on land reform, for example. To overcome this blocking of legislation, in January 1988 Ayatollah Khomeini created a special council to adjudicate conflicts among the Council of Guardians, the Majlis, and the executive. He said the state could set aside provisions of the Quran temporarily if it were for the good of the Islamic community as a whole.

Other than through legislative instititions, political expression occurred in principle through political parties. However, the dominant political faction, the largely clergy-led Islamic Republican Party established in early 1979, was dissolved in 1987 because it had become unmanageable. Subsequently, only one legally recognized political party, the Iran Freedom Movement (Nehzat-e Azadi-yi Iran), which had been established by former Prime Minister Mehdi Bazargan, operated in Iran. Estimates of the number of persons opposed to the government or in prison varied. Officially, the latter number was given as 9,000, but the antigovernment Mojahedin maintained that 140,000 was a more realistic figure. In 1988 opposition parties existed in exile, primarily in Western Europe, and included ethnic Kurdish movements and the Mojahedin Islamic extremists, as well as Marxists and monarchists (see Opposition Political Parties in Exile, ch. 4). The Mojahedin also had created the Iranian National Army of Liberation, which operated out of northern Iraq against the Khomeini regime.

After the Ayatollah's government came to power, it initially executed or imprisoned many members of the shah's regime, including officers of the various armed services. But, following the outbreak of the war with Iraq in 1980, substantial numbers of military men were released from prison to provide essential leadership on the battlefield or in the air war (see Iranian Resistance and Mobilization, ch. 5). As early as June 1979, a counterforce to the regular military was created in the form of the Pasdaran (Pasdaran-e Enghelab-e Islami, or Islamic Revolutionary Guard Corps, or Revolutionary Guards), an organization charged with safeguarding the Revolution. The Pasdaran became a significant military force in its own right and was overseen by a cabinet-level minister (see Special and Irregular Armed Forces, ch. 5).

By 1988 the eight-year-old war with Iraq had evolved through various stages of strategy and tactics (see The Iran-Iraq War, ch. 5). Because Iran's population was approximately three times that of

Iraq, Iran's military manpower pool was vastly superior. Capitalizing on this advantage, in the early stages of the war Iran engaged extensively in "human-wave" assaults against Iraqi positions, frequently using youths in their early teens. This war strategy proved extremely costly to Iran in terms of human casualties; it was estimated that between 180,000 and 250,000 Iranians had been killed by 1987, and estimated losses of matériel were also large. The hostilities included a tanker war in the Persian Gulf and the mining of the Gulf by Iran, events that led to the involvement of the United States and other Western nations, which sought to protect their shipping and safeguard their strategic, economic, and political interests in the area. Furthermore, a "war of cities" was inaugurated in 1985, with each side bombarding the other's urban centers with missiles. Iran expended considerable effort in developing a domestic arms industry capable of manufacturing or modifying weapons and war matériel obtained from outside sources. Iran's principal arms supplier was China, from which it acquired Silkworm HY-2 surface-to-surface missiles, among other weapons systems. Iran received no missiles from the Soviet Union, which attempted to maintain amicable relations with both sides in the Iran-Iraq War. In addition, in the ground war, which initially had favored Iraq but then turned strongly in Iran's favor, in April 1988 Iraq succeeded in regaining the Faw Peninsula. Iraq thus recovered a significant part of the territory it had lost earlier to Iran.

The war has severely strained Iran's economy by depleting its foreign exchange reserves and causing a balance of payments deficit. It has also redirected manpower that would otherwise have increased the ranks of the unemployed (see The War's Impact on the Economy, ch. 3). By 1987 Iran's overall war costs were calculated at approximately US$350 billion. Moreover, wartime damage to urban centers in western Iran, such as Abadan, Ahvaz, Dezful, and Khorramshahr, caused refugees to flood into Tehran and other cities, further aggravating the housing shortage. The destruction of petroleum producing, processing, and shipping installations on the Persian Gulf had reduced Iran's oil production and its export capability, thereby cutting revenues. Sales of other domestic commodities, such as carpets, agricultural products, and caviar, were unable to compensate for the lost oil revenue, which was further reduced by a world oil glut. Thus, in 1988 the revolutionary regime faced a straitened economic future in which basic structural problems—such as the degree of state involvement in the economy and the successful implementation of agricultural reform—remained to be addressed.

Iran's economic situation has influenced its foreign policy to some extent. Although ideological considerations based on revolutionary principles dominated in the early days of the Revolution, Iran's policies became more pragmatic as the war with Iraq continued. For example, because of its need for weapons and other military matériel, the Khomeini regime was willing to purchase arms from Western nations and even from Israel. Initially, the revolutionary government had made a radical foreign policy change from the pro-Western stance of the shah. The United States, because of its support of the shah, was branded as the "Great Satan" and the Soviet Union as the "Lesser Satan." Both capitalism and socialism were condemned as materialistic systems that sought to dominate the Third World. In practice, however, the United States was the major target, as evidenced most clearly in the seizure of the United States embassy in Tehran and the taking of American diplomats as hostages in November 1979.

Because of the Khomeini regime's desire to export revolution, regional monarchies with Western associations, such as Saudi Arabia, the Gulf states, and Jordan, were regarded with some hostility, particularly after these countries came to the support of Iraq in the Iran-Iraq War (see Relations with Regional Powers, ch. 4). Iran's militant foreign policy in the region was reflected in the August 1, 1987, demonstrations during the Mecca pilgrimage. As a result, over 400 pilgrims were killed (the majority of them Iranian). As a protest against Iranian actions in the Gulf, in late April 1988 Saudi Arabia severed diplomatic relations with Iran. Another instance of Iran's militant policy was its funding and sponsorship of Islamic extremist organizations in Lebanon, particularly Islamic Amal and Hizballah, which contributed to the ongoing civil war in Lebanon.

In 1988 the country with which Iran had the most cordial relationship was Syria. Iran also maintained active economic relations with the Soviet Union, especially with respect to direct trade, joint fisheries, and the transshipment of goods via the Soviet Union to Western Europe.

Iran's future course in the late 1980s hinged upon a number of factors. These included the smoothness with which it would be able to make the transition to Ayatollah Khomeini's successor; the duration, cost, and settlement terms of the war with Iraq; the direction of Iran's foreign policy, in relation both to the superpowers and to the remainder of the world, particularly the countries of the region; and the skill of Iranian technocrats in taking the necessary steps to address the country's economic difficulties.

June 20, 1988

*   *   *

After the manuscript was completed in June 1988, two significant events occurred in July 1988 that contributed to Iran's decision on July 18 to accept the United Nations (UN) proposal of 1987 for a cease-fire to the Iran-Iraq War. On July 3, 1988, the United States Navy shot down in error a civilian Iranian airliner that it believed was planning to attack a United States Navy ship in the Persian Gulf. In a step indicative of moderation, Iran took the downing of Iran Air Flight 655 to the UN, a body to which it had paid little heed since 1981 because Iran felt the UN was supporting the Iraqi position in the Iran-Iraq hostilities. Just prior to the UN debate, President Ronald Reagan announced that the United States, without accepting blame for the accident, was prepared to make an *ex gratia* payment to the victims' relatives.

In the more immediate conduct of the war, on July 13 Iraqi forces advanced on the south central front, capturing Dehloran, thirty kilometers inside Iran. They took about 5,000 prisoners as well as substantial amounts of Iranian military equipment during their three-day occupation of the area. Foreign experts surmised that Iraq sought to strengthen its bargaining position in the event peace negotiations were forthcoming.

On July 18 Iran announced its acceptance of UN Resolution 598 of July 1987, which called for a cease-fire. Khomeini, taking responsibility for accepting this "poisonous chalice," while at the same time recognizing the great sacrifices of the nation, stated that, in view of recent "unspecified events" (presumably Iraq's "war of cities" and its use of chemical warfare, together with the intervention of the "Great Satan") and the advice of Iranian political and military experts, he believed the cease-fire to be in the interest of the Revolution. As of mid-May 1989, although the cease-fire was holding, no significant progress had been made in UN-sponsored Iranian-Iraqi peace negotiations, and Iraq was insisting on sovereignty over the entire Shatt al Arab as a condition for the settlement.

Khomeini had often stated that he would not agree to an end of the war without the overthrow of Iraqi President Saddam Husayn's regime. His reversal of position raised questions concerning the future of the Revolution. There was evidence in the spring of 1989 that factionalism was increasing among revolutionary leaders. The most dramatic example of this was Ayatollah Montazeri's being obliged in late March to resign as successor to Khomeini. Montazeri apparently fell from grace because he had become unduly critical in public of the regime's policies. He had repeatedly criticized the continued execution of numerous individuals on the ground that they were hostile to the Revolution and had questioned whether Iran had actually won the war with Iraq.

The realignments taking place among the top hierarchy were not clear as of mid-May 1989. For example, in early March Khomeini had concurred with the appointment of Hojjatoleslam Abdullah Nouri, a friend of Majlis Speaker Ali Akbar Hashemi-Rafsanjani, as his personal representative to the Pasdaran. This move was thought to be part of Rafsanjani's strategy to diminish the influence of the Pasdaran and to integrate them more closely with the army, because the regime considered the army a more loyal force than the Pasdaran in the postwar period. Even before the war ended, in early 1988, the government had begun following a pragmatic policy, seeking to regain friends for Iran in the world community through such means as reestablishing diplomatic relations with France, Canada, and Britain. Relations with Britain were again severed, however, in late February 1989, as a result of Khomeini's imposition of the death sentence on February 14 on British writer Salman Rushdie for his authorship of *The Satanic Verses*.

Since the end of the war in July 1988 a major issue among the different factions in the government has been the degree of foreign involvement to be permitted in Iran's reconstruction. Despite some dissent in this regard, the government has sought to obtain loans and credits for Iran from various West European sources and from Japan because oil income is not projected to be adequate to meet rebuilding needs, let alone allow for development projects. Preoccupation with reconstruction and the lack of funds had obliged the revolutionary regime to postpone, if not abandon, any measures to export the Revolution. Instead, Iran was seeking a reconciliation with some of the Persian Gulf states and with the Soviet Union. Furthermore, it appeared that in its budgetary allocations for the new Iranian year beginning March 21 and for the proposed new five-year development plan, the regime was increasing its spending on agriculture and water projects and stressing education, health, and social measures, all of which were designed to show Islamic concern for the downtrodden.

A second issue among the various factions concerned the extent to which governmental centralization was appropriate. One faction maintained that more centralized policy direction was needed for the successful implementation of reconstruction programs, and that to achieve this end the presidency needed to be strengthened. Rafsanjani supported this position and was one of more than 100 signatories of a proposal made to Khomeini that one of the ways of strengthening the executive would be to eliminate the office of prime minister. In this connection, a letter was published in the Iranian press on April 16, 1989, and signed by 166 Majlis delegates, asking Khomeini to establish a committee to amend the Constitution in three areas: the *faqih,* the presidency, and the judiciary. Khomeini responded in late April by appointing twenty members to a Commission for the Revision of the Constitution, with the Majlis appointing five additional members. Khomeini set out guidelines for the commission to use in looking at eight areas of the Constitution, including the three requested. Other aspects to be examined included the role of the Discernment Council, appointed to reconcile differences among the Council of Guardians, the Majlis, and the government. By mid-May the commission had met several times.

The press has reported that the deliberations included debate on draft proposals for amending the articles of the Constitution pertaining to qualifications for the post of *faqih* so that lower-ranking clergy could serve on a collective council of *faqihs.* This would permit Rafsanjani and Khamenehi, for example, to serve. Other debate centered around proposed changes in the presidency that would entail the elimination of the post of prime minister or allow the president to appoint the prime minister without Majlis approval, thus making the prime minister responsible to the president. As early as January 1989, Rafsanjani had hinted that he might run for president to succeed Khamenehi when the latter's term ended in August 1989. Although as of mid-May Rafsanjani had not publicly committed himself to running, he had gained the endorsement for this post from revolutionary leaders of all factions. It appeared, therefore, that the revolutionary regime was on the way to some major changes in the executive structure and in its leadership.

May 18, 1989   Helen Chapin Metz

                              *   *   *

As this volume was in press, Ayatollah Khomeini died on June 3, 1989, of a heart attack, following intestinal surgery two weeks earlier. After lengthy deliberations, on June 4 President Khamenehi was named Khomeini's successors as *faqih* by a two-thirds majority of the Assembly of Experts. The future of Iran's government in the light of possible collective leadership and the proposed reforms to the constitution affecting the executive, judicial, and administrative structures remained unclear.

June 5, 1989   Helen Chapin Metz

Chapter 1. Historical Setting

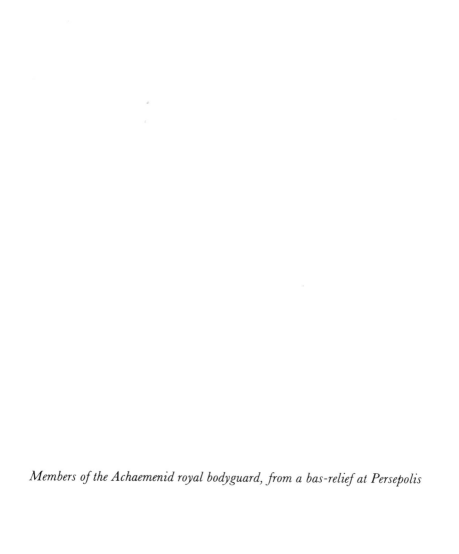

Members of the Achaemenid royal bodyguard, from a bas-relief at Persepolis

THE ISLAMIC REVOLUTION in 1979 brought a sudden end to the rule of the Pahlavi dynasty, which for fifty years had been identified with the attempt to modernize and Westernize Iran. The Revolution replaced the monarchy with an Islamic republic and a secular state with a quasi-theocracy. It brought new elites to power, altered the pattern of Iran's foreign relations, and led to the transfer of substantial wealth from private ownership to state control. There were continuities across the watershed of the Revolution, however; bureaucratic structure and behavior, attitudes toward authority and individual rights, and the arbitrary use of power remained much the same. In 1987, nearly a decade after the Revolution, it was still too early to determine whether the continuities—always striking over the long sweep of Iran's history—or the changes would prove the more permanent.

The Revolution ended a pattern of monarchical rule that, until 1979, had been an almost uninterrupted feature of Iranian government for nearly 500 years. The tradition of monarchy itself is even older. In the sixth century B.C., Iran's first empire, the Achaemenid Empire, was already established. It had an absolute monarch, centralized rule, a highly developed system of administration, aspirations of world rule, and a culture that was uniquely Iranian even as it borrowed, absorbed, and transformed elements from other cultures and civilizations. Although Alexander the Great brought the Achaemenid Empire to an end in 330 B.C., under the Sassanids (A.D. 224–642) Iran once again became the center of an empire and a great civilization.

The impact of the Islamic conquest in the seventh century was profound. It introduced a new religion and a new social and legal system. The Iranian heartland became part of a world empire whose center was not in Iran. Nevertheless, historians have found striking continuities in Iranian social structure, administration, and culture. Iranians contributed significantly to all aspects of Islamic civilization; in many ways they helped shape the new order. By the ninth century, there was a revival of the Persian (Farsi) language and of a literature that was uniquely Iranian but was enriched by Arabic and Islamic influences.

The breakup of the Islamic empire led, in Iran as in other parts of the Islamic world, to the establishment of local dynasties. Iran, like the rest of the Middle East, was affected by the rise to power of the Seljuk Turks and then by the destruction wrought first by

3

the Mongols and then by Timur, also called Tamerlane (Timur the Lame).

With the rise of the Safavids (1501–1732), Iran was reconstituted as a territorial state within borders not very different from those prevailing today. Shia (see Glossary) Islam became the state religion, and monarchy once again became a central institution. Persian became unquestionably the language of administration and high culture. Although historians no longer assert that under the Safavids Iran emerged as a nation-state in the modern sense of the term, nevertheless by the seventeenth century the sense of Iranian identity and Iran as a state within roughly demarcated borders was more pronounced.

The Qajars (1795–1925) attempted to revive the Safavid Empire and in many ways patterned their administration after that of the Safavids. But the Qajars lacked the claims to religious legitimacy available to the Safavids; they failed to establish strong central control; and they faced an external threat from technically, militarily, and economically superior European powers, primarily Russia and Britain. Foreign interference in Iran, Qajar misrule, and new ideas on government led in 1905 to protests and eventually to the Constitutional Revolution (1905–07), which, at least on paper, limited royal absolutism, created in Iran a constitutional monarchy, and recognized the people as a source of legitimacy.

The rise of Reza Shah Pahlavi, who as Reza Khan seized power in 1921 and established a new dynasty in 1925, reflected the failure of the constitutional experiment. His early actions also reflected the aspirations of educated Iranians to create a state that was strong, centralized, free of foreign interference, economically developed, and sharing those characteristics thought to distinguish the more advanced states of Europe from the countries of the East.

This work of modernization and industrialization, expansion of education, and economic development was continued by the second Pahlavi monarch, Mohammad Reza Shah Pahlavi. He made impressive progress in expanding employment and economic and educational opportunities, in building up strong central government and a strong military, in limiting foreign influence, and in giving Iran an influential role in regional affairs.

Such explosions of unrest as occurred during the 1951–53 oil nationalization crisis and the 1963 riots during the Muslim month of Moharram, indicated that there were major unresolved tensions in Iranian society, however. These stemmed from inequities in wealth distribution; the concentration of power in the hands of the crown and bureaucratic, military, and entrepreneurial elites; the demands for political participation by a growing middle class and

members of upwardly mobile lower classes; a belief that Westernization posed a threat to Iran's national and Islamic identity; and
a growing polarization between the religious classes and the state.

These tensions and problems gave rise to the Islamic Revolution. In the late 1980s, they continued to challenge Iran's new rulers.

Ancient Iran

Pre-Achaemenid Iran

Iran's history as a nation of people speaking an Indo-European
language did not begin until the middle of the second millennium
B.C. Before then, Iran was occupied by peoples with a variety of
cultures. There are numerous artifacts attesting to settled agriculture, permanent sun-dried-brick dwellings, and pottery-making
from the sixth millennium B.C. The most advanced area techno-
logically was ancient Susiana, present-day Khuzestan Province (see
fig. 1). By the fourth millennium, the inhabitants of Susiana, the
Elamites, were using semipictographic writing, probably learned
from the highly advanced civilization of Sumer in Mesopotamia
(ancient name for much of the area now known as Iraq), to the west.

Sumerian influence in art, literature, and religion also became
particularly strong when the Elamites were occupied by, or at least
came under the domination of, two Mesopotamian cultures, those
of Akkad and Ur, during the middle of the third millennium. By
2000 B.C. the Elamites had become sufficiently unified to destroy
the city of Ur. Elamite civilization developed rapidly from that
point, and, by the fourteenth century B.C., its art was at its most
impressive.

Immigration of the Medes and the Persians

Small groups of nomadic, horse-riding peoples speaking Indo-
European languages began moving into the Iranian cultural area
from Central Asia near the end of the second millennium B.C.
Population pressures, overgrazing in their home area, and hostile
neighbors may have prompted these migrations. Some of the groups
settled in eastern Iran, but others, those who were to leave significant historical records, pushed farther west toward the Zagros
Mountains.

Three major groups are identifiable—the Scythians, the Medes
(the Amadai or Mada), and the Persians (also known as the Parsua
or Parsa). The Scythians established themselves in the northern
Zagros Mountains and clung to a seminomadic existence in which
raiding was the chief form of economic enterprise. The Medes settled over a huge area, reaching as far as modern Tabriz in the north

and Esfahan in the south. They had their capital at Ecbatana (present-day Hamadan) and annually paid tribute to the Assyrians. The Persians were established in three areas: to the south of Lake Urmia (the traditional name, also cited as Lake Orumiyeh, to which it has reverted after being called Lake Rezaiyeh under the Pahlavis), on the northern border of the kingdom of the Elamites; and in the environs of modern Shiraz, which would be their eventual settling place and to which they would give the name *Parsa* (what is roughly present-day Fars Province).

During the seventh century B.C., the Persians were led by Hakamanish (Achaemenes, in Greek), ancestor of the Achaemenid dynasty. A descendant, Cyrus II (also known as Cyrus the Great or Cyrus the Elder), led the combined forces of the Medes and the Persians to establish the most extensive empire known in the ancient world.

The Achaemenid Empire, 550–330 B.C.

By 546 B.C., Cyrus had defeated Croesus, the Lydian king of fabled wealth, and had secured control of the Aegean coast of Asia Minor, Armenia, and the Greek colonies along the Levant (see fig. 2). Moving east, he took Parthia (land of the Arsacids, not to be confused with Parsa, which was to the southwest), Chorasmis, and Bactria. He besieged and captured Babylon in 539 and released the Jews who had been held captive there, thus earning his immortalization in the Book of Isaiah. When he died in 529, Cyrus's kingdom extended as far east as the Hindu Kush in present-day Afghanistan.

His successors were less successful. Cyrus's unstable son, Cambyses II, conquered Egypt but later committed suicide during a revolt led by a priest, Gaumata, who usurped the throne until overthrown in 522 by a member of a lateral branch of the Achaemenid family, Darius I (also known as Darayarahush or Darius the Great). Darius attacked the Greek mainland, which had supported rebellious Greek colonies under his aegis, but as a result of his defeat at the Battle of Marathon in 490 was forced to retract the limits of the empire to Asia Minor.

The Achaemenids thereafter consolidated areas firmly under their control. It was Cyrus and Darius who, by sound and farsighted administrative planning, brilliant military maneuvering, and a humanistic worldview, established the greatness of the Achaemenids and in less than thirty years raised them from an obscure tribe to a world power.

The quality of the Achaemenids as rulers began to disintegrate, however, after the death of Darius in 486. His son and successor,

Xerxes, was chiefly occupied with suppressing revolts in Egypt and Babylonia. He also attempted to conquer the Greek Peloponnesus, but encouraged by a victory at Thermopylae, he overextended his forces and suffered overwhelming defeats at Salamis and Plataea. By the time his successor, Artaxerxes I, died in 424, the imperial court was beset by factionalism among the lateral family branches, a condition that persisted until the death in 330 of the last of the Achaemenids, Darius III, at the hands of his own subjects.

The Achaemenids were enlightened despots who allowed a certain amount of regional autonomy in the form of the satrapy system. A satrapy was an administrative unit, usually organized on a geographical basis. A satrap (governor) administered the region, a general supervised military recruitment and ensured order, and a state secretary kept official records. The general and the state secretary reported directly to the central government. The twenty satrapies were linked by a 2,500-kilometer highway, the most impressive stretch being the royal road from Susa to Sardis, built by command of Darius. Relays of mounted couriers could reach the most remote areas in fifteen days. Despite the relative local independence afforded by the satrapy system however, royal inspectors, the "eyes and ears of the king," toured the empire and reported on local conditions, and the king maintained a personal bodyguard of 10,000 men, called the Immortals.

The language in greatest use in the empire was Aramaic. Old Persian was the "official language" of the empire but was used only for inscriptions and royal proclamations.

Darius revolutionized the economy by placing it on a silver and gold coinage system. Trade was extensive, and under the Achaemenids there was an efficient infrastructure that facilitated the exchange of commodities among the far reaches of the empire. As a result of this commercial activity, Persian words for typical items of trade became prevalent throughout the Middle East and eventually entered the English language; examples are *bazaar, shawl, sash, turquoise, tiara, orange, lemon, melon, peach, spinach,* and *asparagus.* Trade was one of the empire's main sources of revenue, along with agriculture and tribute. Other accomplishments of Darius's reign included codification of the *data,* a universal legal system upon which much of later Iranian law would be based, and construction of a new capital at Persepolis, where vassal states would offer their yearly tribute at the festival celebrating the spring equinox.

In its art and architecture, Persepolis reflected Darius's perception of himself as the leader of conglomerates of people to whom he had given a new and single identity. The Achaemenid art and architecture found there is at once distinctive and also highly

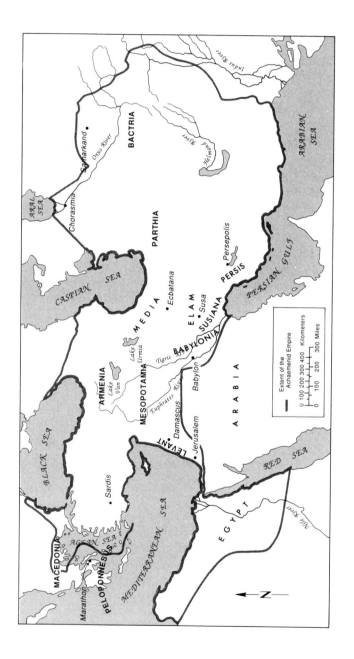

Source: Based on information from *Hammond World Atlas*, Maplewood, New Jersey, 1971; and Herbert Vreeland, *Iran*, New Haven, 1957.

Figure 2. Persian Empire, ca. 500 B.C.

eclectic. The Achaemenids took the art forms and the cultural and religious traditions of many of the ancient Middle Eastern peoples and combined them into a single form. This Achaemenid artistic style is evident in the iconography of Persepolis, which celebrates the king and the office of the monarch.

Alexander the Great, the Seleucids, and the Parthians

Envisioning a new world empire based on a fusion of Greek and Iranian culture and ideals, Alexander the Great of Macedon accelerated the disintegration of the Achaemenid Empire. He was first accepted as leader by the fractious Greeks in 336 B.C. and by 334 had advanced to Asia Minor, an Iranian satrapy. In quick succession he took Egypt, Babylonia, and then, over the course of two years, the heart of the Achaemenid Empire—Susa, Ecbatana, and Persepolis—the last of which he burned. Alexander married Roxana (Roshanak), the daughter of the most powerful of the Bactrian chiefs (Oxyartes, who revolted in present-day Tadzhikistan), and in 324 commanded his officers and 10,000 of his soldiers to marry Iranian women. The mass wedding, held at Susa, was a model of Alexander's desire to consummate the union of the Greek and Iranian peoples. These plans ended in 323 B.C., however, when Alexander was struck with fever and died in Babylon, leaving no heir. His empire was divided among four of his generals. Seleucus, one of these generals, who became ruler of Babylon in 312, gradually reconquered most of Iran. Under Seleucus's son, Antiochus I, many Greeks entered Iran, and Hellenistic motifs in art, architecture, and urban planning became prevalent.

Although the Seleucids faced challenges from the Ptolemies of Egypt and from the growing power of Rome, the main threat came from the province of Fars (Partha to the Greeks). Arsaces (of the seminomadic Parni tribe), whose name was used by all subsequent Parthian kings, revolted against the Seleucid governor in 247 B.C. and established a dynasty, the Arsacids, or Parthians. During the second century, the Parthians were able to extend their rule to Bactria, Babylonia, Susiana, and Media, and, under Mithradates II (123-87 B.C.), Parthian conquests stretched from India to Armenia. After the victories of Mithradates II, the Parthians began to claim descent from both the Greeks and the Achaemenids. They spoke a language similar to that of the Achaemenids, used the Pahlavi script, and established an administrative system based on Achaemenid precedents.

Meanwhile, Ardeshir, son of the priest Papak, who claimed descent from the legendary hero Sasan, had become the Parthian governor in the Achaemenid home province of Persis (Fars). In

A.D. 224 he overthrew the last Parthian king and established the Sassanid dynasty, which was to last 400 years.

The Sassanids, A.D. 224–642

The Sassanids established an empire roughly within the frontiers achieved by the Achaemenids, with the capital at Ctesiphon (see fig. 3). The Sassanids consciously sought to resuscitate Iranian traditions and to obliterate Greek cultural influence. Their rule was characterized by considerable centralization, ambitious urban planning, agricultural development, and technological improvements. Sassanid rulers adopted the title of *shahanshah* (king of kings), as sovereigns over numerous petty rulers, known as *shahrdars.* Historians believe that society was divided into four classes: the priests, warriors, secretaries, and commoners. The royal princes, petty rulers, great landlords, and priests together constituted a privileged stratum, and the social system appears to have been fairly rigid. Sassanid rule and the system of social stratification were reinforced by Zoroastrianism, which became the state religion. The Zoroastrian priesthood became immensely powerful. The head of the priestly class, the *mobadan mobad,* along with the military commander, the *eran spahbod,* and the head of the bureaucracy, were among the great men of the state.

Rome had replaced Greece as Iran's principal Western enemy, and hostilities between the two empires were frequent. Shahpur I (241–72), son and successor of Ardeshir, waged successful campaigns against the Romans and in 260 even took the emperor Valerian prisoner.

Chosroes I (531–79), also known as Anushirvan the Just, is the most celebrated of the Sassanid rulers. He reformed the tax system and reorganized the army and the bureaucracy, tying the army more closely to the central government than to local lords. His reign witnessed the rise of the *dihqans* (literally, village lords), the petty landholding nobility who were the backbone of later Sassanid provincial administration and the tax collection system. Chosroes was a great builder, embellishing his capital, founding new towns, and constructing new buildings. Under his auspices, too, many books were brought from India and translated into Pahlavi. Some of these later found their way into the literature of the Islamic world. The reign of Chosroes II (591–628) was characterized by the wasteful splendor and lavishness of the court.

Toward the end of his reign Chosroes II's power declined. In renewed fighting with the Byzantines, he enjoyed initial successes, captured Damascus, and seized the Holy Cross in Jerusalem. But counterattacks by the Byzantine emperor Heraclius brought enemy forces deep into Sassanid territory.

Years of warfare exhausted both the Byzantines and the Iranians. The later Sassanids were further weakened by economic decline, heavy taxation, religious unrest, rigid social stratification, the increasing power of the provincial landholders, and a rapid turnover of rulers. These factors facilitated the Arab invasion in the seventh century.

Islamic Conquest

The beduin Arabs who toppled the Sassanid Empire were propelled not only by a desire for conquest but also by a new religion, Islam. The Prophet Muhammad, a member of the Hashimite clan of the powerful tribe of Quraysh, proclaimed his prophetic mission in Arabia in 612 and eventually won over the city of his birth, Mecca, to the new faith (see Religious Life, ch. 2). Within one year of Muhammad's death in 632, Arabia itself was secure enough to allow his secular successor, Abu Bakr, the first caliph, to begin the campaign against the Byzantine and Sassanid empires.

Abu Bakr defeated the Byzantine army at Damascus in 635 and then began his conquest of Iran. In 637 the Arab forces occupied the Sassanid capital of Ctesiphon (which they renamed Madain), and in 641–42 they defeated the Sassanid army at Nahavand. After that, Iran lay open to the invaders. The Islamic conquest was aided by the material and social bankruptcy of the Sassanids; the native populations had little to lose by cooperating with the conquering power. Moreover, the Muslims offered relative religious tolerance and fair treatment to populations that accepted Islamic rule without resistance. It was not until around 650, however, that resistance in Iran was quelled. Conversion to Islam, which offered certain advantages, was fairly rapid among the urban population but slower among the peasantry and the *dihqans.* The majority of Iranians did not become Muslim until the ninth century.

Although the conquerors, especially the Umayyads (the Muslim rulers who succeeded Muhammad from 661–750), tended to stress the primacy of Arabs among Muslims, the Iranians were gradually integrated into the new community. The Muslim conquerors adopted the Sassanid coinage system and many Sassanid administrative practices, including the office of vizier, or minister, and the *divan,* a bureau or register for controlling state revenue and expenditure that became a characteristic of administration throughout Muslim lands. Later caliphs adopted Iranian court ceremonial practices and the trappings of Sassanid monarchy. Men of Iranian origin served as administrators after the conquest, and

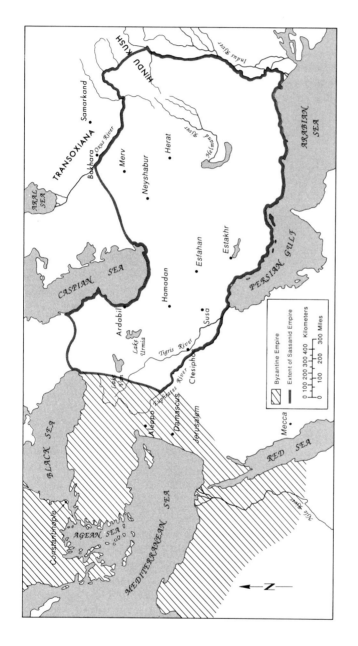

Source: Based on information from *Historical Atlas of the Muslim Peoples*, Amsterdam, 1957; and Jere L. Bacharach, *A Middle East Studies Handbook*, Seattle, 1984.

Figure 3. Sassanid Empire, Sixth Century A.D.

Iranians contributed significantly to all branches of Islamic learning, including philology, literature, history, geography, jurisprudence, philosophy, medicine, and the sciences.

The Arabs were in control, however. The new state religion, Islam, imposed its own system of beliefs, laws, and social mores. In regions that submitted peacefully to Muslim rule, landowners kept their land. But crown land, land abandoned by fleeing owners, and land taken by conquest passed into the hands of the new state. This included the rich lands of the Sawad, a rich, alluvial plain in central and southern Iraq. Arabic became the official language of the court in 696, although Persian continued to be widely used as the spoken language. The *shuubiyya* literary controversy of the ninth through the eleventh centuries, in which Arabs and Iranians each lauded their own and denigrated the other's cultural traits, suggests the survival of a certain sense of distinct Iranian identity. In the ninth century, the emergence of more purely Iranian ruling dynasties witnessed the revival of the Persian language, enriched by Arabic loanwords and using the Arabic script, and of Persian literature.

Another legacy of the Arab conquest was Shia Islam, which, although it has come to be identified closely with Iran, was not initially an Iranian religious movement. It originated with the Arab Muslims. In the great schism of Islam, one group among the community of believers maintained that leadership of the community following the death of Muhammad rightfully belonged to Muhammad's son-in-law, Ali, and to his descendants. This group came to be known as the Shiat Ali, the partisans of Ali, or the Shias. Another group, supporters of Muawiya (a rival contender for the caliphate following the murder of Uthman), challenged Ali's election to the caliphate in 656. After Ali was assassinated while praying in a mosque at Kufa in 661, Muawiya was declared caliph by the majority of the Islamic community. He became the first caliph of the Umayyad dynasty, which had its capital at Damascus.

Ali's youngest son, Husayn, refused to pay the homage commanded by Muawiya's son and successor Yazid I and fled to Mecca, where he was asked to lead the Shias—mostly those living in present-day Iraq—in a revolt. At Karbala, in Iraq, Husayn's band of 200 men and women followers, unwilling to surrender, were finally cut down by about 4,000 Umayyad troops. The Umayyad leader received Husayn's head, and Husayn's death in 680 on the tenth of Moharram continues to be observed as a day of mourning for all Shias (see Religious Life, ch. 2).

The largest concentration of Shias in the first century of Islam was in southern Iraq. It was not until the sixteenth century, under

13

the Safavids, that a majority of Iranians became Shias. Shia Islam became then, as it is now, the state religion.

The Abbasids, who overthrew the Umayyads in 750, while sympathetic to the Iranian Shias, were clearly an Arab dynasty. They revolted in the name of descendants of Muhammad's uncle, Abbas, and the House of Hashim. Hashim was an ancestor of both the Shia and the Abbas, or Sunni (see Glossary), line, and the Abbasid movement enjoyed the support of both Sunni and Shia Muslims. The Abbasid army consisted primarily of Khorasanians and was led by an Iranian general, Abu Muslim. It contained both Iranian and Arab elements, and the Abbasids enjoyed both Iranian and Arab support.

Nevertheless, the Abbasids, although sympathetic to the Shias, whose support they wished to retain, did not encourage the more extremist Shia aspirations. The Abbasids established their capital at Baghdad. Al Mamun, who seized power from his brother, Amin, and proclaimed himself caliph in 811, had an Iranian mother and thus had a base of support in Khorasan. The Abbasids continued the centralizing policies of their predecessors. Under their rule, the Islamic world experienced a cultural efflorescence and the expansion of trade and economic prosperity. These were developments in which Iran shared.

Iran's next ruling dynasties descended from nomadic, Turkic-speaking warriors who had been moving out of Central Asia into Transoxiana for more than a millennium. The Abbasid caliphs began enlisting these people as slave warriors as early as the ninth century. Shortly thereafter the real power of the Abbasid caliphs began to wane; eventually they became religious figureheads while the warrior slaves ruled. As the power of the Abbasid caliphs diminished, a series of independent and indigenous dynasties rose in various parts of Iran, some with considerable influence and power. Among the most important of these overlapping dynasties were the Tahirids in Khorasan (820–72); the Saffarids in Sistan (867–903); and the Samanids (875–1005), originally at Bukhara (also cited as Bokhara). The Samanids eventually ruled an area from central Iran to India. In 962 a Turkish slave governor of the Samanids, Alptigin, conquered Ghazna (in present-day Afghanistan) and established a dynasty, the Ghaznavids, that lasted to 1186.

Several Samanid cities had been lost to another Turkish group, the Seljuks, a clan of the Oghuz (or Ghuzz) Turks, who lived north of the Oxus River (present-day Amu Darya). Their leader, Tughril Beg, turned his warriors against the Ghaznavids in Khorasan. He moved south and then west, conquering but not wasting the cities in his path. In 1055 the caliph in Baghdad gave Tughril Beg robes, gifts, and the title King of the East. Under Tughril Beg's successor, Malik Shah (1072–92), Iran enjoyed a cultural and scientific renaissance, largely attributed to his brilliant Iranian vizier, Nizam al Mulk. These leaders established the observatory where Umar (Omar) Khayyam did much of his experimentation for a new calendar, and they built religious schools in all the major towns. They brought Abu Hamid Ghazali, one of the greatest Islamic theologians, and other eminent scholars to the Seljuk capital at Baghdad and encouraged and supported their work.

A serious internal threat to the Seljuks, however, came from the Ismailis, a secret sect with headquarters at Alumut between Rasht and Tehran. They controlled the immediate area for more than 150 years and sporadically sent out adherents to strengthen their rule by murdering important officials. The word *assassins,* which was applied to these murderers, developed from a European corruption of the name applied to them in Syria, *hashishiyya,* because folklore had it that they smoked hashish before their missions.

Invasions of the Mongols and Tamerlane

After the death of Malik Shah in 1092, Iran once again reverted to petty dynasties. During this time, Genghis (Chinghis) Khan brought together a number of Mongol tribes and led them on a devastating sweep through China. Then, in 1219, he turned his 700,000 forces west and quickly devastated Bukhara, Samarkand, Balkh, Merv, and Neyshabur. Before his death in 1227, he had reached western Azarbaijan, pillaging and burning cities along the way.

The Mongol invasion was disastrous to the Iranians. Destruction of *qanat* irrigation systems destroyed the pattern of relatively continuous settlement, producing numerous isolated oasis cities in a land where they had previously been rare (see Water, ch. 3). A large number of people, particularly males, were killed; between 1220 and 1258, the population of Iran dropped drastically.

Mongol rulers who followed Genghis Khan did little to improve Iran's situation. Genghis's grandson, Hulagu Khan, turned to foreign conquest, seizing Baghdad in 1258 and killing the last Abbasid caliph. He was stopped by the Mamluk forces of Egypt at Ain Jalut in Palestine. Afterward he returned to Iran and spent the rest of his life in Azarbaijan.

A later Mongol ruler, Ghazan Khan (1295–1304), and his famous Iranian vizier, Rashid ad Din, brought Iran a partial and brief economic revival. The Mongols lowered taxes for artisans, encouraged agriculture, rebuilt and extended irrigation works, and improved the safety of the trade routes. As a result, commerce increased dramatically. Items from India, China, and Iran passed easily across the Asian steppes, and these contacts culturally enriched Iran. For example, Iranians developed a new style of painting based on a unique fusion of solid, two-dimensional Mesopotamian painting with the feathery, light brush strokes and other motifs characteristic of China. After Ghazan's nephew, Abu Said, died in 1335, however, Iran again lapsed into petty dynasties—the Salghurid, Muzaffarid, Inju, and Jalayirid—under Mongol commanders, old Seljuk retainers, and regional chiefs.

Tamerlane, variously described as of Mongol or Turkic origin, was the next ruler to achieve emperor status. He conquered Transoxiana proper and by 1381 established himself as sovereign. He did not have the huge forces of earlier Mongol leaders, so his conquests were slower and less savage than those of Genghis Khan or Hulagu Khan. Nevertheless, Shiraz and Esfahan were virtually leveled. Tamerlane's regime was characterized by its inclusion of Iranians in administrative roles and its promotion of architecture and poetry. His empire disintegrated rapidly after his death in 1405, however, and Mongol tribes, Uzbeks, and Bayundur Turkomans ruled roughly the area of present-day Iran until the rise of the Safavid dynasty, the first native Iranian dynasty in almost 1,000 years.

The Safavids, 1501–1722

The Safavids, who came to power in 1501, were leaders of a militant Sufi order. They traced their ancestry to Shaykh Safi ad Din (died circa 1334), the founder of their order, who claimed descent from Shia Islam's Seventh Imam, Musa al Kazim. From their home base in Ardabil, they recruited followers among the Turkoman tribesmen of Anatolia and forged them into an effective fighting force and an instrument for territorial expansion. Sometime in the mid-fifteenth century, the Safavids adopted Shia Islam, and their movement became highly millenarian in character. In 1501, under their leader Ismail, the Safavids seized power in Tabriz, which became their capital. Ismail was proclaimed shah of Iran. The rise of the Safavids marks the reemergence in Iran of a powerful central authority within geographical boundaries attained by former Iranian empires. The Safavids declared Shia Islam the state religion and used proselytizing and force to convert the large majority of Muslims in Iran to the Shia sect. Under the early Safavids, Iran was a theocracy in which state and religion were closely intertwined. Ismail's followers venerated him not only as the *murshid-kamil,* the perfect guide, but also as an emanation of the Godhead. He combined in his person both temporal and spiritual authority. In the

Part of the Porch of Xerxes at Persepolis
Courtesy LaVerle Berry

new state, he was represented in both these functions by the *vakil,* an official who acted as a kind of alter ego. The *sadr* headed the powerful religious organization; the vizier, the bureaucracy; and the *amir alumara,* the fighting forces. These fighting forces, the *qizilbash,* came primarily from the seven Turkic-speaking tribes that supported the Safavid bid for power.

The Safavids faced the problem of integrating their Turkic-speaking followers with the native Iranians, their fighting traditions with the Iranian bureaucracy, and their messianic ideology with the exigencies of administering a territorial state. The institutions of the early Safavid state and subsequent efforts at state reorganization reflect attempts, not always successful, to strike a balance among these various elements. The Safavids also faced external challenges from the Uzbeks and the Ottomans. The Uzbeks were an unstable element along Iran's northeastern frontier who raided into Khorasan, particularly when the central government was weak, and blocked the Safavid advance northward into Transoxiana. The Ottomans, who were Sunnis, were rivals for the religious allegiance of Muslims in eastern Anatolia and Iraq and pressed territorial claims in both these areas and in the Caucasus.

The Safavid Empire suffered a serious setback in 1524, when the Ottoman sultan Selim I defeated the Safavid forces at Chaldiran and occupied the Safavid capital, Tabriz. Although he was forced to withdraw because of the harsh winter and Iran's scorched earth policy, and although Safavid rulers continued to assert claims to spiritual leadership, the defeat shattered belief in the shah as a semidivine figure and weakened the hold of the shah over the *qizilbash* chiefs. In 1533 the Ottoman sultan Süleyman occupied Baghdad and then extended Ottoman rule to southern Iraq. Except for a brief period (1624-38) when Safavid rule was restored, Iraq remained firmly in Ottoman hands. The Ottomans also continued to challenge the Safavids for control of Azarbaijan and the Caucasus until the Treaty of Qasr-e Shirin in 1639 established frontiers both in Iraq and in the Caucasus that remain virtually unchanged in the late twentieth century.

The Safavid state reached its apogee during the reign of Shah Abbas (1587-1629). The shah gained breathing space to confront and defeat the Uzbeks by signing a largely disadvantageous treaty with the Ottomans. He then fought successful campaigns against the Ottomans, reestablishing Iranian control over Iraq, Georgia, and parts of the Caucasus. He counterbalanced the power of the *qizilbash* by creating a body of troops composed of Georgian and Armenian slaves who were loyal to the person of the shah. He extended state and crown lands and the provinces directly administered by the state, at the expense of the *qizilbash* chiefs. He relocated tribes to weaken their power, strengthened the bureaucracy, and further centralized the administration.

Shah Abbas made a show of personal piety and supported religious institutions by building mosques and religious seminaries and by making generous endowments for religious purposes. His reign, however, witnessed the gradual separation of religious institutions from the state and an increasing movement toward a more independent religious hierarchy.

In addition to his political reorganization and his support of religious institutions, Shah Abbas also promoted commerce and the arts. The Portuguese had previously occupied Bahrain and the island of Hormoz off the Persian Gulf coast in their bid to dominate Indian Ocean and Persian Gulf trade, but in 1602 Shah Abbas expelled them from Bahrain, and in 1623 he used the British (who sought a share of Iran's lucrative silk trade) to expel the Portuguese from Hormoz. He significantly enhanced government revenues by establishing a state monopoly over the silk trade and encouraged internal and external trade by safeguarding the roads and welcoming British, Dutch, and other traders to Iran. With the encouragement of the shah, Iranian craftsmen excelled in producing fine silks, brocades, and other cloths, carpets, porcelain, and metalware. When Shah Abbas built a new capital at Esfahan, he adorned it with fine mosques, palaces, schools, bridges, and a bazaar. He patronized the arts, and the calligraphy, miniatures, painting, and agriculture of his period are particularly noteworthy.

Although there was a recovery with the reign of Shah Abbas II (1642–66), in general the Safavid Empire declined after the death of Shah Abbas. The decline resulted from weak rulers, interference by the women of the harem in politics, the reemergence of *qizilbash* rivalries, maladministration of state lands, excessive taxation, the decline of trade, and the weakening of Safavid military organization. (Both the *qizilbash* tribal military organization and the standing army composed of slave soldiers were deteriorating.) The last two rulers, Shah Sulayman (1669–94) and Shah Sultan Hosain (1694–1722), were voluptuaries. Once again the eastern frontiers began to be breached, and in 1722 a small body of Afghan tribesmen won a series of easy victories before entering and taking the capital itself, ending Safavid rule.

Afghan supremacy was brief. Tahmasp Quli, a chief of the Afshar tribe, soon expelled the Afghans in the name of a surviving member of the Safavid family. Then, in 1736, he assumed power in his own name as Nader Shah. He went on to drive the Ottomans from Georgia and Armenia and the Russians from the Iranian coast on the Caspian Sea and restored Iranian sovereignty over Afghanistan. He also took his army on several campaigns into India and in 1739 sacked Delhi, bringing back fabulous treasures. Although Nader Shah achieved political unity, his military campaigns and extortionate taxation proved a terrible drain on a country already ravaged and depopulated by war and disorder, and in 1747 he was murdered by chiefs of his own Afshar tribe.

A period of anarchy and a struggle for supremacy among Afshar, Qajar, Afghan, and Zand tribal chieftains followed Nader Shah's death. Finally Karim Khan Zand (1750–79) was able to defeat his rivals and to unify the country, except for Khorasan, under a loose form of central control. He refused to assume the title of shah, however, and ruled as *vakil al ruaya,* or deputy of the subjects. He is remembered for his mild and beneficent rule.

The Qajars, 1795–1925

At Karim Khan's death, another struggle for power among the Zands, Qajars, and other tribal groups once again plunged the country into disorder and disrupted economic life. This time Aga Mohammad Qajar defeated the last Zand ruler outside Kerman in 1794 and made himself master of the country, beginning the Qajar dynasty that was to last until 1925. Under Fath Ali (1797–1834), Mohammad Shah (1834–48), and Naser ad Din Shah (1848–96) a degree of order, stability, and unity returned to the country. The Qajars revived the concept of the shah as the shadow of God on earth and exercised absolute powers over the servants of the state. They appointed royal princes to provincial governorships and, in the course of the nineteenth century, increased their power in relation to that of the tribal chiefs, who provided contingents for the shah's army. Under the Qajars, the merchants and the ulama, or religious leaders, remained important members of the community. A large bureaucracy assisted the chief officers of the state, and, in the second half of the nineteenth century, new ministries and offices were created. The Qajars were unsuccessful, however, in their attempt to replace the army based on tribal levies with a European-style standing army having regular training, organization, and uniforms.

Early in the nineteenth century, the Qajars began to face pressure from two great world powers, Russia and Britain. Britain's interest in Iran arose out of the need to protect trade routes to India, while Russia's came from a desire to expand into Iranian territory from the north. In two disastrous wars with Russia, which ended with the Treaty of Gulistan (1812) and the Treaty of Turkmanchay (1828), Iran lost all its territories in the Caucasus north of the Aras

*The tomb of Ibn Sina (known as Avicenna by the West),
a famous mathematician who died in A.D. 1037*
Courtesy LaVerle Berry

River. Then, in the second half of the century, Russia forced the
Qajars to give up all claims to territories in Central Asia. Meanwhile, Britain twice landed troops in Iran to prevent the Qajars
from reasserting a claim to Herat, lost after the fall of the Safavids.
Under the Treaty of Paris in 1857, Iran surrendered to Britain
all claims to Herat and territories in present-day Afghanistan.

The two great powers also came to dominate Iran's trade and
interfered in Iran's internal affairs. They enjoyed overwhelming
military and technological superiority and could take advantage
of Iran's internal problems. Iranian central authority was weak;
revenues were generally inadequate to maintain the court,
bureaucracy, and army; the ruling class was divided and corrupt;
and the people suffered exploitation by their rulers and governors.

When Naser ad Din acceded to the throne in 1848, his prime
minister, Mirza Taqi Khan Amir Kabir, attempted to strengthen
the administration by reforming the tax system, asserting central
control over the bureaucracy and the provincial governors, encouraging trade and industry, and reducing the influence of the Islamic
clergy (see Glossary) and foreign powers. He established a new
school, the Dar ol Fonun, to educate members of the elite in the
new sciences and in foreign languages. The power he concentrated
in his hands, however, aroused jealousy within the bureaucracy

21

and fear in the king. He was dismissed and put to death in 1851, a fate shared by earlier powerful prime ministers.

In 1858 officials like Malkam Khan began to suggest in essays that the weakness of the government and its inability to prevent foreign interference lay in failure to learn the arts of government, industry, science, and administration from the advanced states of Europe. In 1871, with the encouragement of his new prime minister, Mirza Hosain Khan Moshir od Dowleh, the shah established a European-style cabinet with administrative responsibilities and a consultative council of senior princes and officials. He granted a concession for railroad construction and other economic projects to a Briton, Baron Julius de Reuter, and visited Russia and Britain himself. Opposition from bureaucratic factions hostile to the prime minister and from clerical leaders who feared foreign influence, however, forced the shah to dismiss his prime minister and to cancel the concession. Nevertheless, internal demand for reform was slowly growing. Moreover, Britain, to which the shah turned for protection against Russian encroachment, continued to urge the shah to undertake reforms and open the country to foreign trade and enterprise as a means of strengthening the country. In 1888 the shah, heeding this advice, opened the Karun River in Khuzestan to foreign shipping and gave Reuter permission to open the country's first bank. In 1890 he gave another British company a monopoly over the country's tobacco trade. The tobacco concession was obtained through bribes to leading officials and aroused considerable opposition among the clerical classes, the merchants, and the people. When a leading cleric, Mirza Hasan Shirazi, issued a *fatva* (religious ruling) forbidding the use of tobacco, the ban was universally observed, and the shah was once again forced to cancel the concession at considerable cost to an already depleted treasury.

The last years of Naser ad Din Shah's reign were characterized by growing royal and bureaucratic corruption, oppression of the rural population, and indifference on the shah's part. The tax machinery broke down, and disorder became endemic in the provinces. New ideas and a demand for reform were also becoming more widespread. In 1896, reputedly encouraged by Jamal ad Din al Afghani (called Asadabadi because he came from Asadabad), the well-known Islamic preacher and political activist, a young Iranian assassinated the shah.

The Constitutional Revolution

The shah's son and successor, Muzaffar ad Din (1896–1907), was a weak and ineffectual ruler. Royal extravagance and the absence of incoming revenues exacerbated financial problems. The shah quickly spent two large loans from Russia, partly on trips to Europe. Public anger fed on the shah's propensity for granting concessions to Europeans in return for generous payments to him and his officials. People began to demand a curb on royal authority and the establishment of the rule of law as their concern over foreign, and especially Russian, influence grew.

The shah's failure to respond to protests by the religious establishment, the merchants, and other classes led the merchants and clerical leaders in January 1906 to protest by taking sanctuary in mosques in Tehran and outside the capital. When the shah reneged on a promise to permit the establishment of a "house of justice," or consultative assembly, 10,000 people, led by the merchants, took sanctuary in June in the compound of the British legation in Tehran. In August the shah was forced to issue a decree promising a constitution. In October an elected assembly convened and drew up a constitution that provided for strict limitations on royal power, an elected parliament, or Majlis (see Glossary), with wide powers to represent the people, and a government with a cabinet subject to confirmation by the Majlis. The shah signed the constitution on December 30, 1906. He died five days later. The Supplementary Fundamental Laws approved in 1907 provided, within limits, for freedom of press, speech, and association, and for security of life and property. According to scholar Ann K.S. Lambton, the Constitutional Revolution marked the end of the medieval period in Iran. The hopes for constitutional rule were not realized, however.

Muzaffar ad Din's successor, Mohammad Ali Shah, was determined to crush the constitution. After several disputes with the members of the Majlis, in June 1908 he used his Russian-officered Persian Cossack Brigade to bomb the Majlis building, arrest many of the deputies, and close down the assembly. Resistance to the shah, however, coalesced in Tabriz, Esfahan, Rasht, and elsewhere. In July 1909, constitutional forces marched from Rasht and Esfahan to Tehran, deposed the shah, and reestablished the constitution. The ex-shah went into exile in Russia.

Although the constitutional forces had triumphed, they faced serious difficulties. The upheavals of the Constitutional Revolution and civil war had undermined stability and trade. In addition, the ex-shah, with Russian support, attempted to regain his throne, landing troops in July 1910. Finally, the hope that the Constitutional Revolution would inaugurate a new era of independence from the great powers ended when, under the Anglo-Russian Agreement of 1907, Britain and Russia agreed to divide Iran into spheres of influence. The Russians were to enjoy exclusive right to pursue their interests in the northern sphere, the British in the south and east; both powers would be free to compete for economic and political advantage in a neutral sphere in the center. Matters came to a head when Morgan Shuster, a United States administrator hired as treasurer general by the Persian government to reform its finances, sought to collect taxes from powerful officials who were Russian protégés and to send members of the treasury gendarmerie, a tax department police force, into the Russian zone. When in December 1911 the Majlis unanimously refused a Russian ultimatum demanding Shuster's dismissal, Russian troops, already in the country, moved to occupy the capital. To prevent this, on December 20 Bakhtiari chiefs and their troops surrounded the Majlis building, forced acceptance of the Russian ultimatum, and shut down the assembly, once again suspending the constitution. There followed a period of government by Bakhtiari chiefs and other powerful notables.

World War I

Iran hoped to avoid entanglement in World War I by declaring its neutrality, but ended up as a battleground for Russian, Turkish, and British troops. When German agents tried to arouse the southern tribes against the British, Britain created an armed force, the South Persia Rifles, to protect its interests. Then a group of Iranian notables led by Nezam os Saltaneh Mafi, hoping to escape Anglo-Russian dominance and sympathetic to the German war effort, left Tehran, first for Qom and then for Kermanshah (renamed Bakhtaran after the fall of Mohammad Reza Shah in 1979), where they established a provisional government. The provisional government lasted for the duration of the war but failed to capture much support.

At the end of the war, because of Russia's preoccupation with its own revolution, Britain was the dominant influence in Tehran. The foreign secretary, Lord Curzon, proposed an agreement under which Britain would provide Iran with a loan and with advisers to the army and virtually every government department. The Iranian prime minister, Vosuq od Dowleh, and two members of his cabinet who had received a large financial inducement from the British, supported the agreement. The Anglo-Persian Agreement of 1919 was widely viewed as establishing a British protectorate over Iran. It aroused considerable opposition, and the Majlis refused to approve it. The agreement was already dead when, in February 1921, Persian Cossack Brigade officer Reza Khan, in collaboration with prominent journalist Sayyid Zia ad Din

Tabatabai, marched into Tehran and seized power, inaugurating a new phase in Iran's modern history.

The Era of Reza Shah, 1921–41

Tabatabai became prime minister and Reza Khan became commander of the armed forces in the new government. Reza Khan, however, quickly emerged as the dominant figure. Within three months, Tabatabai was forced out of the government and into exile. Reza Khan became minister of war. In 1923 Ahmad Shah agreed to appoint Reza Khan prime minister and to leave for Europe. The shah was never to return. Reza Khan seriously considered establishing a republic, as Atatürk had done in Turkey, but abandoned the idea as a result of clerical opposition. In October 1925, a Majlis dominated by Reza Khan's men deposed the Qajar dynasty; in December the Majlis conferred the crown on Reza Khan and his heirs. The military officer who had become master of Iran was crowned as Reza Shah Pahlavi in April 1926.

Even before he became shah, Reza Khan had taken steps to create a strong central government and to extend government control over the country. Now, as Reza Shah, with the assistance of a group of army officers and younger bureaucrats, many trained in Europe, he launched a broad program of change designed to bring Iran into the modern world (see Historical Background, ch. 5). To strengthen the central authority, he built up Iran's heterogeneous military forces into a disciplined army of 40,000, and in 1926 he persuaded the Majlis to approve a law for universal military conscription. Reza Shah used the army not only to bolster his own power but also to pacify the country and to bring the tribes under control. In 1924 he broke the power of Shaykh Khazal, who was a British protégé and practically autonomous in Khuzestan. In addition, Reza Shah forcibly settled many of the tribes.

To extend government control and promote Westernization, the shah overhauled the administrative machinery and vastly expanded the bureaucracy. He created an extensive system of secular primary and secondary schools and, in 1935, established the country's first European-style university in Tehran. These schools and institutions of higher education became training grounds for the new bureaucracy and, along with economic expansion, helped create a new middle class. The shah also expanded the road network, successfully completed the trans-Iranian railroad, and established a string of state-owned factories to produce such basic consumer goods as textiles, matches, canned goods, sugar, and cigarettes.

Many of the Shah's measures were consciously designed to break the power of the religious hierarchy. His educational reforms ended the clerics' near monopoly on education. To limit further the power of the clerics, he undertook a codification of the laws that created a body of secular law, applied and interpreted by a secular judiciary outside the control of the religious establishment. He excluded the clerics from judgeships, created a system of secular courts, and transferred the important and lucrative task of notarizing documents from the clerics to state-licensed notaries. The state even encroached on the administration of *vaqfs* (religious endowments) and on the licensing of graduates of religious seminaries.

Among the codes comprising the new secular law were the civil code, the work of Justice Minister Ali Akbar Davar, enacted between 1927 and 1932; the General Accounting Act (1934–35), a milestone in financial administration; a new tax law; and a civil service code.

Determined to unify what he saw as Iran's heterogeneous peoples, end foreign influence, and emancipate women, Reza Shah imposed European dress on the population. He opened the schools to women and brought them into the work force. In 1936 he forcibly abolished the wearing of the veil.

Reza Shah initially enjoyed wide support for restoring order, unifying the country, and reinforcing national independence, and for his economic and educational reforms. In accomplishing all this, however, he took away effective power from the Majlis, muzzled the press, and arrested opponents of the government. His police chiefs were notorious for their harshness. Several religious leaders were jailed or sent into exile. In 1936, in one of the worst confrontations between the government and religious authorities, troops violated the sanctity of the shrine of Imam Reza in Mashhad, where worshipers had gathered to protest Reza Shah's reforms. Dozens of worshipers were killed and many injured. In addition, the shah arranged for powerful tribal chiefs to be put to death; bureaucrats who became too powerful suffered a similar fate. Reza Shah jailed and then quietly executed Abdul Hosain Teimurtash, his minister of court and close confidant; Davar committed suicide.

As time went on, the shah grew increasingly avaricious and amassed great tracts of land. Moreover, his tax policies weighed heavily on the peasants and the lower classes, the great landowners' control over land and the peasantry increased, and the condition of the peasants worsened during his reign. As a result, by the mid-1930s there was considerable dissatisfaction in the country.

Meanwhile, Reza Shah initiated changes in foreign affairs as well. In 1928 he abolished the capitulations under which Europeans in Iran had, since the nineteenth century, enjoyed the privilege of being subject to their own consular courts rather than to the Iranian judiciary. Suspicious of both Britain and the Soviet Union, the shah circumscribed contacts with foreign embassies. Relations with the Soviet Union had already deteriorated because of that country's commercial policies, which in the 1920s and 1930s adversely affected Iran. In 1932 the shah offended Britain by canceling the agreement under which the Anglo-Persian Oil Company produced and exported Iran's oil. Although a new and improved agreement was eventually signed, it did not satisfy Iran's demands and left bad feeling on both sides. To counterbalance British and Soviet influence, Reza Shah encouraged German commercial enterprise in Iran. On the eve of World War II, Germany was Iran's largest trading partner.

World War II and the Azarbaijan Crisis

At the outbreak of World War II, Iran declared its neutrality, but the country was soon invaded by both Britain and the Soviet Union. Britain had been annoyed when Iran refused Allied demands that it expel all German nationals from the country. When Hitler invaded the Soviet Union in 1941, the Allies urgently needed to transport war matériel across Iran to the Soviet Union, an operation that would have violated Iranian neutrality. As a result, Britain and the Soviet Union simultaneously invaded Iran on August 26, 1941, the Soviets from the northwest and the British across the Iraqi frontier from the west and at the head of the Persian Gulf in the south. Resistance quickly collapsed. Reza Shah knew the Allies would not permit him to remain in power, so he abdicated on September 16 in favor of his son, who ascended the throne as Mohammad Reza Shah Pahlavi. Reza Shah and several members of his family were taken by the British first to Mauritius and then to Johannesburg, South Africa, where Reza Shah died in July 1944.

The occupation of Iran proved of vital importance to the Allied cause and brought Iran closer to the Western powers. Britain, the Soviet Union, and the United States together managed to move over 5 million tons of munitions and other war matériel across Iran to the Soviet Union. In addition, in January 1942 Iran signed a tripartite treaty of alliance with Britain and the Soviet Union under which Iran agreed to extend nonmilitary assistance to the war effort. The two Allied powers, in turn, agreed to respect Iran's independence and territorial integrity and to withdraw their troops from Iran within six months of the end of hostilities. In September 1943, Iran declared war on Germany, thus qualifying for membership in the United Nations (UN). In November at the Tehran Conference, President Franklin D. Roosevelt, Prime Minister Winston Churchill, and Prime Minister Josef Stalin reaffirmed a commitment to

Iran's independence and territorial integrity and a willingness to extend economic assistance to Iran.

The effects of the war, however, were very disruptive for Iran. Food and other essential items were scarce. Severe inflation imposed great hardship on the lower and middle classes, while fortunes were made by individuals dealing in scarce items. The presence of foreign troops accelerated social change and also fed xenophobic and nationalist sentiments. An influx of rural migrants into the cities added to political unrest. The Majlis, dominated by the propertied interests, did little to ameliorate these conditions. With the political controls of the Reza Shah period removed, meanwhile, party and press activity revived. The communist Tudeh Party was especially active in organizing industrial workers. Like many other political parties of the left and center, it called for economic and social reform.

Eventually, collusion between the Tudeh and the Soviet Union brought further disintegration to Iran. In September 1944, while American companies were negotiating for oil concessions in Iran, the Soviets requested an oil concession in the five northern provinces. In December, however, the Majlis passed a law forbidding the government to discuss oil concessions before the end of the war. This led to fierce Soviet propaganda attacks on the government and agitation by the Tudeh in favor of a Soviet oil concession. In December 1945, the Azarbaijan Democratic Party, which had close links with the Tudeh and was led by Jafar Pishevari, announced the establishment of an autonomous republic. In a similar move, activists in neighboring Kordestan established the Kurdish Republic of Mahabad. Both autonomous republics enjoyed the support of the Soviets, and Soviet troops remained in Khorasan, Gorgan, Mazandaran, and Gilan. Other Soviet troops prevented government forces from entering Azarbaijan and Kordestan. Soviet pressure on Iran continued as British and American troops evacuated in keeping with their treaty undertakings. Soviet troops remained in the country. Prime Minister Ahmad Qavam had to persuade Stalin to withdraw his troops by agreeing to submit a Soviet oil concession to the Majlis and to negotiate a peaceful settlement to the Azarbaijan crisis with the Pishevari government. In April the government signed an oil agreement with the Soviet Union; in May, partly as a result of United States, British, and UN pressure, Soviet troops withdrew from Iranian territory. Qavam took three Tudeh members into his cabinet. Qavam was able to reclaim his concessions to the Soviet Union, however. A tribal revolt in the south, partly to protest communist influence, provided an opportunity to dismiss the Tudeh cabinet officers. In December, ostensibly in preparation for new Majlis elections, he sent the Iranian army into Azarbaijan. Without Soviet backing, the Pishevari government collapsed, and Pishevari himself fled to the Soviet Union. A similar fate befell the Kurdish Republic of Mahabad. In the new Majlis, a strong bloc of deputies, organized in the National Front and led by Mohammad Mossadeq, helped defeat the Soviet oil concession agreement by 102 votes to 2. The Majlis also passed a bill forbidding any further foreign oil concessions and requiring the government to exploit oil resources directly.

Soviet influence diminished further in 1947, when Iran and the United States signed an agreement providing for military aid and for a United States military advisory mission to help train the Iranian army. In February 1949, the Tudeh was blamed for an abortive attempt on the shah's life, and its leaders fled abroad or were arrested. The party was banned.

Mossadeq and Oil Nationalization

From 1949 on, sentiment for nationalization of Iran's oil industry grew. In 1949 the Majlis approved the First Development Plan (1948–55), which called for comprehensive agricultural and industrial development of the country (see The Beginnings of Modernization: The Post-1925 Period, ch. 3). The Plan Organization was established to administer the program, which was to be financed in large part from oil revenues. Politically conscious Iranians were aware, however, that the British government derived more revenue from taxing the concessionaire, the Anglo-Iranian Oil Company (AIOC—formerly the Anglo-Persian Oil Company), than the Iranian government derived from royalties. The oil issue figured prominently in elections for the Majlis in 1949, and nationalists in the new Majlis were determined to renegotiate the AIOC agreement. In November 1950, the Majlis committee concerned with oil matters, headed by Mossadeq, rejected a draft agreement in which the AIOC had offered the government slightly improved terms. These terms did not include the fifty-fifty profit-sharing provision that was part of other new Persian Gulf oil concessions.

Subsequent negotiations with the AIOC were unsuccessful, partly because General Ali Razmara, who became prime minister in June 1950, failed to persuade the oil company of the strength of nationalist feeling in the country and in the Majlis. When the AIOC finally offered fifty-fifty profit-sharing in February 1951, sentiment for nationalization of the oil industry had become widespread. Razmara advised against nationalization on technical grounds and was assassinated in March 1951 by Khalil Tahmasebi, a member of the militant Fadayan-e Islam. On March 15, the Majlis voted to nationalize the oil industry. In April the shah yielded to Majlis pressure and demonstrations in the streets by naming Mossadeq prime minister.

Oil production came to a virtual standstill as British technicians left the country, and Britain imposed a worldwide embargo on the purchase of Iranian oil. In September 1951, Britain froze Iran's sterling assets and banned export of goods to Iran. It challenged the legality of the oil nationalization and took its case against Iran to the International Court of Justice at The Hague. The court found in Iran's favor, but the dispute between Iran and the AIOC remained unsettled. Under United States pressure, the AIOC improved its offer to Iran. The excitement generated by the nationalization issue, anti-British feeling, agitation by radical elements, and the conviction among Mossadeq's advisers that Iran's maximum demands would, in the end, be met, however, led the government to reject all offers. The economy began to suffer from the loss of foreign exchange and oil revenues.

Whereas Mossadeq's popularity was growing, political disorder also increased, leading to United States intervention. Mossadeq had come to office on the strength of support from the National Front and other parties in the Majlis and as a result of his great popularity. His popularity, growing power, and intransigence on the oil issue were creating friction between the prime minister and the shah. In the summer of 1952, the shah refused the prime minister's demand for the power to appoint the minister of war (and, by implication, to control the armed forces). Mossadeq resigned, three days of pro-Mossadeq rioting followed, and the shah was forced to reappoint Mossadeq to head the government.

As domestic conditions deteriorated, however, Mossadeq's populist style grew more autocratic. In August 1952, the Majlis acceded to his demand for full powers in all affairs of government for a six-month period. These special powers were subsequently extended for a further six-month term. He also obtained approval for a law to reduce, from six years to two years, the term of the Senate (established in 1950 as the upper house of the legislature), and thus brought about the dissolution of that body. Mossadeq's support in the lower house, the Majlis, was dwindling, however, so on August 3, 1953, the prime minister organized a plebiscite for the dissolution of the Majlis, claimed a massive vote in favor of the proposal, and dissolved the legislative body.

The administration of President Harry S Truman initially had been sympathetic to Iran's nationalist aspirations. Under the administration of President Dwight D. Eisenhower, however, the

United States came to accept the view of the British government that no reasonable compromise with Mossadeq was possible and that, by working with the Tudeh, Mossadeq was making probable a communist-inspired takeover. Mossadeq's intransigence and inclination to accept Tudeh support, the Cold War atmosphere, and the fear of Soviet influence in Iran also shaped United States thinking. In June 1953, the Eisenhower administration approved a British proposal for a joint Anglo-American operation, code-named Operation Ajax, to overthrow Mossadeq. Kermit Roosevelt of the United States Central Intelligence Agency (CIA) traveled secretly to Iran to coordinate plans with the shah and the Iranian military, which was led by General Fazlollah Zahedi.

In accord with the plan, on August 13 the shah appointed Zahedi prime minister to replace Mossadeq. Mossadeq refused to step down and arrested the shah's emissary. This triggered the second stage of Operation Ajax, which called for a military coup. The plan initially seemed to have failed, the shah fled the country, and Zahedi went into hiding. After four days of rioting, however, the tide turned. On August 19, pro-shah army units and street crowds defeated Mossadeq's forces. The shah returned to the country. Mossadeq was sentenced to three years' imprisonment for trying to overthrow the monarchy, but he was subsequently allowed to remain under house arrest in his village outside Tehran until his death in 1967. His minister of foreign affairs, Hosain Fatemi, was sentenced to death and executed. Hundreds of National Front leaders, Tudeh Party officers, and political activists were arrested; several Tudeh army officers were also sentenced to death.

The Post-Mossadeq Era and the Shah's White Revolution

To help the Zahedi government through a difficult period, the United States arranged for immediate economic assistance of US$45 million. The Iranian government restored diplomatic relations with Britain in December 1953, and a new oil agreement was concluded in the following year (see Concession Agreements, ch. 3). The shah, fearing both Soviet influence and internal opposition, sought to bolster his regime by edging closer to Britain and the United States. In October 1955, Iran joined the Baghdad Pact, which brought together the "northern tier" countries of Iraq, Turkey, and Pakistan in an alliance that included Britain, with the United States serving as a supporter of the pact but not a full member. (The pact was renamed the Central Treaty Organization—CENTO—after Iraq's withdrawal in 1958.) In March 1959, Iran signed a bilateral defense agreement with the United States (see Foreign Influences in Weapons, Training, and Support Systems, ch. 5). In the Cold War atmosphere, relations with the Soviet Union were correct but not cordial. The shah visited the Soviet Union in 1956, but Soviet propaganda attacks and Iran's alliance with the West continued. Internally, a period of political repression followed the overthrow of Mossadeq, as the shah concentrated power in his own hands. He banned or suppressed the Tudeh, the National Front, and other parties; muzzled the press; and strengthened the secret police, SAVAK (Sazman-e Ettelaat va Amniyat-e Keshvar—see Law Enforcement Agencies, ch. 5). Elections to the Majlis in 1954 and 1956 were closely controlled. The shah appointed Hosain Ala to replace Zahedi as prime minister in April 1955 and thereafter named a succession of prime ministers who were willing to do his bidding.

Attempts at economic development and political reform were inadequate. Rising oil revenues allowed the government to launch the Second Development Plan (1955–62) in 1956 (see The Beginnings of Modernization: The Post-1925 Period, ch. 3). A number of large-scale industrial and agricultural projects were initiated, but economic recovery from the disruptions of the oil nationalization period was slow. The infusion of oil money led to rapid inflation and spreading discontent, and strict controls provided no outlets for political unrest. When martial law, which had been instituted in August 1953 after the coup, ended in 1957, the shah ordered two of his senior officials to form a majority party and a loyal opposition as the basis for a two-party system. These became known as the Melliyun and the Mardom parties. These officially sanctioned parties did not satisfy demands for wider political representation, however. During Majlis elections in 1960, contested primarily by the Melliyun and the Mardom parties, charges of widespread fraud could not be suppressed, and the shah was forced to cancel the elections. Jafar Sharif-Emami, a staunch loyalist, became prime minister. After renewed and more strictly controlled elections, the Majlis convened in February 1961. But as economic conditions worsened and political unrest grew, the Sharif-Emami government fell in May 1961.

Yielding both to domestic demands for change and to pressure for reform from President John F. Kennedy's administration, the shah named Ali Amini, a wealthy landlord and senior civil servant, as prime minister. Amini was known as an advocate of reform. He received a mandate from the shah to dissolve parliament and rule for six months by cabinet decree. Amini loosened controls on the press, permitted the National Front and other political parties to resume activity, and ordered the arrest of a number of former senior officials on charges of corruption. Under Amini, the cabinet approved the Third Development Plan (1962–68) and undertook a program to reorganize the civil service. In January 1962, in the single most important measure of the fourteen-month Amini government, the cabinet approved a law for land distribution.

The Amini government, however, was beset by numerous problems. Belt-tightening measures ordered by the prime minister were necessary, but in the short term they intensified recession and unemployment. This recession caused discontent in the bazaar and business communities. In addition, the prime minister acted in an independent manner, and the shah and senior military and civilian officials close to the court resented this challenge to royal authority. Moreover, although enjoying limited freedom of activity for the first time in many years, the National Front and other opposition groups pressed the prime minister for elections and withheld their cooperation. Amini was unable to meet a large budget deficit; the shah refused to cut the military budget, and the United States, which had previously supported Amini, refused further aid. As a result, Amini resigned in July 1962.

He was replaced by Asadollah Alam, one of Mohammad Reza Shah's close confidants. Building on the credit earned in the countryside and in urban areas by the land distribution program, the shah in January 1963 submitted six measures to a national referendum. In addition to land reform, these measures included profit-sharing for industrial workers in private sector enterprises, nationalization of forests and pastureland, sale of government factories to finance land reform, amendment of the electoral law to give more representation on supervisory councils to workers and farmers, and establishment of a Literacy Corps to allow young men to satisfy their military service requirement by working as village literacy teachers. The shah described the package as his White Revolution (see Glossary), and when the referendum votes were counted, the government announced a 99-percent majority in favor of the program. In addition to these other reforms, the shah announced in February that he was extending the right to vote to women.

These measures earned the government considerable support among certain sectors of the population, but they did not deal immediately with sources of unrest. Economic conditions were still difficult for the poorer classes. Many clerical leaders opposed land reform and the extension of suffrage to women. These leaders were also concerned about the extension of government and royal authority that the reforms implied. In June 1963, Ayatollah Sayyid Ruhollah Musavi Khomeini, a religious leader in Qom, was arrested after a fiery speech in which he directly attacked the shah.

The arrest sparked three days of the most violent riots the country had witnessed since the overthrow of Mossadeq a decade earlier. The shah severely suppressed these riots, and, for the moment, the government appeared to have triumphed over its opponents.

State and Society, 1964–74

Elections to the twenty-first Majlis in September 1963 led to the formation of a new political party, the Iran Novin (New Iran) Party, committed to a program of economic and administrative reform and renewal. The Alam government had opened talks with the National Front leaders earlier in the year, but no accommodation had been reached, and the talks had broken down over such issues as freedom of activity for the front. As a result, the front was not represented in the elections, which were limited to the officially sanctioned parties, and the only candidates on the slate were those presented by the Union of National Forces, an organization of senior civil servants and officials and of workers' and farmers' representatives, put together with government support.

After the elections, the largest bloc in the new Majlis, with forty seats, was a group called the Progressive Center. The center, an exclusive club of senior civil servants, had been established by Hasan Ali Mansur in 1961 to study and make policy recommendations on major economic and social issues. In June 1963, the shah had designated the center as his personal research bureau. When the new Majlis convened in October, 100 more deputies joined the center, giving Mansur a majority. In December, Mansur converted the Progressive Center into a political party, the Iran Novin. In March 1964, Alam resigned and the shah appointed Mansur prime minister, at the head of an Iran Novin-led government.

The events leading to the establishment of the Iran Novin and the appointment of Mansur as prime minister represented a renewed attempt by the shah and his advisers to create a political organization that would be loyal to the crown, attract the support of the educated classes and the technocratic elite, and strengthen the administration and the economy. The Iran Novin drew its membership almost exclusively from a younger generation of senior civil servants, Western-educated technocrats, and business leaders. Initially, membership was limited to 500 hand-picked persons, and it was allowed to grow very slowly. In time it came to include leading members of the provincial elite and its bureaucratic, professional, and business classes. Even in the late 1960s and early 1970s, when trade unions and professional organizations affiliated themselves with the party, full membership was reserved for a limited group.

In carrying out economic and administrative reforms, Mansur created four new ministries and transferred the authority for drawing up the budget from the Ministry of Finance to the newly created Budget Bureau. The bureau was attached to the Plan Organization and was responsible directly to the prime minister. In subsequent years it introduced greater rationality in planning and budgeting. Mansur appointed younger technocrats to senior civil service posts, a policy continued by his successor. He also created the Health Corps, modeled after the Literacy Corps, to provide primary health care to rural areas.

In the Majlis the government enjoyed a comfortable majority, and the nominal opposition, the Mardom Party, generally voted with the government party. An exception, however, was the general response to the Status of Forces bill, a measure that granted diplomatic immunity to United States military personnel serving in Iran, and to their staffs and families. In effect, the bill would allow these Americans to be tried by United States rather than Iranian courts for crimes committed on Iranian soil. For Iranians the bill recalled the humiliating capitulatory concessions extracted from Iran by the imperial powers in the nineteenth century. Feeling against the bill was sufficiently strong that sixty-five deputies absented themselves from the legislature, and sixty-one opposed the bill when it was put to a vote in October 1964.

The measure also aroused strong feeling outside the Majlis. Khomeini, who had been released from house arrest in April 1964, denounced the measure in a public sermon before a huge congregation in Qom. Tapes of the sermon and a leaflet based on it were widely circulated and attracted considerable attention. Khomeini was arrested again in November, within days of the sermon, and sent into exile in Turkey. In October 1965, he was permitted to take up residence in the city of An Najaf, Iraq—the site of numerous Shia shrines—where he was to remain for the next thirteen years.

Although economic conditions were soon to improve dramatically, the country had not yet fully recovered from the recession of the 1959–63 period, which had imposed hardships on the poorer classes. Mansur attempted to make up a budget deficit of an estimated US$300 million (at then prevalent rates of exchange) by imposing heavy new taxes on gasoline and kerosene and on exit permits for Iranians leaving the country. Because kerosene was the primary heating fuel for the working classes, the new taxes proved highly unpopular. Taxicab drivers in Tehran went on strike, and Mansur was forced to rescind the fuel taxes in January, six weeks after they had been imposed. An infusion of US$200 million in new revenues (US$185 million from a cash bonus for five offshore oil concessions granted to United States and West European firms and US$15 million from a supplementary oil agreement concluded with the Consortium, a group of foreign oil companies) helped the government through its immediate financial difficulties.

With this assistance, Mohammad Reza Shah was able to maintain political stability despite the assassination of his prime minister and an attempt on his own life. On January 21, 1965, Mansur was assassinated by members of a radical Islamic group. Evidence made available after the Islamic Revolution revealed that the group had affiliations with clerics close to Khomeini. A military tribunal sentenced six of those charged to death and the others to long prison terms. In April there was also an attempt on the shah's life, organized by a group of Iranian graduates of British universities. To replace Mansur as prime minister, the shah appointed Amir Abbas Hoveyda, a former diplomat and an executive of the National Iranian Oil Company (NIOC—see Oil and Gas Industry, ch. 3). Hoveyda had helped Mansur found the Progressive Center and the Iran Novin and had served as his minister of finance.

Hoveyda's appointment marked the beginning of nearly a decade of impressive economic growth and relative political stability at home. During this period, the shah also used Iran's enhanced economic and military strength to secure for the country a more influential role in the Persian Gulf region, and he improved relations with Iran's immediate neighbors and the Soviet Union and its allies. Hoveyda remained in office for the next twelve years, the longest term of any of Iran's modern prime ministers. During this decade, the Iran Novin dominated the government and the Majlis. It won large majorities in both the 1967 and the 1971 elections. These elections were carefully controlled by the authorities. Only the Mardom Party and, later, the Pan-Iranist Party, an extreme nationalist group, were allowed to participate in them. Neither party was able to secure more than a handful of Majlis seats, and neither engaged in serious criticism of government programs.

In 1969 and again in 1972, the shah appeared ready to permit the Mardom Party, under new leadership, to function as a genuine opposition, i.e., to criticize the government openly and to contest elections more energetically, but these developments did not occur. The Iran Novin's domination of the administrative machinery was further made evident during municipal council elections held in 136 towns throughout the country in 1968. The Iran Novin won control of a large majority of the councils and every seat in 115 of them. Only 10 percent of eligible voters cast ballots in Tehran, however, a demonstration of public indifference that was not confined to the capital.

Under Hoveyda the government improved its administrative machinery and launched what was dubbed "the education revolution." It adopted a new civil service code and a new tax law and appointed better qualified personnel to key posts. Hoveyda also created several additional ministries in 1967, including the Ministry of Science and Higher Education, which was intended to help meet expanded and more specialized manpower needs. In mid-1968 the government began a program that, although it did not resolve problems of overcrowding and uneven quality, increased the number of institutions of higher education substantially, brought students from provincial and lower middle-class backgrounds into the new community colleges, and created a number of institutions of high academic standing, such as Tehran's Arya Mehr Technical University (see Education, ch. 2).

The shah had remarried in 1959, and the new queen, Farah Diba Pahlavi, had given birth to a male heir, Reza, in 1960. In 1967, because the crown prince was still very young, steps were taken to regularize the procedure for the succession. Under the constitution, if the shah were to die before the crown prince had come of age, the Majlis would meet to appoint a regent. There might be a delay in the appointment of a regent, especially if the Majlis was not in session. A constituent assembly, convened in September 1967, amended the constitution, providing for the queen automatically to act as regent unless the shah in his lifetime designated another individual. In October 1967, believing his achievements finally justified such a step, the shah celebrated his long-postponed coronation. Like his father, he placed the crown on his own head. To mark the occasion, the Majlis conferred on the shah the title of Arya-Mehr, or "Light of the Aryans."

This glorification of the monarchy and the monarch, however, was not universally popular with the Iranians. In 1971 celebrations were held to mark what was presented as 2,500 years of uninterrupted monarchy (there were actually gaps in the chronological record) and the twenty-fifth centennial of the founding of the Iranian empire by Cyrus the Great. The ceremonies were designed primarily to celebrate the institution of monarchy and to affirm the position of the shah as the country's absolute and unchallenged ruler. The lavish ceremonies (which many compared to a Hollywood-style extravaganza), the virtual exclusion of Iranians from the celebrations in which the honored guests were foreign heads of state, and the excessive adulation of the person of the shah in official propaganda generated much adverse domestic comment. A declaration by Khomeini condemning the celebrations and the regime received wide circulation. In 1975, when the Majlis, at government instigation, voted to alter the Iranian calendar so that year one of the calendar coincided with the first year of the reign of Cyrus rather than with the beginning of the Islamic era, many Iranians viewed the move as an unnecessary insult to religious sensibilities.

Iran, meantime, experienced a period of unprecedented and sustained economic growth. The land distribution program launched in 1962, along with steadily expanding job opportunities, improved living standards, and moderate inflation between 1964 and 1973, help explain the relative lack of serious political unrest during this period.

In foreign policy, the shah used the relaxation in East-West tensions to improve relations with the Soviet Union. In an exchange of notes in 1962, he gave Moscow assurances he would not allow Iran to become a base for aggression against the Soviet Union or permit foreign missile bases to be established on Iranian soil. In 1965 Iran and the Soviet Union signed a series of agreements under which the Soviets provided credits and technical assistance to build Iran's first steel mill in exchange for shipments of Iranian natural gas. This led to the construction of the almost 2,000-kilometer-long trans-Iranian gas pipeline from the southern fields to the Iranian-Soviet frontier. The shah also bought small quantities of arms from the Soviet Union and expanded trade with East European states. Although Soviet officials did not welcome the increasingly close military and security cooperation between Iran and the United States, especially after 1971, Moscow did not allow this to disrupt its own rapprochement with Tehran.

In 1964 the shah joined the heads of state of Turkey and Pakistan to create an organization, Regional Cooperation for Development (RCD), for economic, social, and cultural cooperation among the three countries "outside the framework of the Central Treaty Organization." The establishment of RCD was seen as a sign of the diminishing importance of CENTO and, like the rapprochement with the Soviet Union, of the shah's increasing independence in foreign policy. The three RCD member states undertook a number of joint economic and cultural projects, but never on a large scale.

The shah also began to play a larger role in Persian Gulf affairs. He supported the royalists in the Yemen Civil War (1962–70) and, beginning in 1971, assisted the sultan of Oman in putting down a rebellion in Dhofar (see Historical Background, ch. 5). He also reached an understanding with Britain on the fate of Bahrain and

Shah Mohammad Reza Pahlavi distributes land deeds
to a peasant woman under a land reform program
Courtesy United States Information Agency

three smaller islands in the Gulf that Britain had controlled since the nineteenth century but that Iran continued to claim. Britain's decision to withdraw from the Gulf by 1971 and to help organize the Trucial States into a federation of independent states (eventually known as the United Arab Emirates—UAE) necessitated resolution of that situation. In 1970 the shah agreed to give up Iran's long-standing claim to Bahrain and to abide by the desire of the majority of its inhabitants that Bahrain become an independent state. The shah, however, continued to press his claim to three islands, Abu Musa (controlled by the shaykh of Sharjah) and the Greater and Lesser Tunbs (controlled by the shaykh of Ras al Khaymah). He secured control of Abu Musa by agreeing to pay the shaykh of Sharjah an annual subsidy, and he seized the two Tunbs by military force, immediately following Britain's withdrawal.

This incident offended Iraq, however, which broke diplomatic relations with Iran as a result. Relations with Iraq remained strained until 1975, when Iran and Iraq signed the Algiers Agreement, under which Iraq conceded Iran's long-standing demand for equal navigation rights in the Shatt al Arab, and the shah agreed to end support for the Kurdish rebellion in northern Iraq.

With the other Persian Gulf states, Tehran maintained generally good relations. Iran signed agreements with Saudi Arabia and other Gulf states delimiting frontiers along the continental shelf in the Persian Gulf, began cooperation and information-sharing on security matters with Saudi Arabia, and encouraged closer cooperation among the newly independent Gulf shaykhdoms through the Gulf Cooperation Council.

To enhance Iran's role in the Gulf, the shah also used oil revenues to expand and equip the Iranian army, air force, and navy. His desire that, in the aftermath of the British withdrawal, Iran would play the primary role in guaranteeing Gulf security coincided with President Richard M. Nixon's hopes for the region. The Nixon Doctrine, enunciated in 1969, sought to encourage United States allies to shoulder greater responsibility for regional security. Then, during his 1972 visit to Iran, Nixon took the unprecedented step of allowing the shah to purchase any conventional weapon in the United States arsenal in the quantities the shah believed necessary for Iran's defense (see Foreign Influences in Weapons, Training, and Support Systems, ch. 5). United States-Iranian military cooperation deepened when the shah allowed the United States to establish two listening posts in Iran to monitor Soviet ballistic missile launches and other military activity.

Renewed Opposition

In the years that followed the riots of June 1963, there was little overt political opposition. The political parties that had been prominent in the 1950–63 period were weakened by arrests, exile, and internal splits. Political repression continued, and it proved more difficult to articulate a coherent policy of opposition in a period of economic prosperity, foreign policy successes, and such reform measures as land distribution. Nonetheless, opposition parties gradually reorganized, new groups committed to more violent forms of struggle were formed, and more radical Islamic ideologies were developed to revive and fuel the opposition movements.

Both the Tudeh and the National Front underwent numerous splits and reorganizations. The Tudeh leadership remained abroad, and the party did not play a prominent role in Iran until after the Islamic Revolution. Of the National Front parties that managed to survive the post-1963 clampdown, the most prominent was the Nehzat-e Azadi-yi Iran, or the Iran Freedom Movement (IFM), led by Mehdi Bazargan. Bazargan worked to establish links between his movement and the moderate clerical opposition. Like others who looked to Islam as a vehicle for political mobilization, Bazargan was active in preaching the political pertinence of Islam to a younger generation of Iranians. Among the best known thinkers associated with the IFM was Ali Shariati, who argued for an Islam committed to political struggle, social justice, and the cause of the deprived classes.

Khomeini, in exile in Iraq, continued to issue antigovernment statements, to attack the shah personally, and to organize supporters. In a series of lectures delivered to his students in An Najaf in 1969 and 1970 and later published in book form under the title of *Velayat-e Faqih* (The Vice Regency of the Islamic Jurist), he argued that monarchy was a form of government abhorrent to Islam, that true Muslims must strive for the establishment of an Islamic state, and that the leadership of the state belonged by right to the *faqih,* or Islamic jurist. A network of clerics worked for Khomeini in Iran, returning from periods of imprisonment and exile to continue their activities. Increasing internal difficulties in the early 1970s gradually won Khomeini a growing number of followers.

In the meantime, some younger Iranians, disillusioned with what they perceived to be the ineffectiveness of legal opposition to the regime and attracted by the example of guerrilla movements in Cuba, Vietnam, and China, formed a number of underground groups committed to armed struggle. Most of these groups were uncovered and broken up by the security authorities, but two survived: the Fadayan (Cherikha-ye Fadayan-e Khalq, or People's Guerrillas), and the Mojahedin (Mojahedin-e Khalq, or People's Struggle). The Fadayan were Marxist in orientation, whereas the Mojahedin sought to find in Islam the inspiration for an ideology of political struggle and economic radicalism (see Antiregime Opposition Groups, ch. 5). Nevertheless, both movements used similar tactics in attempting to overthrow the regime: attacks on police stations; bombing of United States, British, and Israeli commercial or diplomatic offices; and assassination of Iranian security officers and United States military personnel stationed in Iran. In February 1971, the Fadayan launched the first major guerrilla action against the state with an armed attack on an Imperial Iranian Gendarmerie (the internal security and border guard) post at Siahkal in the Caspian forests of northern Iran. Several similar actions followed. A total of 341 members of these guerrilla movements died between 1971 and 1979 in armed confrontations with security forces, by execution or suicide, or while in the hands of their jailers. Many more served long terms in prison.

The Coming of the Revolution

By late 1976 and early 1977, it was evident that the Iranian economy was in trouble. The shah's attempt to use Iran's vastly expanded oil revenues after 1973 for an unrealistically ambitious industrial and construction program and a massive military buildup

41

greatly strained Iran's human and institutional resources and caused severe economic and social dislocation. Widespread official corruption, rapid inflation, and a growing gap in incomes between the wealthier and the poorer strata of society fed public dissatisfaction.

In response, the government attempted to provide the working and middle classes with some immediate and tangible benefits of the country's new oil wealth. The government nationalized private secondary schools, declared that secondary education would be free for all Iranians, and started a free meal program in schools. It took over private community colleges and extended financial support to university students. It lowered income taxes, inaugurated an ambitious health insurance plan, and speeded up implementation of a program introduced in 1972, under which industrialists were required to sell 49 percent of the shares of their companies to their employees.

The programs were badly implemented, however, and did not adequately compensate for the deteriorating economic position of the urban working class and those, who, like civil servants, were on fixed salaries. To deal with the disruptive effects of excessive spending, the government adopted policies that appeared threatening to the propertied classes and to bazaar, business, and industrial elements who had benefited from economic expansion and might have been expected to support the regime. For example, in an effort to bring down rents, municipalities were empowered to take over empty houses and apartments and to rent and administer them in place of the owners. In an effort to bring down prices in 1975 and 1976, the government declared a war on profiteers, arrested and fined thousands of shopkeepers and petty merchants, and sent two prominent industrialists into exile.

Moreover, by 1978 there were 60,000 foreigners in Iran—45,000 of them Americans—engaged in business or in military training and advisory missions. Combined with a superficial Westernization evident in dress, life styles, music, films, and television programs, this foreign presence tended to intensify the perception that the shah's modernization program was threatening the society's Islamic and Iranian cultural values and identity. Increasing political repression and the establishment of a one-party state in 1975 further alienated the educated classes.

The shah was aware of the rising resentment and dissatisfaction in the country and the increasing international concern about the suppression of basic freedoms in Iran. Organizations such as the International Council of Jurists and Amnesty International were drawing attention to mistreatment of political prisoners and violation of the rights of the accused in Iranian courts. More important, President Jimmy Carter, who took office in January 1977, was making an issue of human rights violations in countries with which the United States was associated. The shah, who had been pressed into a program of land reform and political liberalization by the Kennedy administration, was sensitive to possible new pressures from Washington.

Beginning in early 1977, the shah took a number of steps to meet both domestic and foreign criticism of Iran's human rights record. He released political prisoners and announced new regulations to protect the legal rights of civilians brought before military courts. In July the shah replaced Hoveyda, his prime minister of twelve years, with Jamshid Amuzegar, who had served for over a decade in various cabinet posts. Unfortunately for the shah, however, Amuzegar also became unpopular, as he attempted to slow the overheated economy with measures that, although generally thought necessary, triggered a downturn in employment and private sector profits that would later compound the government's problems.

Leaders of the moderate opposition, professional groups, and the intelligentsia took advantage of the shah's accommodations and the more helpful attitude of the Carter administration to organize and speak out. Many did so in the form of open letters addressed to prominent officials in which the writers demanded adherence to the constitution and restoration of basic freedoms. Lawyers, judges, university professors, and writers formed professional associations to press these demands. The National Front, the IFM, and other political groups resumed activity.

The protest movement took a new turn in January 1978, when a government-inspired article in *Etalaat,* one of the country's leading newspapers, cast doubt on Khomeini's piety and suggested that he was a British agent. The article caused a scandal in the religious community. Senior clerics, including Ayatollah Kazem Shariatmadari, denounced the article. Seminary students took to the streets in Qom and clashed with police, and several demonstrators were killed. The Esfahan bazaar closed in protest. On February 18, mosque services and demonstrations were held in several cities to honor those killed in the Qom demonstrations. In Tabriz these demonstrations turned violent, and it was two days before order could be restored. By the summer, riots and anti-government demonstrations had swept dozens of towns and cities. Shootings inevitably occurred, and deaths of protesters fueled public feeling against the regime.

The cycle of protests that began in Qom and Tabriz differed in nature, composition, and intent from the protests of the preceding year. The 1977 protests were primarily the work of middle-class intellectuals, lawyers, and secular politicians. They took the form of letters, resolutions, and declarations and were aimed at the restoration of constitutional rule. The protests that rocked Iranian cities in the first half of 1978, by contrast, were led by religious elements and were centered on mosques and religious events. They drew on traditional groups in the bazaar and among the urban working class for support. The protesters used a form of calculated violence to achieve their ends, attacking and destroying carefully selected targets that represented objectionable features of the regime: nightclubs and cinemas as symbols of moral corruption and the influence of Western culture; banks as symbols of economic exploitation; Rastakhiz (the party created by the shah in 1975 to run a one-party state) offices and police stations as symbols of political repression. The protests, moreover, aimed at more fundamental change: in slogans and leaflets, the protesters attacked the shah and demanded his removal, and they depicted Khomeini as their leader and an Islamic state as their ideal. From his exile in Iraq, Khomeini continued to issue statements calling for further demonstrations, rejected any form of compromise with the regime, and called for the overthrow of the shah.

The government's position deteriorated further in August 1978, when more than 400 people died in a fire at the Rex Cinema in Abadan. Although evidence available after the Revolution suggested that the fire was deliberately started by religiously inclined students, the opposition carefully cultivated a widespread conviction that the fire was the work of SAVAK agents. Following the Rex Cinema fire, the shah removed Amuzegar and named Jafar Sharif-Emami prime minister. Sharif-Emami, a former minister and prime minister and a trusted royalist, had for many years served as president of the Senate. The new prime minister adopted a policy of conciliation. He eased press controls and permitted more open debate in the Majlis. He released a number of imprisoned clerics, revoked the imperial calendar, closed gambling casinos, and obtained from the shah the dismissal from court and public office of members of the Bahai religion, a sect to which the clerics strongly objected (see Non-Muslim Minorities, ch. 2). These measures, however, did not quell public protests. On September 4, more than 100,000 took part in the public prayers to mark the end of Ramazan, the Muslim fasting month. The ceremony became an occasion for anti-government demonstrations that continued for the next two days, growing larger and more radical in composition and in the slogans of the participants. The government declared martial law in Tehran and eleven other cities on the night of September 7–8, 1978. The next day, troops fired into a a crowd of demonstrators at Tehran's Jaleh Square. A large number of protesters, certainly many more than the official figure of eighty-seven, were killed. The Jaleh Square shooting came to be known as "Black Friday." It considerably radicalized the opposition movement and made compromise with the regime, even by the moderates, less likely.

In October the Iraqi authorities, unable to persuade Khomeini to refrain from further political activity, expelled him from the country. Khomeini went to France and established his headquarters at Neauphle-le-Château, outside Paris. Khomeini's arrival in France provided new impetus to the revolutionary movement. It gave Khomeini and his movement exposure in the world press and media. It made possible easy telephone communication with lieutenants in Tehran and other Iranian cities, thus permitting better coordination of the opposition movement. It allowed Iranian political and religious leaders, who were cut off from Khomeini while he was in Iraq, to visit him for direct consultations. One of these visitors was National Front leader Karim Sanjabi. After a meeting with Khomeini early in November 1978, Sanjabi issued a three-point statement that for the first time committed the National Front to the Khomeini demand for the deposition of the shah and the establishment of a government that would be "democratic and Islamic."

Scattered strikes had occurred in a few private sector and government industries between June and August 1978. Beginning in September, workers in the public sector began to go on strike on a large scale. When the demands of strikers for improved salary and working benefits were quickly met by the Sharif-Emami government, oil workers and civil servants made demands for changes in the political system. The unavailability of fuel oil and freight transport and shortages of raw materials resulting from a customs strike led to the shutting down of most private sector industries in November.

On November 5, 1978, after violent demonstrations in Tehran, the shah replaced Sharif-Emami with General Gholam-Reza Azhari, commander of the Imperial Guard. The shah, addressing the nation for the first time in many months, declared he had heard the people's "revolutionary message," promised to correct past mistakes, and urged a period of quiet and order so that the government could undertake the necessary reforms. Presumably to placate public opinion, the shah allowed the arrest of 132 former leaders and government officials, including former Prime Minister Hoveyda, a former chief of SAVAK, and several former cabinet ministers. He also ordered the release of more than 1,000 political prisoners, including a Khomeini associate, Ayatollah Hosain Ali Montazeri.

The appointment of a government dominated by the military brought about some short-lived abatement in the strike fever, and oil production improved. Khomeini dismissed the shah's promises as worthless, however, and called for continued protests. The Azhari government did not, as expected, use coercion to bring striking government workers back to work. The strikes resumed, virtually shutting down the government, and clashes between demonstrators and troops became a daily occurrence. On December 9 and 10, 1978, in the largest antigovernment demonstrations in a year, several hundred thousand persons participated in marches in Tehran and the provinces to mark Moharram, the month in which Shia mourning occurs.

In December 1978, the shah finally began exploratory talks with members of the moderate opposition. Discussions with Karim Sanjabi proved unfruitful: the National Front leader was bound by his agreement with Khomeini. At the end of December another National Front leader, Shapour Bakhtiar, agreed to form a government on condition the shah leave the country. Bakhtiar secured a vote of confidence from the two houses of the Majlis on January 3, 1979, and presented his cabinet to the shah three days later. The shah, announcing he was going abroad for a short holiday, left the country on January 16, 1979. As his aircraft took off, celebrations broke out across the country.

The Bakhtiar Government

Once installed as prime minister, Bakhtiar took several measures designed to appeal to elements in the opposition movement. He lifted restrictions on the press; the newspapers, on strike since November, resumed publication. He set free remaining political prisoners and promised the dissolution of SAVAK, the lifting of martial law, and free elections. He announced Iran's withdrawal from CENTO, canceled US$7 billion worth of arms orders from the United States, and announced Iran would no longer sell oil to South Africa or Israel.

Although Bakhtiar won the qualified support of moderate clerics like Shariatmadari, his measures did not win him the support of Khomeini and the main opposition elements, who were now committed to the overthrow of the monarchy and the establishment of a new political order. The National Front, with which Bakhtiar had been associated for nearly thirty years, expelled him from the movement. Khomeini declared Bakhtiar's government illegal. Bazargan, in Khomeini's name, persuaded the oil workers to pump enough oil to ease domestic hardship, however, and some normalcy returned to the bazaar in the wake of Bakhtiar's appointment. But strikes in both the public and the private sector and large-scale demonstrations against the government continued. When, on January 29, 1979, Khomeini called for a street "referendum" on the monarchy and the Bakhtiar government, there was a massive turnout.

Bakhtiar sought unsuccessfully to persuade Khomeini to postpone his return to Iran until conditions in the country were normalized. Khomeini refused to receive a member of the regency council Bakhtiar sent as an emissary to Paris and after some hesitation rejected Bakhtiar's offer to come to Paris personally for consultations. Bakhtiar's attempt to prevent Khomeini's imminent return by closing the Mehrabad Airport at Tehran on January 26, 1979, proved to be only a stopgap measure.

Khomeini arrived in Tehran from Paris on February 1, 1979, received a rapturous welcome from millions of Iranians, and announced he would "smash in the mouth of the Bakhtiar government." He labeled the government illegal and called for the strikes and demonstrations to continue. A girls' secondary school at which Khomeini established his headquarters in Tehran became the center of opposition activity. A multitude of decisions, and the coordination of the opposition movement, were handled here by what came to be known as the *komiteh-ye Imam,* or the Imam's committee. On February 5, Khomeini named Mehdi Bazargan as prime minister of a provisional government. Although Bazargan did not immediately announce a cabinet, the move reinforced the conditions of dual authority that increasingly came to characterize the closing days of the Pahlavi monarchy. In many large urban centers local *komitehs* (revolutionary committees) had assumed responsibility for municipal functions, including neighborhood security and the distribution of such basic necessities as fuel oil. Government ministries and such services as the customs and the posts remained largely paralyzed. Bakhtiar's cabinet ministers proved unable to assert their authority or, in many instances, even to enter their offices. The loyalty of the armed forces was being seriously eroded by months of confrontation with the people on the streets. There were instances of troops who refused to fire on the crowds, and desertions were rising. In late January, air force technicians at the Khatami Air Base in Esfahan became involved in a confrontation with their officers.

In his statements, Khomeini had attempted to win the army rank and file over to the side of the opposition. Following Khomeini's

47

arrival in Tehran, clandestine contacts took place between Khomeini's representatives and a number of military commanders. These contacts were encouraged by United States ambassador William Sullivan, who had no confidence in the Bakhtiar government, thought the triumph of the Khomeini forces inevitable, and believed future stability in Iran could be assured only if an accommodation could be reached between the armed forces and the Khomeini camp. Contacts between the military chiefs and the Khomeini camp were also being encouraged by United States general Robert E. Huyser, who had arrived in Tehran on January 4, 1979, as President Carter's special emissary. Huyser's assignment was to keep the Iranian army intact, to encourage the military to maintain support for the Bakhtiar government, and to prepare the army for a takeover, should that become necessary. Huyser began a round of almost daily meetings with the service chiefs of the army, navy, and air force, plus heads of the National Police and the Gendarmerie who were sometimes joined by the chief of SAVAK. He dissuaded those so inclined from attempting a coup immediately upon Khomeini's return to Iran, but he failed to get the commanders to take any other concerted action. He left Iran on February 3, before the final confrontation between the army and the revolutionary forces.

On February 8, uniformed airmen appeared at Khomeini's home and publicly pledged their allegiance to him. On February 9, air force technicians at the Doshan Tappeh Air Base outside Tehran mutinied. Units of the Imperial Guard failed to put down the insurrection. The next day, the arsenal was opened, and weapons were distributed to crowds outside the air base. The government announced a curfew beginning in the afternoon, but the curfew was universally ignored. Over the next twenty-four hours, revolutionaries seized police barracks, prisons, and buildings. On February 11, twenty-two senior military commanders met and announced that the armed forces would observe neutrality in the confrontation between the government and the people. The army's withdrawal from the streets was tantamount to a withdrawal of support for the Bakhtiar government and acted as a trigger for a general uprising. By late afternoon on February 12, Bakhtiar was in hiding, and key points throughout the capital were in rebel hands. The Pahlavi monarchy had collapsed.

The Revolution

Bazargan and the Provisional Government

Mehdi Bazargan became the first prime minister of the revolutionary regime in February 1979. Bazargan, however, headed a government that controlled neither the country nor even its own bureaucratic apparatus. Central authority had broken down. Hundreds of semi-independent revolutionary committees, not answerable to central authority, were performing a variety of functions in major cities and towns across the country. Factory workers, civil servants, white-collar employees, and students were often in control, demanding a say in running their organizations and choosing their chiefs. Governors, military commanders, and other officials appointed by the prime minister were frequently rejected by the lower ranks or local inhabitants. A range of political groups, from the far left to the far right, from secular to ultra-Islamic, were vying for political power, pushing rival agendas, and demanding immediate action from the prime minister. Clerics led by Ayatollah Mohammad Beheshti established the Islamic Republican Party (IRP). The party emerged as the organ of the clerics around Khomeini and the major political organization in the country. Not to be outdone, followers of more moderate senior cleric Shariatmadari established the Islamic People's Republican Party (IPRP) in 1979, which had a base in Azarbaijan, Shariatmadari's home province.

Moreover, multiple centers of authority emerged within the government. As the supreme leader, Khomeini did not consider himself bound by the government. He made policy pronouncements, named personal representatives to key government organizations, established new institutions, and announced decisions without consulting his prime minister. The prime minister found he had to share power with the Revolutionary Council, which Khomeini had established in January 1979 and which initially was composed of clerics close to Khomeini, secular political leaders identified with Bazargan, and two representatives of the armed forces. With the establishment of the provisional government, Bazargan and his colleagues left the council to form the cabinet. They were replaced by Khomeini aides from the Paris period, such as Abolhassan Bani Sadr and Sadeq Qotbzadeh, and by protégés of Khomeini's clerical associates. The cabinet was to serve as the executive authority. But the Revolutionary Council was to wield supreme decision-making and legislative authority.

Differences quickly emerged between the cabinet and the council over appointments, the role of the revolutionary courts and other revolutionary organizations, foreign policy, and the general direction of the Revolution. Bazargan and his cabinet colleagues were eager for a return to normalcy and rapid reassertion of central authority. Clerics of the Revolutionary Council, more responsive to the Islamic and popular temper of the mass of their followers, generally favored more radical economic and social measures. They also proved more willing and able to mobilize and to use the street crowd and the revolutionary organizations to achieve their ends.

In July 1979, Bazargan obtained Khomeini's approval for an arrangement he hoped would permit closer cooperation between the Revolutionary Council and the cabinet. Four clerical members of the council joined the government, one as minister of interior and three others as undersecretaries of interior, education, and defense, while Bazargan and three cabinet colleagues joined the council. (All eight continued in their original positions as well.) Nevertheless, tensions persisted.

Even while attempting to put in place the institutions of the new order, the revolutionaries turned their attention to bringing to trial and punishing members of the former regime whom they considered responsible for carrying out political repression, plundering the country's wealth, implementing damaging economic policies, and allowing foreign exploitation of Iran. A revolutionary court set to work almost immediately in the school building in Tehran where Khomeini had set up his headquarters. Revolutionary courts were established in provincial centers shortly thereafter. The Tehran court passed death sentences on four of the shah's generals on February 16, 1979; all four were executed by firing squad on the roof of the building housing Khomeini's headquarters. More executions, of military and police officers, SAVAK agents, cabinet ministers, Majlis deputies, and officials of the shah's regime, followed on an almost daily basis.

The activities of the revolutionary courts became a focus of intense controversy. On the one hand, left-wing political groups and populist clerics pressed hard for "revolutionary justice" for miscreants of the former regime. On the other hand, lawyers' and human rights' groups protested the arbitrary nature of the revolutionary courts, the vagueness of charges, and the absence of defense lawyers. Bazargan, too, was critical of the courts' activities. At the prime minister's insistence, the revolutionary courts suspended their activities on March 14, 1979. On April 5, new regulations governing the courts were promulgated. The courts were to be established at the discretion of the Revolutionary Council and with Khomeini's permission. They were authorized to try a variety of broadly defined crimes, such as "sowing corruption on earth," "crimes against the people," and "crimes against the Revolution." The courts resumed their work on April 6. On the following day, despite international pleas for clemency, Hoveyda, the shah's prime minister for twelve years, was put to death. Attempts by Bazargan to have the revolutionary courts placed under the judiciary and to secure protection for potential victims through amnesties issued by Khomeini also failed. Beginning in August 1979, the courts tried and passed death sentences on members of ethnic minorities involved in antigovernment movements. Some 550 persons had been executed by the time Bazargan resigned in November 1979.

Bazargan had also attempted, but failed, to bring the revolutionary committees under his control. The committees, whose members were armed, performed a variety of duties. They policed neighborhoods in urban areas, guarded prisons and government buildings, made arrests, and served as the execution squads of the revolutionary tribunals. The committees often served the interests of powerful individual clerics, revolutionary personalities, and political groups, however. They made unauthorized arrests, intervened in labor-management disputes, and seized property. Despite these abuses, members of the Revolutionary Council wanted to bring the committees under their own control, rather than eliminate them. With this in mind, in February 1979 they appointed Ayatollah Mohammad Reza Mahdavi-Kani head of the Tehran revolutionary committee and charged him with supervising the committees countrywide. Mahdavi-Kani dissolved many committees, consolidated others, and sent thousands of committeemen home. But the committees, like the revolutionary courts, endured, serving as one of the coercive arms of the revolutionary government.

In May 1979 Khomeini authorized the establishment of the Pasdaran (Pasdaran-e Enghelab-e Islami, Islamic Revolutionary Guard Corps or Revolutionary Guards—see Special and Irregular Armed Forces, ch. 5). The Pasdaran was conceived by the men around Khomeini as a military force loyal to the Revolution and the clerical leaders, as a counterbalance for the regular army, and as a force to use against the guerrilla organizations of the left, which were also arming. Disturbances among the ethnic minorities accelerated the expansion of the Pasdaran.

Two other important organizations were established in this formative period. In March Khomeini established the Foundation for the Disinherited (Bonyad-e Mostazafin—see Treatment of Veterans and Widows, ch. 5). The organization was to take charge of the assets of the Pahlavi Foundation and to use the proceeds to assist low-income groups. The new foundation in time came to be one of the largest conglomerates in the country, controlling hundreds of expropriated and nationalized factories, trading firms, farms, and apartment and office buildings, as well as two large newspaper chains. The Crusade for Reconstruction (Jihad-e Sazandegi or Jihad), established in June, recruited young people for construction of clinics, local roads, schools, and similar facilities in villages and rural areas. The organization also grew rapidly, assuming functions in rural areas that had previously been handled by the Planning and Budget Organization (which replaced the Plan Organization in 1973) and the Ministry of Agriculture.

Trouble broke out among the Turkomans, the Kurds, and the Arabic-speaking population of Khuzestan in March 1979 (see Peoples and Languages, ch. 2). The disputes in the Turkoman region of Gorgan were over land rather than claims for Turkoman cultural identity or autonomy. Representatives of left-wing movements, active in the region, were encouraging agricultural workers to seize land from the large landlords. These disturbances were put down, but not without violence. Meanwhile, in Khuzestan, the center of Iran's oil industry, members of the Arabic-speaking population organized and demanded a larger share of oil revenues for the region, more jobs for local inhabitants, the use of Arabic as a semi-official language, and a larger degree of local autonomy. Because Arab states, including Iraq, had in the past laid claim to Khuzestan as part of the "Arab homeland," the government was bound to regard an indigenous movement among the Arabic-speaking population with suspicion. The government also suspected that scattered instances of sabotage in the oil fields were occurring with Iraqi connivance. In May 1979, government forces responded to these disturbances by firing on Arab demonstrators in Khorramshahr. Several demonstrators were killed; others were shot on orders of the local revolutionary court. The government subsequently quietly transferred the religious leader of the Khuzestan Arabs, Ayatollah Mohammad Taher Shubayr al Khaqani, to Qom, where he was kept under house arrest. These measures ended further protests.

The Kurdish uprising proved more deep-rooted, serious, and durable. The Kurdish leaders were disappointed that the Revolution had not brought them the local autonomy they had long desired. Scattered fighting began in March 1979 between government and Kurdish forces and continued after a brief cease-fire; attempts at negotiation proved abortive. One faction, led by Ahmad Muftizadeh, the Friday prayer leader in Sanandaj, was ready to accept the limited concessions offered by the government, but the Kurdish Democratic Party, led by Abdol-Rahman Qasemlu, and a more radical group led by Shaykh Ezz ad Din Husaini issued demands that the authorities in Tehran did not feel they could accept. These included the enlargement of the Kordestan region to include all Kurdish-speaking areas in Iran, a specified share of the national revenue for expenditure in the province, and complete autonomy in provincial administration. Kurdish was to be recognized as an official language for local use and for correspondence with the central government. Kurds were to fill all local government posts and to be in charge of local security forces. The central government would remain responsible for national defense, foreign affairs, and central banking functions. Similar autonomy would be granted other ethnic minorities in the country. With the rejection of these demands, serious fighting broke out in August 1979. Khomeini, invoking his powers as commander in chief, used the army against other Iranians for the first time since the Revolution. No settlement was reached with the Kurds during Bazargan's prime ministership.

Because the Bazargan government lacked the necessary security forces to control the streets, such control passed gradually into the hands of clerics in the Revolutionary Council and the IRP, who ran the revolutionary courts and had influence with the Pasdaran, the revolutionary committees, and the club-wielding *hezbollahis* (see Glossary), or "partisans of the party of God." The clerics deployed these forces to curb rival political organizations. In June the Revolutionary Council promulgated a new press law and began a crackdown against the proliferating political press. On August 8, 1979, the revolutionary prosecutor banned the leading left-wing newspaper, *Ayandegan*. Five days later *hezbollahis* broke up a Tehran rally called by the National Democratic Front, a newly organized left-of-center political movement, to protest the *Ayandegan* closing. The Revolutionary Council then proscribed the front itself and issued a warrant for the arrest of its leader. *Hezbollahis* also attacked the headquarters of the Fadayan organization and forced the Mojahedin to evacuate their headquarters. On August 20, forty-one opposition papers were proscribed. On September 8, the two largest newspaper chains in the country, Kayhan and Etalaat, were expropriated and transferred to the Foundation for the Disinherited.

In June and July 1979, the Revolutionary Council also passed a number of major economic measures, whose effect was to transfer considerable private sector assets to the state. It nationalized banks, insurance companies, major industries, and certain categories of urban land; expropriated the wealth of leading business and industrial families; and appointed state managers to many private industries and companies.

The New Constitution

Khomeini had charged the provisional government with the task of drawing up a draft constitution. A step in this direction was taken on March 30 and 31, 1979, when a national referendum was held to determine the kind of political system to be established. Khomeini rejected demands by various political groups and by Shariatmadari that voters be given a wide choice. The only form of government to appear on the ballot was an Islamic republic, and voting was not by secret ballot. The government reported an overwhelming majority of over 98 percent in favor of an Islamic republic. Khomeini proclaimed the establishment of the Islamic Republic of Iran on April 1, 1979.

The Khomeini regime unveiled a draft constitution on June 18. Aside from substituting a strong president, on the Gaullist model, for the monarchy, the constitution did not differ markedly from the 1906 constitution and did not give the clerics an important role in the new state structure (see Constitutional Framework, ch. 4). Khomeini was prepared to submit this draft, virtually unmodified, to a national referendum or, barring that, to an appointed council of forty representatives who could advise on, but not revise, the document. Ironically, as it turned out, it was the parties of the left who most vehemently rejected this procedure and demanded that the constitution be submitted for full-scale review by a constituent assembly. Shariatmadari supported these demands.

A newly created seventy-three-member Assembly of Experts convened on August 18, 1979, to consider the draft constitution. Clerics, and members and supporters of the IRP dominated the assembly, which revamped the constitution to establish the basis for a state dominated by the Shia clergy. The Assembly of Experts completed its work on November 15, and the Constitution was approved in a national referendum on December 2 and 3, 1979, once again, according to government figures, by over 98 percent of the vote.

In October 1979, when it had become clear that the draft constitution would institutionalize clerical domination of the state, Bazargan and a number of his cabinet colleagues had attempted to persuade Khomeini to dissolve the Assembly of Experts, but Khomeini refused. Now opposition parties attempted to articulate their objections to the Constitution through protests led by the IPRP. Following the approval of the Constitution, Shariatmadari's followers in Tabriz organized demonstrations and seized control of the radio station. A potentially serious challenge to the dominant clerical hierarchy fizzled out, however, when Shariatmadari wavered in his support for the protesters, and the pro-Khomeini forces organized massive counterdemonstrations in the city in 1979. In fear of condemnation by Khomeini and of IRP reprisals, the IPRP in December 1979 announced the dissolution of the party.

Few foreign initiatives were possible in the early months of the Revolution. The Bazargan government attempted to maintain correct relations with the Persian Gulf states, despite harsh denunciations of the Gulf rulers by senior clerics and revolutionary leaders. Anti-American feeling was widespread and was fanned by Khomeini himself, populist preachers, and the left-wing parties. Bazargan, however, continued to seek military spare parts from Washington and asked for intelligence information on Soviet and Iraqi activities in Iran. On November 1, 1979, Bazargan met with President Carter's national security adviser, Zbigniew K. Brzezinski, in Algiers, where the two men were attending Independence Day celebrations. Meanwhile, the shah, who was seriously ill, was admitted to the United States for medical treatment. Iranians feared that the shah would use this visit to the United States to secure United States support for an attempt to overthrow the Islamic Republic. On November 1, 1979, hundreds of thousands marched in Tehran to demand the shah's extradition, while the press denounced Bazargan for meeting with a key United States official. On November 4, young men who later designated themselves "students of the Imam's line" (imam—see Glossary), occupied the United States embassy compound and took United States diplomats hostage. Bazargan resigned two days later; no prime minister was named to replace him.

The Revolutionary Council took over the prime minister's functions, pending presidential and Majlis elections. The elections for the new president were held in January 1980; Bazargan, fearing further personal attacks, did not run. The three leading candidates were Jalal od Din Farsi, representing the IRP, the dominant clerical party; Abolhasan Bani Sadr, an independent associated with Khomeini who had written widely on the relationship of Islam to politics and economics; and Admiral Ahmad Madani, a naval officer who had served as governor of Khuzestan Province and commander of the navy after the Revolution. Farsi, however, was disqualified because of his Afghan origin, leaving Bani Sadr and Madani as the primary challengers. Bani Sadr was elected by 75 percent of the vote.

The Bani Sadr Presidency

Bani Sadr's program as president was to reestablish central authority, gradually to phase out the Pasdaran and the revolutionary courts and committees and to absorb them into other government organizations, to reduce the influence of the clerical hierarchy, and to launch a program for economic reform and development. Against the wishes of the IRP, Khomeini allowed Bani Sadr to be sworn in as president in January 1980, before the convening of the Majlis. Khomeini further bolstered Bani Sadr's position by appointing him chairman of the Revolutionary Council and delegating to the president his own powers as commander in chief of the armed forces. On the eve of the Iranian New Year, on March 20, Khomeini issued a message to the nation designating the coming year as "the year of order and security" and outlining a program reflecting Bani Sadr's own priorities.

Nevertheless, the problem of multiple centers of power and of revolutionary organizations not subject to central control persisted to plague Bani Sadr. Like Bazargan, Bani Sadr found he was competing for primacy with the clerics and activists of the IRP. The struggle between the president and the IRP dominated the political life of the country during Bani Sadr's presidency. Bani Sadr failed to secure the dissolution of the Pasdaran and the revolutionary courts and committees. He also failed to establish control over the judiciary or the radio and television networks. Khomeini himself appointed IRP members Ayatollah Mohammad Beheshti as chief justice and Ayatollah Abdol-Karim Musavi-Ardabili as prosecutor general (also seen as attorney general). Bani Sadr's appointees to head the state broadcasting services and the Pasdaran were forced to resign within weeks of their appointments.

Parliamentary elections were held in two stages in March and May 1980, amid charges of fraud. The official results gave the IRP and its supporters 130 of 241 seats decided (elections were not completed in all 270 constituencies). Candidates associated with Bani Sadr and with Bazargan's IFM each won a handful of seats; other left-of-center secular parties fared no better. Candidates of the radical left-wing parties, including the Mojahedin, the Fadayan, and the Tudeh, won no seats at all. IRP dominance of the Majlis was reinforced when the credentials of a number of deputies representing the National Front and the Kurdish-speaking areas, or standing as independents, were rejected. The consequences of this distribution of voting power soon became evident. The Majlis began its deliberations in June 1980. Hojjatoleslam Ali Akbar Hashemi-Rafsanjani, a cleric and founding member of the IRP, was elected Majlis speaker. After a two-month deadlock between the president and the Majlis over the selection of the prime minister, Bani Sadr was forced to accept the IRP candidate, Mohammad Ali Rajai. Rajai, a former street peddler and schoolteacher, was a Beheshti protégé. The designation of cabinet ministers was delayed because Bani Sadr refused to confirm cabinet lists submitted by Rajai. In September 1980, Bani Sadr finally confirmed fourteen of a list of twenty-one ministers proposed by the prime minister. Some key cabinet posts, including the ministries of foreign affairs, labor, commerce, and finance, were filled only gradually over the next six

Demonstrators outside the United States Embassy
in Tehran in late 1979
Copyright Lehtikuva/PHOTRI

months. The differences between president and prime minister over cabinet appointments remained unresolved until May 1981, when the Majlis passed a law allowing the prime minister to appoint caretakers to ministries still lacking a minister.

The president's inability to control the revolutionary courts and the persistence of revolutionary temper were demonstrated in May 1980, when executions, which had become rare in the previous few months, began again on a large scale. Some 900 executions were carried out, most of them between May and September 1980, before Bani Sadr left office in June 1981. In September the chief justice finally restricted the authority of the courts to impose death sentences. Meanwhile a remark by Khomeini in June 1980 that "royalists" were still to be found in government offices led to a resumption of widespread purges. Within days of Khomeini's remarks some 130 unofficial purge committees were operating in government offices. Before the wave of purges could be stopped, some 4,000 civil servants and between 2,000 and 4,000 military officers lost their jobs. Around 8,000 military officers had been dismissed or retired in previous purges.

The Kurdish problem also proved intractable. The rebellion continued, and the Kurdish leadership refused to compromise on its demands for local autonomy. Fighting broke out again in April

1980, followed by another cease-fire on April 29. Kurdish leaders and the government negotiated both in Mahabad and in Tehran, but, although Bani Sadr announced he was prepared to accept the Kurdish demands with "modifications," the discussions broke down and fighting resumed. The United States hostage crisis was another problem that weighed heavily on Bani Sadr. The "students of the Imam's line" and their IRP supporters holding the hostages were using the hostage issue and documents found in the embassy to radicalize the public temper, to challenge the authority of the president, and to undermine the reputations of moderate politicians and public figures. The crisis was exacerbating relations with the United States and West European countries. President Carter had ordered several billion dollars of Iranian assets held by American banks in the United States and abroad to be frozen. Bani Sadr's various attempts to resolve the crisis proved abortive. He arranged for the UN secretary general to appoint a commission to investigate Iranian grievances against the United States, with the understanding that the hostages would be turned over to the Revolutionary Council as a preliminary step to their final release. The plan broke down when, on February 23, 1980, the eve of the commission's arrival in Tehran, Khomeini declared that only the Majlis, whose election was still several months away, could decide the fate of the hostages.

The shah had meantime made his home in Panama. Bani Sadr and Foreign Minister Qotbzadeh attempted to arrange for the shah to be arrested by the Panamanian authorities and extradited to Iran. But the shah abruptly left Panama for Egypt on March 23, 1980, before any summons could be served.

In April the United States attempted to rescue the hostages by secretly landing aircraft and troops near Tabas, along the Dasht-e Kavir desert in eastern Iran. Two helicopters on the mission failed, however, and when the mission commander decided to abort the mission, a helicopter and a C–130 transport aircraft collided, killing eight United States servicemen.

The failed rescue attempt had negative consequences for the Iranian military. Radical factions in the IRP and left-wing groups charged that Iranian officers opposed to the Revolution had secretly assisted the United States aircraft to escape radar detection. They renewed their demand for a purge of the military command. Bani Sadr was able to prevent such a purge, but he was forced to reshuffle the top military command. In June 1980, the chief judge of the Army Military Revolutionary Tribunal announced the discovery of an antigovernment plot centered on the military base in Piranshahr in Kordestan. Twenty-seven junior and warrant officers were arrested. In July the authorities announced they had uncovered a plot centered on the Shahrokhi Air Base in Hamadan. Six hundred officers and men were implicated. Ten of the alleged plotters were killed when members of the Pasdaran broke into their headquarters. Approximately 300 officers, including two generals, were arrested, and warrants were issued for 300 others. The government charged the accused with plotting to overthrow the state and seize power in the name of exiled leader Bakhtiar. Khomeini ignored Bani Sadr's plea for clemency and said those involved must be executed. As many as 140 officers were shot on orders of the military tribunal; wider purges of the armed forces followed.

In September 1980, perhaps believing the hostage crisis could serve no further diplomatic or political end, the Rajai government indicated to Washington through a diplomat of the Federal Republic of Germany (West Germany) that it was ready to negotiate in earnest for the release of the hostages. Talks opened on September 14 in West Germany and continued for the next four months, with the Algerians acting as intermediaries. The hostages were released on January 20, 1981, concurrently with President Ronald Reagan's taking the oath of office. The United States in return released US$11 to US$12 billion in Iranian funds that had been frozen by presidential order. Iran, however, agreed to repay US$5.1 billion in syndicated and nonsyndicated loans owed to United States and foreign banks and to place another US$1 billion in an escrow account, pending the settlement of claims filed against Iran by United States firms and citizens. These claims, and Iranian claims against United States firms, were adjudicated by a special tribunal of the International Court of Justice at The Hague, established under the terms of the Algiers Agreement. As of 1987, the court was still reviewing outstanding cases, of which there were several thousand.

The hostage settlement served as a further bone of contention between the Rajai government, which negotiated the terms, and Bani Sadr. The president and the governor of the Central Bank (Central Bank of the Islamic Republic of Iran—established originally in 1960 as Bank Markazi Iran), a presidential appointee, charged the Iranian negotiators with accepting terms highly disadvantageous to Iran.

One incentive to the settling of the hostage crisis had been that in September 1980 Iran became engaged in full-scale hostilities with Iraq. The conflict stemmed from Iraqi anxieties over possible spillover effects of the Iranian Revolution. Iranian propagandists were spreading the message of the Islamic Revolution throughout the Gulf, and the Iraqis feared this propaganda would infect the Shia Muslims who constituted a majority of Iraq's population.

59

The friction between Iran and Iraq led to border incidents, beginning in April 1980. The Iraqi government saw in the disturbed situation in Iran the opportunity to undo the 1975 Algiers Agreement concluded with the shah (not to be confused with the 1980 United States-Iran negotiations). There is also evidence the Iraqis hoped to bring about the overthrow of the Khomeini regime and to establish a more moderate government in Iran. On September 17, President Saddam Husayn of Iraq abrogated the Algiers Agreement. Five days later Iraqi troops and aircraft began a massive invasion of Iran (see The Iran-Iraq War, ch. 5).

The war did nothing to moderate the friction between Bani Sadr and the Rajai government with its clerical and IRP backers. Bani Sadr championed the cause of the army; his IRP rivals championed the cause of the Pasdaran, for which they demanded heavy equipment and favorable treatment. Bani Sadr accused the Rajai government of hampering the war effort; the prime minister and his backers accused the president of planning to use the army to seize power. The prime minister also fought the president over the control of foreign and domestic economic policy. In late October 1980, in a private letter to Khomeini, Bani Sadr asked Khomeini to dismiss the Rajai government and to give him, as president, wide powers to run the country during the war emergency. He subsequently also urged Khomeini to dissolve the Majlis, the Supreme Judicial Council, and the Council of Guardians so that a new beginning could be made in structuring the government. In November Bani Sadr charged that torture was taking place in Iranian prisons and that individuals were executed ''as easily as one takes a drink of water.'' A commission Khomeini appointed to investigate the torture charges, however, claimed it found no evidence of mistreatment of prisoners.

There were others critical of the activities of the IRP, the revolutionary courts and committees, and the club-wielding *hezbollahis* who broke up meetings of opposition groups. In November and December, a series of rallies critical of the government was organized by Bani Sadr supporters in Mashhad, Esfahan, Tehran, and Gilan. In December, merchants of the Tehran bazaar who were associated with the National Front called for the resignation of the Rajai government. In February 1981, Bazargan denounced the government at a mass rally. A group of 133 writers, journalists, and academics issued a letter protesting the suppression of basic freedoms. Senior clerics questioned the legitimacy of the revolutionary courts, widespread property confiscations, and the power exercised by Khomeini as *faqih*. Even Khomeini's son, Ahmad Khomeini, initially spoke on the president's behalf. The IRP retaliated by using its *hezbollahi* gangs to break up Bani Sadr rallies in various cities and to harass opposition organizations. In November it arrested Qotbzadeh, the former foreign minister, for an attack on the IRP. Two weeks later, the offices of Bazargan's paper, *Mizan,* were smashed.

Khomeini initially sought to mediate the differences between Bani Sadr and the IRP to prevent action that would irreparably weaken the president, the army, or the other institutions of the state. He ordered the cancellation of a demonstration called for December 19, 1980, to demand the dismissal of Bani Sadr as commander in chief. In January 1981, he urged nonexperts to leave the conduct of the war to the military. The next month he warned clerics in the revolutionary organizations not to interfere in areas outside their competence. On March 16, after meeting with and failing to persuade Bani Sadr, Rajai, and clerical leaders to resolve their differences, he issued a ten-point declaration confirming the president in his post as commander in chief and banning further speeches, newspaper articles, and remarks contributing to factionalism. He established a three-man committee to resolve differences between Bani Sadr and his critics and to ensure that both parties adhered to Khomeini's guidelines. This arrangement soon broke down. Bani Sadr, lacking other means, once again took his case to the public in speeches and newspaper articles. The adherents of the IRP used the revolutionary organizations, the courts, and the *hezbollahi* gangs to undermine the president.

The three-man committee appointed by Khomeini returned a finding against the president. In May, the Majlis passed measures to permit the prime minister to appoint caretakers to ministries still lacking a minister, to deprive the president of his veto power, and to allow the prime minister rather than the president to appoint the governor of the Central Bank. Within days the Central Bank governor was replaced by a Rajai appointee.

By the end of May, Bani Sadr appeared also to be losing Khomeini's support. On May 27, Khomeini denounced Bani Sadr, without mentioning him by name, for placing himself above the law and ignoring the dictates of the Majlis. On June 7, *Mizan* and Bani Sadr's newspaper, *Enqelab-e Eslami,* were banned. Three days later, Khomeini removed Bani Sadr from his post as the acting commander in chief of the military. Meanwhile, gangs roamed the streets calling for Bani Sadr's ouster and death and clashed with Bani Sadr supporters. On June 10, participants in a Mojahedin rally at Revolution Square in Tehran clashed with *hezbollahis.* On June 12, a motion for the impeachment of the president was presented by 120 deputies. On June 13 or 14, Bani Sadr, fearing for his life, went into hiding. The speaker of the Majlis, after initially blocking the motion, allowed it to go forward on June 17. The next day, the Mojahedin issued a call for "revolutionary resistance in all its forms." The government treated this as a call for rebellion and moved to confront the opposition on the streets. Twenty-three protesters were executed on June 20 and 21, as the Majlis debated the motion for impeachment. In the debate, several speakers denounced Bani Sadr; only five spoke in his favor. On June 21, with 30 deputies absenting themselves from the house or abstaining, the Majlis decided for impeachment on a vote of 177 to 1. The revolutionary movement had brought together a coalition of clerics, middle-class liberals, and secular radicals against the shah. The impeachment of Bani Sadr represented the triumph of the clerical party over the other members of this coalition.

Terror and Repression

Following the fall of Bani Sadr, opposition elements attempted to reorganize and to overthrow the government by force. The government responded with a policy of repression and terror. The government also took steps to impose its version of an Islamic legal system and an Islamic code of social and moral behavior.

Bani Sadr remained in hiding for several weeks. Believing he was illegally impeached, he maintained his claim to the presidency, formed an alliance with Mojahedin leader Masoud Rajavi, and in July 1981 escaped with Rajavi from Iran to France. In Paris, Bani Sadr and Rajavi announced the establishment of the National Council of Resistance (NCR) and committed themselves to work for the overthrow of the Khomeini regime. They announced a program that emphasized a form of democracy based on elected popular councils; protection for the rights of the ethnic minorities; special attention to the interests of shopkeepers, small landowners, and civil servants; limited land reform; and protection for private property in keeping with the national interest. The Kurdish Democratic Party, the National Democratic Front, and a number of other small groups and individuals subsequently announced their adherence to the NCR.

Meanwhile, violent opposition to the regime in Iran continued. On June 28, 1981, a powerful bomb exploded at the headquarters of the IRP while a meeting of party leaders was in progress. Seventy-three persons were killed, including the chief justice and party secretary general Mohammad Beheshti, four cabinet ministers, twenty-seven Majlis deputies, and several other government officials. Elections for a new president were held on July 24, and Rajai, the prime minister, was elected to the post. On August 5, 1981, the Majlis approved Rajai's choice of Ayatollah Mohammad Javad-Bahonar as prime minister.

Rajai and Bahonar, along with the chief of the Tehran police, lost their lives when a bomb went off during a meeting at the office of the prime minister on August 30. The Majlis named another cleric, Mahdavi-Kani, as interim prime minister. In a new round of elections on October 2, Hojjatoleslam Ali Khamenehi was elected president. Division within the leadership became apparent, however, when the Majlis rejected Khamenehi's nominee, Ali Akbar Velayati, as prime minister. On October 28, the Majlis elected Mir-Hosain Musavi, a protégé of the late Mohammad Beheshti, as prime minister.

Although no group claimed responsibility for the bombings that had killed Iran's political leadership, the government blamed the Mojahedin for both. The Mojahedin did, however, claim responsibility for a spate of other assassinations that followed the overthrow of Bani Sadr. Among those killed in the space of a few months were the Friday prayer leaders in Tabriz, Kerman, Shiraz, Yazd, and Bakhtaran; a provincial governor; the warden of Evin Prison, the chief ideologue of the IRP; and several revolutionary court judges, Majlis deputies, minor government officials, and members of revolutionary organizations.

In September 1981, expecting to spark a general uprising, the Mojahedin sent their young followers into the streets to demonstrate against the government and to confront the authorities with their own armed contingents. On September 27, the Mojahedin used machine guns and rocket-propelled grenade launchers against units of the Pasdaran. Smaller left-wing opposition groups, including the Fadayan, attempted similar guerrilla activities. In July 1981, members of the Union of Communists tried to seize control of the Caspian town of Amol. At least seventy guerrillas and Pasdaran members were killed before the uprising was put down. The government responded to the armed challenge of the guerrilla groups by expanded use of the Pasdaran in counterintelligence activities and by widespread arrests, jailings, and executions. The executions were facilitated by a September 1981 Supreme Judicial Council circular to the revolutionary courts permitting death sentences for "active members" of guerrilla groups. Fifty executions a day became routine; there were days when more than 100 persons were executed. Amnesty International documented 2,946 executions in the 12 months following Bani Sadr's impeachment, a conservative figure because the authorities did not report all executions. The pace of executions slackened considerably at the end of 1982, partly as a result of a deliberate government decision but primarily because, by then, the back of the armed resistance movement had largely been broken. The radical opposition had, however, eliminated several key clerical leaders, exposed vulnerabilities in the state's security apparatus, and posed the threat, never realized, of sparking a wider opposition movement.

By moving quickly to hold new elections and to fill vacant posts, the government managed to maintain continuity in authority, however, and by repression and terror it was able to crush the guerrilla movements. By the end of 1983, key leaders of the Fadayan, Paykar (a Marxist-oriented splinter group of the Mojahedin), the Union of Communists, and the Mojahedin in Iran had been killed, thousands of the rank and file had been executed or were in prison, and the organizational structure of these movements was gravely weakened. Only the Mojahedin managed to survive, and even it had to transfer its main base of operations to Kordestan, and later to Kurdistan in Iraq, and its headquarters to Paris (see Antiregime Opposition Groups, ch. 5).

During this period, the government was also able to consolidate its position in Kordestan. Fighting had resumed between government forces and Kurdish rebels after the failure of talks under Bani Sadr in late 1980. The Kurds held parts of the countryside and were able to enter the major cities at will after dark. With its takeover of Bukan in November 1981, however, the government reasserted control over the major urban centers. Further campaigns in 1983 reduced rebel control over the countryside, and the Kurdish Democratic Party had to move its headquarters to Iraq, from which it made forays into Iran. The Kurdish movement was further weakened when differences between the Kurdish Democratic Party and the more radical Komala (Komala-ye Shureshgari-ye Zahmat Keshan-e Kordestan-e Iran, or Committee of the Revolutionary Toilers of Iranian Kordestan), a Kurdish Marxist guerrilla organization, resulted in open fighting in 1985.

The government also moved against other active and potential opponents. In April 1982, the authorities arrested former Khomeini aide and foreign minister Qotbzadeh and charged him with plotting with military officers and clerics to kill Khomeini and to overthrow the state. Approximately 170 others, including 70 military men, were also arrested. The government implicated the respected religious leader Shariatmadari, whose son-in-law had allegedly served as the intermediary between Qotbzadeh and Shariatmadari. At his trial, Qotbzadeh denied any design on Khomeini's life and claimed he had wanted only to change the government, not to overthrow the Islamic Republic. Shariatmadari, in a television interview, said he had been told of the plot but did not actively support it. Qotbzadeh and the military men were executed, and Shariat-madari's son-in-law was jailed. In an unprecedented move, members of the Association of the Seminary Teachers of Qom voted to strip Shariatmadari of his title of *marja-e taqlid* (a jurist who is also an object of emulation). Shariatmadari's Center for Islamic Study and Publications was closed, and Shariatmadari was placed under virtual house arrest.

In June 1982, the authorities captured Qashqai leader Khosrow Qashqai, who had returned to Iran after the Revolution and had led his tribesmen in a local uprising. He was tried and publicly hanged in October.

All these moves to crush opposition to the Republic gave freer rein to the Pasdaran and revolutionary committees. Members of these organizations entered homes, made arrests, conducted searches, and confiscated goods at will. The government organized "Mobile Units of God's Vengeance" to patrol the streets and to impose Islamic dress and Islamic codes of behavior. Instructions issued by Khomeini in December 1981 and in August 1982 admonishing the revolutionary organizations to exercise proper care in entering homes and making arrests were ignored. "Manpower renewal" and "placement" committees in government ministries and offices resumed widescale purges in 1982, examining office-holders and job applicants on their beliefs and political inclinations. Applicants to universities and military academies were subjected to similar examinations.

By the end of 1982, the country experienced a reaction against the numerous executions and a widespread feeling of insecurity because of the arbitrary actions of the revolutionary organizations and the purge committees. The government saw that insecurity was also undermining economic confidence and exacerbating economic difficulties. Accordingly, in December 1982 Khomeini issued an eight-point decree prohibiting the revolutionary organizations from entering homes, making arrests, conducting searches, and confiscating property without legal authorization. He also banned unauthorized tapping of telephones, interference with citizens in the privacy of their homes, and unauthorized dismissals from the civil service. He urged the courts to conduct themselves so that the people felt their life, property, and honor were secure.

The government appointed a follow-up committee to ensure adherence to Khomeini's decree, to look into the activities of the revolutionary organizations, and to hear public complaints against government officials. Some 300,000 complaints were filed within a few weeks. The follow-up committee was soon dissolved, but the decree nevertheless led to a marked decrease in executions, tempered the worst abuses of the Pasdaran and revolutionary committees, and brought a measure of security to individuals not engaged in opposition activity.

The December decree, however, implied no increased tolerance for the political opposition. The Tudeh had secured itself a measure of freedom during the first three years of the Revolution by declaring loyalty to Khomeini and supporting the clerics against liberal and left-wing opposition groups. But the government showed less tolerance for the party after the impeachment of Bani Sadr and the repression of left-wing guerrilla organizations. The party's position further deteriorated in 1982, as relations between Iran and the Soviet Union grew more strained over such issues as the war with Iraq and the Soviet presence in Afghanistan. The government began closing down Tudeh publications as early as June 1981, and in 1982 officials and senior clerics publicly branded the members of the Tudeh as agents of a foreign power.

In February 1983, the government arrested Tudeh leader Nureddin Kianuri, other members of the party Central Committee, and more than 1,000 party members. The party was proscribed, and Kianuri confessed on television to spying for the Soviet Union and to "espionage, deceit, and treason." Possibly because of Soviet intervention, none of the leading members of the party was brought to trial or executed, although the leaders remained in prison. Many rank and file members, however, were put to death.

By 1983 Bazargan's IFM was the only political group outside the factions of the ruling hierarchy that was permitted any freedom of activity. Even this group was barely tolerated. For example, the party headquarters was attacked in 1983, and two party members were assaulted on the floor of the Majlis.

In 1984 Khomeini denounced the Hojjatiyyeh, a fundamentalist religious group that rejected the role assigned to the *faqih* under the Constitution. The organization, taking this attack as a warning, dissolved itself.

Consolidation of the Revolution

As the government eliminated the political opposition and successfully prosecuted the war with Iraq, it also took further steps to consolidate and to institutionalize the achievements of the Revolution. The government took several measures to regularize the status of revolutionary organizations. It reorganized the Pasdaran and the Crusade for Reconstruction as ministries (the former in November 1982 and the latter in November 1983), a move designed to bring these bodies under the aegis of the cabinet, and placed the revolutionary committees under the supervision of the minister of interior. The government also nominally incorporated the revolutionary courts into the regular court system and in 1984 reorganized the security organization led by Mohammadi Rayshahri, concurrently the head of the Army Military Revolutionary Tribunal, as the Ministry of Information and Security. These measures met with only limited success in reducing the considerable autonomy, including budgetary independence, enjoyed by the revolutionary organizations.

An Assembly of Experts (not to be confused with the constituent assembly that went by the same name) was elected in December 1982 and convened in the following year to determine the successor to Khomeini. Khomeini's own choice was known to be Montazeri. The assembly, an eighty-three-member body that is required to convene once a year, apparently could reach no agreement on a successor during either its 1983 or its 1984 session, however. In 1985 the Assembly of Experts agreed, reportedly on a split vote, to name Montazeri as Khomeini's "deputy" (*qaem maqam*), rather than "successor" (*ja-neshin*), thus placing Montazeri in line for the succession without actually naming him as the heir apparent (see The Faqih, ch. 4).

Elections to the second Majlis were held in the spring of 1984. The IFM, doubting the elections would be free, did not participate, so the seats were contested only by candidates of the IRP and other groups and individuals in the ruling hierarchy. The campaign revealed numerous divisions within the ruling group, however, and the second Majlis, which included several deputies who had served in the revolutionary organizations, was more radical than the first. The second Majlis convened in May 1984 and, with some prodding from Khomeini, gave Mir-Hosain Musavi a renewed vote of confidence as prime minister. In 1985 it elected Khamenehi, who was virtually unchallenged, to another four-year term as president.

Bazargan, as leader of the IFM, continued to protest the suppression of basic freedoms. He addressed a letter on these issues to Khomeini in August 1984 and issued a public declaration in February 1985. He also spoke out against the war with Iraq and urged a negotiated settlement. In April 1985 Bazargan and forty members of the IFM and the National Front urged the UN secretary general to negotiate a peaceful end to the conflict. In retaliation, in February 1985, the *hezbollahis* smashed the offices of the party, and the party newspaper was once again shut down. Bazargan was denounced from pulpits and was not allowed to run for president in the 1985 elections.

There were, however, increasing signs of factionalism within the ruling group itself over questions of social justice in relation to economic policy, the succession, and, in more muted fashion, foreign

67

policy and the war with Iraq. The debate on economic policy arose partly from disagreement over the more equitable distribution of wealth and partly from differences between those who advocated state control of the economy and those who supported private sector control. Divisions also arose between the Majlis and the Council of Guardians, a group composed of senior Islamic jurists and other experts in Islamic law and empowered by the Constitution to veto, or demand the revision of, any legislation it considers in violation of Islam or the Constitution. In this dispute, the Council of Guardians emerged as the collective champion of private property rights.

In May 1982, the Council of Guardians had vetoed a law that would have nationalized foreign trade. In the fall of 1982, the council forced the Majlis to pass a revised law regarding the state takeover of urban land and to give landowners more protection. In January of the following year, the council vetoed the Law for the Expropriation of the Property of Fugitives, a measure that would have allowed the state to seize the property of any Iranian living abroad who did not return to the country within two months.

In December 1982, the Council of Guardians also vetoed the Majlis' new and more conservative land reform law. This law had been intended to help resolve the issue of land distribution, left unresolved when the land reform law was suspended in November 1980. The suspension had also left unsettled the status of 750,000 to 850,000 hectares of privately owned land that, as a result of the 1979–80 land seizures and redistributions, was being cultivated by persons other than the owners, but without transfer of title.

The debate between proponents of state and of private sector control over the economy was renewed in the winter of 1983–84, when the government came under attack and leaflets critical of the Council of Guardians were distributed. Undeterred, the council blocked attempts in 1984 and 1985 to revive measures for nationalization of foreign trade and for land distribution, and it vetoed a measure for state control over the domestic distribution of goods. As economic conditions deteriorated in 1985, there was an attempt in the Majlis to unseat the prime minister. Khomeini, however, intervened to maintain the incumbent government in office (see The Consolidation of Theocracy, ch. 4).

These differences over major policy issues persisted even as the Revolution was institutionalized and the regime consolidated its hold over the country. The differences remained muted, primarily because of Khomeini's intervention, but the debate threatened to grow more intense and more divisive in the post-Khomeini period. Moreover, while in 1985 Montazeri appeared slated to succeed Khomeini as Iran's leader, there was general agreement that he would be a far less dominant figure as head of the Islamic Republic than Khomeini has been.

*   *   *

The projected eight-volume *The Cambridge History of Iran* provides learned and factual essays by specialists on history, literature, the sciences, and the arts for various periods of Iranian history from the earliest times. Six volumes, covering history through the Safavid era, had been published by 1987.

For the history of ancient Iran and the period from the Achaemenids up to the Islamic conquest, R. Ghirshman's *Iran: From the Earliest Times to the Islamic Conquest* and A.T. Olmstead's *History of the Persian Empire* are somewhat dated but continue to be standard works. More recent books on the period are Richard Frye's *The Heritage of Persia* and its companion volume *The Golden Age of Persia*.

For the early Islamic period, there are few books devoted specifically to Iran, and readers must consult standard works on early Islamic history. A good study to consult is Marshall G.S. Hodgson's three-volume work, *The Venture of Islam*. Much useful information, for the early as well as the later Islamic period, can be culled from E.G. Browne's four-volume *A Literary History of Persia*. Ann K.S. Lambton's *Landlord and Peasant in Persia* is excellent for both administrative history and land administration until the 1950s.

For studies of single Islamic dynasties in Iran, the following are interesting and competent: E.C. Bosworth's *The Ghaznavids,* Vasilii Bartold's *Turkestan to the Mongol Invasion,* Bertold Spuler's *Die Mongolen in Iran,* and Roy P. Mottahedeh's study of the Buyids, *Loyalty and Leadership in an Early Islamic Society*.

On the Safavid and post-Safavid periods, in addition to the excellent pieces by H.R. Roemer and others in *The Cambridge History of Iran,* volume 6, there is also Laurence Lockhart's *The Fall of the Safavid Dynasty and the Afghan Occupation of Persia* and his *Nadir Shah* and Roger Savory's *Iran under the Safavids.* Said Amir Arjomand's *The Shadow of God and the Hidden Imam* focuses on the relationship of the religious establishment to the state under the Safavids. The Zand period is covered in straightforward fashion by John R. Perry in *Karim Khan Zand*.

For the modern period, *Roots of Revolution* by Nikki R. Keddie provides an interpretative survey from the rise of the Qajars in 1795 to the fall of the Pahlavis in 1979; *Iran Between Two Revolutions* by Ervand Abrahamian is a detailed political history of Iran from the period of the Constitutional Revolution of 1905–1907 to the Islamic

Revolution of 1979. Ruhollah K. Ramazani's *The Foreign Policy of Iran, 1500–1941* is factual and comprehensive on foreign policy issues for the period from 1800 to the abdication of Reza Shah. On nineteenth-century economic history, Charles Issawi's *The Economic History of Iran, 1800–1914,* a collection of documents with extensive commentary, is still unsurpassed.

For the period of Reza Shah, *A History of Modern Iran* by Joseph M. Upton is concise and incisive. *Modern Iran* by L.P. Elwell-Sutton, although written in the 1940s, is still a useful study; and Amin Banani's *The Modernization of Iran, 1921–1941,* covering the same period and along the same lines, looks less at political developments under Reza Shah than at the changes introduced in such areas as industry, education, legal structure, and women's emancipation. Donald Wilber's *Riza Shah Pahlavi, 1878–1944* is basically a factual but not strongly interpretative biography of the founder of the Pahlavi dynasty. J. Bharier's *Economic Development in Iran, 1900–1970,* as the name suggests, provides an economic history of the late Qajar and much of the Pahlavi period.

For the period of Mohammad Reza Shah, in addition to books by Abrahamian and Keddie (cited above), *Iran: The Politics of Groups, Classes, and Modernization* by James A. Bill and *The Political Elite of Iran* by Marvin Zonis are both studies of elite politics and elite structure. Fred Halliday's *Iran: Dictatorship and Development* is a critical account of the nature of the state and the shah's rule, and Robert Graham's *Iran: The Illusion of Power* casts an equally critical eye on the last years of the shah's reign. More sympathetic assessments can be found in George Lenczowski's *Iran under the Pahlavis.* Relations between the state and the religious establishment for the whole of the Pahlavi period are covered in Shahrough Akhavi's *Religion and Politics in Contemporary Iran.* Iran's foreign policy is surveyed in Ramazani's *Iran's Foreign Policy, 1941–1973.*

The United States-Iranian relationship in the period 1941–80 is the focus of Barry Rubin's *Paved with Good Intentions.* The United States-Iranian relationship in the period following the Islamic Revolution is covered in Gary Sick's *All Fall Down.* The foreign policy of the Islamic Republic is covered in Ramazani's *Revolutionary Iran. Reign of the Ayatollahs* by Shaul Bakhash is a political history of the Islamic Revolution up to 1986. *The State and Revolution in Iran, 1962–1982* by Hossein Bashiriyeh is an interpretative essay on the Revolution and its background. Roy P. Mottahedeh's *The Mantle of the Prophet* is at once a biography of a modern-day Iranian cleric, a study of religious education in Iran, and an intriguing interpretation of Iran's cultural history. (For further information and complete citations, see Bibliography.)

Chapter 2. The Society and Its Environment

Two men who came to pay tribute to Darius, ca. 500 B.C., from a bas-relief at Persepolis

IRAN HAS BEEN EXPERIENCING significant social changes since the 1979 Islamic Revolution that overthrew the monarchy. Ayatollah Sayyid Ruhollah Musavi Khomeini, the spiritual leader of the Revolution, and his supporters, who were organized in the Islamic Republican Party (IRP), were determined to desecularize Iranian society. They envisaged the destruction of the royal regime as a prelude to the creation of an Islamic society whose laws and values were derived from the Quran and religious texts sacred to Shia (see Glossary) Islam. The flight into foreign exile of the royal family and most of the prerevolutionary political elite, and the imprisonment or cooptation of those who chose to remain, effectively enabled the Shia Islamic clergy (see Glossary) to take over governmental institutions and to use the power and authority of the central government to implement programs designed to accomplish this goal.

The creation of the Islamic Republic of Iran in 1979 resulted in the destruction of the power and influence of the predominantly secular and Western-oriented political elite that had ruled Iran since the early part of the twentieth century. The new political elite that emerged was composed of Shia clergymen and lay technocrats of middle-class origins. The major consequence of their programs has been cultural, that is, the desecularization of public life in Iran. By 1987 this new political elite had not adopted policies that would have caused any major restructuring of the country's economy. While there has been controversy regarding the appropriate role of the government in regulating the national economy, the overall philosophy of this new political elite has been that private property is respected and protected under Islam.

The establishment of an "ideal" religious society has been impeded by foreign war. Iran became involved in a protracted war with its neighbor, Iraq, in September 1980, when the latter country invaded Iran's oil-rich southwestern province of Khuzestan. This conflict has meant a total war for Iran. By 1987 at least 200,000 Iranians had been killed and another 350,000 to 500,000 wounded. At any one time, 600,000 men were under arms. Property destruction, including the complete leveling of one major city, several towns, and scores of villages, as well as extensive damage to industrial infrastructure and residential neighborhoods of other urban areas, was estimated at billions of dollars. The war also created the need to provide for as many as 1.5 million persons who had become refugees; to ration a wide variety of foodstuffs; to retool most major industries for the production of war-related goods; and to expend a substantial proportion of government resources, including revenues from the sale of petroleum, on the war effort.

Although the war with Iraq has imposed extraordinary burdens on the economy and society, the government of the Republic has continued its efforts to recast society according to religiously prescribed behavioral codes. These policies have resulted in a significant enhancement of the role that the mosque plays in society. The Shia clergy have become the major political actors not only at the national level but also at the local level, where the chief cleric in each town has assumed the functions of a de facto district governor (see Local Government, ch. 4). Thus, local mosques, in addition to fulfilling their traditional roles as places for prayer, have become primary sources of social services that formerly were obtained from various government ministries. Mosques also have become one of the principal institutions for enforcing the observance of public morals.

All the major cultural and social groups in Iran have been affected by the changes resulting from the establishment of the Republic. The secularized, Western-educated, upper and middle classes of the prerevolutionary period have been frequent targets of criticism by the clergy and lay political leaders, who have accused them of "immoral life-styles." These secular groups have tended to resent the laws that regulate individual behavior. In particular, they dislike *hejab* (see Glossary), the dress codes that require women to be covered in public except for their faces and hands, and the prohibition of all alcoholic beverages. Members of these classes, who predominated in the upper levels of the civil service and in the professions, have also been compelled to undergo "re-education classes" in Islam to retain their positions.

In contrast, the religious middle class, generally identified as the bazaar class, has tended to support the laws the secularized groups disliked because these laws reflect the ideal life-style that the bazaar traditionally has tried to follow. Similarly, the lower classes in both urban and rural areas have not necessarily tended to perceive laws regulating behavior as intrusions because the religious sanctions have for the most part merely reinforced the values of their generally conservative life-styles.

Geography

Iran is one of the world's most mountainous countries. Its mountains have helped to shape both the political and the economic history of the country for several centuries. The mountains enclose several broad basins, or plateaus, on which major agricultural and urban settlements are located. Until the twentieth century, when major highways and railroads were constructed through the mountains to connect the population centers, these basins tended to be relatively isolated from one another. Typically, one major town dominated each basin, and there were complex economic relationships between the town and the hundreds of villages that surrounded it. In the higher elevations of the mountains rimming the basins, tribally organized groups practiced transhumance, moving with their herds of sheep and goats between traditionally established summer and winter pastures. There are no major river systems in the country, and historically transportation was by means of caravans that followed routes traversing gaps and passes in the mountains. The mountains also impeded easy access to the Persian Gulf and the Caspian Sea.

With an area of 1,648,000 square kilometers, Iran ranks sixteenth in size among the countries of the world. Iran is about one-fifth the size of the continental United States, or slightly larger than the combined area of the contiguous states of California, Arizona, Nevada, Oregon, Washington, and Idaho.

Located in southwestern Asia, Iran shares its entire northern border with the Soviet Union. This border extends for more then 2,000 kilometers, including nearly 650 kilometers of water along the southern shore of the Caspian Sea. Iran's western borders are with Turkey in the north and Iraq in the south, terminating at the Shatt al Arab (which Iranians call the Arvand Rud). The Persian Gulf and Gulf of Oman littorals form the entire 1,770-kilometer southern border. To the east lie Afghanistan on the north and Pakistan on the south. Iran's diagonal distance from Azarbaijan in the northwest to Baluchestan va Sistan in the southeast is approximately 2,333 kilometers.

Topography

Iran consists of rugged, mountainous rims surrounding high interior basins. The main mountain chain is the Zagros Mountains, a series of parallel ridges interspersed with plains that bisect the country from northwest to southeast. Many peaks in the Zagros exceed 3,000 meters above sea level, and in the south-central region of the country there are at least five peaks that are over 4,000 meters. As the Zagros continue into southeastern Iran, the average elevation of the peaks declines dramatically to under 1,500 meters. Rimming the Caspian Sea littoral is another chain of mountains, the narrow but high Alborz Mountains. Volcanic Mount Damavand (5,600 meters), located in the center of the Alborz, is not only the

75

country's highest peak but also the highest mountain on the Eurasian landmass west of the Hindu Kush (see fig. 4).

The center of Iran consists of several closed basins that collectively are referred to as the Central Plateau. The average elevation of this plateau is about 900 meters, but several of the mountains that tower over the plateau exceed 3,000 meters. The eastern part of the plateau is covered by two salt deserts, the Dasht-e Kavir and the Dasht-e Lut. Except for some scattered oases, these deserts are uninhabited.

Iran has only two expanses of lowlands: the Khuzestan plain in the southwest and the Caspian Sea coastal plain in the north. The former is a roughly triangular-shaped extension of the Mesopotamia plain and averages about 160 kilometers in width. It extends for about 120 kilometers inland, barely rising a few meters above sea level, then meets abruptly with the first foothills of the Zagros. Much of the Khuzestan plain is covered with marshes. The Caspian plain is both longer and narrower. It extends for some 640 kilometers along the Caspian shore, but its widest point is less than 50 kilometers, while at some places less than 2 kilometers separate the shore from the Alborz foothills. The Persian Gulf coast south of Khuzestan and the Gulf of Oman coast have no real plains because the Zagros in these areas come right down to the shore.

There are no major rivers in the country. Of the small rivers and streams, the only one that is navigable is the Karun, which shallow-draft boats can negotiate from Khorramshahr to Ahvaz, a distance of about 180 kilometers. Several other permanent rivers and streams also drain into the Persian Gulf, while a number of small rivers that originate in the northwestern Zagros or Alborz drain into the Caspian Sea. On the Central Plateau, numerous rivers, most of which have dry beds for the greater part of the year, form from snow melting in the mountains during the spring and flow through permanent channels, draining eventually into salt lakes that also tend to dry up during the summer months. There is a permanent salt lake, Lake Urmia (the traditional name, also cited as Lake Urmiyeh, to which it has reverted after being called Lake Rezaiyeh under Mohammad Reza Shah), in the northwest, whose brine content is too high to support fish or most other forms of aquatic life. There are also several connected salt lakes along the Iran-Afghanistan border in the province of Baluchestan va Sistan.

Climate

Iran has a variable climate. In the northwest, winters are cold with heavy snowfall and subfreezing temperatures during December and January. Spring and fall are relatively mild, while summers are dry and hot. In the south, winters are mild and the summers are very hot, having average daily temperatures in July exceeding 38° C. On the Khuzestan plain, summer heat is accompanied by high humidity.

In general, Iran has an arid climate in which most of the relatively scant annual precipitation falls from October through April. In most of the country, yearly precipitation averages 25 centimeters or less. The major exceptions are the higher mountain valleys of the Zagros and the Caspian coastal plain, where precipitation averages at least 50 centimeters annually. In the western part of the Caspian, rainfall exceeds 100 centimeters annually and is distributed relatively evenly throughout the year. This contrasts with some basins of the Central Plateau that receive ten centimeters or less of precipitation annually.

Population

In November 1986, the government reported that the preliminary count in the fourth national census, which had been conducted during October, showed a total population of 48,181,463. According to the government, this total included about 2.6 million refugees who had come from Afghanistan and Iraq since 1980. The population of Iranian nationals, approximately 45.6 million, represented an increase of about 12 million over the 33.7 million enumerated in the 1976 census. This indicated that the Iranian population had grown at an annual rate of 3.6 percent between 1976 and 1986. A population increase in excess of 3.3 percent per year puts Iran's population growth rate among the higher rates in the world.

The preliminary report on the 1986 census showed that Iran's population had been growing at a faster rate since 1976 than during earlier periods. Throughout the first half of the twentieth century, estimates and scattered population surveys indicated that the average population growth rate was less than 2 percent annually. After World War II, however, the population growth rate began to rise. Between the first national census in 1956, when Iran's population numbered 19 million, and the second national census in 1966, when the population count was 25.3 million, the annual growth rate averaged 2.9 percent. The results of the 1976 national census, however, indicated a slight decrease in the average annual growth rate to 2.7 percent.

The sharp increase in the population growth rate from 2.7 percent to nearly 3.6 percent per year between 1976 and 1986 appeared to be related to the Revolution in 1979. Prior to the Revolution, the government had promoted a family planning program; however, following the Revolution, the new government ceased all official

77

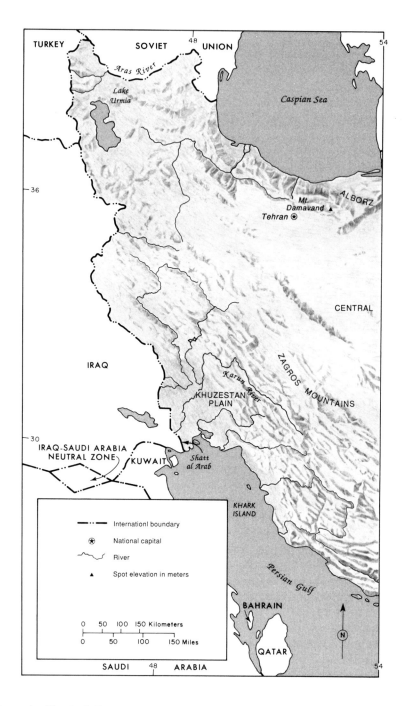

Figure 4. Physical Features

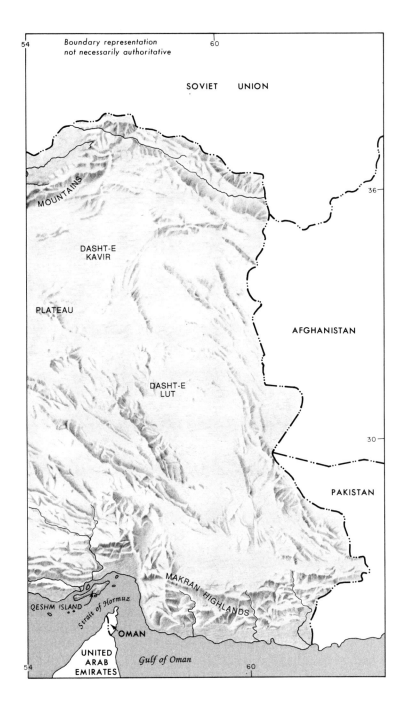

involvement in family planning. Although there has been no religious prohibition on birth control, government pronouncements and literature have tended to extol the virtues of large families.

In mid-1987, data on vital statistics from the 1986 preliminary census were incomplete, but some demographic changes were already evident. The 1976 census data had indicated that 51.4 percent of the population was male and 48.6 was female. The median age of the population was 16.5 years, and less than 3.5 percent of the population was over 65. The relatively large population increase between 1976 and 1986 had the effect of increasing the already extreme youthfulness of the population. In 1986 the government announced that 50 percent of the population was under 15 years of age, and about 45 percent was in the 15- to 59-year age group, while only 5 percent was over the age of 60.

According to the preliminary results of the 1986 census, the average population density for the country was twenty-nine persons per square kilometer. In some regions, especially along the Caspian coast and in East Azarbaijan, the average density was significantly higher, while in the more arid regions of the Central Plateau and Baluchestan va Sistan, average population density was ten or fewer persons per square kilometer.

Major Cities

Tehran, the capital, is the country's largest city and the second most populous city in the Middle East after Cairo. Tehran is a comparatively young city, the origins of which date back about 700 years. The old part of the city is a few kilometers to the northwest of ancient Rey, an important city that was destroyed by the Mongol invasions of the thirteenth century. Tehran was founded by refugees from Rey, but remained an insignificant small town until the end of the eighteenth century, when the founder of the Qajar dynasty chose it to be his capital (see The Qajars, 1795–1925, ch. 1). Tehran has been the capital of the country ever since.

The centralization of the government and the expansion of the bureaucracy under the Pahlavis, the last royal dynasty, were major factors in Tehran's rapid growth after 1925. The city's population doubled between 1926 and 1940 and tripled between 1940 and 1956, when it reached more than 1.5 million. Tehran's population continued to grow rapidly, exceeding 2.7 million by 1966. Its population in the 1986 census was slightly over 6 million. This figure represented a 35 percent increase over the 1976 census of slightly under 4.5 million.

In 1986 Iran had one other city, Mashhad, with a population over 1 million. Mashhad's population of more than 1.4 million represented an increase of 110 percent since 1976. Much of its growth was attributed to the large number of Afghan refugees, approximately 450,000, who were living in the city. The historical origins of Mashhad are similar to those of Tehran inasmuch as the city essentially developed after the centuries-old city of Tus, near modern Mashhad, was destroyed by the Mongols. Mashhad has served as the principal commercial center of Khorasan since the nineteenth century, although its major growth has occurred only since the mid-1950s. It also has become an important manufacturing center and has numerous carpet, textile, and food-processing factories.

Iran's other major cities include Esfahan, Tabriz, and Shiraz, all of which had populations of 800,000 or more in 1986. Like Mashhad, these cities have experienced relatively rapid growth since the mid-1950s. All three of these cities are important manufacturing centers, especially Esfahan, where many of Iran's heavy industries are concentrated. Smaller cities (populations of 100,000 to 500,000) such as Ahvaz, Bakhtaran (before the Revolution Kermanshah), Hamadan, Karaj, Kerman, Qazvin, Qom, Rasht, and Urumiyeh (or Urmia, formerly known as Rezaiyeh) also have grown considerably since 1956 (see table 2, Appendix). A total of 30 cities, more than double the number in the 1966 census, had populations exceeding 100,000 in 1986.

Emigration

Since the Revolution, there has been a small but steady emigration of educated Iranians. Estimates of the number vary from 750,000 to 1.5 million. Most such emigrants have preferred to settle in Western Europe or the United States, although there are also sizable communities of Iranians in Turkey. Newspapers in Istanbul claimed during 1986 that as many as 600,000 Iranians were living in Turkey, although the Turkish Ministry of Interior has reported that there are only about 30,000 Iranians in the country. The United States census for 1980 found 122,000 Iranians living in the United States. By 1987 it was estimated this number exceeded 200,000, with the largest concentration found in southern California.

Iranian emigrants tended to be highly educated, many holding degrees from American and West European universities. A sizable proportion were members of the prerevolutionary political elite. They had been wealthy before the Revolution, and many succeeded in transferring much of their wealth out of Iran during and after the Revolution.

Other Iranians who have emigrated include members of religious minorities, especially Bahais and Jews; intellectuals who had

81

opposed the old regime, which they accused of suppressing free thought and who have the same attitude toward the Islamic Republic; members of ethnic minorities; political opponents of the government in Tehran; and some young men who deserted from the military or sought to avoid conscription. There were virtually no economic emigrants from Iran, although a few thousand Iranians have continued to work in Kuwait, Qatar, and other Persian Gulf states, as before the Revolution.

Refugees

The preliminary 1986 national census figures included approximately 2.6 million persons listed as refugees of foreign nationality. The largest number, consisting of slightly more than 2.3 million, were Afghans. The refugees from Afghanistan were concentrated in several refugee camps in eastern Iran, but approximately one-third of them were living in such cities as Mashhad, Shiraz, and Tehran at the time of the census. In addition, there were nearly 300,000 refugees from Iraq, with which Iran had been at war since 1980.

The influx of foreign refugees was the direct result of war on Iran's borders. Since early 1980, the Afghan refugees had been fleeing the fighting in their country between various Afghan resistance groups and government forces assisted by more than 100,000 Soviet troops. The Iraqi refugees were expelled by their own government, which claimed that they were really Iranian descendants of persons who had immigrated to Iraq from Iran many years ago. In addition to refugees of foreign origins, Tehran has had to cope with several hundred thousand Iranian civilian refugees from the war zones.

The Iraqi advance into Khuzestan in the fall of 1980 resulted in extensive damage to the residential areas of two of Iran's major cities, Abadan and Khorramshahr, as well as the destruction of numerous small towns and villages (see The Original Iraq Offensive, ch. 5). The intensive shelling of the large cities of Ahvaz and Dezful also destroyed residential neighborhoods. Consequently, tens of thousands of civilians fled southwestern Iran in 1980 and 1981, and the government set up refugee reception areas in Shiraz, Tehran, and other cities removed from the battle zone. During the Iraqi occupation of Khuzestan, the government had to shelter up to 1.5 million refugees. Efforts to resettle at least some of the refugees were undertaken in 1983 after Iran had recaptured much of Khuzestan from Iraq; however, continued fighting in the area and Iraqi air strikes on cities and towns in western Iran resulted in a steady stream of displaced civilians in need of food and shelter.

During the period 1980 to 1981, the government of Iraq expelled into Iran about 200,000 persons whom it claimed were Iranians. Most were Iraqi citizens, sometimes whole families, who were or had been residents of Iraq's Shia shrine cities and also were descendants of Iranian clergy and pilgrims who had settled in the religious centers as far back as the eighteenth century. In most cases, the refugees had never been to Iran and could speak no Persian (Farsi). Furthermore, they were required to leave the greater part of their possessions in Iraq. Thus, the Iranian government had to provide them with basic food and shelter.

Developing policies to deal with the Afghan refugees became a major burden for the government as early as 1984 because the number of Afghan refugees had continued to increase almost daily since the first group crossed the border in 1980. Iran, however, received virtually no international assistance for the Afghan refugees. It set up several camps in eastern Iran where the refugees were processed and provided with basic shelter and rations. These camps were located in or near towns in Khorasan and were provided with certain municipal services such as free access to public schools for registered refugee children. Although no data have been published on the gender and age composition of the refugees, press reports indicate that most were probably women, children, and men too old to fight, as in the Afghan refugee camps in Pakistan. Most of the young men probably remained with the Afghan resistance forces for the greater part of the year.

Although the Afghans were required to live in the special refugee camps, by 1986 an estimated one-third of them had left the camps and were living in residential areas of large cities such as Mashhad, Shiraz, and Tehran. The Afghans apparently came to the cities in order to earn money to support families who remained in the camps. They engaged in street vending and worked on construction sites or in factories. The Iranian press periodically reported on the roundup of such Afghans and their forcible return to the camps. The Afghans needed special work permits, but it was not clear whether these were difficult or easy to obtain or whether private employers required them as a condition of employment.

Peoples and Languages

Iran has a heterogeneous population speaking a variety of Indo-Iranian, Semitic, and Turkic languages. The largest language group consists of the speakers of Indo-Iranian languages, who in 1986 comprised about 70 percent of the population. The speakers of Indo-Iranian languages are not, however, a homogeneous group. They include speakers of Persian, the official language of the country, and its various dialects; speakers of Kirmanji, the term for related dialects spoken by the Kurds who live in the cities, towns, and villages of western Iran and adjacent areas of Iraq and Turkey; speakers of Luri, the language of the Bakhtiaris and Lurs who live in the Zagros; and Baluchi, the language of the seminomadic people who live in southeastern Iran and adjacent areas of Afghanistan and Pakistan. Approximately 28 percent of the population speaks various dialects of Turkish. Speakers of Semitic languages include Arabs and Assyrians (see fig. 5).

The Persian Language

The official language of Iran is Persian (the Persian term for which is Farsi). It is the language of government and public instruction and is the mother tongue of half of the population. Persian is spoken as a second language by a large proportion of the rest. Many different dialects of Persian are spoken in various parts of the Central Plateau, and people from each city can usually be identified by their speech. Some dialects, such as Gilaki and Mazandari, are distinct enough to be virtually unintelligible to a Persian speaker from Tehran or Shiraz.

Persian is an ancient language that has developed through three historical stages. Old Persian dates back to at least 514 B.C. and was used until about A.D. 250. It was written in cuneiform and used exclusively for royal proclamations and announcements. Middle Persian, also known as Pahlavi, was in use from about A.D. 250 to 900. It was the official language of the Sassanid Empire and of the Zoroastrian priesthood. It was written in an ideographic script called Huzvaresh.

Modern Persian is a continually evolving language that began to develop about A.D. 900. Following the Arab conquest of the Sassanid Empire in the seventh century and the gradual conversion of the population to Islam, Arabic became the official, literary, and written language, but Persian remained the language of court records. Persian, however, borrowed heavily from Arabic to enrich its own vocabulary and eventually adopted the Arabic script. In subsequent centuries, many Turkic words also were incorporated into Persian.

As part of the Indo-European family of languages, Persian is distantly related to Latin, Greek, the Slavic and Teutonic languages, and English. This relationship can be seen in such cognates as *beradar* (brother), *pedar* (father), and *mader* (mother). It is a relatively easy language for English-speaking people to learn compared with any other major language of the Middle East. Verbs tend to be regular, nouns lack gender and case distinction, prepositions are much used, noun plural formation tends to be regular, and word order is important. The difficulty of the language lies in the subtlety and variety of word meanings according to context. Persian is written right to left in the Arabic script with several modifications. It has four more consonants than Arabic—*pe, che, zhe,* and *gaf*—making a total of thirty-two letters. Most of the letters have four forms in writing, depending on whether they occur at the beginning, in the middle, or at the end of a word or whether they stand separately. The letters stand for the consonants and the three long vowels; special marks written above or below the line are used to denote short vowels. These signs are used only in dictionaries and textbooks, so that a reader must have a substantial vocabulary to understand a newspaper, an average book, or handwriting.

Persian is the most important of a group of several related languages that linguists classify as Indo-Iranian. Persian speakers regard their language as extremely beautiful, and they take great pleasure in listening to the verses of medieval poets such as Ferdowsi, Hafez, and Sadi. The language is a living link with the past and has been important in binding the nation together.

There is no accepted standard transliteration of Persian into Latin letters, and Iranians write their names for Western use in a variety of ways, often following French spelling. Among scholars and librarians a profound dispute exists between those who think Persian should be transliterated in conformity with the rules for Arabic and those who insist that Persian should have its own rules because it does not use all of the same sounds as Arabic.

Among educated Persians, there have been sporadic efforts as far back as the tenth century to diminish the use of Arabic loanwords in their language. Both Pahlavi shahs supported such efforts in the twentieth century. During the reign of Reza Shah Pahlavi (1925–41), serious consideration was given to the possibility of Romanizing the writing of Persian as had been done with Turkish, but these plans were abandoned. Since the Revolution, a contrary tendency to increase the use of Arabic words in both spoken and written Persian has emerged among government leaders.

The Persian-speaking People

The Persians constitute the largest ethnic component in Iran. They predominate in the major urban areas of central and eastern Iran—in the cities of Tehran, Esfahan, Mashhad, Shiraz, Arak, Kashan, Kerman, Qom, and Yazd—and in the villages of the Central Plateau. An estimated 50 to 60 percent of the population speaks Persian as a first language.

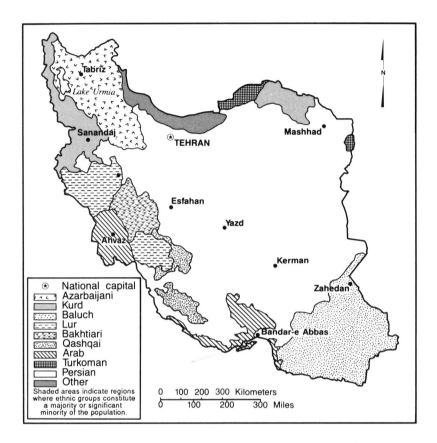

Figure 5. Major Ethnic Groups

In music, poetry, and art the Persians consider themselves—and are generally considered by other groups—as the leaders of the country. This feeling is strengthened by a consciousness of a heroic past and a rich literary heritage. Both before the Revolution and since, Persians have filled the majority of government positions.

The vast majority of Persians are Shia Muslims (see Shia Islam in Iran, this ch.). The Shia religion serves as a source of unity among Persians and other Iranian Shias. Since at least the beginning of the nineteenth century, Persians have dominated the higher ranks of the Shia clergy and have provided important clerical revolutionary leaders such as ayatollahs Khomeini and Hosain Ali Montazeri. Fewer than 500,000 Persians are followers of other faiths. These include Bahais, Jews, or members of the pre-Islamic Zoroastrian faith.

Indo-Iranian-speaking Groups

Lurs and Bakhtiaris

In the central and southern Zagros live the Bakhtiaris and the Lurs, two groups that speak Luri, a language closely related to Persian. Linguists have identified two Luri dialects: Lur Buzurg, which is spoken by the Bakhtiari, Kuhgiluyeh, and Mamasani tribes; and Lur Kuchik, which is spoken by the Lurs of Lorestan. Like the Persians, the Bakhtiaris and Lurs are Shia Muslims. Historically, each of the two groups was organized into several tribes. The tribal leaders or *khans*, especially those of the Bakhtiari tribes, were involved in national politics and were considered part of the prerevolutionary elite (see table 3, Appendix).

The Bakhtiaris have been considered both a political and a tribal entity separate from other Lurs for at least two centuries. They are concentrated in an area extending southward from Lorestan Province to Khuzestan Province and westward from Esfahan to within eighty kilometers of the present-day Iraqi border. A pastoral nomadic tribe called Bakhtiari can be traced back in Iranian history to as early as the fourteenth century, but the important Bakhtiari tribal confederation dates only from the nineteenth century. At the height of Bakhtiari influence, roughly from 1870 to 1930, the term *Bakhtiari* came to be associated not just with the nomadic tribes that provided the military prowess of the confederation but also with the villagers and even town dwellers who were under Bakhtiari jurisdiction. Thus, some Arabic-, Persian-, and Turkic-speaking peasants were considered part of the Bakhtiari. Beginning in the 1920s, the Pahlavi shahs gradually succeeded in establishing the authority of the central government in the Bakhtiari area. Several campaigns also were undertaken to settle forcibly the nomadic pastoral component of the Bakhtiari. The combined political and economic pressures resulted in a significant decline in the power of the Bakhtiari confederation. Detribalized Bakhtiaris, especially those who settled in urban areas and received an education in state schools, tended to be assimilated into Persian culture. By the time of the Revolution in 1979 the term *Bakhtiari* tended to be restricted to an estimated 250,000 tribespeople, most of whom still practiced pastoral nomadism.

Historically, the Bakhtiaris have been divided into two main tribal groups. The Chahar Lang are located in the northwest of the Bakhtiari country and until the middle of the nineteenth century retained the leadership of all the Bakhtiari tribes. The Haft Lang, the southwestern group, have been more closely associated with modern Iranian politics than the Chahar Lang and in some instances have exercised significant influence.

The Lurs (closely related to the Bakhtiaris) live in the Zagros to the northwest, west, and southeast of the Bakhtiaris. There were about 500,000 Lurs in Iran in the mid-1980s. The Lurs are divided into two main groups, the Posht-e Kuhi and the Pish-e Kuhi. These two groups are subdivided into more than sixty tribes, the most important of which include the Boir Ahmadi, the Kuhgiluyeh, and the Mamasani. Historically, the Lurs have included an urban segment based in the town of Khorramabad, the provincial capital of Lorestan. Prior to 1900, however, the majority of Lurs were pastoral nomads. Traditionally, they were considered among the fiercest of Iranian tribes and had acquired an unsavory reputation on account of their habit of preying on both Lur and non-Lur villages. During the 1920s and 1930s, the government of Reza Shah undertook several coercive campaigns to settle the nomadic Lurs. Following the abdication of Reza Shah in 1941, many of the recently settled tribes reverted to nomadism. Mohammad Reza Shah Pahlavi's government attempted with some success through various economic development programs to encourage the remaining nomadic Lurs to settle. By 1986 a majority of all Lurs were settled in villages and small towns in the traditional Lur areas or had migrated to cities.

Baluchis

The Baluchis—who constitute the majority of the population in Baluchestan va Sistan—numbered approximately 600,000 in Iran in the mid-1980s. They are part of a larger group that forms the majority of the population of Baluchistan Province in Pakistan and of some areas in southern Afghanistan. In Iran the Baluchis are concentrated in the Makran highlands, an area that stretches eastward along the Gulf of Oman coast to the Pakistan border and includes some of the most desolate country in the world. The Baluchis speak an Indo-Iranian language that is distantly related to Persian and more closely related to Pashtu, one of the major languages of Afghanistan and Pakistan. Historically, Baluchi has been only an oral language, although educated Baluchis in Pakistan have developed a written script that employs the Arabic alphabet. Unlike the majority of Persians, the majority of Baluchis are Sunni (see Glossary) rather than Shia Muslims. This religious difference has been a source of tension in the past, especially in the ethnically mixed provincial capital of Zahedan. Religious tensions have been exacerbated since the establishment of the Republic.

About half of the Baluchis are seminomadic or nomadic; the remainder are settled farmers or townsmen. Tribal organization remains intact among nomadic and seminomadic Baluchis; tribal patterns of authority and obligation have also been retained by the majority of settled Baluchis. The Baluchis have been one of the most difficult tribal groups for the central government to control, in large part because of poor communications between Tehran and Baluchestan va Sistan. With the exception of the city of Zahedan, neither the monarchy nor the Republic invested any significant funds in local development projects. As a result, the Baluchis are one of the poorest and least educated peoples in Iran. Most of the principal Baluchi tribes in Iran border Pakistan or Afghanistan. They include the Yarahmadzai, the Nauri, the Gomshadzai, the Saravan, the Lashari, and the Barazani. Along the coast of the Gulf of Oman live the important tribes of Sadozai and Taherza.

Kurds

The Kurds speak a variety of closely related dialects, which in Iran are collectively called Kirmanji. The dialects are divided into northern and southern groups, and it is not uncommon for the Kurds living in adjoining mountain valleys to speak different dialects. There is a small body of Kurdish literature written in a modified Arabic script. Kurdish is more closely related to Persian than is Baluchi and also contains numerous Persian loanwords. In large Kurdish cities, the educated population speaks both Persian and Kurdish.

There are approximately 4 million Kurds in Iran. They are the third most important ethnic group in the country after the Persians and Azarbaijanis and account for about 9 percent of the total population (see Turkic-speaking Groups, this ch.). They are concentrated in the Zagros Mountain area along the western frontiers with Turkey and Iraq and adjacent to the Kurdish populations of both those countries. Kurds also live in the Soviet Union and Syria. The Kurdish area of Iran includes most of West Azarbaijan, all of Kordestan, much of Bakhtaran (formerly known as Kermanshahan) and Ilam, and parts of Lorestan. Historically, the Kurds of Iran have been both urban and rural, with as much as half the rural population practicing pastoral nomadism in different periods of history. By the mid-1970s, fewer than 15 percent of all Kurds were nomadic. In addition, during the 1970s there was substantial migration of rural Kurds to such historic Kurdish cities as Bakhtaran (known as Kermanshah until 1979), Sanandaj, and Mahabad, as well as to larger towns such as Baneh, Bijar, Ilam, Islamabad (known as Shahabad until 1979), Saqqez, Sar-e Pol-e Zahab, and Sonqor. Educated Kurds also migrated to non-Kurdish cities such as Karaj, Tabriz, and Tehran.

There are also scatterings of Kurds in the provinces of Fars, Kerman, and Baluchestan va Sistan, and there is a large group of approximately 350,000 living in a small area of northern Khorasan. These are all descendants of Kurds whom the government forcibly removed from western Iran during the seventeenth century.

Most of the rural Kurds retain a tribal form of social organization, although the position of the chief is less significant among the majority of Kurds who live in villages than it is among the unsettled pastoralists. An estimated forty Kurdish tribes and confederations of tribes were still recognized in the mid-1980s. Many of these were organized in the traditional manner, which obligated several subordinate clans to pay dues in cash or produce and provide allegiance to a chief clan. The land reform program of the 1960s did not disrupt this essentially feudal system among most tribally organized Kurds.

The majority of both rural and urban Kurds in West Azarbaijan and Kordestan practice Sunni Islam. There is more diversity of religious practice in southern Kurdish areas, especially in the Bakhtaran area, where many villagers and townspeople follow Shia beliefs. Schismatic Islamic groups, such as the Ahl-e Haqq and the Yazdis, both of which are considered heretical by orthodox Shias, traditionally have had numerous adherents among the Kurds of the Bakhtaran region. A tiny minority of Kurds are adherents of Judaism.

The Kurds have manifested an independent spirit throughout modern Iranian history, rebelling against central government efforts to restrict their autonomy during the Safavid, Qajar, and Pahlavi periods. The most recent Kurdish uprising took place in 1979 following the Revolution. Mahabad, which has been a center of Kurdish resistance against Persian authority since the time of the Safavid monarch Shah Abbas (1587-1629), was again at the forefront of the Kurdish autonomy struggle. Intense fighting between government forces and Kurdish guerrillas occurred from 1979 to 1982, but since 1983 the government has asserted its control over most of the Kurdish area.

Other Groups

Scattered throughout central, southern, and eastern Iran are small groups speaking many different Indo-Iranian languages. In the southern part of the Central Plateau are such small nomadic and seminomadic tribes. Other tribes, related to groups in neighboring Afghanistan and the Soviet Union, are found in Khorasan. Also in Khorasan are an estimated 25,000 Tajiks, a settled farming people related to the Tajiks of Afghanistan and the Soviet

Union. Distinguishable, but comparatively smaller, Indo-Iranian-speaking minorities are the following tribally organized settled groups: the Hazareh, Barbai, Teimuri, Jamshidi, and Afghani in Khorasan; the Qadikolahi and Palavi in Mazandaran; and the Sasani and Agajani in the Talesh region of Gilan.

Turkic-speaking Groups

The second major element of the population is composed of various Turkic-speaking groups. The Turkic languages belong to the Ural-Altaic family, which includes many languages of Soviet Central Asia and western China, as well as Turkish, Hungarian, and Finnish. The various Turkic languages spoken in Iran tend to be mutually intelligible. Of these, only Azarbaijani is written to any extent. In Iran it is written in the Arabic script, in contrast to the Azarbaijani in Turkey, which is written in the Roman script, and that of the Soviet Union, which is written in the Cyrillic script. Unlike Indo-European languages, Turkic languages are characterized by short base words to which are added numerous prefixes and suffixes, each addition changing the meaning of the base. They are also distinguished by their vowel harmony, which means that the kind of vowel used in the base word and the additives must agree. Thus, lengthy words might be filled with ''o's'' and ''u's'' or with ''a's'' and ''e's,'' but not with mixtures of the two.

Turkic speakers make up as much as 25 percent of Iran's total population. They are concentrated in northwestern Iran, where they form the overwhelming majority of the population of East Azarbaijan and a majority of West Azarbaijan. They also constitute a significant minority in the provinces of Fars, Gilan, Hamadan, Khorasan, Mazandaran, and Tehran. Except for the Azarbaijanis, most of the Turkic groups are tribally organized. Some of the Turkic tribes continue to follow a nomadic or semi-nomadic life. Educated Turkic speakers in the large cities speak and understand Persian.

Azarbaijanis

By far the largest Turkic-speaking group are the Azarbaijanis, who account for over 85 percent of all Turkic speakers in Iran. Most of the Azarbaijanis are concentrated in the northwestern corner of the country, where they form the majority population in an area between the Caspian Sea and Lake Urmia and from the Soviet border south to the latitude of Tehran. Their language, Azarbaijani (also called Azeri or Turkish), is structurally similar to the Turkish spoken in Turkey but with a strikingly different accent. About half of all Azarbaijanis are urban. Major Azarbaijani cities include Tabriz, Urmia, Ardabil, Zanjan, Khoy, and Maragheh. In addition, an estimated one-third of the population of Tehran is Azarbaijani and there are sizable Azarbaijani minorities in other major cities, such as Hamadan, Karaj, and Qazvin. The life styles of urban Azarbaijanis do not differ from those of Persians, and there is considerable intermarriage among the upper classes in cities of mixed populations. Similarly, customs among Azarbaijani villagers do not appear to differ markedly from those of Persian villagers. The majority of Azarbaijanis, like the majority of Persians, are Shia Muslims. A tiny minority of Azarbaijanis are Bahais (see Non-Muslim Minorities, this ch.).

Qashqais

The Qashqais are the second largest Turkic group in Iran. The Qashqais are a confederation of several Turkic-speaking tribes in Fars Province numbering about 250,000 people. They are pastoral nomads who move with their herds of sheep and goats between summer pastures in the higher elevations of the Zagros south of Shiraz and winter pastures at low elevations north of Shiraz. Their migration routes are considered to be among the longest and most difficult of all of Iran's pastoral tribes. The majority of Qashqais are Shias.

The Qashqai confederation emerged in the eighteenth century when Shiraz was the capital of the Zand dynasty. During the nineteenth century, the Qashqai confederation became one of the best organized and most powerful tribal confederations in Iran, including among its clients hundreds of villages and some non-Turkic-speaking tribes. Under the Qashqais' most notable leader, Khan Solat ad Doleh, their strength was great enough to defeat the British-led South Persia Rifles in 1918. Reza Shah's campaigns against them in the early 1930s were successful because the narrow pass on the route from their summer to winter pastures was blocked, and the tribe was starved into submission. Solat and his son were imprisoned in Tehran, where Solat was subsequently murdered. Many Qashqais were then settled on land in their summer pastures, which averages 2,500 meters above sea level.

The Qashqais, like the Bakhtiaris and other forcibly settled tribes, returned to nomadic life upon Reza Shah's exile in 1941. Army and government officials were driven out of the area, but the Qashqais, reduced in numbers and disorganized after their settlement, were unable to regain their previous strength and independence. In the post-World War II period, the Qashqai khans supported the National Front of Prime Minister Mohammad Mossadeq. Following the 1953 royalist coup d'état against Mossadeq,

A nomadic Qashqai family moving to new grazing ground
Courtesy United Nations (S. Jackson)

the Qashqai khans were exiled, and army officers were appointed to supervise tribal affairs. The Qashqais revolted again in the period 1962 to 1964, when the government attempted to take away their pastures under the land reform program. A full-fledged military campaign was launched against them, and the area was eventually pacified. Since the mid-1960s, many Qashqais have settled in villages and towns. According to some estimates, as many as 100,000 Qashqais may have been settled by 1986. This change from pastoral nomadism to settled agriculture and urban occupations proved to be an important factor hindering the Qashqai tribes from organizing effectively against the central government after the Revolution in 1979 when exiled tribal leaders returned to Iran hoping to rebuild the confederation.

By the 1980s, the terms *Qashqai* and *Turk* tended to be used interchangeably in Fars, especially by non-Turkic speakers. Many Turkic groups, however, such as the urban Abivardis of Shiraz and their related village kin in nearby rural areas and the Baharlu, the Inalu, and other tribes, were never part of the Qashqai confederation. The Baharlu and Inalu tribes actually were part of the Khamseh confederacy created to counterbalance the Qashqais. Nevertheless, both Qashqai and non-Qashqai Turks in Fars recognize a common ethnic identity in relation to non-Turks. All of these Turks speak mutually intelligible dialects that are closely related to Azarbaijani. The total Turkic-speaking population of Fars was estimated to be about 500,000 in 1986.

Other Groups

Many other Turkic-speaking groups are scattered throughout Iran, but mainly along the northern tier of provinces. In the northeastern part of East Azarbaijan live some fifty tribes collectively called the Ilsavan (formerly known as Shahsavan). The Ilsavan, who may number as many as 100,000, are pastoral and take their flocks to summer pastures on the high slopes of Mount Sabalan and to winter pastures in the Dasht-e Moghan, adjacent to the Aras River, which forms the frontier between Iran and the Soviet Union. The Ilsavan first appeared in Iranian history as staunch supporters of the Safavid dynasty, which originated during the fifteenth century in Ardabil, a town located in a valley on the south side of Mount Sabalan.

The Qajars, from whom came the royal family that Reza Shah dethroned, form a Turkic-speaking enclave among the Mazandarani. Some are settled agriculturists while others are pastoral nomads. In the northeastern part of Mazandaran, in a region known as the Turkoman Sahra, live several tribes of Turkomans, some of which are sections of larger tribes living across the border in the Soviet Union. In 1986 the number of Turkomans in Iran was estimated to be about 250,000. Several small, nomadic, Turkic-speaking groups, including Qarapakhs and Uzbeks, live in Khorasan. Small numbers of Qarapakhs also live in northwestern Iran along the southern shore of Lake Urmia.

The Afshars are one of the most scattered of the Turkic-speaking groups. A seminomadic people who speak a dialect akin to Azarbaijani, they are found along the shore of Lake Urmia, around Zanjan, along the borders of Kordestan, south of Kerman, and in Khorasan. These separated groups are estimated to total 100,000, but they do not share any consciousness of a common identity nor do they have any political unity. Nevertheless, they all refer to themselves as Afshars and differentiate themselves from other groups, both Turk and non-Turk, that surround them.

Semitic Language Groups

Arabic and Assyrian are the two Semitic languages spoken in Iran. The Arabic dialects are spoken in Khuzestan and along the Persian Gulf coast. They are modern variants of the older Arabic that formed the base of the classical literary language and all the colloquial languages of the Arabic-speaking world. As a Semitic language, Arabic is related to Hebrew, Syriac, and Ethiopic. Like these other Semitic languages, Arabic is based on three-consonant roots, whose meanings vary according to the combinations of vowels that are used to separate the consonants. Written Arabic often is difficult to learn because of the tendency not to indicate short vowels by diacritical marks. There is no linguistic family relationship between Arabic and Persian, although Persian vocabulary has been heavily influenced by Arabic. The Arabic loanwords incorporated into Persian have been modified to fit the Persian sound patterns. Arabic also continues to be the language of prayer of all Muslims in Iran. Children in school learn to read the Quran in Arabic. Persian- and Turkic-speaking Iranians who have commercial interests in the Persian Gulf area often learn Arabic for business purposes.

In 1986 there were an estimated 530,000 Arabs in Iran. A majority lived in Khuzestan, where they constituted a significant ethnic minority. Most of the other Arabs lived along the Persian Gulf coastal plains, but there also were small scattered tribal groups living in central and eastern Iran. About 40 percent of the Arabs were urban, concentrated in such cities as Abadan, Ahvaz, and Khorramshahr. The majority of urban Arab adult males were unskilled workers, especially in the oil industry. Arabs also worked in commerce and services, and there was a small number of Arab professionals. Some urban Arabs and most rural Arabs are tribally organized. The rural Arabs of Khuzestan tend to be farmers and fishermen. Many of the Arabs who live along the Persian Gulf coastal plains are pastoral nomads who keep herds of cattle, sheep, and camels.

Both the urban and the rural Arabs of Khuzestan are intermingled with the Persians, Turks, and Lurs who also live in the province. The Khuzestan Arabs are Shias. While this physical and spiritual closeness has facilitated intermarriage between the Arabs and other Iranians, the Arabs have tended to regard themselves as separate from non-Arabs and have usually been so regarded by other Iranians. Among the Khuzestan Arabs there has been a sense of ethnic solidarity for many years. The government of neighboring Iraq, both before and after the 1979 Revolution in Iran, has claimed that the Khuzestan Arabs are discriminated against and has asserted at various times that it has assisted those desiring ''liberation'' from Tehran. When Iraq invaded Iran in 1980 and occupied much of Khuzestan for nearly two years, however, an anticipated uprising of the Arab population did not occur, and most of the local Arabs fled the area along with the non-Arab population.

Apart from Khuzestan there is little sense of ethnic unity among the scattered Arab settlements. The Arabs in the area stretching

95

from Bushehr to Bandar-e Abbas tend to be Sunnis. This has helped to strengthen their differentiation from most non-Arab Iranians and even from the Arabs of Khuzestan.

The other Semitic people of Iran are the Assyrians, a Christian group that speaks modern dialects of Assyrian, an Aramaic language that evolved from old Syriac. Language and religion provide a strong cohesive force and give the Assyrians a sense of identity with their coreligionists in Iraq, in other parts of the Middle East, and also in the United States. Most Assyrians adhere to the Assyrian Church of the East (sometimes referred to as the Chaldean Church or Nestorian Church). Many theologians regard this church as the oldest in Christendom. In the nineteenth century, Protestant and Roman Catholic missionaries proselytized among the Assyrians and converted many of them.

There were about 32,000 Assyrians in Iran at the time of the 1976 census. Many of them emigrated after the Revolution in 1979, but at least 20,000 were estimated still to be living in Iran in 1987. The traditional home of the Assyrians in Iran is along the western shore of Lake Urmia. During World War I virtually the entire Assyrian population fled the area, which had become a battleground for opposing Russian and Turkish armies. Thousands of Assyrians perished on the overland flight through the Zagros to the safety of British-controlled Iraq. Eventually, many of the Iranian Assyrians settled among the Assyrian population of Iraq or emigrated to the United States. During the reign of Reza Shah, Assyrians were invited back to Iran to repopulate their villages. A few thousand did return, but, since the 1940s, most young Assyrians have migrated to Tehran and other urban centers.

Armenians

Armenians, a non-Muslim minority that traditionally has lived in northwestern Iran adjacent to the historic Armenian homeland located in what today are eastern Turkey and Soviet Armenia, speak an Indo-European language that is distantly related to Persian. There were an estimated 300,000 Armenians in the country at the time of the Revolution in 1979. There has been considerable emigration of Armenians from Iran since, although in 1986 the Armenian population was still estimated to be 250,000. In the past there were many Armenian villages, especially in the Esfahan area, where several thousand Armenian families had been forcibly resettled in the early seventeenth century during the reign of the Safavid ruler, Shah Abbas. By the 1970s, the Armenians were predominantly urban. Approximately half lived in Tehran, and there were sizable communities in Esfahan, Tabriz, and other cities. The Armenians tend to be relatively well educated and maintain their own schools and Armenian-language newspapers.

Most Armenians are Gregorian Christians, although there are some Roman Catholic and Protestant Armenians as a result of European and American missionary work in Iran during the nineteenth and early twentieth centuries. The Armenian Orthodox Church is divided between those who give their allegiance to the patriarch based at Echmiadzin, near Yerevan in the Armenian Soviet Socialist Republic, and those who support his rival, the patriarch of Cicile at Antilyas, near Beirut in Lebanon. Since 1949 a majority of Armenian Gregorians have followed the patriarch of Cicile. Clergy from Soviet Armenia were at one time active among the Iranian Armenians and had some success in exploiting their sense of community with their coreligionists in the Soviet Union. Several thousand Armenians emigrated from Iran to Soviet Armenia during World War II, and, except for occasional interruptions by one government or another, such emigration has continued. There has also been steady emigration of Iranian Armenians from Iran to the United States.

Structure of Society

Iranians have a very strong sense of class structure. In the past they referred to their society as being divided into tiers, or *tabagheh,* which were identified by numbers: the first tier corresponded to the upper classes; the second, to the middle classes; and the third, to the lower classes. Under the influence of revolutionary ideology, society is now perceived as being divided into the wealthy, a term generally prefixed with negative adjectives; the middle classes; and the *mostazafin,* a term that literally means disinherited. In reality, Iranian society has always been more complex than a three-tier division implies because each of the three broad classes is subdivided into several social groups. These divisions have existed in both urban and rural areas.

Urban Society

Historically, towns in Iran have been administrative, commercial, and manufacturing centers. The traditional political elite consisted of families whose wealth was derived from land and/or trade and from which were recruited the official representatives of the central government. In larger cities, these families could trace their power and influence back several generations. Influential families were also found among the Shia clergy in the largest cities. The middle stratum included merchants and owners of artisan workshops.

The lowest class of urban society included the artisans, laborers, and providers of personal services, such as barbers, bath attendants, shoemakers, tailors, and servants. Most of these, especially the artisans, who were organized into trade associations or guilds, worked in the covered bazaars of the towns.

The urban bazaar historically has been the heart of the Iranian town. In virtually all towns the bazaar is a covered street, or series of streets and alleyways, lined with small shops grouped by service or product. One part of the bazaar contains the shops of cloth and apparel dealers; another section those of carpet makers and merchants; and still another, the workshops of artisans making goods of copper, brass, or other metals, leather, cotton, and wool. In small towns the bazaar might be the equivalent of a narrow, block-long street; in the largest cities, such as Tehran, Esfahan, Mashhad, Tabriz, and Shiraz, the bazaar is a warren of streets that contains warehouses, restaurants, baths, mosques, schools, and gardens in addition to hundreds and hundreds of shops.

The modernization policies of the Pahlavi shahs both preserved and transformed all of these aspects of urban society. This process also led to the rapid growth of the urban population. The extension of central government authority throughout the country fostered the expansion of administrative apparatuses in all major provincial centers. By the 1970s, such cities were sites not just of the principal political and security offices but also of the local branches of diverse government offices such as education, justice, taxation, and telecommunications.

The establishment of modern factories displaced the numerous artisan workshops. Parts of old bazaars were destroyed to create wide streets. Merchants were encouraged to locate retail shops along these new streets rather than in the bazaars. Many of the stores that opened to meet the increased demand for commerce and services from the rapidly expanding urban population were in the new streets. The political elite in the last years of the Pahlavi dynasty spoke of the bazaars as symbols of backwardness and advanced plans to replace some of them with modern shopping malls.

The Urban Political Elite

Prior to the Revolution of 1979, the political elite of the towns consisted of the shah and his family and court in Tehran and the representatives of the monarchy in the provincial towns. These representatives included provincial governors and city mayors, all of whom were appointed by Tehran; high-level government officials; high-ranking military officers; the wealthiest industrialists and financiers; the most prominent merchants; and the best known

professionals in law, medicine, and education. The highest ranks
of the Shia clergy—the clerics who had obtained the status of
ayatollah—were no longer considered part of the national elite by
the mid-1970s, although this social group had been very important in the elite from the seventeenth to the mid-twentieth century.

The Revolution of 1979 swept aside this old elite. Although the
old political elite was not physically removed, albeit many of its
members voluntarily or involuntarily went into exile, it was stripped
of its political power. The new elite consisted first and foremost
of the higher ranks of the Shia clergy. The most important administrative, military, and security positions were filled by lay politicians who supported the rule of the clergy. The majority of the
lay political elite had their origins in the prerevolutionary middle
class, especially the bazaar families (see Political Dynamics, ch. 4).

The Bazaar

Opposing the political elite through much of the twentieth century has been the bazaar, an important political, economic, and
social force in Iran since at least the time of the Qajar dynasty.
The Pahlavi shahs viewed the bazaar as an impediment to the
modern society that they wished to create and sought to enact policies that would erode the bazaar's importance. They were aware
that the alliance of the mercantile and artisan forces of the bazaar
with the Shia clergy posed a serious threat to royal government,
as occurred in 1890 and again during the Constitutional Revolution of 1905–07. The emergence of such an alliance in the period
from 1923 to 1924 is believed by many scholars to have convinced
Reza Shah not to establish a republic, as Atatürk had done in Turkey, but to establish a new dynasty based upon his family.

Reza Shah recognized the potential power of the bazaar, and
he was apparently determined to control it. As his secularization
programs had adversely affected the clergy, many of his economic
reforms hurt the bazaar. His son also sought to control the influence
of the bazaar. As a consequence, the bazaar remained a locus of
opposition to both Pahlavi shahs. During 1978 the bazaar spear-
headed the strikes that paralyzed some sectors of the economy and
provided support for the political actions of the Shia clergy. In
essence, the feared alliance of the bazaar and clergy had once again
come to play a pivotal role in effecting political change in Iran.

The Republic has been much more solicitous of the bazaar than
was the Pahlavi dynasty. Several of the early economic programs
implemented by the governments of the Republic have benefited
the interests of the bazaar; nevertheless, the complexities of managing an economy under the impact of a total war have also forced

the central government to adopt economic policies that the bazaar has opposed. Generally, the government leaders have favored varying degrees of state regulation over such economic issues as the pricing of basic commodities and foreign trade, while entrepreneurs, bazaar merchants, and some prominent clergy have opposed such restrictions. These economic issues have been among the main reasons for the emergence of two contentious factions among the political elite (see The Consolidation of Theocracy, ch. 4).

Social Class in Contemporary Iran

Prior to the Revolution of 1979, political connections were considered a key measure of one's social status. In other words, the amount of access that one was perceived to have to the highest levels of decision making was the major determinant of prestige. Wealth was important, but acquiring and maintaining wealth tended to be closely intertwined with access to political power. Consequently, members of the political elite were generally involved in numerous complex interrelationships. For example, some members of the Senate (the upper house of the parliament, or Majlis—see Glossary), a legislative body that included many members of the political elite appointed by the shah, were also on the boards of several industrial and commercial enterprises and were owners of extensive agricultural lands. Since being part of an elite family was an important prerequisite for entry into the political elite, marital relationships tended to bind together important elite families.

The other classes attempted to emulate the political elite in seeking connections to those with political power, whether on the provincial, town, or village level. By the 1970s, however, the nonelite of all classes perceived education as important for improving social status. Education was seen as providing entry into high-status jobs that in turn would open up opportunities for making connections with those who had political power. Despite a great expansion in educational opportunities, the demand far outstripped the ability or willingness of the elite to provide education; this in turn became a source of resentment. By the late 1970s, the nonelite groups, especially the middle classes, rather than admiring the elite and desiring to emulate them, tended to resent the elite for blocking opportunities to compete on an equal basis.

As a result of the lack of field research in Iran after the Revolution, it was difficult in the late 1980s to determine whether the traditional bases for ascribing class status had changed. It is probable that access to political power continued to be important for ascribing status even though the composition of the political elite had changed. It also appears that education continued to be an important basis for determining status.

The Upper Classes

The postrevolutionary upper classes consisted of some of the same elements as the old elite, such as large landowners, industrialists, financiers, and large-scale merchants. They remained part of the upper class by virtue of having stayed in Iran and having retained a considerable part of their wealth. For the most part, however, such persons no longer had any political influence, and in the future the absence of such influence could impede the acquisition of new wealth. The element of the upper classes with greatest political influence was a new group, the senior clergy. Wealth was apparently no longer an attribute of authority, as the example of Khomeini demonstrated. Religious expertise and piety became the major criteria for belonging to the new political elite. Thus, key government administrators held their positions because of their perceived commitment to Shia Islam. They were part of the new political elite, although not members of the old social elite.

The Middle Classes

After the Revolution of 1979, the composition of the middle class was no different from what it had been under the monarchy. There were several identifiable social groups, including entrepreneurs, bazaar merchants, professionals, managers of private and nationalized concerns, the higher grades of the civil service, teachers, medium-scale landowners, military officers, and the junior ranks of the Shia clergy. Some middle-class groups apparently had more access to political power than they had had before the Revolution because the new political elite had been recruited primarily from the middle class.

Prior to the Revolution, the middle class was divided between those possessed of a Western education, who had a secular outlook, and those suspicious of Western education, who valued a role for religion in both public and private life. In general, the more secularly oriented tended to be found among those employed in the bureaucracy, the professions, and the universities, while the more religiously oriented were concentrated among bazaar merchants and the clergy. Among entrepreneurs and especially primary and secondary school teachers, the secular and religious points of view may have had roughly equal numbers of proponents. Since the Revolution, these two outlooks have been in contention. The religious outlook has dominated politics and society, but it appears that the secular middle class has resented laws and regulations that were perceived as interfering with personal liberties.

The middle class was divided by other issues as well. Before the Revolution, an extremely high value had been placed upon obtaining a foreign education. The new political elite, however, regarded a foreign education with suspicion; accordingly, many members of the middle class who were educated abroad have been required to undergo special Islamic indoctrination courses to retain their jobs. In some cases, refusal to conform to religiously prescribed dress and behavior codes has resulted in the loss of government jobs. As a result of these tensions, thousands of Western-educated Iranians have emigrated since 1979.

The Working Class

The working class has been in the process of formation since the early twentieth century. The industrialization programs of the Pahlavi shahs provided the impetus for the expansion of this class. By the 1970s, a distinct working-class identity, *kargar,* had been established, although those who applied this term to themselves did not actually constitute a unified group. The working class was divided into various groups of workers: those in the oil industry, manufacturing, construction, and transportation; and mechanics and artisans in bazaar workshops. The most important component, factory workers, numbered about 2.5 million on the eve of the Revolution, double the number in 1965, and they accounted for 25 percent of Iran's total employed labor force (see Labor Force, ch. 3).

The workers within any one occupation, rather than sharing a common identity, were divided according to perceived skills. For example, skilled construction workers, such as carpenters, electricians, and plumbers, earned significantly higher wages than the more numerous unskilled workers and tended to look down upon them. Similar status differences were common among workers in the oil industry, textile manufacturing, and metal goods production. The heaviest concentration of unskilled workers was in construction, which on the eve of the Revolution employed 9 percent of the entire labor force. In addition to relatively low wages, unskilled construction workers had no job security.

The unions played only a passive role from the viewpoint of workers. Under both the monarchy and the Republic, union activity was strictly controlled by the government. Both the shah and the government of the Islamic Republic considered strikes to be unpatriotic and generally suppressed both strikes and independent efforts to organize workers. Although strikes played an important role in undermining the authority of the government during the final

An elderly, blind cleric
Courtesy United Nations
(John Isaac)

months of the monarchy, once the Republic had been established the new government embraced the view of its royalist predecessor regarding independent labor activities. Thus the government has considered strikes to be un-Islamic and has forcibly suppressed them. A long history of factionalism among different working-class occupational groups and between skilled and unskilled workers within an industry traditionally has contributed to the relative success of governments in controlling the working class.

The Lower Class

Members of the urban lower class can be distinguished by their high illiteracy rate, performance of manual labor, and generally marginal existence. The lower class is divided into two groups: those with regular employment and those without. Those who have regular work include domestic servants, bath attendants, porters, street cleaners, peddlers, street vendors, gardeners, office cleaners, laundry workers, and bakery workers. Thousands work only occasionally or seasonally at these or other jobs. Among the marginally employed there is much reliance on begging. In the past, some members of this group also resorted to prostitution, gambling, smuggling, and drug selling. Since the Revolution, there have been severe penalties for persons convicted of moral offenses, although newspaper reports of the uncovering of various crime rings would indicate that the new codes have not been successful in eliminating such activities.

At the time of the Revolution, it was estimated that as much as one-third of the population of Tehran and one-quarter of the population of other large cities consisted of persons living on the margins of urban society. Life was typified by squalid slums, poverty, malnutrition, lack of health and educational facilities, and crime. In 1987 there was no evidence of measures undertaken by the new government to alleviate conditions in the urban slums.

Urban Migration

A main characteristic of the working class has been its peasant origins. The rapid growth of the working class in the 1960s and 1970s was the result of migration from villages to cities. There also has been some migration from small towns to larger cities and from economically depressed areas, such as Baluchestan and Kordestan, to more economically vital regions. The result of these population transfers has been an inability of urban services to keep pace with the population growth and the consequent spread of slum areas. In 1987 south Tehran was still Iran's most extensive urban slum, but other large cities also had notable slum sections. It was in these areas that marginally employed and unskilled workers were concentrated. Immediately after the Revolution, the government announced its intention of making living and working conditions in rural areas more attractive as a means of stemming rural-to-urban migration. Although the slowdown in the economy since the Revolution may have contributed to a generally reduced rate of urban growth, there was no evidence that migration from the villages had ceased. The preliminary results from the 1986 census indicated that such cities as Mashhad and Shiraz have grown at even faster rates than before the Revolution.

Rural Society

At the time of the Revolution there were about 68,000 villages in Iran. They varied from mere hamlets of a few families up to sizable settlements with populations of 5,000. Social organization in these villages was less stratified than in urban areas, but a hierarchy of political and social relationships and patterns of interaction could be identified. At the top of the village social structure was the largest landowner or owners. In the middle stratum were peasants owning medium to small farms. In the larger villages the middle stratum also included local merchants and artisans. The lowest level, which predominated in most villages, consisted of landless villagers.

Immediately before the Revolution in 1979, Iran's agriculturally productive land totaled about 16.6 million hectares. Approximately one-half of this land was owned by some 200,000 absentee landlords who resided in urban areas. Such owners were represented in the villages by agents who themselves were generally large landowners. The property of the large-scale owners tended to be among the most fertile in the country and generally was used for the production of such cash crops as cotton, sugar beets, fruit, and high-demand vegetables. Agricultural workers were recruited from among the landless villagers and were given either a share of the crop or a cash wage. In some cases, landlords contracted with small peasant owners to farm their fields in return for a share of the crop. Such agreements netted for the landlords from 20 to 70 percent of the harvest, depending upon the crop and the particular inputs provided by the respective parties.

In 1979 about 7 million hectares were divided among approximately 2 million peasant families, whose holdings ranged from less than 1 hectare up to 50. They had acquired ownership as a result of a land reform program implemented between 1962 and 1971. In a typical village a few families owned sufficient land—ten or more hectares—to engage in farming for profit. About 75 percent of the peasant owners, however, had less than 7 hectares, an amount generally insufficient for anything but subsistence agriculture.

Approximately 50 percent of all villagers owned no land. Within individual villages the landless population varied from as little as 10 percent of the total to more than 75 percent. The landless villagers were composed of three distinct social groups: village merchants, village artisans and service workers, and agricultural laborers. Village merchants were found primarily in the larger villages. Their interests tended to coincide with those of the peasant owners, and it was not uncommon for the better-off merchants to acquire agricultural landholdings. Village artisans included blacksmiths, carpenters, cobblers, and coppersmiths. The increasing availability of urban-manufactured goods throughout the 1960s and 1970s had caused a sharp decline in the numbers of village artisans, although carpenters were still important in the larger villages.

The largest group of landless villagers consisted of agricultural laborers who subsisted by contracting with landlords and larger peasant owners to work in their fields on a daily or seasonal basis. In return for their labor they received a wage, based upon the nature of the work performed, or, in some cases, a share of the crop. This group also provided many of the migrants from rural areas in the 1970s. In some areas the migration rate was so great that landlords were compelled to import foreign workers, primarily unskilled

Afghans, to work their lands. The Afghan and other foreign workers were rounded up immediately after the Revolution and expelled from Iran.

Traditionally, in each village the *kadkhuda* (see Glossary)—not to be confused with the head of the smallest tribal unit, a clan— was responsible for administering its affairs and for representing the village in relations with governmental authorities and other outsiders. Before land reform, landlords appointed the *kadkhudas* from among the peasants. Sometimes *kadkhudas* also served as the landlord's agent in the village, although the tendency was for these two positions to be filled by separate persons. After land reform, the office of *kadkhuda* became, at least in theory, elective. However, since the *kadkhuda* was the primary channel through which the government transacted its affairs with the villages, any villager desiring to be a *kadkhuda* had to demonstrate that he had sufficient political access to government officials in the nearest town to protect the interests of the village. In effect, this meant that *kadkhudas* were actually selected by government officials. In general, "elected" *kadkhudas* tended to be among the richest peasant landowners. The land reform and various rural development programs undertaken prior to the Revolution did not produce positive results for the majority of villagers. Economic conditions for most village families stagnated or deteriorated precisely at the time that manufacturing and construction were experiencing an economic boom in urban areas. Consequently, there was a significant increase in rural-to-urban migration. Between the 1966 and the 1976 censuses, a period when the population of the country as a whole was growing at the rate of 2.7 percent per year, most villages actually lost population, and the overall growth rate for the rural population was barely 0.5 percent annually. This migration was primarily of young villagers attracted to cities by the prospect of seasonal or permanent work opportunities. By the late 1970s, this migration had seriously depleted the labor force of many villages. This was an important factor in the relative decline in production of such basic food crops as cereals because many farming families were forced to sow their agricultural land with less labor-intensive crops.

The problems of rural stagnation and agricultural decline had already surfaced in public debate by the eve of the Revolution. During the immediate turmoil surrounding the fall of the monarchy, peasants in many villages took advantage of the unsettled conditions to complete the land redistribution begun under the shah, i.e., they expropriated the property of landlords whom they accused of being un-Islamic. In still other villages, former landlords who had lost property as a result of land reform tried to regain it by flaunting their commitment to Islam and their antagonism to the deposed shah.

Thus, from the beginning the republican government was compelled to tackle the land problem. This proved to be a difficult issue because of the differences among the political elite with respect to the role of private property under Islam. Some officials wanted to legitimize the peasant expropriations as a means of resolving the problem of inequitable land distribution resulting from the shah's land reform program. Such officials generally believed in the principle that the peasant who actually tilled the soil should also be the owner. In contrast, other officials opposed legitimizing land expropriations on the ground that private property is both sanctioned and protected by Islamic law. By 1987 no consensus had been reached, and the question of land redistribution remained unresolved.

The government, however, has demonstrated considerable interest in rural development. A new organization for rebuilding villages, the Crusade for Reconstruction (Jihad-e Sazandegi or Jihad), was created in 1979. It consisted of high-school-educated youth, largely from urban areas, who were charged with such village improvement tasks as providing electrification and piped water, building feeder roads, constructing mosques and bath houses, and repairing irrigation networks.

Nomadic Society

There has never been a census of pastoral nomads in Iran. In 1986 census officials estimated that nomads totaled 1.8 million. The number of tribally organized people, both nomadic and sedentary, may be twice that figure, or nearly 4 million. The nomadic population practices transhumance, migrating in the spring and in the fall. Each tribe claims the use of fixed territories for its summer and winter pastures and the right to use a specified migration route between these areas. Frequently summer and winter camps are widely separated, in some cases by as much as 300 kilometers. Consequently, the semiannual migrations, with families, flocks, and household equipment, may take up to two months to complete. The nomadic tribes are concentrated in the Zagros, but small groups are also found in northeastern and southeastern Iran.

The movements of the tribes appear to be an adaptation to the ecology of the Zagros. In the summer, when the low valleys are parched from insufficient rainfall, the tribes are in the higher elevations. When the snows begin to fall and cover the pastures of the higher valleys, the tribes migrate to low-lying pastures that remain green throughout the winter because of the seasonal rainfall.

Traditionally, the nomadic tribes have kept large herds of sheep and goats, which have provided the main source of red meat for Iran. During migrations the tribes trade their live animals, wool, hair, hides, dairy products, and various knotted and woven textiles with villagers and townspeople in return for manufactured and agricultural goods that the nomads are unable to produce. This economic interdependence between the nomadic and settled populations of Iran has been an important characteristic of society for several centuries.

During the Qajar period (1795–1925), when the central government was especially weak, the nomadic tribes formed tribal confederations and acquired a great deal of power and influence. In many areas these tribal confederations were virtually autonomous and negotiated with the local and national governments for extensive land rights. The largest tribal confederations, such as those of the Bakhtiari and the Qashqai, were headed by a paramount leader, or *ilkhan*. Individual tribes within a confederation were headed by a *khan, beg, shaykh,* or *sardar*. Subtribes, generally composed of several clans, were headed by *kalantars*. The head of the smallest tribal unit, the clan, was called a *kadkhuda*.

Reza Shah moved against the tribes with the new national army that he began creating while minister of war and prime minister (1921–25). After he became shah, his tribal policy had two objectives: to break the authority and power of the great tribal confederation leaders, whom he perceived as a threat to his goal of centralizing power, and to gain the allegiance of urban political leaders who had historically resented the power of the tribes. In addition to military maneuvers against the tribes, Reza Shah used such economic and administrative techniques as confiscation of tribal properties and the holding of chiefs' sons as hostages. Eventually, many nomads were subdued and placed under army control. Some were given government-built houses and forced to follow a sedentary life. As a result, the herds kept by the nomads were unable to obtain adequate pasturage, and there was a drastic decline in livestock. When Reza Shah abdicated in 1941, many nomadic tribes returned to their former life-styles.

Mohammad Reza Shah continued the policy of weakening the political power of the nomadic tribes, but efforts to coerce them to settle were abandoned. Several tribal leaders were exiled, and the military was given greater authority to regulate tribal migrations. Tribal pastures were nationalized during the 1960s as a means of permitting the government to control access to grazing. In addition, various educational, health, and vocational training programs were implemented to encourage the tribes to settle voluntarily.

Following the Revolution, several former tribal leaders attempted to revitalize their tribes as major political and economic forces. Many factors impeded this development, including the hostile attitude of the central government, the decline in nomadic populations as a result of the settlement of large numbers of tribespeople in the 1960s and 1970s, and the consequent change in attitudes, especially of youth raised in villages and towns.

By the mid-1980s, it seemed that the nomadic tribes were no longer a political force in Iranian society. For one thing, the central government had demonstrated its ability to control the migration routes. Moreover, the leadership of the tribes, while formally vested in the old families, effectively was dispersed among a new generation of nonelite tribespeople who tended to see themselves as ethnic minorities and did not share the views of the old elite.

The Family

For most Iranians the reciprocal obligations and privileges that define relations between kinsfolk—from the parent-child bond to more distant ones—have been more important than those associated with any other kind of social alignment. Economic, political, and other forms of institutional activity have been significantly colored by family ties. This has been true not only for the nuclear family of parents and offspring but also for the aggregate kinsfolk, near and distant, who together represent the extended family at its outermost boundary.

Historically, an influential family was one that had its members strategically distributed throughout the most vital sectors of society, each prepared to support the others in order to ensure family prestige and family status. Since the Revolution, this has meant that each of the elite families of Tehran and the major provincial centers included a cadre of clergy, bureaucrats, and Pasdaran (Pasdaran-e Enghelab-e Islami, or Islamic Revolutionary Guard Corps, or Revolutionary Guards—see Special and Irregular Armed Forces, ch. 5). Business operations have continued to be family affairs; often large government loans for business ventures have been obtained simply because the owners were recognized as members of families with good Islamic and revolutionary credentials. Political activities also followed family lines. Several brothers or first cousins might join the Islamic Republican Party. Another group of siblings might become members of a clandestine opposition group such as the Mojahedin (Mojahedin-e Khalq, or People's Struggle) (see Opposition Political Parties in Exile, ch. 4). Similarly, one member of a family might join the clergy, another the Pasdaran or the armed forces. Successful members were expected to assist less successful ones to get their start. Iranians have viewed this inherent nepotism as a positive value, not as a form of corruption. A person without family ties has little status in the society at large. The severing of ties is acceptable only if a family member has done something repugnant to Islam. Even then, the family is encouraged to make the person aware of his deviance and encourage repentance.

Religious law supports the sanctity of the family in diverse ways, defining the conditions for marriage, divorce, inheritance, and guardianship. Additional laws have been passed by the Majlis that reinforce and refine religious law and are designed to protect the integrity of the family (see The Judiciary, ch. 4).

The head of the household—the father and the husband—expects obedience and respect from others in the family. In return, he is obligated to support them and to satisfy their spiritual, social, and material needs. In practice, he is more a strict disciplinarian. He also may be a focus of love and affection, and family members may feel a strong sense of duty toward him. Considerable conflict and irresolution have resulted in many families, especially in urban areas, because young Iranians, imbued with revolutionary religious views or secular values, have not been able to reconcile these new ideas with the traditional values of their fathers.

Marriage regulations are defined by Shia religious law, although non-Shias are permitted to follow their own religious practices. Before the Revolution, the legal marriage age was eighteen for females and twenty-one for males, although in practice most couples, especially among lower-class urban and rural families, actually were younger than the law permitted when they married. Consequently, the average marriage age for both sexes was 18.9 years. Since the Revolution, the minimum legal age for marriage for both males and females has been lowered to fifteen and thirteen years, respectively, although even younger boys and girls may be married with the permission of their fathers. The average age of marriage is believed to have fallen as a result of official encouragement of earlier marriages.

The selection of a marriage partner is normally determined by customary preference, economic circumstances, and geographic considerations. Among the Christians, Jews, and Zoroastrians, the choice may be restricted by religious practice. There is a distinct preference for marriage within extended kin networks, and a high incidence of marriages among first and second cousins exists. A traditionally preferred marriage is between the children of two brothers, although this kind of consanguineous marriage was declining among the old regime elite and secular middle class by the eve of the Revolution.

Marriage arrangements in villages and among the lower and traditional middle classes of urban areas tend to follow traditional patterns. When a young man is judged ready for marriage, his parents will visit the parents of a girl whom they believe to be a suitable match. In many cases, the man will have already expressed an interest in the girl and have asked his parents to begin these formalities. If the girl's parents show similar interest in the union, the conversation quickly turns to money. There must be an agreement on the amount of the bride-price that will be given to the bride's family at the time of marriage. In principle this payment is supposed to compensate the girl's family for her loss, but in practice it is used primarily to finance the cost of the wedding. The exact sum varies according to the wealth, social position, and degree of kinship of the two families.

Once the two families have agreed to the marriage, the prospective bride and groom are considered engaged. The courtship period now commences and may extend for a year or more, although generally the engagement lasts less than twelve months. The actual wedding involves a marriage ceremony and a public celebration. The ceremony is the signing of a marriage contract in the presence of a mullah (see Glossary). One significant feature of the marriage contract is the *mahriyeh,* a stipulated sum that the groom gives to his new bride. The *mahriyeh* usually is not paid at the time of the marriage, especially in marriages between cousins. The contract notes that it is to be paid, however, in the event of divorce or, in case of the husband's death, to be deducted from his estate before the inheritance is divided according to religious law. If the *mahriyeh* is waived, as sometimes happens in urban areas, this too must be stipulated in the marriage contract.

Marriage customs among the secularized middle and upper classes tend to follow practices in the United States and Europe. The prenuptial bride-price may be paid in installments or even eliminated altogether, especially if a substantial *mahriyeh* is guaranteed. It is typical for the marriage partners to have chosen one another. The bride and groom usually sit together at the reception, to which both male and female guests are invited.

Polygyny in Iran is regulated by Islamic custom, which permits a man to have as many as four wives simultaneously, provided that he treats them equally. During the reign of Mohammad Reza Shah, the government attempted to discourage polygyny through legal restrictions, such as requiring the permission of the first wife before the state would register a second marriage. The practice of kin marriages also tended to work against polygynous marriages, since families would exert pressure on men not to take a second wife.

No reliable figures existed on the number of polygynous marriages in the 1960s and 1970s, but they were believed to be on the decline and largely confined to the older generation. After the Revolution, the republican government abolished the secular codes relating to marriage and decreed polygyny acceptable as long as such marriages were in accordance with Shia religious law.

Shia Islam, unlike Sunni Islam, also recognizes a special form of temporary marriage called *muta*. In a *muta* marriage, the man and woman sign a contract agreeing to live together as husband and wife for a specified time, which can be as brief as several hours or as long as ninety-nine years. The man agrees to pay a certain amount of money for the duration of the contract. Provision is also made for the support of any offspring. There is no limit on the number of *muta* marriages that a man may contract. Traditionally, *muta* marriages have been common in Shia pilgrimage centers such as Mashhad and An Najaf in Iraq. Under the monarchy, the government refused to grant any legal recognition to *muta* marriages in an effort to discourage the practice. Since the Revolution, however, *muta* marriages have again become acceptable.

Under both Islamic law and traditional practice, divorce in Iran historically has been easier for a man to obtain than for a woman. Men could exercise the right of repudiation of wives according to the guidelines of Islamic law. Women were permitted to leave their husbands on narrowly defined grounds, such as insanity or impotence. Beginning in the mid-1960s, the royal government attempted to broaden the grounds upon which women could seek divorce through the Family Protection Law. This legislation was frequently criticized by the clergy and was one of the first laws abrogated after the Revolution. In 1985, however, legislation was passed permitting women to initiate divorce proceedings in certain limited circumstances.

Statistics on divorce since the Revolution were unavailable in early 1987. The government claimed that the divorce rate in Iran was much lower than in industrialized countries. Furthermore, members of the clergy have preached that divorce is ''reprehensible'' under Islam even though it is tolerated.

The Sexes
Traditional Attitudes Toward Segregation of the Sexes

With the notable exception of the Westernized and secularized upper and middle classes, Iranian society before the Revolution practiced public segregation of the sexes. Women generally practiced use of the *chador* (or veil) when in public or when males not

112

related to them were in the house. In the traditional view, an ideal society was one in which women were confined to the home, where they performed the various domestic tasks associated with managing a household and rearing children. Men worked in the public sphere, that is, in the fields, factories, bazaars, and offices. Deviations from this ideal, especially in the case of women, tended to reflect adversely upon the reputation of the family. The strength of these traditional attitudes was reflected in the public education system, which maintained separate schools for boys and girls from the elementary through the secondary levels.

The traditional attitudes on the segregation of women clashed sharply with the views and customs of the secularized upper and middle classes, especially those in Tehran. Mixed gatherings, both public and private, were the norm. During the Pahlavi era the government was the main promoter of change in traditional attitudes toward sexual segregation. It sought to discourage veiling of women at official functions and encouraged mixed participation in a variety of public gatherings. The result was to bring the government into social conflict with the Shia clergy, who sought to defend traditional values.

Impact of Western Ideas on the Role of Women

Among the ideas imported into Iran from the West was the notion that women should participate in the public sphere. The Pahlavi government encouraged women to get as much education as possible and to participate in the labor force at all levels. After 1936, when Reza Shah banned the *chador,* veiling came to be perceived among the minority of elite and secular middle-class women as a symbol of oppression. Before the Revolution, Iranian society was already polarized between the traditionally minded majority and a minority of involved women who were dedicated to improving the status of women. As early as 1932, Iranian women held a meeting of the Oriental Feminine Congress in Tehran at which they called for the right of women to vote, compulsory education for both boys and girls, equal salaries for men and women, and an end to polygyny. In 1963 women were given the right to vote and to hold public office.

Female Participation in the Work Force

Prior to the Revolution, three patterns of work existed among women. Among the upper classes, women either worked as professionals or undertook voluntary projects of various kinds. Whereas secular middle-class women aspired to emulate such women, traditional middle-class women worked outside the home only from dire

113

necessity. Lower class women frequently worked outside the home, especially in major cities, because their incomes were needed to support their households.

Women were active participants in the Revolution that toppled the shah. Most activists were professional women of the secular middle classes, from among whom political antagonists to the regime had long been recruited. Like their male counterparts, such women had nationalist aspirations and felt that the shah's regime was a puppet of the United States. Some women also participated in the guerrilla groups, especially the Mojahedin and the Fadayan (see Anti-Regime Opposition Groups, ch. 5). More significant, however, were the large numbers of lower class women in the cities who participated in street demonstrations during the latter half of 1978 and early 1979. They responded to the call of Khomeini that it was necessary for all Muslims to demonstrate their opposition to tyranny.

Following the Revolution, the status of women changed. The main social group to inherit political power—the traditional middle class—valued most highly the traditional role of women in a segregated society. Accordingly, laws were enacted to restrict the role of women in public life; these laws affected primarily women of the secularized middle and upper classes. *Hejab,* or properly modest attire for women, became a major issue. Although it was not mandated that women who had never worn a *chador* would have to wear this garment, it was required that whenever women appeared in public they had to have their hair and skin covered, except for the face and hands. The law has been controversial among secularized women, although for the majority of women, who had worn the *chador* even before the Revolution, the law probably has had only negligible impact.

Religious Life

The overwhelming majority of Iranians—at least 90 percent of the total population—are Muslims who adhere to Shia Islam. In contrast, the majority of Muslims throughout the world follow Sunni Islam. Of the several Shia sects, the Twelve Imam (see Glossary) or Twelver (*ithna-ashari*), is dominant in Iran; most Shias in Bahrain, Iraq, and Lebanon also follow this sect. All the Shia sects originated among early Muslim dissenters in the first three centuries following the death of the Prophet Muhammad in A.D. 632 (see Islamic Conquest, ch. 1).

The principal belief of Twelvers, but not of other Shias, is that the spiritual and temporal leadership of the Muslim community passed from Muhammad to Ali and then sequentially to eleven of

Esfahan women attend a literacy class concerned with home economics
Courtesy United Nations

Ali's direct male descendants, a tenet rejected by Sunnis. Over the centuries various other theological differences have developed between Twelver Shias and Sunnis.

Shia Islam in Iran

Distinctive Beliefs

Although Shias have lived in Iran since the earliest days of Islam, and there was one Shia dynasty in part of Iran during the tenth and eleventh centuries, it is believed that most Iranians were Sunnis until the seventeenth century. The Safavid dynasty made Shia Islam the official state religion in the sixteenth century and aggressively proselytized on its behalf. It is also believed that by the mid-seventeenth century most people in what is now Iran had become Shias, an affiliation that has continued.

All Shia Muslims believe there are seven pillars of faith, which detail the acts necessary to demonstrate and reinforce faith. The first five of these pillars are shared with Sunni Muslims. They are *shahada,* or the confession of faith; *namaz,* or ritualized prayer; *zakat,* or almsgiving; *sawm,* fasting and contemplation during daylight hours during the lunar month of Ramazan; and hajj, or pilgrimage to the holy cities of Mecca and Medina once in a lifetime if financially feasible. The other two pillars, which are not shared with

115

Sunnis, are jihad—or crusade to protect Islamic lands, beliefs, and institutions, and the requirement to do good works and to avoid all evil thoughts, words, and deeds.

Twelver Shia Muslims also believe in five basic principles of faith: there is one God, who is a unitary divine being in contrast to the trinitarian being of Christians; the Prophet Muhammad is the last of a line of prophets beginning with Abraham and including Moses and Jesus, and he was chosen by God to present His message to mankind; there is a resurrection of the body and soul on the last or judgment day; divine justice will reward or punish believers based on actions undertaken through their own free will; and Twelve Imams were successors to Muhammad. The first three of these beliefs are also shared by non-Twelver Shias and Sunni Muslims.

The distinctive dogma and institution of Shia Islam is the Imamate, which includes the idea that the successor of Muhammad be more than merely a political leader. The Imam must also be a spiritual leader, which means that he must have the ability to interpret the inner mysteries of the Quran and the *shariat* (see Glossary). The Twelver Shias further believe that the Twelve Imams who succeeded the Prophet were sinless and free from error and had been chosen by God through Muhammad.

The Imamate began with Ali, who is also accepted by Sunni Muslims as the fourth of the "rightly guided caliphs" to succeed the Prophet. Shias revere Ali as the First Imam, and his descendants, beginning with his sons Hasan and Husayn (also seen as Hosein), continue the line of the Imams until the Twelfth, who is believed to have ascended into a supernatural state to return to earth on judgment day. Shias point to the close lifetime association of Muhammad with Ali. When Ali was six years old, he was invited by the Prophet to live with him, and Shias believe Ali was the first person to make the declaration of faith in Islam. Ali also slept in Muhammad's bed on the night of the *hijra,* or migration from Mecca to Medina, when it was feared that the house would be attacked by unbelievers and the Prophet stabbed to death. He fought in all the battles Muhammad did except one, and the Prophet chose him to be the husband of his favorite daughter, Fatima.

In Sunni Islam an imam is the leader of congregational prayer. Among the Shias of Iran the term *imam* traditionally has been used only for Ali and his eleven descendants. None of the Twelve Imams, with the exception of Ali, ever ruled an Islamic government. During their lifetimes, their followers hoped that they would assume the rulership of the Islamic community, a rule that was believed to have been wrongfully usurped. Because the Sunni caliphs were cognizant of this hope, the Imams generally were persecuted during the

Umayyad and Abbasid dynasties. Therefore, the Imams tried to be as unobtrusive as possible and to live as far as was reasonable from the successive capitals of the Islamic empire.

During the ninth century Caliph Al Mamun, son of Caliph Harun ar Rashid, was favorably disposed toward the descendants of Ali and their followers. He invited the Eighth Imam, Reza (A.D. 765–816), to come from Medina to his court at Marv (Mary in the present-day Soviet Union). While Reza was residing at Marv, Mamun designated him as his successor in an apparent effort to avoid conflict among Muslims. Reza's sister Fatima journeyed from Medina to be with her brother but took ill and died at Qom. A shrine developed around her tomb, and over the centuries Qom has become a major Shia pilgrimage and theology center.

Mamun took Reza on his military campaign to retake Baghdad from political rivals. On this trip Reza died unexpectedly in Khorasan. Reza was the only Imam to reside or die in what is now Iran. A major shrine, and eventually the city of Mashhad, grew up around his tomb, which has become the most important pilgrimage center in Iran. Several important theological schools are located in Mashhad, associated with the shrine of the Eighth Imam.

Reza's sudden death was a shock to his followers, many of whom believed that Mamun, out of jealousy for Reza's increasing popularity, had him poisoned. Mamun's suspected treachery against Reza and his family tended to reinforce a feeling already prevalent among his followers that the Sunni rulers were untrustworthy.

The Twelfth Imam is believed to have been only five years old when the Imamate descended upon him in A.D. 874 at the death of his father. The Twelfth Imam is usually known by his titles of Imam-e Asr (the Imam of the Age) and Sahib az Zaman (the Lord of Time). Because his followers feared he might be assassinated, the Twelfth Imam was hidden from public view and was seen only by a few of his closest deputies. Sunnis claim that he never existed or that he died while still a child. Shias believe that the Twelfth Imam remained on earth, but hidden from the public, for about seventy years, a period they refer to as the lesser occultation (*gheybat-e sughra*). Shias also believe that the Twelfth Imam has never died, but disappeared from earth in about A.D. 939. Since that time the greater occultation (*gheybat-e kubra*) of the Twelfth Imam has been in force and will last until God commands the Twelfth Imam to manifest himself on earth again as the Mahdi, or Messiah. Shias believe that during the greater occultation of the Twelfth Imam he is spiritually present—some believe that he is materially present as well—and he is besought to reappear in various invocations and prayers. His name is mentioned in wedding invitations, and his birthday is one of the most jubilant of all Shia religious observances.

The Shia doctrine of the Imamate was not fully elaborated until the tenth century. Other dogmas were developed still later. A characteristic of Shia Islam is the continual exposition and reinterpretation of doctrine. The most recent example is Khomeini's expounding of the doctrine of *velayat-e faqih* (see Glossary), or the political guardianship of the community of believers by scholars trained in religious law. This has not been a traditional idea in Shia Islam and is, in fact, an innovation. The basic idea is that the clergy, by virtue of their superior knowledge of the laws of God, are the best qualified to rule the society of believers who are preparing themselves on earth to live eternally in heaven. The concept of *velayat-e faqih* thus provides the doctrinal basis for theocratic government, an experiment that Twelver Imam Shias had not attempted prior to the Iranian Revolution in 1979.

Religious Obligations

In addition to the seven principal tenets of faith, there are also traditional religious practices that are intimately associated with Shia Islam. These include the observance of the month of martyrdom, Moharram, and pilgrimages to the shrines of the Twelve Imams and their various descendants. The Moharram observances commemorate the death of the Third Imam, Husayn, who was the son of Ali and Fatima and the grandson of Muhammad. He was killed near Karbala in modern Iraq in A.D. 680 during a battle with troops supporting the Umayyad caliph. Husayn's death is commemorated by Shias with passion plays and is an intensely religious time.

Pilgrimage to the shrines of imams is a specific Shia custom. The most important shrines in Iran are those for the Eighth Imam in Mashhad and for his sister Fatima in Qom. There are also important secondary shrines for other relatives of the Eighth Imam in Rey, adjacent to south Tehran, and in Shiraz. In virtually all towns and in many villages there are numerous lesser shrines, known as *imamzadehs,* which commemorate descendants of the imams who are reputed to have led saintly lives. Shia pilgrims visit these sites because they believe that the imams and their relatives have power to intercede with God on behalf of petitioners. The shrines in Iraq at Karbala and An Najaf are also revered by Shias.

Religious Institutions and Organizations

Historically, the single most important religious institution in Iran has been the mosque. In towns, congregational prayers, as well as prayers and rites associated with religious observances and important phases in the lives of Muslims, took place in mosques. Iranian Shias before the Revolution did not generally attach great significance to institutionalization, however, and there was little emphasis on mosque attendance, even for the Friday congregational prayers. Mosques were primarily an urban phenomenon, and in most of the thousands of small villages there were no mosques. Mosques in the larger cities began to assume more important social roles during the 1970s; during the Revolution they played a prominent role in organizing people for the large demonstrations that took place in 1978 and 1979. Since that time their role has continued to expand, so that in 1987 mosques played important political and social roles as well as religious ones.

Another religious institution of major significance was a special building known as a *hoseiniyeh*. *Hoseiniyehs* existed in urban areas and traditionally served as sites for recitals commemorating the martyrdom of Husayn, especially during the month of Moharram. In the 1970s, some *hoseiniyehs*, such as the Hoseiniyeh Irshad in Tehran, became politicized as prominent clerical and lay preachers used the symbol of the deaths as martyrs of Husayn and the other Imams as thinly veiled criticism of Mohammad Reza Shah's regime, thus helping to lay the groundwork for the Revolution in 1979.

Institutions providing religious education include *madrasehs* and *maktabs*. *Madrasehs*, or seminaries, historically have been important for advanced training in Shia theology and jurisprudence. *Madrasehs* are generally associated with noted Shia scholars who have attained the rank of ayatollah. There are also some older *madrasehs*, established initially through endowments, at which several scholars may teach. Students, known as *talabehs*, live on the grounds of the *madrasehs* and are provided stipends for the duration of their studies, usually a minimum of seven years, during which they prepare for the examinations that qualify a seminary student to be a low-level preacher, or mullah. At the time of the Revolution, there were slightly more than 11,000 *talabehs* in Iran; approximately 60 percent of these were studying at the *madrasehs* in the city of Qom, another 25 percent were enrolled in the important *madrasehs* of Mashhad and Esfahan, and the rest were at *madrasehs* in Tabriz, Yazd, Shiraz, Tehran, Zanjan, and other cities.

Maktabs, primary schools run by the clergy, were the only educational institutions prior to the end of the nineteenth century when the first secular schools were established. *Maktabs* declined in numbers and importance as the government developed a national public school system beginning in the 1930s. Nevertheless, *maktabs*

120

A prayer meeting at the University of Tehran
Courtesy United Nations (John Isaac)

continued to exist as private religious schools right up to the Revolution. Since 1979 the public education system has been desecularized and the *maktabs* and their essentially religious curricula merged with government schools (see Education, this ch.).

Another major religious institution in Iran is the shrine. There are more than 1,100 shrines that vary from crumbling sites associated with local saints to the imposing shrines of Imam Reza and his sister Fatima in Mashhad and Qom, respectively. These more famous shrines are huge complexes that include the mausoleums of the venerated Eighth Imam and his sister, tombs of former shahs, mosques, *madrasehs,* and libraries. Imam Reza's shrine is the largest and is considered to be the holiest. In addition to the usual shrine accoutrements, Imam Reza's shrine contains hospitals, dispensaries, a museum, and several mosques located in a series of courtyards surrounding his tomb. Most of the present shrine dates from the early fourteenth century, except for the dome, which was rebuilt after being damaged in an earthquake in 1673. The shrine's endowments and gifts are the largest of all religious institutions in the country. Traditionally, free meals for as many as 1,000 people per day are provided at the shrine. Although there are no special times for visiting this or other shrines, it is customary for pilgrimage traffic to be heaviest during Shia holy periods. It has been estimated that more than 3 million pilgrims visit the shrine annually.

Visitors to Imam Reza's shrine represent all socioeconomic levels. Whereas piety is a motivation for many, others come to seek the spiritual grace or general good fortune that a visit to the shrine is believed to ensure. Commonly a pilgrimage is undertaken to petition Imam Reza to act as an intermediary between the pilgrim and God. Since the nineteenth century, it has been customary among the bazaar class and members of the lower classes to recognize those who have made a pilgrimage to Mashhad by prefixing their names with the title *mashti.*

The next most important shrine is that of Imam Reza's sister, Fatima, known as Hazarat-e Masumeh (the Pure Saint). The present shrine dates from the early sixteenth century, although some later additions, including the gilded tiles, were affixed in the early nineteenth century. Other important shrines are those of Shah Abdol Azim, a relative of Imam Reza, who is entombed at Rey, near Tehran, and Shah Cheragh, a brother of Imam Reza, who is buried in Shiraz. A leading shrine honoring a person not belonging to the family of Imams is that of the Sufi master Sayyid Nimatollah Vali near Kerman. Shias make pilgrimages to these shrines and the hundreds of local *imamzadehs* to petition the saints to grant them special favors or to help them through a period of troubles.

Because Shias believe that the holy Imams can intercede for the dead as well as for the living, cemeteries traditionally have been located adjacent to the most important shrines in both Iran and Iraq. Corpses were transported overland for burial in Karbala in southern Iraq until the practice was prohibited in the 1930s. Corpses are still shipped to Mashhad and Qom for burial in the shrine cemeteries of these cities.

The constant movement of pilgrims from all over Iran to Mashhad and Qom has helped bind together a linguistically heterogeneous population. Pilgrims serve as major sources of information about conditions in different parts of the country and thus help to mitigate the parochialism of the regions.

A traditional source of financial support for all religious institutions has been the *vaqf,* a religious endowment by which land and other income-producing property is given in perpetuity for the maintenance of a shrine, mosque, *madraseh,* or charitable institution such as a hospital, library, or orphanage. A *mutavalli* administers a *vaqf* in accordance with the stipulations in the donor's bequest. In many *vaqfs* the position of *mutavalli* is hereditary. Under the Pahlavis, the government attempted to exercise control over the administration of *vaqfs,* especially those of the larger shrines. This was a source of conflict with the clergy, who perceived the government's efforts as lessening their influence and authority in traditional religious matters.

The government's interference with the administration of *vaqfs* led to a sharp decline in the number of *vaqf* bequests. Instead, wealthy and pious Shias chose to give financial contributions directly to the leading ayatollahs in the form of *zakat,* or obligatory alms. The clergy in turn used the funds to administer their *madrasehs* and to institute various educational and charitable programs, which indirectly provided them with more influence in society. The access of the clergy to a steady and independent source of funding was an important factor in their ability to resist state controls and ultimately helped them direct the opposition to the shah.

Religious Hierarchy

From the time that Twelver Shia Islam emerged as a distinct religious denomination in the early ninth century, its clergy, or ulama, have played a prominent role in the development of its scholarly and legal tradition; however, the development of a distinct hierarchy among the Shia clergy dates back only to the early nineteenth century. Since that time the highest religious authority has been vested in the *mujtahids,* scholars who by virtue of their erudition in the science of religion (the Quran, the traditions of

Muhammad and the imams, jurisprudence, and theology) and their attested ability to decide points of religious conduct, act as leaders of their community in matters concerning the particulars of religious duties. Lay Shias and lesser members of the clergy who lack such proficiency are expected to follow *mujtahids* in all matters pertaining to religion, but each believer is free to follow any *mujtahid* he chooses. Since the mid-nineteenth century it has been common for several *mujtahids* concurrently to attain prominence and to attract large followings. During the twentieth century, such *mujtahids* have been accorded the title of *ayatollah*. Occasionally an ayatollah achieves almost universal authority among Shias and is given the title of *ayatollah ol ozma*, or grand ayatollah. Such authority was attained by as many as seven *mujtahids* simultaneously, including Ayatollah Khomeini, in the late 1970s.

To become a *mujtahid*, it is necessary to complete a rigorous and lengthy course of religious studies in one of the prestigious *madrasehs* of Qom or Mashhad in Iran or An Najaf in Iraq and to receive an authorization from a qualified *mujtahid*. Of equal importance is either the explicit or the tacit recognition of a cleric as a *mujtahid* by laymen and scholars in the Shia community. There is no set time for studying a particular subject, but serious preparation to become a *mujtahid* normally requires fifteen years to master the religious subjects deemed essential. It is uncommon for any student to attain the status of *mujtahid* before the age of thirty; more commonly students are between forty and fifty years old when they achieve this distinction.

Most seminary students do not complete the full curriculum of studies to become *mujtahids*. Those who leave the *madrasehs* after completing the primary level can serve as prayer leaders, village mullahs, local shrine administrators, and other religious functionaries. Those who leave after completing the second level become preachers in town and city mosques. Students in the third level of study are those preparing to become *mujtahids*. The advanced students at this level are generally accorded the title of *hojjatoleslam* when they have completed all their studies.

The Shia clergy in Iran wear a white turban and an *aba*, a loose, sleeveless brown cloak, open in front. A *sayyid*, who is a clergyman descended from Muhammad, wears a black turban and a black *aba*.

Unorthodox Shia Religious Movements

Shah Ismail, the founder of the Safavid dynasty, who established Twelver Shia Islam as the official religion of Iran at the beginning of the sixteenth century, was revered by his followers as a Sufi master. Sufism, or Islamic mysticism, has a long tradition in Iran. It developed there and in other areas of the Islamic empire during the ninth century among Muslims who believed that worldly pleasures distracted from true concern with the salvation of the soul. Sufis generally renounced materialism, which they believed supported and perpetuated political tyranny. Their name is derived from the Arabic word for wool, *suf,* and was applied to the early Sufis because of their habit of wearing rough wool next to their skin as a symbol of their asceticism. Over time a great variety of Sufi brotherhoods was formed, including several that were militaristic, such as the Safavid order, of which Ismail was the leader.

Although Sufis were associated with the early spread of Shia ideas in the country, once the Shia clergy had consolidated their authority over religion by the early seventeenth century, they tended to regard Sufis as deviant. At various periods during the past three centuries some Shia clergy have encouraged persecution of Sufis, but Sufi orders have continued to exist in Iran. During the Pahlavi period, some Sufi brotherhoods were revitalized. Some members of the secularized middle class were especially attracted to them, but the orders appear to have had little following among the lower classes. The largest Sufi order was the Nimatollahi, which had *khanehgahs,* or teaching centers, in several cities and even established new centers in foreign countries. Other important orders were the Dhahabi and Kharksar brotherhoods. Sufi brotherhoods such as the Naqshbandi and the Qadiri also existed among Sunni Muslims in Kordestan. There is no evidence of persecution of Sufis under the Republic, but the brotherhoods are regarded suspiciously and generally have kept a low profile.

Iran also contains Shia sects that many of the Twelver Shia clergy regard as heretical. One of these is the Ismaili, a sect that has several thousand adherents living primarily in northeastern Iran. The Ismailis, of whom there were once several different sects, trace their origins to the son of Ismail who predeceased his father, the Sixth Imam. The Ismailis were very numerous and active in Iran from the eleventh to the thirteenth century; they are known in history as the ''Assassins'' because of their practice of killing political opponents. The Mongols destroyed their center at Alamut in the Alborz Mountains in 1256. Subsequently, their living imams went into hiding from non-Ismailis. In the nineteenth century, their leader emerged in public as the Agha Khan and fled to British-controlled India, where he supervised the revitalization of the sect. The majority of the several million Ismailis in the 1980s live outside Iran.

Another Shia sect is the Ahl-e Haqq. Its adherents are concentrated in Lorestan, but small communities also are found in

Kordestan and Mazandaran. The origins of the Ahl-e Haqq are believed to lie in one of the medieval politicized Sufi orders. The group has been persecuted sporadically by orthodox Shias. After the Revolution, some of the sect's leaders were imprisoned on the ground of religious deviance.

Sunni Muslims

Sunni Muslims constitute approximately 8 percent of the Iranian population. A majority of Kurds, virtually all Baluchis and Turkomans, and a minority of Arabs are Sunnis, as are small communities of Persians in southern Iran and Khorasan. The main difference between Sunnis and Shias is that the former do not accept the doctrine of the Imamate. Generally speaking, Iranian Shias are inclined to recognize Sunnis as fellow Muslims, but as those whose religion is incomplete. Shia clergy tend to view missionary work among Sunnis to convert them to true Islam as a worthwhile religious endeavor. Since the Sunnis generally live in the border regions of the country, there has been no occasion for Shia-Sunni conflict in most of Iran. In those towns with mixed populations in West Azarbaijan, the Persian Gulf region, and Baluchestan va Sistan, tensions between Shias and Sunnis existed both before and after the Revolution. Religious tensions have been highest during major Shia observances, especially Moharram.

Non-Muslim Minorities

Bahais

The largest non-Muslim minority in Iran is the Bahais. There were an estimated 350,000 Bahais in Iran in 1986 (see table 4, Appendix). The Bahais are scattered in small communities throughout Iran with a heavy concentration in Tehran. Most Bahais are urban, but there are some Bahai villages, especially in Fars and Mazandaran. The majority of Bahais are Persians, but there is a significant minority of Azarbaijani Bahais, and there are even a few among the Kurds.

Bahaism is a religion that originated in Iran during the 1840s as a reformist movement within Shia Islam. Initially it attracted a wide following among Shia clergy and others dissatisfied with society. The political and religious authorities joined to suppress the movement, and since that time the hostility of the Shia clergy to Bahaism has remained intense. In the latter half of the nineteenth century, the Bahai leader fled to Ottoman Palestine—roughly present-day Israel—where he and his successors continued to elaborate Bahai doctrines by incorporating beliefs from other world religions. By the early twentieth century, Bahaism had evolved into a new religion that stressed the brotherhood of all peoples, equality of the sexes, and pacifism.

The Shia clergy, as well as many Iranians, have continued to regard Bahais as heretics from Islam. Consequently, Bahais have encountered much prejudice and have sometimes been the objects of persecution. The situation of the Bahais improved under the Pahlavi shahs when the government actively sought to secularize public life. Bahais were permitted to hold government posts (despite a constitutional prohibition) and allowed to open their own schools, and many were successful in business and the professions. Their position was drastically altered after 1979. The Islamic Republic did not recognize the Bahais as a religious minority, and the sect has been officially persecuted. More than 700 of their religious leaders were arrested, and several of them were executed for apostasy; their schools were closed; their communal property was confiscated; they were prohibited from holding any government employment; and they were not issued identity cards. In addition, security forces failed to protect Bahais and their property from attacks by mobs.

Christians

Iran's indigenous Christians include an estimated 250,000 Armenians, some 32,000 Assyrians, and a small number of Roman Catholic, Anglican, and Protestant Iranians converted by missionaries in the nineteenth and twentieth centuries. The Armenians are predominantly urban and are concentrated in Tehran and Esfahan; smaller communities exist in Tabriz, Arak, and other cities. A majority of the Assyrians are also urban, although there are still several Assyrian villages in the Lake Urmia region. Armenians and Assyrians were recognized as official religious minorities under the 1906 constitution. Although Armenians and Assyrians have encountered individual prejudice, they have not been subjected to persecution. During the twentieth century, Christians in general have participated in the economic and social life of Tehran. The Armenians, especially, achieved a relatively high standard of living and maintained a large number of parochial primary and secondary schools.

The new, republican Constitution of 1979 also recognized the Armenians and Assyrians as official religious minorities (see Constitutional Framework, ch. 4). They are entitled to elect their own representatives to the Majlis and are permitted to follow their own religious laws in matters of marriage, divorce, and inheritance. Other Christians have not received any special recognition, and there have been a number of incidents of persecution of Iranian

Anglicans. All Christians are required to observe the new laws relating to attire, prohibition of alcohol, and segregation by sex at public gatherings. Christians have resented these laws because they have infringed on their traditional religious practices. In addition, the administration of the Armenian schools has been a source of tension between Christians and the government. The Ministry of Education has insisted that the principals of such schools be Muslims, that all religion courses be taught in Persian, that any Armenian literature classes have government approval, and that all female students observe *hejab* inside the schools.

Jews

In 1986 there were an estimated 50,000 Jews in Iran, a decline from about 85,000 in 1978. The Iranian Jewish community is one of the oldest in the world, being descended from Jews who remained in the region following the Babylonian captivity, when the Achaemenid rulers of the first Iranian empire permitted Jews to return to Jerusalem. Over the centuries the Jews of Iran became physically, culturally, and linguistically indistinguishable from the non-Jewish population. The overwhelming majority of Jews speak Persian as their mother language, and a tiny minority, Kurdish. The Jews are predominantly urban and by the 1970s were concentrated in Tehran, with smaller communities in other cities, such as Shiraz, Esfahan, Hamadan, and Kashan.

Until the twentieth century the Jews were confined to their own quarters in the towns. In general the Jews were an impoverished minority, occupationally restricted to small-scale trading, money-lending, and working with precious metals. Since the 1920s, Jews have had greater opportunities for economic and social mobility. They have received assistance from a number of international Jewish organizations, including the American Joint Distribution Committee, which introduced electricity, piped water, and modern sanitation into Jewish neighborhoods. The Jews have gradually gained increased importance in the bazaars of Tehran and other cities, and after World War II some educated Jews entered the professions, particularly pharmacy, medicine, and dentistry.

The Constitution of 1979 recognized Jews as an official religious minority and accorded them the right to elect a representative to the Majlis. Like the Christians, the Jews have not been persecuted. Unlike the Christians, the Jews have been viewed with suspicion by the government, probably because of the government's intense hostility toward Israel. Iranian Jews generally have many relatives in Israel—some 45,000 Iranian Jews emigrated from Iran to Israel between 1948 and 1977—with whom they are in regular contact.

Since 1979 the government has cited mail and telephone communications as evidence of "spying" in the arrest, detention, and even execution of a few prominent Jews. Although these individual cases have not affected the status of the community as a whole, they have contributed to a pervasive feeling of insecurity among Jews regarding their future in Iran and have helped to precipitate large-scale emigration. Most Jews who have left since the Revolution have settled in the United States.

Zoroastrians

In 1986 there were an estimated 32,000 Zoroastrians in Iran. They speak Persian and are concentrated in Tehran, Kerman, and Yazd. Zoroastrianism initially developed in Iran during the seventh century B.C. Later, it became the official religion of the Sassanid Empire, which ruled over Iran for approximately four centuries before being destroyed by the Arabs in the seventh century A.D. After Iran's incorporation into the Islamic empire, the majority of its population was gradually converted from Zoroastrianism to Islam, a process that was probably completed by the tenth century.

During the Qajar era there was considerable prejudice against Zoroastrians. In the mid-nineteenth century, several thousand Zoroastrians emigrated from Iran to British-ruled India to improve their economic and social status. Many eventually acquired wealth in India and subsequently expended part of their fortunes on upgrading conditions in the Zoroastrian communities of Iran. The emphasis placed on Iran's pre-Islamic heritage by the Pahlavis also helped Zoroastrians to achieve a more respected position in society. Many of them migrated from Kerman and Yazd to Tehran, where they accumulated significant wealth as merchants and in real estate. By the 1970s, younger Zoroastrians were entering the professions.

Like the Christians and Jews, the Zoroastrians are recognized as an official religious minority under the Constitution of 1979. They are permitted to elect one representative to the Majlis and, like the other legally accepted minorities, may seek employment in the government. They generally enjoy the same civil liberties as Muslims. Although Zoroastrians probably have encountered individual instances of prejudice, they have not been persecuted because of their religious beliefs.

Education

Prior to the mid-nineteenth century, it was traditional in Iran for education to be associated with religious institutions. The clergy, both Shia and non-Shia, assumed responsibility for instructing youth in basic literacy and the fundamentals of religion. Knowledge of reading and writing was not considered necessary for all the population, and thus education generally was restricted to the sons of the economic and political elite. Typically, this involved a few years of study in a local school, or *maktab*. Those who desired to acquire more advanced knowledge could continue in a religious college, or *madraseh,* where all fields of religious science were taught. A perceived need to provide instruction in subjects that were not part of the traditional religious curriculum, such as accounting, European languages, military science, and technology, led to the establishment of the first government school in 1851. For many years this remained the only institution of higher learning in the country.

By the early twentieth century there were several schools teaching foreign languages and sciences, including a few for girls. These schools were run by foreign missionaries, private Iranians, and the government. Their function was to educate the children of the elite. During the Constitutional Revolution (1905–1907), a number of reform-minded individuals proposed the establishment of a nationwide, public, primary school system. Progress in opening new schools was steady but slow, and by the end of the Qajar dynasty (1925) there were approximately 3,300 government schools with a total enrollment of about 110,000 students.

During the Pahlavi era (1925–79), the government implemented a number of policies aimed at modernizing the country and expanded the education system. The Ministry of Education was given responsibility for regulating all public and private schools and drafted a uniform curriculum for primary and for secondary education. The entire public system was secular and for many years remained based upon the French model. Its objective was to train Iranians for modern occupations in administration, management, science, and teaching. This education system was the single most important factor in the creation of the secularized middle class.

The goal of creating a nationwide education system was never achieved during the Pahlavi era. In 1940 only 10 percent of all elementary-age children were enrolled in school, and less than 1 percent of youths between the ages of 12 and 20 were in secondary school. These statistics did not increase significantly until the early 1960s, when the government initiated programs to improve and expand the public school system. By 1978 approximately 75 percent of all elementary-age children were enrolled in primary schools, while somewhat less than 50 percent of all teenagers were attending secondary schools.

Modern college and university education also was developed under the Pahlavis; by the 1920s, the country had several institutes of higher education. In 1934 the institutes associated with government ministries were combined to form the University of Tehran, which was coeducational from its inception. Following World War II, universities were founded in other major cities, such as Tabriz, Esfahan, Mashhad, Shiraz, and Ahvaz. During the 1970s, these universities were expanded, and colleges and vocational institutes were set up in several cities.

One of the first measures adopted by the government after the Revolution in 1979 was the desecularization of the public school system. This was a three-pronged program that involved purging courses and textbooks believed to slander Islam and substituting courses on religion; purging teachers to ensure that only those who understood the true meaning of Islam (i.e., were not secular) remained in the schools; and regulating the behavior and dress of students.

Although the government reintroduced the study of religion into the public school curriculum from primary grades through college, it did not act to alter the basic organization of the education system. Thus, as late as the school year 1986–1987, schools had not changed significantly from the pattern prior to the Revolution. Students studied in primary schools for five years, beginning the first grade at about age seven. Then they spent three years, designated the guidance cycle, in a middle school. In this cycle, the future training of students was determined by their aptitude as demonstrated on examinations. Students were then directed into one of three kinds of four-year high schools: the academic cycle, preparing for college; the science and mathematics cycle, preparing for university programs in engineering and medicine; and the vocational technical cycle.

The Ministry of Education announced that nearly 11.5 million students were registered for elementary and secondary schools during the academic year 1986–1987. Statistics on the percentage of young people aged seven through nineteen enrolled in school have not been available since the Revolution. It is generally estimated that the percentages have remained similar to those before the Revolution: school attendance of about 78 percent of elementary-age children and less than 50 percent of secondary-age youth.

Since the Revolution, higher education has experienced significantly more drastic changes than elementary and secondary education. The university campuses became centers of conflict between students who supported a thorough desecularization of administrations, faculties, and curricula and students who wanted to retain a secular system. There were violent clashes at several universities in the 1979–1980 school year; as a result the government closed all 200 institutes of higher learning in April 1980. The universities then were purged of professors and students considered insufficiently Islamic and were not completely reopened until the fall of 1983. When the colleges resumed classes, they enrolled only a fraction of the 1979 to 1980 student body. At the University of Tehran, Iran's largest, student enrollment was reduced from 17,000 to 4,500; similarly large declines were registered at other institutions. The decline in the number of female students was even more dramatic: whereas on the eve of the revolution women had constituted about 40 percent of the total number of students in higher education, after 1983 they formed only 10 percent.

An educational problem in Iran since the early twentieth century has been the general perception among the upper and middle classes that foreign education is superior to Iranian. Thus, there have been large numbers of Iranians studying abroad. As long as the foreign-educated students returned to Iran, they were able to apply their skills for the overall benefit of the country; however, under both the monarchy and the Republic, thousands of Iranians have elected not to return to their homeland, creating a veritable "brain drain." Since the Revolution, the government has tried to discourage Iranians from going abroad to study, although it has not prevented the practice.

Health and Welfare

Medical Personnel and Facilities

According to the Iranian Medical Association (IMA), in 1986 there were 12,300 physicians and 1,700 dentists in Iran. Medical support personnel of all kinds were in short supply, with the total number of nurses estimated at around 7,000. There were about 550 hospitals throughout the country, with a total of 62,100 beds.

The regional distribution of medical personnel was uneven. The ratio of patients to physicians in 1986 averaged more than 1,000 to 1 for Tehran, Mashhad, Esfahan, and Shiraz; more than 2,000 to 1 in all other large cities (with more than 100,000 in population); and more than 4,500 to 1 elsewhere. An estimated 70 percent of all specialists practiced in Tehran.

Even before the Revolution there was a high rate of emigration of physicians, most of whom settled in the United States. In March 1976 when there were 12,196 physicians practicing in Iran, there were an estimated 10,000 other Iranian physicians practicing abroad. During the revolution there was a major exodus of physicians; the IMA has estimated that about 7,000—40 percent of the

A worker sprays to rid area of mosquitoes during a malaria-eradication campaign Courtesy World Health Organization

total—have left the country since the Revolution, contributing to a severe shortage.

The Islamic Republic has sought to increase the number of all medical personnel and to expand medical facilities. Health clinics and dispensaries have been constructed in lower income neighborhoods of the large cities, in small towns, and in villages. The medical schools at Tehran and Shiraz universities have developed programs for training paramedical personnel, and more students have been admitted to medical schools. Nevertheless, the facilities for training physicians remained inadequate, and fewer than 750 doctors were graduated from medical schools between 1980 and 1986. The IMA has said that Iran needs a total of at least 50,000 physicians to provide the whole population with minimally adequate health care.

Health Hazards and Preventive Medicine

During the 1970s, apart from a high infant mortality rate, the chief causes of death were gastrointestinal, respiratory, and parasitic diseases. The incidence of cancer, diabetes, and heart disease was increasing. Several contagious diseases, such as grippe and influenza, conjunctivitis, scarlet fever, whooping cough, pulmonary tuberculosis, and typhoid fever were common. There is no evidence that the incidence of these diseases or the major causes of mortality have declined during the 1980s.

Drug addiction was a serious problem before the Revolution and reportedly has worsened since 1979. The Ministry of Health estimated in 1986 that there may have been as many as 1 million addicts in the country. Opium is the most commonly used drug. Since the end of the nineteenth century, opium has been smoked as a recreational drug at social gatherings. The Shia clergy have tried to discourage this practice by declaring the use of opium religiously prohibited. There is also some heroin use in the country.

In the 1970s and 1980s, the Ministry of Health carried out vaccination campaigns in both urban and rural areas. Periodic campaigns have included immunizations against measles, tuberculosis, diphtheria, tetanus, whooping cough, and poliomyelitis for infants and children, and general vaccinations against smallpox and cholera. These campaigns have prevented the outbreak of major epidemics.

Water Supply and Sanitation

In the mid-1980s, polluted water supplies remained one of the main reasons for the high incidence of parasitic and gastrointestinal diseases. Tehran and other large cities had chlorinated water systems, but contaminated water has continued to be a major problem in the smaller towns and villages. The disposal of waste also remained unsatisfactory. Tehran in 1986 still did not have a sewage system serving the entire city. Most of the other cities had only partial sewage systems, and in small towns and villages there were none at all.

Welfare

Religious and social traditions profoundly influence attitudes toward welfare. There is a general belief that fate determines living conditions, but most Iranians feel an obligation to help the needy in accordance with religious tenets. This idea has been reinforced since the Revolution by the persistent exhortations of the clergy to help the poorest people in society, the *mostazafin*. The giving of alms (*zakat*) is one of the mandatory obligations of the Islamic faith. As a consequence, donors of real property and monetary bequests are anxious that their names be attached to their gifts. Charitable donations may be distributed at any time, but Friday, the day of congregational prayers, is regarded as a particularly appropriate day, and even those of modest means regularly distribute food to the poor.

There is a long history in Iran of wealthy individuals' bequeathing part of their estates in the form of perpetual endowments, *vaqfs,* for a specified charitable purpose (see Religious Institutions and

Organizations, this ch.). The last dynasty established the Pahlavi Foundation, which funded programs ranging from low-cost housing projects to the preservation of national relics. After the Revolution, the government took over administration of the Pahlavi Foundation and renamed it the Foundation for the Disinherited (Bonyad-e Mostazafin). Some of its former programs, such as granting scholarships and operating cooperatives, have been continued, but others were redesigned or dropped entirely in favor of new projects that are in accord with religious ideology.

Government-funded social insurance programs have not been as important as the private *vaqfs*. The first workers in the country to benefit from a public retirement program were government employees. Legislation during the 1960s and 1970s provided for the extension of social security benefits to broader categories of employees, but by the time of the Revolution less than 10 percent of the total work force was actually covered by social security. The government of the Islamic Republic has said that extending coverage to all employed persons is one of its priorities, but as of 1986 no information was available about what measures may have been adopted to extend coverage.

The first public housing projects were built in the 1960s in the southern part of Tehran. These were developments of small, single-family homes that were sold to the occupants at subsidized cost over several years. Public housing projects expanded to other cities during the 1970s. After the Revolution, the Republic continued to budget funds for the construction of low-cost public housing, although prior to 1985 its efforts in this area focused primarily on the provision of interest-free, long-term loans to encourage private construction on public land.

Since 1985 the government has built low-cost public housing, particularly in Tehran and in large cities that suffered considerable damage during the war, such as Ahvaz and Dezful. Priority for such housing has been given to widows of men killed during the war.

This housing is an example of the kind of social program that the revolutionary regime felt ideologically committed to provide as a way of assisting the less fortunate, the *mostazafin*. Other examples of concern for the poorer elements of society were the construction of elementary schools, bathhouses, and health clinics in villages and low-income urban areas and the emphasis on religious charitable giving to the disadvantaged. This concern for the deprived members of society was a traditional element of Islam

135

that had been neglected to a considerable degree under the shah but which was being emphasized by the revolutionary government.

* * *

The most complete analysis of Iranian society prior to the Revolution is *Iran Between Two Revolutions* by Ervand Abrahamian. *Roots of Revolution* by Nikki R. Keddie is an excellent study of the cultural tensions between the secularized middle and upper classes and the religiously oriented bazaar class, and it examines the relationship of this social conflict to the Revolution. The background of Shia clerical opposition to secular state policies is thoroughly examined in Shahrough Akhavi's *Religion and Politics in Contemporary Iran*. The most detailed study of social class divisions is *Iran: Dictatorship and Development* by Fred Halliday. A detailed analysis of several important policies implemented during the early years of the Republic is *The Reign of the Ayatollahs* by Shaul Bakhash. A fascinating fictionalized account of how the secularized classes have reacted to the Islamic Republic is *Sorraya in a Coma* by Ismail Fassih. (For further information and complete citations, see Bibliography.)

Chapter 3. The Economy

A ninth century ceramic plate from Neyshabur

REGARDLESS OF THE CHANGES in politics and ideology brought about by each successive regime in Iran, the one constant has been lack of fundamental economic change for the majority of Iran's people. Since the Islamic Revolution in 1979, Iran has repudiated the Western-style modernization initiated by Reza Shah Pahlavi and continued by his son, Mohammad Reza Shah Pahlavi. The postrevolutionary government of Ayatollah Sayyid Ruhollah Musavi Khomeini condemned the Pahlavi policy of allowing all countries to invest in, and trade freely with, Iran as unsatisfactory on political and cultural grounds and initiated a program of "self-reliance." Moreover, the modern production techniques introduced by the Pahlavis had eventually proved inappropriate for Iran because they required large capital investments. Having rejected Western models as inimical to the needs of Iran and being obliged to manage a wartime economy, the post-revolutionary government cut imports of luxury goods, began rationing subsistence items, nationalized industries, and expanded direct taxation. By late 1987, the result was a shortage of many goods that had once been imported, an insufficiently productive agricultural system, high unemployment, and a greater dependence than ever on revenues from oil and gas exports.

In the early 1920s, only a few large or modern industrial plants were in operation in Iran. The population was overwhelmingly rural, and transportation remained primitive. Except for the petroleum industry, still in its formative stage, production was geared to small, local markets. Increasing quantities of oil were produced for the international market, but with little impact on the domestic economy.

After establishing the Pahlavi dynasty in 1925, Reza Shah began to modernize Iran by developing a strong central government and entering Western markets. The results were mixed. The government improved communications, built an education system modeled on the Western example, and began construction of the Trans-Persian Railway. Centralization led, however, to authoritarianism, a state monopoly on foreign trade, and stagnant agricultural productivity. Many Iranians continued to reside in small, isolated settlements, and an estimated one-quarter of the population consisted of fiercely independent nomadic tribesmen. Modernization threatened the nomads' way of life and generally brought little benefit to Iran's undereducated, underemployed population because it focused on the development of capital-intensive industries rather than of labor-intensive enterprises.

When Mohammad Reza assumed power in 1941, he attempted to continue his father's modernization efforts (see The Post-Mossadeq Era and the Shah's White Revolution, ch. 1). By 1978 Iran had experienced great changes, but progress had been uneven for various elements of the population and different parts of the country over the preceding half-century. The Revolution of 1979 substituted "self-reliance" for Westernization as the focus of development. The importing of luxury goods, such as color televisions and stereos, was stopped, and the funding for development and construction in particular was cut significantly. Reductions in construction spending affected the entire economy and sent the gross national product (GNP—see Glossary) on a downward spiral. The budget cuts made in the name of "self-reliance," after the Revolution in 1979 and the onset of the war with Iraq in 1980, did additional damage to the economy.

During the 1970s, oil and gas exports remained Iran's main source of foreign exchange. This dependence increased in the years immediately following the Revolution, as the price of oil peaked at US$40 per barrel. Although non-oil exports began to drop sharply because of the 1980 international recession, earnings from oil exports remained high until the mid-1980s, when the price of oil began to decline. Oil revenues began to fall in 1984 and by 1985 averaged only US$1 billion per month, the approximate equivalent of the cost of continuing the war with Iraq. By 1986 monthly oil revenues averaged US$6.5 million per month. After 1984 the decline in oil revenues and the cost of the war created budget deficits. Consequently, the government reduced nonmilitary spending, which did further damage to the national economy. Domestic food production became insufficient, which forced Iran to import 65 percent of the food that it needed and to ration essential items such as meat, rice, and dairy products. Black marketing, long lines for consumer goods, and high unemployment exacerbated the effects of nonmilitary budget cuts. To ameliorate the situation, the government tried to reduce its dependence on declining oil revenues by investing in other key industries, such as copper and steel production. As of late 1987, however, economic problems remained severe and essential commodities scarce.

The Revolution of 1979 held forth to the Iranian populace the promise of "national integrity" through "self-reliance." Although intended to change Iran's economic and political course, the Revolution had produced no structural changes in the economy by late

1987. The growing need to sell oil on the international market demonstrated Iran's continuing inability to isolate its economy.

By late 1987, Iran was actually more dependent on oil than ever before. As in Reza Shah's time, attempts at modernization had been initiated by an autocratic government that stressed Iran's "unique" identity. In the late 1980s, that identity increasingly has been defined by Islam, rather than by any particular economic policy. Although much economic activity has occurred within Iran since 1979, the lack of fundamental change has been the constant. Oil earnings have fluctuated, banks have been nationalized, industries have developed—yet the power structure has merely shifted from the shah's circle to the clerical class.

Role of the Government

The central economic role of government in post-World War II Iran has been the manipulation and allocation of oil revenues. Since the beginning of the production of petroleum in commercial quantities in the 1920s, government oil policies have reflected the varying priorities of the different regimes and have exacerbated economic and cultural cleavages within the society.

During the reign of Reza Shah (1925–41), oil revenues were modest, and most of the proceeds from oil went to Britain through the Anglo-Iranian Oil Company (AIOC). For its revenues, the regime relied upon indirect taxes (customs duties and excise taxes) on items such as tea and sugar. In contrast, after 1951, the government of Mohammad Reza Shah (1941–79) relied on oil income to finance the policies of centralization by which it was able to control most aspects of Iranian society until nearly the end of the shah's rule.

Reza Shah's regime financed its development programs through modest oil royalties, customs revenues, personal income taxes, and state monopolies. During his reign, oil production royalties, although still low, quadrupled in terms of the rial (for value of the rial—see Glossary); this money was spent on defense and industrial development. Between 1926 and 1941, higher tariffs boosted annual customs revenues from approximately US$5.6 million to US$16.3 million. Institution of a small income tax replaced the local levies and enabled the government to extend its influence into the provinces; by 1941 the income tax provided annual revenues of US$10.8 million. Finally, the government relied upon state monopolies on consumer goods such as sugar, tobacco, tea, and fuel, which contributed approximately US$46.5 million annually by the early 1940s.

The Beginnings of Modernization: The Post-1925 Period

Reza Shah introduced the concept of centralized economic planning to Iran at the expense of older societal values and traditions (see The Era of Reza Shah, 1921–41, ch. 1). Reza Shah consolidated power by developing support in three areas: the army, the government bureaucracy, and the court circle. Once his power was consolidated, he pursued economic, social, and cultural reforms. Reza Shah believed that the secret of modernization lay in replacing many religious and social norms of traditional society with the values of a twentieth-century nation-state. Reza Shah's policies favored the urban over the rural, the wealthy over other classes, and industry in general over agriculture. Developing this "new order" gradually cost Reza Shah most of his base of support. Nevertheless, government centralization enabled him to achieve full control over the economy.

Economic development began with the expansion of the transportation system. The first project was the expansion of the Trans-Persian Railway. In the first five years of his reign, Reza Shah developed a network of railroads that connected ports to inland cities, thereby encouraging trade between rural and urban centers. By 1941 railroads crossed Iran from north to south and from east to west (see Transportation and Telecommunications, this ch.).

The existence of a modern transportation system by the 1930s encouraged industrial growth, which was further promoted by government financial incentives. Construction of modern manufacturing plants was a high priority, as was the development of whole industries rather than small, individual factories. Financial incentives included government-sanctioned monopolies, low-interest loans to prospective factory owners, and financial backing for plants and equipment by the Ministry of Industry. The number of industrial plants (excluding those processing petroleum) increased 1,700 percent during Reza Shah's reign.

In 1925 only about twenty modern plants existed, of which five were relatively large, employing about fifty workers each. By 1941 the number of modern plants had risen to 346, of which 146 were large installations. These large plants included thirty-seven textile mills, eight sugar refineries, eleven match factories, eight chemical companies, two glassworks, one tobacco-processing plant, and five tea-processing plants.

Between 1926 and 1941, the oil industry labor force increased from 20,000 to 31,000. By 1941 the oil industry employed 16,000 workers at the Abadan refinery and another 4,800 at drilling sites in Khuzestan. These wage earners, in conjunction with those

A copper artisan plies his trade on a street in Esfahan
Courtesy United Nations

employed in emerging modern industrial enterprises, formed a working class of about 170,000 and represented about 4 percent of the total labor force in 1941.

Rapid industrial growth created a modern, urban working class that nonetheless coexisted with people who had more traditional occupations, values, and ways of life. This new industrial work force developed in the five major centers, where 75 percent of the modern factories were located: the towns of Tehran, Tabriz, and Esfahan, and the provinces of Gilan and Mazandaran. Tehran's population alone increased from more than 196,000 in 1922 to about 700,000 by 1941. Modernization accelerated the pace of life through changes in culture, education, and traditional social norms, including those governing the role of women.

The cost of developing the military establishment, centralized ministries, large-scale industrial plants, and institutions of higher education increased the budget nearly 1,800 percent during Reza Shah's reign. The Iranian national budget grew from approximately US$15 million in 1925 to US$166.5 million in 1941 (based on the 1936 exchange rate). Because industrial development was predicated on oil revenues, the government's lack of control over the oil industry created periodic tensions with foreign oil companies. The emphasis on industrial development also demonstrated the need for development planning.

143

The concept of development planning by the government dates back to 1947, when it was initiated by Mohammad Reza Shah's government as a series of seven-year cycles. The Plan Organization consisted of leading government officials, who provided guidelines from which a development strategy was formed. Planning had a direct impact on the public sector because of its effect on allocations of capital expenditures. In Iran's mixed economy, however, the planners had no direct power over private sector investments and development; instead, they had to rely on indirect measures, such as fiscal and financial incentives.

The First Development Plan (1948–55) failed, except for strengthening the role of the Plan Organization, which, after 1973 was called the Planning and Budget Organization and in January 1985 was transformed by the parliament, or Majlis (see Glossary), into a ministry. The basic development strategy was the pragmatic approach of accelerating growth by incorporating the latest technology into large-scale, capital-intensive industry. Expansion of the infrastructure, however, preceded the development of industry. The planners often built ahead of demand, creating physical and economic incentives for the private sector. Diversification of industry was also a goal, although the planners recognized that the excessive dependence on oil revenues would have to continue at first to provide the capital to diversify. Diversification was intended to facilitate import substitution, and development of large-scale industry meant that many plants producing for export could achieve economies of scale.

The Second Development Plan (1955–62) focused on public sector expenditures, with an investment program to be funded by foreign loans and 80 percent of oil revenues. The government spent so much money, however, that the regime faced severe inflation and depleted foreign currency reserves by fiscal year (FY—see Glossary) 1959. Although Iran was experiencing economic problems, the plan provided for the construction of several reservoir dams, the most important of which were located on the Dez, Safid, and Karaj rivers. Simultaneously, private sector investment in light industry remained strong until the economic crisis that began in 1959.

During the middle and late 1950s, economic instability exacerbated chronic social problems, such as overcentralization of government, concentration of land in the hands of relatively few wealthy landlords, enormous bureaucracy, and regressive tax laws. As early as 1949, the shah voiced his intention to consider needed changes, especially in land reform. It was not until the 1960s, however, that he actually instituted agrarian reform. The intervening decade was a period of consolidation following the regime of Reza Shah; it also featured a period of government control by Mohammad Mossadeq (see Mossadeq and Oil Nationalization, ch. 1).

Oil Revenues and the Acceleration of Modernization, 1960–79

During the reign of Mohammad Reza Shah, significant increases in oil revenues, coincident with the centralization of the economy, compounded societal stress and imbalance. The modernization that continued throughout the shah's rule affected the economic infrastructure but not the monarchical political structure. The gap between the two was accentuated by the Western industrial policies promulgated by the shah.

In the 1960s, economic planning focused on four main goals. The first was rapid development of large industries by capital-intensive methods and the use of the latest technology; the second was employment of foreign advisers and technicians to guide the modern industrial complex. The third was encouragement of large industrial profits, and the fourth was control of wages by reallocating savings from labor costs to capital investment. It was assumed that wealthy industrialists would reinvest their capital in the economy, thereby stimulating economic development. But such investment did not occur, and the gap in income between industrial owners and the commercial class, or bazaar (traditional middle class merchants), was never closed, which contributed to the revolutionary pressures that eventually brought down the regime. The bazaar did not benefit from the 1974–78 oil boom; as a consequence, bazaar members helped lead and finance the Revolution.

The series of national reforms and development programs that Mohammad Reza Shah had embarked on in the 1950s came to be known in 1963 as the "White Revolution" (see The Post-Mossadeq Era and the Shah's White Revolution, ch. 1). The White Revolution was simultaneously the shah's attempt at economic modernization and his attempt at political stabilization. He intended to accelerate nation-building and to enhance his regime's image as the promoter and guardian of the public welfare.

Land reform was a major element of the shah's economic development program. Land reform affected both the economic structure and the social mores of the agrarian component of society. The Third Development Plan (1962–68) and the Fourth Development Plan (1968–73) together infused US$1.2 billion into agriculture through land reclamation, subsidized irrigation projects, and land redistribution programs. These programs undermined traditional rural authority figures, encouraged commercial farming, and transformed the rural class structure. By the 1970s, the rural class was divided into three components: absentee farmers, independent farmers, and rural wage earners (see Land Use, this ch.).

The third plan was transitional to a new time frame of five years for development plans. Oil revenues supported the US$1.9 billion national budget, which fostered an economic boom in the public and private sectors. The government concentrated its activities on heavy industries, dam building, and public utilities, as well as on expansion of oil and gas production. Private industry benefited from bank credits given as part of the third plan.

The fourth plan accelerated economic growth and integrated sectoral and regional concerns into a national development program. During the fourth plan, the annual rate of growth in gross domestic product (GDP—see Glossary) averaged 11.8 percent, which exceeded the growth target. The strongest growth occurred in industry, petroleum, transportation, and communications. Several large projects under construction during the fourth plan included a steel mill, an aluminum smelter, a petrochemical complex, a tractor plant, and a gas pipeline leading to the Soviet border. Farming and crop production were given low priority during this period of industrialization, which widened the large gap between the industrial and agricultural sectors.

The third and fourth development plans affected the urban population in particular because of the emphasis on the increased production of consumer goods and the expansion of industries such as gas and oil. Between 1963 and 1977, many industrial facilities were constructed, primarily in urban areas.

The Fifth Development Plan (1973–78) set investment at US$36.5 billion; this figure almost doubled to US$70 billion as a result of large increases in oil revenues during the period. Almost two-thirds of the capital allocated under the fifth plan was concentrated in housing, manufacturing and mining, oil and gas projects, and transportation and communications. Some additional oil revenues were spent on ad hoc defense and construction projects rather than on the fifth plan's priority areas.

In the period between the quadrupling of oil prices in 1973 and mid-1977, Mohammad Reza Shah pushed both industrialization and the establishment of a modern, mechanized military much too rapidly. As a result, inflation increased, corruption became commonplace, and rural-to-urban migration intensified. In addition, because of a lack of technically trained Iranian personnel, the shah increasingly brought foreign consultants into Iran. This further exacerbated an already severe housing shortage in Tehran.

In mid-1977, the shah appointed Jamshid Amuzegar as prime minister, and the latter immediately launched a deflationary program. This sudden slowdown in the economy led to widespread unemployment, especially among unskilled and semiskilled workers, which further increased the gap between rich and poor. The economic slowdown was a major factor in radicalizing large segments of the population and turning them against the shah.

Some argue that rapid modernization created the disequilibrium that brought about the shah's fall. Others, however, stress the importance of the way in which the rapid modernization was implemented. After the economy's initial development, inequalities in income distribution were not addressed. Those at the lower end of the economic spectrum—for example, small merchants and businessmen, urban migrants, and artisans—felt disadvantaged in relation to workers in large businesses, industries, and enterprises with foreign associations. Western-educated Iranians rapidly became a well-paid elite, as did factory workers. Bazaar merchants, students, and the ulama, however, did not benefit so directly from modernization.

The increased availability of health and educational resources in towns and cities that resulted from Mohammad Reza Shah's programs contributed to an explosion of the urban population. In the 1950s, urban areas accounted for 31 percent of the population; by the late 1970s, that number had increased to about 50 percent. The urban population became stratified into an upper class, a propertied middle class, a salaried (managerial) class that included the bazaar, and a wage-earning working class.

The Post-1979 Period

The disparity between the economic promises of the shah's regime and the results as perceived by the majority of Iran's citizens contributed to a revolutionary climate in the late 1970s. When the revolutionary regime came to power in 1979 (on the heels of the economic downturn of the late 1970s), it claimed that modernization and Westernization had nothing to offer Iran, as the recession had made evident. Islam, not economic planning, was cited as the basis for correcting the perceived ills of Iranian society stemming from the alleged excesses of the shah. The regime came to power criticizing Mohammad Reza Shah's failed agricultural policies and promising self-sufficiency and economic independence. The government adopted an emphasis on agriculture as the foundation of its program. To consolidate power quickly among the rural poor, the Khomeini regime capitalized on popular resentment of the shah for having largely ignored the agricultural sector.

All six of the development plans designed under the shah aimed at economic development; the Sixth Development Plan, intended for 1978–83, was never implemented because the Revolution occurred in early 1979. The First Development Plan of the Islamic Republic (1983–88) proclaimed that its goals were to establish Iran's economic independence through self-sufficiency in foodstuffs and to reduce the country's dependence on oil exports.

The first "republican" plan focused on five points: expanding education, representing the interests of the *mostazafin* (the disinherited), achieving economic independence, diversifying the economy to lessen the dependence on oil and gas exports, and developing agriculture. The development plan did not include a factor for defense expenditures. Criticism of this plan resulted in its revision in 1984, although the changes were not approved by the Majlis until January 1986. The revision included an increase in the investment in agriculture (from 15.5 to 16.7 percent of the national budget) and a smaller investment in non-oil industry (the share fell to 52 percent). Projected oil revenues in this version of the plan were based on the lower oil price prevailing in 1985.

The budget for the first republican plan was US$166 billion, but the allocation of funds was delayed because of political and economic pressures. The political pressures came from newly empowered groups and individuals interested in using the social disruption caused by the Revolution to create their own financial empires, free of state control. The war with Iraq also affected funding for the first republican plan.

Oil revenue shortfalls caused the first republican plan to be revised again in early 1987. The shortfalls, in combination with the expenses associated with the Iran-Iraq War, resulted in nearly half the budget being allocated to military goods. Imports of consumer products were cut in half, and projects under the development plan were given low priority (see fig. 6). Austerity measures and increased unemployment resulted.

Gauging the relationship between government economic policy and actual operation of the economy subsequent to the Revolution of 1979 is difficult because official economic policy has been obscured by religious and ideological themes. Iran's financial system began adhering to Islamic principles after the Revolution, a process that accelerated in the 1980s. Although the Planning and Budget Organization prepared budgets, in coordination with several other ministries, the Majlis, the majority of whose members were Muslim religious leaders, was responsible for ratification (see The Majlis, ch. 4).

The budget presented a financial outline within which outlays were planned for military purposes, education, and other government activities. There was an increasing discrepancy between budget estimates for the war and actual costs. Whereas the government claimed in 1982 that 13 percent of the total budget was spent on defense, independent analysts claimed that the figure rose from 11.5 percent of the budget in 1979 to 46.9 percent in 1982. However unreliable the Iranian claims about defense spending, one thing was increasingly clear: the Iranian government dedicated virtually all foreign exchange resources, including both advance drawings on revenues and uncollectible receivables (which were counted as assets), to prosecution of the war.

Inflation was a serious issue in the mid-1980s. The increase in prices, which was beyond the control of the monetary authorities and the Central Bank—founded originally in 1960 as Bank Markazi Iran and renamed Central Bank (Bank Markazi) of the Islamic Republic of Iran in December 1983—began in the 1970s with the rapid rise in oil revenues and equally rapid increases in government expenditures. The latter had a multiplier effect on the money supply and added to the demand for goods and services, thereby inducing price rises. The monetary authorities attempted to minimize the multiplier effect by increasing the cost of borrowing and tightening credit. Imports increased as a result of lower duties, relaxed quotas, and an increase in government purchases of foreign goods. Bottlenecks at the ports and elsewhere in the transportation system limited the capacity of imports to satisfy demand, however.

Efforts to reduce inflation date to 1973, when a serious price control program was initiated. The government took additional measures to curb inflation in May 1980 by linking the rial to the Special Drawing Rights (SDRs—see Glossary) of the International Monetary Fund (IMF—see Glossary) instead of the United States dollar and by encouraging investment in the private sector and growth in non-oil industries. In addition, subsidies on basic goods were increased to keep their prices down. Nevertheless, a 30-percent inflation rate persisted, a black market rate on the United States dollar flourished, and foreign exchange controls continued.

Inflation was continually understated by the government. The government asserted that the inflation rate had fallen from 32.5 percent in FY 1980 to 17 percent in FY 1983 and to 5.5 percent in FY 1985; independent analysts, however, claimed that a more accurate inflation rate for 1985 was 50 percent. As essential goods grew scarcer in the wartime economy, import controls fed inflation. Prices of basic foodstuffs and consumer goods increased faster than the Central Bank admitted. The increasing cost of rental property in urban areas and continued subsidies for consumers on basic foods reflected a serious inflationary problem in the mid-1980s.

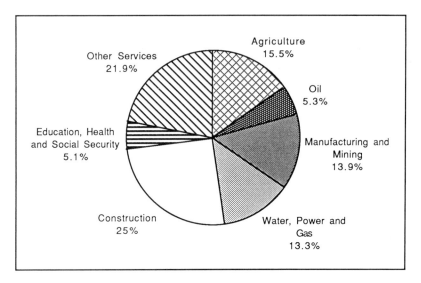

Source: Based on information from Iranian government publications and Economist Intelligence Unit, *Iran Country Profile, 1986–87,* London, 1987.

Figure 6. First Development Plan of Islamic Republic of Iran, 1983–88

To the surprise of many, the Majlis increased the FY 1986 budget in March 1986, even though oil revenues were projected downward. The increase went mainly to finance military spending and the steel and nuclear industries. The rising costs of the war, coupled with falling oil prices in 1986, led to the use of non-oil exports to generate revenue because oil income was no longer a guaranteed source of foreign currency (see Non-Oil Exports, this ch.). To finance short-term debts, Iran drained its small reserve of foreign currency by allowing advance drawing on revenues.

The FY 1987 budget also reflected the priority of the war effort. The government again promised to curb inflation, to continue to subsidize basic foodstuffs, and to make available to the import sector a revolving fund of US$7 billion, presumably for consumer use.

Monetary and Fiscal Policy

The Iranian fiscal year begins on March 21 and runs through March 20 of the following calendar year. The budget, presented to the Majlis by the Planning and Budget Organization, consists of three sections: ordinary, plan, and defense allocations. Because of conflict between the Revolution's stated opposition to the massive defense expenditures of the shah and the high cost of the war with Iraq that began less than one year after the Revolution, as of late 1987 there had been no fiscal year in which defense expenditures were not severely understated for domestic political reasons. As a result, attempting to set forth actual figures on the money supply, especially as a function of fiscal policy, was almost pointless.

Banking

Western-style banks and insurance came late to Iran, but protected and stimulated by the government and fed by expanding economic activity, banking became one of the fastest growing sectors of the economy in the 1960s. The insurance industry had barely started in 1960 and had a negligible role in the accumulation of funds to finance development, largely because insurance was not used by most of the population.

Before the modern era in Iranian banking, which dates to the opening of a branch of a British bank in 1888, credit was available only at high rates from noninstitutional lenders such as relatives, friends, wealthy landowners, and bazaar moneylenders. In 1988 these noninstitutional sources of credit were still available, particularly in the more isolated rural communities. Institutional banking spread rapidly in the late 1960s; by 1988 almost all small towns were served by at least one bank. None of these operations were private because banks were nationalized in 1979.

In 1960 Bank Markazi Iran was established as the central bank. Later legislation further defined its powers and responsibilities. The bank issued notes and acted as banker for the government, keeping accounts, marketing government securities, maintaining foreign exchange reserves, and overseeing international transactions. It also set standards for the supervised financial institutions, established credit and monetary policies, and took measures to enforce credit and monetary policies. The banking laws limited foreign participation to 40 percent in any banks operated in Iran (except the Soviet bank, which had been founded much earlier). Subsequently, the Central Bank limited foreign ownership in new banks to 35 percent.

By 1977 the banking system consisted of the Central Bank, twenty-four commercial banks, twelve specialized banks, and three savings and loan associations (these numbers decreased after the Revolution). The commercial banks had more than 7,400 branches, including a few in other countries. The specialized banks focused mostly on a particular kind of lending (e.g., industrial or agricultural loans), although three regional banks specialized in financing local development projects. In addition, in 1977 approximately seventy foreign banks (primarily from the major industrial nations)

151

had representative offices in Iran, but they conducted no local banking business. Their purpose was to facilitate trade relations.

All domestic banks and insurance companies in Iran were nationalized in 1979. In 1980 the twenty-nine domestic banks remaining after the Revolution were consolidated into nine units. Foreign banks in Iran declined in number to thirty by 1987 and included the representative office of a small Soviet bank that financed trade. French banks were excluded from the Iranian market in 1983, leaving those of the Federal Republic of Germany (West Germany), as well as Swiss, Japanese, and British banks to finance about 30 percent of total trade.

Immediately after the Revolution, the government called for the establishment of an Islamic banking system (which became law in March 1984) that would replace interest payments with profit sharing. In Islamic terms, this meant that profit (interest) was acceptable only if a lender's money were "not at risk." The introduction of Islamic banking procedures was gradual; confusion and delays disrupted the initial stages of implementation. In March 1985, the Islamic code was extended to include bank loans and advances. By late 1987, however, only certain banks were fully Islamicized, and only about 10 percent of private deposits were subject to Islamic rules.

The Central Bank controlled the issuance of letters of credit. These were deferred payment instruments that relieved the cash-flow problem Iran experienced after oil prices began to decline in 1983. The government financed many imports with these high-interest letters of credit. Originally a letter of credit was to be repaid within 180 days, but by 1987 Iranian customers wanted 720 days' credit. Up to US$4 billion in letters of credit remained outstanding in early 1987, but the government did not include these supplier credits when assessing its foreign debt.

The Central Bank established a good reputation in international banking circles in the 1980s. It had practically no long-term foreign debt in early 1987—only US$5 million—and was recognized as an international creditor. Between 1979 and 1984, the government paid cash for US$66 billion worth of imports, and it repaid immediately US$7 billion of existing debts. The Central Bank's reputation for honoring its financial obligations, however, did not change the attitudes of West European bankers, who, in a 1987 poll, expressed their unwillingness to lend money to Iran. To help relieve its cash-flow problem after 1983, the government sought repayment from several countries of money they borrowed from Iran during the reign of the Mohammad Reza Shah.

In the first quarter of 1986, Iranian deposits in international banks fell by US$570 million, reducing Iran's holdings to US$7.1 billion. This reduction coincided with the continued fall in oil revenues, and foreign exchange deposits were expected to decrease further in the late 1980s.

Taxes

In the past, Iranian officials had focused on increasing non-oil tax revenues, particularly through direct taxes on personal and business income. A major reform of the tax laws in 1967 nearly doubled direct tax revenues within two years. Additional legislation in the 1970s had the effect of increasing the importance of direct taxes, which grew to US$2.5 billion in FY 1976, up from US$156 million in FY 1967.

Like most developing countries that produced oil, Iran had relied on indirect taxes (customs duties and excise taxes) for most of its non-oil revenue. Indirect taxes accounted for 72 percent of non-oil tax revenues in FY 1962, 60 percent in FY 1972, and 45 percent in FY 1976. In FY 1986, indirect taxes fell 12 percent as a result of a 30-percent reduction in customs duties.

The rapid increase in oil production and oil revenues in the 1970s freed Iranian officials from having to develop the tax system. As a consequence, the narrow tax base focused on consumers generally and on the urban, salaried middle class specifically. In 1977 fiscal authorities attempted to reform the tax system. But the numerous exemptions, particularly those that had been granted to industries to encourage private investment, presented obstacles to the continued expansion of direct taxes.

By 1985 government workers were paying a disproportionate amount of Iran's taxes—nearly three-quarters of all taxes in FY 1984—according to the government. For example, in the last few months of 1984 about US$16 million was collected from individuals in the private sector and US$510 million (or 76 percent of tax revenues) from government employees.

Taxes were expected to contribute US$15.7 billion to the budget in FY 1987, an amount 11.2 percent less than that approved the previous year. In the FY 1987 budget, direct taxes were reduced to a level that accounted for 46 percent of tax income, while indirect taxes accounted for 53 percent. Companies accounted for most of the direct taxes (54 percent). Of the indirect taxes, 40 percent came from taxes on imports, and 60 percent from consumption and sales taxes. A decrease in imports resulted in an overall decline in tax revenue.

The decline in revenue from indirect taxes (such as customs duties) in FY 1986 caused total tax revenues to fall 1 percent below the FY 1985 level. The collection of direct taxes simultaneously increased by 9.5 percent, partly because of a new option that permitted payment of taxes into a regional development fund. Businesses paid income taxes at a higher rate than individuals, and the tax rate on government corporations was higher than that on private businesses.

The War's Impact on the Economy

Iraq's attack on Iran in September 1980 provided the new Iranian government with an external scapegoat to divert attention from its own economic mismanagement. The war created economic dislocation, decreased industrial and petroleum development, and caused further deterioration of the agricultural sector, which had already suffered from the flight of landlords in 1979 and 1980.

Oil Exports

Iraq attacked Iranian ports, the oil terminal at Khark (then the main export terminal for crude oil, also cited as Kharg) Island and, beginning in 1984, tankers shuttling between Khark and Sirri islands in the Persian Gulf. The heavy damage to refineries and pipelines, factories, and industrial sites hurt oil production but did not significantly slow the export of oil until 1986; between 1982 and 1986, Iran produced 2.3 million barrels per day (bpd—see Glossary) on average (see table 5, Appendix). The combined effects of decreased oil production and falling oil prices, however, created an economic crisis and a shortage of foreign exchange by 1986. The destruction in 1980 of the important Abadan refinery (which produced an average of 628,000 bpd), the bombing of refineries and shuttle tankers, and the continued embargo on purchases of Iranian oil by Japan, the United States, and France contributed to the crisis. By November 1987, Iranian oil exports were estimated at 1 million bpd, down from an estimated 1.9 million bpd the previous month.

The Iraqi strategy of interrupting Iran's export supply line dated back to February 1984, when Iraq attacked tankers shuttling between Khark and Sirri islands. The terminal and cargo handling jetties on Khark Island were hit, reducing the island's export capacity from 6.5 million bpd to 2.5 million bpd within 3 months. This new tactic did not halt Iranian oil exports, but it did decrease them. As a consequence of lower export earnings, the new budgets showed deficits in fiscal years 1985 and 1986.

After the bombings of Khark Island, Iran developed Sirri Island as an alternate terminal. Operations began on Sirri Island in February 1985. Iraq attacked the refinery there on August 12, 1986, temporarily disrupting Iran's oil exports, and again in the fall of 1986, this time inflicting damage from which Iran took longer to recover.

As a consequence of the early 1984 bombings, insurance rates for tankers in the Gulf increased. The increase prompted Iran to extend special incentives to tankers to compensate for the risk involved. During the Iraqi attacks, Iran's main crude oil customer, Japan, banned its tankers from the Khark-Sirri shuttle. After Iran began giving preferential treatment to certain customers, Japan resumed its shipments in July 1984.

The August 1986 attacks on Sirri Island caused oil exports to fall to about one-third of their normal volume (from 1.6 million bpd to 600,000 bpd). An effort was made to develop Larak Island as a loading point, but monsoon winds temporarily closed Abu al Bukush, Larak Island's main oil terminal, in September 1986. Iraqi attacks on Larak Island's chief remaining oil export terminal in November and December 1986 further damaged it. By November 1987, Larak Island had recovered and had become Iran's main export point because of its distance from Iraq's air bases and because of its air defense system.

The oil export terminal at Lavan Island, which for years had exported 200,000 bpd, was also severely damaged in an attack in September 1986. The success of this attack made it clear that Iraq was gradually destroying Iran's export industry. By the end of 1986, the Iraqis had bombed Khark, Sirri, and Larak islands, as well as the shuttle tankers to Sirri and Larak; thirteen tankers had been damaged in missile attacks in August 1986 alone. The war also postponed the completion (projected for 1989) of a large petrochemical plant at Bandar-e Khomeini (formerly known as Bandar Shahpur, but renamed after the Revolution), an Iranian-Japanese venture.

War Costs

Half of Iran's revenue was spent on arms imports in the mid-1980s. In order to dedicate half its budget to military expenditures, Iran was forced to reduce such essential imports as food, for which it spent about US$4 billion annually from 1983 to 1987. Rationing of essentials such as meat, rice, and dairy products after the beginning of the war resulted in long lines at shops and an active black market. Sometimes the need occurred, as in the spring of 1987, to add nonfood consumer items to the rationing list. These austerity measures gave rise to the possibility of political instability.

Because of the war, trade had to be rerouted through the Soviet Union and Turkey, which increased transportation costs. The war also caused Iran to deplete its foreign reserves and to depend on foreign suppliers for needed goods. Military equipment accounted for about 25 percent of total imports by the mid-1980s, and the budget for FY 1987 showed that funds for the war exceeded financial allocations to all other economic sectors. The total cost of the war from its beginning in 1980 until early 1987 was more than US$240 billion (based on a total of US$200 billion by the end of 1984 and a cost of US$20 billion for each year thereafter). If lost oil revenues were taken into account, the cost of the war through 1987 would be even higher.

Labor Force

Data on Iran's labor force after the Revolution were incomplete in mid-1987, but the economically active population was estimated to be about 12.5 million. Unemployment had been a serious problem since 1979. In the autumn of 1986, the government announced that 1.8 million persons—about 14.5 percent of the labor force—were registered as unemployed. This was a high percentage by comparison with the 1975 International Labour Organisation's unemployment estimate of 3.5 percent. In 1987 economists believed that underemployment was also relatively high.

Agriculture remained the principal source of employment in the late 1980s. The decline in the size of the agricultural work force had been much more gradual since the Revolution than during 1949-79. At the end of World War II, approximately 60 percent of the work force was employed in agriculture; by 1979 the percentage of workers in agriculture had fallen to just under 40 percent. In 1987 an estimated 38 percent of the work force, or nearly 4.8 million workers, was employed in agriculture.

The industrial sector in 1987 employed about 31 percent of the work force, the same percentage as on the eve of the Revolution. From the 1920s until 1978, the industrial work force grew rapidly, especially during the 1970s, when industrial employment grew at an annual rate of 14 percent. The relative stasis of industrial employment in comparison to its rapid expansion before the Revolution has been attributed by economists to the war with Iraq, especially to the destruction of important industrial infrastructure in the southwestern part of the country (see fig. 7).

According to an Iranian government report for FY 1984, the industrial work force employed in factories with 10 or more laborers totaled some 593,000. About 25 percent of this number, or 145,000 workers, was employed in the textile and leather industries. Another 141,000 workers were employed in heavy industries.

The service sector employed about 31 percent of the work force in 1987. All commercial activity and most civil service jobs were considered part of this sector. A substantial proportion of service sector employment, however, was in marginal activities such as custodial work, street vending, and personal services such as barbering, attendant work at public baths, consumer goods repairs, and the performance of porter duties in town bazaars.

At the time of the Revolution in 1979, an estimated 1.3 million Iranians (13 percent of the work force) were women. (Rural women working the fields were not counted as part of the work force.) Female employment was highest in manufacturing, which accounted for an estimated 60 percent of all working females. Women were employed extensively in the textile mills and in labor-intensive manufacturing jobs requiring few skills and offering relatively low pay, such as carpet making and other handicrafts undertaken in factories, small workshops, and homes. Many women were employed in services as well. About 20 percent of working females were employed in domestic and other personal services and accounted for nearly 17 percent of all employment in this category. Less than 20 percent of working women were government employees, and a tiny minority held professional positions.

After the Revolution, work opportunities for professional women and those working in offices were severely constricted. The government opposed having women work in jobs that would enable them to render legal opinions or supervise males. Official statistics, however, indicated that the number of women in the labor force remained relatively constant because women were needed to work in war-related plant jobs. The government survey for FY 1984 reported that females made up more than 12.6 percent of the urban labor force and 6 percent of the industrial work force. The total number of women in the labor force in 1985 was 1.6 million, of whom about 18 percent were unemployed. Of the 1.3 million women actively employed, approximately 43 percent worked in urban areas; 61 percent of urban women workers were government employees.

Two factors for which there were no reliable data in 1988 affected the labor force after 1980: the war with Iraq and the presence of Afghan refugees. On the one hand, more than 500,000 working-age males were removed from the labor force at any given time for military service. War-related casualties removed additional tens of thousands of potential workers. On the other hand, many Afghan refugees, of whom there were slightly more than 2.3 million

Iran: A Country Study

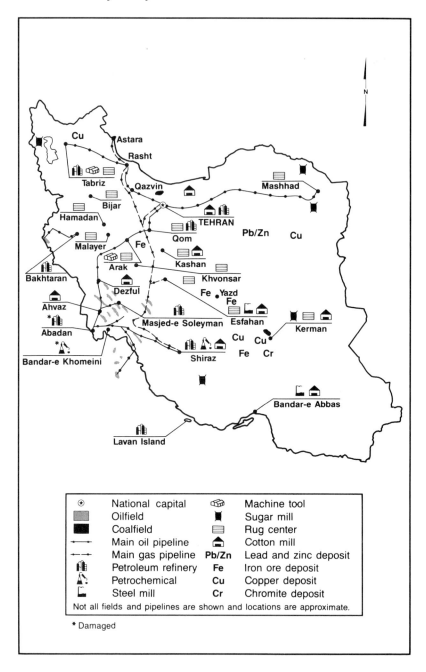

Figure 7. Industry and Mining, 1987

158

according to the preliminary 1986 figures, were working in Iran after 1980, most in unskilled jobs (see Refugees, ch. 2). There were no meaningful estimates of the number of workers who may have lost jobs because of the extensive war-inflicted destruction of industrial sites and commercial enterprises between 1980 and 1987.

Petroleum Industry

Following the quadrupling of oil prices in the last quarter of 1973, prices remained relatively stable from 1975 to 1978. During this period, Mohammad Reza Shah encouraged a high level of oil production and increased spending on imported goods and services and on military and economic aid to a small number of Iran's allies. Khomeini's government shifted the emphasis by decreeing a policy of oil conservation, with production reduced to a level sufficient to do no more than meet foreign exchange needs.

The efforts, initiated by the shah, to develop the petrochemical industry were thwarted by the Iran-Iraq War. The shah had begun a large petrochemical plant at Bandar Shahpur (now Bandar-e Khomeini) to produce fertilizers and sulfur; the plan was to expand production to include aromatics and olefins in a joint venture with Mitsui, a Japanese consortium. The plant, which cost US$3 billion, had almost been completed at the time of the Revolution. Iraqi planes bombed the still-unfinished plant in late 1986. Other petrochemical plants were completed soon after 1979, including the Khemco sulfur plant on Khark Island and a fertilizer plant at Marv Dasht near Shiraz.

The global recession of the early 1980s depressed the demand for oil. Iranian exports were also affected by the increased production by countries that were not members of the Organization of Petroleum Exporting Countries (OPEC—see Glossary). The resulting glut on the market caused a decline in Iranian oil revenues, which in turn lowered the value of the Iranian GNP. From September to October 1980, output fell from 1.3 million bpd to 450,000 bpd. Iran's petroleum production increased, however, to 2.4 million bpd in both 1982 and 1983, which enabled the government to end domestic rationing (see table 5, Appendix). However, production fell again in 1986 to 1.9 million bpd. OPEC prices for crude oil meanwhile fell from US$34 per barrel in 1982 to US$29 in March 1983. The government reduced oil exports in the early 1980s to promote a higher price per barrel and to foster conservation. Oil production fell as planned, although not as low as during 1980–81. By 1987 oil and gas exports produced only enough revenue to meet basic needs.

Oil revenues financed the import of weapons, food, medicine, and other critical goods and services by the mid-1980s. Whether or not the oil sector would be able to sustain losses as Iraq continued to target Iranian oil production and transportation facilities remained to be seen in late 1987. In addition to bombings of Iranian shuttle tankers, the Iranian oil industry was also troubled by fluctuating prices. Oil revenues decreased in 1985 and early 1986, remained steady in late 1986, and rose gradually in 1987. The government attempted to compensate for lost revenues in 1987 by further reductions in nonmilitary programs.

Oil and Gas Industry

Petroleum has been the main industry in Iran since the 1920s. Iran was the world's fourth largest producer of crude oil and the second largest exporter of petroleum at the peak of its oil industry in the mid-1970s. The war with Iraq cut Iran's production in the 1980s, although Iranian oil reserves remained the fourth largest in the world.

Nationalization of the oil industry in 1951 resulted in temporary political and financial chaos. Production did not resume until late 1954 (see Mossadeq and Oil Nationalization, ch. 1). As part of the nationalization process, the government formed the National Iranian Oil Company (NIOC). As owner, the government directed NIOC policy. As a result of the Consortium Agreement reached in 1954 between the government and a consortium of foreign oil companies, industry control of the oil companies was left virtually intact, but the agreement greatly increased the government's share of income from each barrel of oil produced. The combination of the larger share of income and rising oil production provided the government with increased revenues with which to finance industrial development. In addition, slow but steady progress was made in reestablishing Iran's relations with Western powers in the aftermath of nationalization. The resolution of the oil crisis in 1954 (nationalization of oil and the signing of the Consortium Agreement) led to a policy of increased economic and political cooperation between Iran and states outside the Soviet sphere of influence. In 1961 Iran joined with other major oil-exporting countries to form OPEC, whose members acted in concert to increase each country's control over its own production and to maximize its revenues.

When Iran's economy worsened after the outbreak of war with Iraq, its willingness to abide by OPEC guidelines decreased. From 1983 to 1984, OPEC priced oil at US$29 per barrel, but Iran undercut OPEC prices at US$28 per barrel through October 1984 and subsequently reduced it even further to US$26.50 per barrel. Iran continued deliberate undercutting until the pricing crisis in July 1986, when prices dropped below US$10 per barrel and the oil-exporting countries met to reach agreement on both price and production levels. The thirteen members of OPEC, and several non-OPEC countries, agreed in December 1986 to a price of US$18 per barrel, with a maximum differential of US$2.65 between light and heavy crude oil. (Light crude is the source of products such as gasoline and is more expensive, whereas heavy crude provides the components used in products such as residual fuel, oil coke, and waxes.) By January 1987, as a result of war damage and government conservation policies, crude production averaged 2.2 million bpd, about 100,000 bpd below Iran's OPEC quota.

Production and Reserves

In 1986 Iran's reported crude oil reserves of 48.5 billion barrels ranked behind only those of Saudi Arabia, the Soviet Union, and Kuwait. By February 1987, the NIOC estimated that Iran's recoverable oil reserves had nearly doubled from the 1986 level to 93 billion barrels, a figure that could not be verified by outside specialists. In the first half of 1986, Iran had produced 1.9 million bpd of oil, of which 800,000 bpd went for domestic consumption and 1.1 million bpd for export. Production dropped during 1986 as a result of the oil pricing crisis and the bombings of Khark Island and Sirri Island. By early 1987, oil exports had increased and neared the level set in OPEC's December 1986 agreement, averaging 1.5 to 1.7 million bpd.

Iran made strides in the development of the gas industry as well, with efforts dating back to the 1960s. One area of emphasis was the extraction of ''associated'' gas, natural gas found in solution with oil, which previously had been flared. In 1966 Iran reached agreement with the Soviet Union to deliver up to 28 million cubic meters of gas per day. In return, the Soviets committed equipment and expertise to build a steel mill, an engineering plant, and other related facilities. In 1966 the government also formed the National Iranian Gas Company, a wholly owned subsidiary of NIOC, to produce gas for both domestic consumption and export. By October 1970, the Iranian gas trunkline had been completed, capable of moving gas from the southwestern Iranian oil fields to the Soviet border at Astara on the Caspian Sea. Spur lines branched off the trunkline to major Iranian cities, supplying gas primarily for industrial use. Pipeline capacity reached 45.3 million cubic meters per day by 1975. Iran had made a heavy investment in developing the gas industry by 1977, anticipating a decline in oil production in the early 1980s.

Gas production increased from 20 billion cubic meters in 1980 to about 35 billion cubic meters in 1985. Much of this increased production, however, was flared (an inefficient but inexpensive process), peaking in 1982 at over 50 percent of gas produced (14.2 billion cubic meters flared of 24.5 billion cubic meters produced), largely as a result of Iraqi destruction of facilities for producing and reinjecting natural gas. Recovery of natural gas improved thereafter, with flaring accounting for less than 22 percent of production in 1984 and 17 percent in 1985.

The development of the Iranian gas industry was bolstered by the discovery of several natural gas fields in 1973 and 1974. Reserves in 1974 stood at 7.5 trillion cubic meters, and by 1977 known natural gas reserves amounted to 10.6 trillion cubic meters. According to Iranian sources, natural gas reserves in Iran were the second largest in the world at 13.8 trillion cubic meters in proven reserves as of 1987. This was more than the combined reserves of the entire Western world. Additional gas deposits were discovered in Baluchestan va Sistan Province in August 1986. Only Soviet reserves, estimated to be some 3.5 times larger, surpassed Iran's. Despite its enormous reserves, Iran exported no gas from 1980, when a pricing agreement with the Soviet Union was canceled and the gas trunkline to the Soviet Union was closed, to 1987. Because the Soviets refused to pay Iran's price, Iran turned its gas reserves to domestic industrial, commercial, and residential use. In August 1986, Iran announced that it would resume the export of natural gas to the Soviet Union, with the expectation of returning eventually to the previous export level of 10 billion cubic meters per year. Subsequently, the resumption of natural gas export was postponed and no deliveries had occurred as of the end of 1987.

Concession Agreements

Commercial extraction of oil began at the turn of the century, when exploration and exploitation rights were granted to foreigners. The first of these was an Englishman, W.K. D'Arcy, who in 1908 discovered commercial quantities of petroleum. D'Arcy's discovery led to the formation of the Anglo-Persian Oil Company in 1909, which, after 1935, operated as the Anglo-Iranian Oil Company (AIOC).

Disagreements over revenues arose almost immediately between the government and the newly formed oil company. The interpretative agreement reached in 1920 temporarily quieted matters. When revenues fell sharply at the beginning of the Great Depression, however, Iran canceled the concession, causing Britain to take the case to the League of Nations in 1932. Before the league came to

Petroleum is the engine that drives the Iranian economy
Courtesy United Nations (E. Adams)

a decision, a significant modification of the original concession was negotiated by Iran and the company acting on their own. Royalty payments, previously a share of company profits, were supplanted by a fixed payment per ton of oil produced. Minimum payments to the government were established, and the life of the concession was extended by 32 years (until 1993), although the concession area was reduced about 80 percent.

After continued disputes over the terms of the contract with the AIOC, the Majlis voted to nationalize the petroleum industry in 1951. In 1954 the AIOC was renamed the Consortium, reflecting the 40-percent ownership held by British Petroleum, 14 percent by Royal Dutch Shell; 7 percent each by Gulf Oil, Socony-Mobil, Esso (later Exxon), Standard Oil of California, and Texaco; 6 percent by Compagnie Française des Pétroles; and 5 percent by various interests collectively known as the Iricon Agency. The Consortium's concession was to run through 1979, with the expectation of negotiable fifteen-year options. Instead, at the request of the Iranian government, in 1973 the Consortium agreed to form a new agency to market Iranian petroleum. The Consortium members in return received a privileged buyer status for a twenty-year supply of crude petroleum.

This agreement was interrupted because of strikes in the oil fields in 1978 during the rebellion against Mohammad Reza Shah.

163

Petroleum exporting was not resumed until his departure on January 16, 1979. Subsequently, the NIOC canceled the 1973 marketing agreement with former Consortium members, offering them instead a special nine-month supply agreement, after which they lost special buyer status.

Refining and Transport

At the beginning of 1977, Iran had six refineries in operation, with a combined capacity of more than 800,000 bpd. In 1986 Iran had refineries operating in Esfahan, Tabriz, Bakhtaran (formerly known as Kermanshah), Shiraz, Qom, Tehran, and Lavan Island, with a combined capacity of more than 1 million bpd. All contributed to the domestic supply of petroleum products, but the Abadan refinery in the late 1970s produced primarily for export. The high cost of transportation led to regional location of refineries. Pipelines brought the crude oil from the fields to the refineries for processing and regional distribution of products.

The Abadan refinery, located on the Persian Gulf, was completed in 1912 and, until bombed and destroyed in 1980 by Iraq, remained one of the world's largest, with a capacity of 628,000 bpd. Foreign oil companies had operated it until the 1973 NIOC takeover. About 20 percent of its production had gone to the domestic market in the early 1970s, but in 1973 the NIOC geared the industry toward domestic needs and local consumption. The Abadan refinery was linked by pipeline to several fields and a seaport; the pipeline ran from Abadan north to Tehran, and then along Iran's northern border from Tabriz in the west to Mashhad in the east.

The other refineries were smaller than the one at Abadan. Two, built and operated by the NIOC, were located near Tehran to supply that market; one was completed in 1968 and the other in 1975. Both were supplied by pipelines from the southwestern oil fields. An additional pipeline also carried petroleum products from the Abadan refinery for distribution in the Tehran area.

Crude oil for the Bakhtaran refinery came from a field close to the Iraqi border; the Shiraz refinery, completed in 1973 with a capacity of 40,000 bpd, distributed its products in the southern and eastern parts of the country. A topping plant (see Glossary), constructed in the 1930s, operated at Masjed-e Soleyman in southwestern Iran. It supplied oil for the domestic market and sent distillates by pipeline to the Abadan refinery.

A refinery in Tabriz, constructed in 1975 and having a capacity of 80,000 bpd, supplied the northwestern area of the country. Petroleum consumption had increased rapidly in the northwest, and a pipeline was completed by 1976 from Tehran to Tabriz to supply crude to the refinery.

Khark Island, located 483 kilometers from the mouth of the Persian Gulf and about 25 kilometers off the coast of Iran, was the principal sea terminal until bombed by the Iraqis in 1985 and 1986; it had been the world's largest offshore crude oil terminal. Export of refined products then reverted to the terminal at Bandar-e Mashur in southwestern Iran, which had been used before the construction of the Khark Island installation.

The availability of new oil terminals allowed Iran to expand its oil production. In the 1960s, crude was sent to Abadan, then exported from Abadan and Bandar-e Mashur. The construction of the Khark Island terminal to export crude oil permitted use of Bandar-e Mashur exclusively for product exports. Some 95 percent of the crude oil came from the producing fields of Agha Jari, Karenj, Marun, Pariz, Bibi Hakimeh, and Ahvaz.

During the 1980s, the Khark Island terminal continued to be responsible for 80 percent of oil exports. Khark Island had two terminals, one on a jetty and the other on a small island off the west coast of the island. The first was a complete complex, and the second was used for quick loading of ships. The jetty was bombed by Iraq to disrupt Iran's main shipping point in early 1985 and again more heavily in September 1985. Shipments were slowed at the jetty, and the island terminal section was devastated.

Aside from Bandar-e Mashur, other export facilities were developed both inside and outside the Persian Gulf. To reduce the threat from Iraq, facilities were expanded at the port of Jask, located just outside the Persian Gulf on the Gulf of Oman, and Sirri Island became an alternative loading point. A petroleum shuttle was initiated between Khark and Sirri islands, and Khark Island continued to export most of the country's oil until additional Iraqi bombing in January 1986. Reduced exports remained possible through the use of the shuttle service to Sirri Island, with its floating terminal for storage and reloading. The August 1986 bombing of shuttle tankers to Sirri and the resulting increase in insurance rates, however, prevented even this level of exports. Because the pipelines for Khark converge at a pumping station at Ganaveh (about forty kilometers northeast of Khark on the Gulf) before going underwater, Ganaveh replaced Khark as the western terminus of the oil shuttle to Sirri Island in the mid-1980s.

Non-Oil Industry

Government incentives to bolster domestic industry were offered in the mid-1980s, but they were offset by the effects of the war.

Factories were forced to lay off workers or to shut down because of declines in imports of as much as nearly 50 percent. This decline resulted in raw material shortages. Other state and private industrial enterprises converted to production of military matériel.

In the mid-1980s, Iran halted importation of domestically producible machinery. As an incentive to domestic production, industries that produced war matériel were granted about US$400 million to replace items whose import value would have exceeded US$1.3 billion. Domestic production increases by 1986 resulted in local manufacture of 80 percent of required munitions, including an antitank missile and such items as gas masks for protection against Iraqi chemical weapons. Industrial production held steady in early 1987, following a 20 percent drop in 1985 from 1984. The Ministry of Heavy Industries anticipated US$75 million in industrial exports in FY 1986.

Among the projects scheduled for funding in FY 1987 were a pesticides plant at Qazvin and the completion of a steel plant at Mobarakeh. There were also plans to construct mineral processing plants in the northwestern city of Zanjan that would produce 40,000 tons of lead and 60,000 tons of zinc annually.

The non-oil industrial sector represented a small portion of the economy, but it provided labor-intensive domestic employment, such as the hand knotting of rugs. Foreign sales of Iran's non-oil products also generated badly needed hard currency. Iran exported US$2.3 billion worth of non-oil goods between 1982 and 1987. Of this total, agricultural products accounted for 32.2 percent, carpets 29.3 percent, textiles 10.9 percent, and caviar 4.9 percent (see Non-Oil Exports, this ch.).

In 1986 Iran started placing greater emphasis on non-oil sectors to offset falling oil prices and revenue. Non-oil revenue totaled about US$700 million in 1986, in comparison with oil revenues of less than US$1 billion. Although it had increased by US$200 million over the previous year, non-oil revenue fell short of the official goal of US$1 billion. Carpet sales accounted for most of the increase, whereas exports of such items as industrial goods and minerals decreased. The FY 1987 target for non-oil exports was doubled to US$1.4 billion, including US$50 million in locally made goods.

Carpets

After the 1979 Revolution, the customary high volume of carpet exports was sharply reduced because of the new regime's policy of conserving carpets as national treasures and its refusal to export them to ''corrupt Westerners.'' This policy was abandoned in 1984

*The manufacturing of carpets and rugs
is an important element in Iran's economy
Courtesy United Nations (John Isaac)*

in view of carpets' importance as a source of foreign exchange. Carpet exports more than tripled in value (from US$35 million to US$110 million) and doubled in weight (from 1,154 tons to 2,845 tons) between March and August 1986, which contributed to a fall in world carpet prices.

Construction

The economic prosperity fueled by the growing oil revenues of the mid-1970s encouraged a construction boom. The expansion of the construction industry slowed, however, and all but stopped after the Revolution. Construction continued to decline until 1984. The domestic recession, created by deliberate government reductions in oil production in 1979, caused a drop in new construction starts, fewer buyers, and a decreased demand for materials.

In FY 1983, the government decided once again to encourage private sector participation in construction. The subsequent increase in loans to private industries by commercial banks revived the construction industry by 1984, although it could not keep pace with housing needs in urban areas.

The housing shortage became severe by 1986. Exacerbated by population pressures, the shortage was an especially serious problem in Tehran. The allocation of credit for building construction accounted for 7 to 8 percent of the GNP. Half of all the 900,000 housing applicants countrywide were in Tehran, yet only half of these received housing. Tehran issued 25 percent of the country's housing permits, with fixed construction investment accounting for 2 percent of the GNP. The government deliberately discouraged further expansion in Tehran, and new building construction regulations in 1986 tied construction permits to the ownership of land through an earlier order from a religious magistrate. According to the director of the Urban Land Organization, a government body created in June 1979 to administer the transfer of nationalized land to deserving families for housing purposes, the housing sector in early 1986 needed about US$10 billion to alleviate the shortage. The banks could only provide about US$4 billion of this total.

Manufacturing and Industrial Development

The first phase of modern industrial development occurred under Reza Shah in the 1930s. When Mohammad Reza Shah succeeded his father in 1941, he began a planning process designed to hasten economic modernization. During the mid-1950s, the state encouraged and supported the building of fertilizer, sugar-refining, cement, textile, and milling plants. By the late 1950s, the government had provided a role for private business by authorizing generous credits from the Plan Organization.

Industrialization led to a rapid increase in manufacturing output. Many new industries were established between 1962 and 1972. The impressive new range of domestic manufacturing enterprises included iron and steel, machine tools, agricultural implements, tractors, communications equipment, television sets, refrigerators, car and bus assembly, and petrochemical products.

Higher oil revenues in the 1970s accelerated economic development. A number of large-scale industrial projects were undertaken during the period of the Fifth Development Plan (1973–78), with government investments concentrated in petrochemicals and basic metal industries as well as crude oil production. Domestic and international private investment was projected to furnish 64 percent of a planned total of US$11 billion for manufacturing investments between FY 1973 and FY 1977. The economy proved incapable of absorbing such feverish growth, however; some projects were postponed, and completion dates were extended for others. Nevertheless, industrial production grew at close to 20 percent per year, and a diversified industrial base was established. By FY 1975, manufacturing and mining (excluding electric power and construction) contributed about 10 percent of GDP.

Shortages of skilled labor and equipment adversely affected production from 1977 onward. Business failures and a generally declining economy led to strikes and political instability in 1978 and 1979. The flight of capital and factory owners after the 1979 Revolution led to the nationalization of industries in the summer of 1979. The decline of the industrial sector was hastened by the war with Iraq; Iraqi bombing of petrochemical and steel plants in Abadan, Ahvaz, and Bandar-e Khomeini in 1980 and 1981 caused further disruption. Recovery began in 1982, but only among smaller industries. Efforts to revive the larger industrial and petrochemical plants began in 1982 and 1983. As a result of technical advances, the Esfahan steel mill was expected to produce 700,000 tons of iron rods in FY 1987—enough to meet domestic needs. In May 1987, Iran's minister of mines and metals reported that twenty exploration projects were under way, aimed at supplying raw materials for the country's steel plants.

The war with Iraq slowed industrial production but also created a new industry, the manufacture of prosthetics. In August 1986, the head of the Iranian Rehabilitation Agency stated that more than 2 million handicapped individuals had sought the rehabilitation services offered by his agency in 1985 but that the agency was capable of serving only 40,000 newly handicapped persons annually. In response to this need, Iran reportedly planned to increase to six the number of factories producing artificial limbs and other prosthetic devices.

Mining and Quarrying

Iran's mineral wealth, in addition to oil and gas, includes chromite, lead, zinc, copper, coal, gold, tin, iron, manganese, ferrous oxide, and tungsten. Commercial extraction of significant reserves of turquoise, fireclay, and kaolin is also possible. Most mining was small scale until modernization efforts in the 1960s led to the systematic recording of known deposits, as well as the systematic search for new ones. Industrialization increased the need for steel, which in turn boosted demand for coal, iron ore, and limestone. Construction of new roads and railroads since the 1960s improved transportation among mining centers throughout the country, especially around the Kerman-Bafq area of south-central Iran.

Prior to the Revolution in 1979, the government intended to develop the copper industry to the point that it would rival oil as a source of foreign exchange. Iranian copper deposits are among the world's largest, and mining is particularly advanced southwest of Kerman near Sirjan. The Iran-Iraq War risks and declining world copper prices inhibited copper extraction, which prior to

FY 1982 had remained insignificant. The government, however, promoted private sector investment in copper in FY 1982, which may have been responsible for the improved copper output in 1983.

In the 1980s, Iran's major nonmetallic mineral exports were chromite and construction stone. Iran's total chromite reserves were estimated at 20 to 30 million tons in 1987. Exports of construction stone to the Persian Gulf countries increased 200 percent in 1986 over the previous year.

The government conducted surveys in the 1970s to ascertain the commercial potential of known mineral deposits. By 1977 about half the country had been surveyed from the air, but less than one-fifth had been explored on the ground. Studies of mineral deposits throughout the country were completed in the mid-1980s, detailing the most recent discoveries of reserves of silica, limestone, granite, and iron ore. In addition, several uranium deposits were discovered in Baluchestan va Sistan in August 1986, and in September 1986 another 750,000 tons of white kaolin deposits on the Iran-Afghanistan border near Birjand were reported.

The extent of mineral resources was indicated by the fact that approximately 2.7 million tons of minerals were extracted from 27 active mines in Yazd Province in FY 1986. Iran earned a total of US$85 million from mineral exports in that year.

Utilities

In 1963 the Iranian government created a hydroelectric management authority. Its functions were incorporated into the Ministry of Water and Power in 1967. The electric power industry had been nationalized in 1965 so that a large, integrated system might be built. In 1967 all water resources were nationalized except generators attached to industrial plants (see Water, this ch.).

The Fourth Development Plan (1968–73) ushered in a new phase of utility development designed to add 4,915 million cubic meters of storage capacity for water, which in turn would generate electricity. Projects designed under this program were completed after the Revolution; they included dam projects in Halil Rud (Jiroft), Shahrud (Taleghan), Lar, Minab, and Qeshlaq.

By 1972, about one-quarter of the population had electricity, and approximately 3,218 kilometers of transmission and distribution lines had been constructed as the start of a national system. Two smaller, separate networks were centered on Kerman in the south central area and Mashhad in the northeast.

During the 1960s and early 1970s, the rapid growth of manufacturing, increasing urbanization, and the extension of electrical service to more of the population put great pressure on planners to

Laborers weigh and process jute in a small mill
Courtesy United States Information Agency

build ahead of demand. They did not always succeed, even with extensive foreign advice. For example, industrial development was temporarily held up in the vicinity of Bandar-e Abbas because of insufficient power, and by mid-1977 brownouts and blackouts were frequently disrupting industry. Nevertheless, many experts favored building a network with large, interconnected power stations rather than the more costly and inefficient construction of separate facilities to head off each impending local shortage. The near doubling of investment goals for the fifth plan compounded the problem of keeping the power supply ahead of demand, however, for it meant a substantial increase in the number of industrial consumers.

In the 1980s, the government began to emphasize the development of steam-powered plants, as part of a plan to reduce hydroelectric power from 25 percent to 10 percent of available national energy by the end of the century. Reversing this policy in the mid-1980s, Minister of Energy Mohammad Taqi Banki stated that hydroelectric power had once again been given priority for reasons of environmental safety and higher productivity.

By the end of 1986, 17 dams were operating with a total energy generation capacity of 7,000 megawatts, a 10-percent increase over 1985. Construction on the Qom River of a US$130 million dam with a 200-million-cubic-meter capacity was scheduled to begin in December 1986. It would supply the northern city of Qom, seventy kilometers away, with drinking and irrigation water. A three-megawatt power station was planned nearby. A feasibility study for a US$1 billion hydroelectric dam on the Karun River was submitted in early 1987. This dam, which would take 6 years to build, would generate 800 megawatts of electricity and replace 2 other proposed dams.

Iran's total electric power capacity was approximately 12 million kilowatts in 1985, the most recent year for which statistics were available in 1987. It produced almost 42 billion kilowatt-hours in 1985, compared with 33 billion kilowatt-hours in 1983. In the FY 1987 budget, the Ministry of Water and Power was authorized to raise electricity rates for consumers who used more than 250 kilowatts, with a further increase for those using more than 400 kilowatts, in order to boost revenues by US$830.4 million.

The national supply of electricity dropped 40 percent in early 1986 because of Iraqi bombing of power plants. The minister of energy announced that the shortages began in January because of severe gas shortages at the power plants in Esfahan, Lowshan, Rasht, Rey, and several other locations. Again, in December 1986, the minister of energy announced impending power cuts as a result of shortfalls in generation.

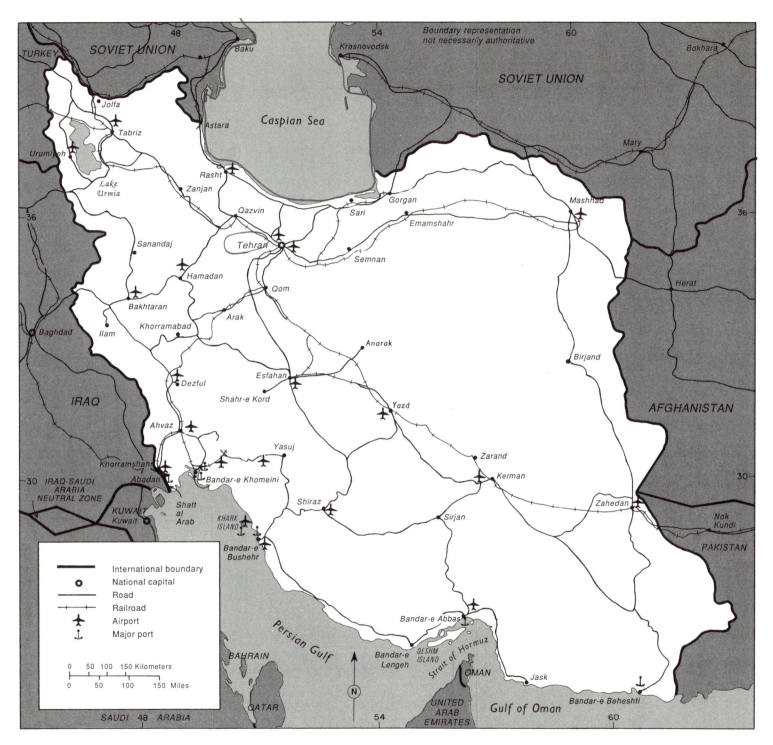

Figure 8. Transportation System, 1987

174

Iranian officials had earlier opted for nuclear power plants to meet part of the demand for electricity, entering into discussions with representatives from West Germany and France. The plants under consideration were pressurized water reactors using enriched uranium. They were to be built near the Persian Gulf because of the need for large quantities of water for cooling. The decision in favor of nuclear power stemmed from policy decisions to develop non-oil energy sources.

Nuclear power was not abandoned in the 1980s. The Atomic Energy Organization of Iran, set up in 1973 to produce nuclear energy for electricity needs, focused in 1987 on the exploration and use of uranium deposits and on the use of nuclear energy in industry, agriculture, and medicine. The construction of the nuclear power plant in Bushehr ceased in 1982 as a result of a fire in the plant; additional damage stemmed from three Iraqi attacks in 1985 and 1986. In 1987 an Argentine-Spanish firm was negotiating to finish construction of the nuclear power plant. Designed to have two 1,200-megawatt reactors, it was expected to take 3 years to complete.

Transportation and Telecommunications

As part of Reza Shah's development plan, modernization of the transportation and telecommunications sectors began in the 1930s and received huge infusions of capital investment from the mid-1960s onward under Mohammad Reza Shah's regime. In May 1979, Mehdi Bazargan's government created an organization called the Crusade for Reconstruction (Jihad-e Sazandegi or Jihad), which focused on rural reconstruction. In 1982 the organization claimed to have built 12,872 kilometers of roads, or nearly 1 kilometer per village.

Transportation

The rugged terrain and sheer size of Iran made the expansion of transportation facilities difficult. Emphasis was placed on linking the major population centers and economic centers by rail and road; superimposed on a map, such main arteries would form a "T," with the crossbar extending from the northwestern corner to the northeast along the southern coast of the Caspian Sea. The vertical line would run through Tehran down to the Gulf (see fig. 8).

In 1925 Iran had only 3,218 kilometers of railroad—much of it in disrepair, but in 1931 a railroad was built to link the two bodies of water on Iran's northern and southern borders, the port of Bandar-e Shah (known as Bandar-e Torkaman after the Revolution of 1979) on the Caspian Sea near Gorgan was linked by rail to the port of Bandar-e Shahpur (known as Bandar-e Khomeini after the 1979 Revolution) on the southwestern coast, passing through Tehran, and in 1941 the northern regions of Iran were connected by rail from west to east (from Tabriz to Mashhad). This was accomplished with the aid of foreign technicians and engineers. The railroad had expanded southeast from Tabriz to Kerman by 1977, and roads and air travel linked many parts of the country. Roads in good condition in 1941 totaled 22,526 kilometers; by 1984 there were 51,389 kilometers of paved roads. These roads, built primarily for military use, had the effect of stimulating development.

The leg of the "T" from Tehran to the Gulf was the most intensively used transportation corridor, accounting for half of all road traffic and two-thirds of all rail traffic by 1978. Domestic and foreign trade from the Gulf traversed this portion of road. Key ports were connected to each other and to Tehran through the "T" network. Foreign trade came through the Gulf ports of Khorramshahr, Bandar-e Shahpur, Bushehr, and Bandar-e Abbas. Khorramshahr handled trade primarily for the private sector, and Bandar-e Shahpur handled imports for the governments. Other foreign trade traversed the northwestern part of Iran. This area was connected by road and railroad with Turkey and the Soviet Union and with two minor ports on the Caspian Sea.

The transportation system became incapable of meeting trade demands during the oil boom of the mid-1970s. Neither the ports nor the transportation infrastructure leading from the ports could handle the volume of goods. As a consequence, long lines of ships formed, some waiting months to unload and adding more than US$1 billion a year to freight costs. Perishable goods spoiled, and delayed deliveries of durable goods disrupted production and construction schedules. Consequently, the government gave the expansion of port and transportation facilities high priority. By 1976 the 6 major ports of Bandar-e Abbas, Bandar-e Shahpur, Chah Bahar (known as Bandar-e Beheshti after the 1979 Revolution), Bushehr, Abadan, and Khorramshahr had a capacity of 12 million tons, with expansion projects underway. By late 1977, unloading delays were no longer a problem. As a result of war damage, the ports of Abadan and Khorramshahr were closed in 1980, leaving the other four main ports and twelve minor ports in operation.

The construction of fourteen jetties along the Gulf coast was planned in 1986; one of these, at Jask near the Strait of Hormuz, opened in February 1986. Built at a cost of approximately US$20 million, it included a covered warehouse, a passenger terminal building, and a 130-meter-long jetty for the use of small ships up to 2,000 tons. Especially after the Revolution, the government expanded roads as well as port facilities. The total length of roads in 1974 was about 50,000 kilometers, of which 14 percent was hard-surfaced. A major post-1979 increase in road construction helped boost total road length in 1984 to 136,381 kilometers, of which 41 percent was paved. Main or national roads comprised 16,551 kilometers and secondary roads 34,838 kilometers of this total.

Post-Revolution maintenance of roads and railroads suffered, as did road access to the ports. The State Railways Organization extended Iran's 4,567 kilometers of railroad track by the completion in 1987 of approximately 130 kilometers of electrified track in the north between Tabriz and Jolfa for imports from the Soviet Union. An additional 1,300 kilometers were scheduled to be added to the network by 1989, although war conditions made it unlikely that this goal would be realized. Other legs were planned between Mashhad in the northeast and the Soviet border at Sarakhs and in the north from Gorgan to Gonbad. A joint economic agreement between Iran and the Soviet Union in August 1987 reportedly called for a railroad route for the export of Soviet goods through Iran to the Gulf. A 560-kilometer extension to the World War II-era railroad linking Iran to Pakistan via Zahedan in southeastern Iran was completed in 1987 to join Zahedan to Kerman and thence to Tehran.

Iran's two principal international airports were located in Tehran (Mehrabad Airport) and Abadan. A new international airport in Esfahan began operations in 1986, and another airport forty kilometers south of Tehran was under construction in 1987. In addition, an international airport was scheduled to be built at Gorgan, east of the Caspian Sea. In developments affecting smaller, national airports, the runway at Kerman was extended in FY 1986. Plans in 1987 called for the airports at Ardabil, Iranshahr, Mashhad, Sari, and Zabol to be lengthened and widened to accommodate larger airplanes and for a new runway to be built at Zahedan.

Telecommunications

Reza Shah emphasized telecommunications as a focus of modernization in the 1930s. Telecommunications was reemphasized in the 1960s as part of Mohammad Reza Shah's White Revolution (see Glossary). Development was financed by a consortium of international firms that established satellite links for Iran's telecommunications. By the late 1970s, Iran had telegraph, television, and data communications capabilities. The National Iranian Radio and Television Organization had sufficient television transmission capability and enough relay stations to reach about 60 percent of the population. Iran had 1.7 million television sets in 1976 and 2.1 million by 1984.

The principal complaint about the telecommunications system remained the average citizen's inability to obtain a telephone. Although the number of telephone lines increased from 400,000 to 800,000 between 1972 and 1977, hundreds of thousands of customers waited as long as two years for a telephone. By 1980 the number of telephones had increased to about 1.2 million, and by 1986 to 1.5 million. About 3,000 of 70,000 rural communities had telephones in 1987, compared with 300 in 1979. To meet the demand for telephones, authorities decided to seek local production of digital equipment, and in May 1987 the British company Plessey Major Systems was negotiating a US$166.3 million contract to supply the Ministry of Posts, Telephones, and Telegraph with almost 1 million lines of telephone exchange equipment. Automatic telephone facilities were also included in project planning.

As a result of the opening of additional microwave links between Tehran, Ankara, and Karachi, international service generally improved in the early 1980s. Temporary disruption was caused, however, by an Iraqi attack on a communications installation near Hamadan on June 8, 1986.

Tourism

The disincentives resulting from the war, the anti-Western stance of the revolutionary regime, and the restrictions on visas all discouraged tourism after 1979. Visitors to the famous sites of Persepolis, Pasargard, and Esfahan dwindled; the number of tourists fell from a high of 695,500 in 1977 to 62,373 in 1982. By 1984, however, the number of tourists had increased to 157,000. This increase had a virtually negligible effect, however, on the economy.

Agriculture

After nearly achieving agricultural self-sufficiency in the 1960s, Iran reached the point in 1979 where 65 percent of its food had to be imported. Declining productivity was blamed on the use of modern fertilizers, which had inadvertently scorched the thin Iranian soil. Unresolved land reform issues, a lack of economic incentives to raise surplus crops, and low profit ratios combined to drive increasingly large segments of the farm population into urban areas.

The 1979 Revolution sought self-sufficiency in foodstuffs as part of its overall goal of decreased economic dependence on the West. Higher government subsidies for grain and other staples and expanded short-term credit and tax exemptions for farmers complying with government quotas were intended by the new regime to promote self-sufficiency. But by early 1987, Iran was actually more dependent on agricultural imports than in the 1970s.

Water

Iran's land surface covers 165 million hectares, more than half of which is uncultivable. A total of 11.5 million hectares is under cultivation at any time, of which 3.5 million hectares were irrigated in 1987, and the rest watered by rain. Only 10 percent of the country receives adequate rainfall for agriculture; most of this area is in western Iran. The water shortage is intensified by seasonal rainfalls. The rainy season occurs between October and March, leaving the land parched for the remainder of the year. Immense seasonal variations in flow characterize Iran's rivers. The Karun River and other rivers passing through Khuzestan (in the southwest at the head of the Gulf) carry water during periods of maximum flow that is ten times the amount borne in dry periods. Several of the government's dam projects are on these rivers. In numerous localities, there may be no precipitation until sudden storms, accompanied by heavy rains, dump almost the entire year's rainfall in a few days. Often causing floods and local damage, the runoffs are so rapid that they cannot be used for agricultural purposes.

Water shortages are compounded by the unequal distribution of water. Near the Caspian Sea, rainfall averages about 128 centimeters per year, but in the Central Plateau and in the lowlands to the south it seldom exceeds 10 to 12 centimeters, far below the 26 to 31 centimeters usually required for dry farming (see Climate, ch. 2).

Scarcity of water and of the means for making use of it have constrained agriculture since ancient times. To make use of the limited amounts of water, the Iranians centuries ago developed manmade underground water channels called *qanats* that were still in use in 1987. They usually are located at the foot of a mountain and are limited to land with a slope. A *qanat* taps water that has seeped into the ground and channels it via straight tunnels to the land surface. The *qanats* are designed to surface in proximity to village crops.

The chief advantage of the *qanat* is that its underground location prevents most of the evaporation to which water carried in surface channels is subject. In addition, the *qanat* is preferable to the modern power-operated deep well because it draws upon underground water located far from the villages. The chief disadvantages of the *qanat* are the costs of construction and maintenance and a lack of flexibility; the flow cannot be controlled, and water is lost when it is not being used to irrigate crops.

In the late 1980s, an estimated 60,000 *qanats* were in use, and new units were still being dug (although not in western Iran, where rainfall is adequate). To assist villagers, the government undertook a program to clean many *qanats* after the Revolution in 1979. *Qanat* water is distributed in various ways: by turn, over specified periods; by division into shares; by damming; and by the opening of outlets through which the water flows to each plot of land. So important is the *qanat* system to the agricultural economy and so complex is the procedure for allocating water rights (which are inherited), that a large number of court cases regularly deal with adjudication of conflicting claims.

Construction of large reservoir dams since World War II has made a major contribution to water management for both irrigation and industrial purposes. Dam construction has centered in the province of Khuzestan in the southwest as a result of the configuration of its rivers flowing from the Zagros Mountains. The upper courses flow in parallel stretches before cutting through the surrounding mountains in extremely narrow gorges called *tangs*. The terrain in Khuzestan provides good dam sites. The government set up the Khuzestan Water and Power Authority in 1959 to manage natural resources in that province. All economic development plans emphasized the need to improve water supplies and reservoirs so as to improve crop production. Large reservoirs were built throughout the country, beginning with the Second Development Plan. The first dams were built on the Karaj, Safid, and Dez rivers.

The first of the major dams had a significant impact on the Iranian economy. Completed in 1962, the Mohammad Reza Shah Dam on the Dez River was designed to irrigate the Khuzestan plain and to supply electricity to the province. After several years of operation, the dam had achieved only a small part of its goals, and the government decided that the lands below the dam and other dams nearing completion required special administration. As a consequence, a law was passed in 1969 nationalizing irrigable lands downstream from dams. The lands below the Mohammad Reza Shah Dam were later leased to newly established domestic and foreign companies that became known as agribusinesses.

Land Use

Desert, wasteland, and barren mountain ranges cover about half of Iran's total land area. Of the rest, in the 1980s about 11 percent was forested, about 8 percent was used for grazing or pastureland, and about 1.5 percent was made up of cities, villages, industrial centers, and related areas. The remainder included land that was cultivated either permanently or on a rotation, dry-farming basis (about 14 percent) and land that could be farmed with adequate

Siphon irrigation being used in a sugar-beet field near Qazvin
Courtesy United Nations

irrigation (about 15 to 16 percent). Some observers considered the latter category as pastureland.

In most regions, the natural cover is insufficient to build up much organic soil content, and on the steeper mountain slopes much of the original earth cover has been washed away. Although roughly half of Iran is made up of the arid Central Plateau, some of the gentler slopes and the Gulf lowlands have relatively good soils but poor drainage. In the southeast, a high wind that blows incessantly from May to September is strong enough to carry sand particles with it. Vegetation can be destroyed, and the lighter soils of the region have been stripped away.

In mountain valleys and in areas where rivers descending from the mountains have formed extensive alluvial plains, much of the soil is of medium to heavy texture and is suited to a variety of agricultural uses when brought under irrigation. Northern soils are the richest and the best watered. The regions adjacent to Lake Urmia (also cited as Lake Urumiyeh and formerly known as Lake Rezaiyeh under the Pahlavis) and the Caspian Sea make up only about 25 percent of the country's area but produce 60 percent or more of its major crops.

The land reform program of 1962 affected agricultural lands and the production of crops. Implemented in three stages, the program redistributed agricultural lands to the peasantry, thereby lessening the power of the feudal landlords. By the time the program was declared complete in 1971, more than 90 percent of the farmers who held rights to cultivation had become owners of the land they farmed. The new owners, however, became disillusioned with the government and its policies as their real economic situation worsened by the late 1970s.

On average, the minimal landholding for subsistence farming in Iran is about seven hectares. If each of the 3.5 million sharecroppers and landowners in villages (as of 1981) were given an equal share of land (from the 16.6 million hectares of cropland), each family would be entitled to only 4.7 hectares, not enough land for subsistence farming. Even if there were sufficient arable land, many of the sharecroppers could not afford to buy more than four of the seven hectares needed for subsistence farming.

The basic rural landholding infrastructure did not change after the Revolution. A minority of landowners continued to profit by exploiting the labor of sharecroppers. Prior to the land reform program, feudal and absentee landlords, including religious leaders responsible for *vaqf* land, comprised the ruling elite. Over the years, *vaqf* landholdings grew considerably, providing many Iranian clergy with a degree of economic independence from the central government. Redistribution of the land resulted in power being transferred to farmers who acquired ten or more hectares of land and to the rural bourgeoisie (see State and Society, 1964–74, ch. 1). Uncertainty about the prospect of effective land reform under Khomeini contributed to a massive loss of farm labor—5 million people—between 1982 and 1986.

Emphasis on subsistence agriculture persisted because of the lack of capital allocated after the Revolution, perhaps because the regime's technocrats were from urban areas and therefore uninformed about agriculture, or because the bazaar class, which constituted a disproportionate share of the 1979 government, did not represent the interests of agriculture. Uncertainties about future landownership, as well as the war with Iraq, caused further disruption of agriculture. Ten percent of agricultural land fell into Iraqi hands between 1980 and 1982, although the territory was subsequently regained by Iran. The war stifled agricultural development by causing a loss of revenue and by draining the already shrinking agricultural labor pool through heavy conscription.

Crop Production

By 1987, eight years after the Revolution, there had been no progress toward agricultural self-sufficiency. By the end of the first year following the 1979 Revolution, agricultural output had fallen

by 3.5 percent, and it continued to decline, except for those growing seasons characterized by above-normal rainfall, such as FY 1982
and FY 1985. Sugar, wheat, cotton, and rice production increased
in FY 1982, whereas wheat, barley, and rice production increased
in FY 1985. Iran was the largest world supplier of pistachios, with
95,000 tons produced in 1982 to 1983 and 97,000 tons in 1986.
The war did not inhibit the production of pistachios, which are
grown in south-central Iran (see table 6, Appendix).

Grains

Overall grain production increased throughout the 1970s, peaking
in the late 1970s and again in the early 1980s and decreasing somewhat by 1985. Wheat is Iran's main grain crop; its production
increased in the early 1980s from that in the 1970s, along with that
of barley.

Wheat is a staple for most of the population. Bread is the most
important single item in the Iranian diet, except in certain parts
of the Caspian lowlands where rice is more commonly grown.
Wheat and barley are planted on dry-farmed and irrigated lands
and on mountain slopes and plains. Wheat is used almost exclusively for human consumption, and barley is used mainly as animal
feed.

Rice is the only crop grown exclusively under irrigation. The
long-grain rice of Iran grows primarily in the wet Caspian lowlands
in the northern provinces of Gilan and Mazandaran, where heavy
rainfall facilitates paddy cultivation. Population growth and the
rising standard of living stimulated production of the high-quality
rice that could be used for export. Although the Ministry of Agriculture and Rural Development sought to develop rice as an export
crop as early as 1977, by the end of that year 326,000 tons of rice
had to be imported to meet domestic needs. In 1985 rice imports
increased 3 percent over the previous year's 710,000 tons.

Other grain imports fell in 1985 by 43 percent compared with
1984 levels. Wheat, flour, and feed grain imports declined as output increased.

Sugar

During the early and mid-1970s, sugar output increased annually at a rate of 5 to 6 percent, but consumption rose at a rate of
10 percent or more. With an increased production of beet and cane
sugar in the early 1970s, it was expected that Iran would export
sugar by 1977. Instead, 300,000 tons of raw sugar were imported
that year. To supplement sugar production, the government in 1976
initiated a large beekeeping and honey-processing operation at a

site near Qom, which produced about 2,000 tons of honey annually.

The production of raw sugar decreased from 687,000 tons in 1976 to 412,000 tons in 1985. Sugar production dropped to a low of 380,000 tons in 1980.

Sugar cane production increased from about 1.7 million tons in FY 1981 to about 2 million tons in FY 1983. Sugar beet production, however, declined by 15.5 percent, from 4.3 million tons in FY 1982 to 3.7 million tons in FY 1983.

Livestock

The value of livestock increased annually after 1981, but the decreases in livestock in the early revolutionary period were such that by 1985 the overall value of livestock remained below the 1976 level. Severe shortages of meat and eggs, coupled with high demand and the absence of price controls, encouraged the raising of livestock and were expected to improve livestock availability.

Livestock-raising methods were generally unsophisticated. Sheep and goats were kept by nomadic tribesmen and by sedentary villagers who supported a few animals as a sideline to farming. These animals had diets of grass and shrubs that often left them diseased and malnourished; in turn, the herders obtained little profit in the way of meat, milk, hair, and hides.

Fisheries

The Caspian Sea and the Persian Gulf remained the country's two largest fishing areas. A variety of fish were found in both bodies of water; catches totaled 44,800 tons in 1981 and 34,500 tons in 1983. Fishing in the Persian Gulf has declined since the onset of war with Iraq. By 1986 national freshwater catches totaled only 25,000 to 35,000 tons per year.

Commercial fishing was controlled by two state-owned enterprises, the Northern Fishing Company operating in the Caspian Sea and the Southern Fisheries Company in the Persian Gulf and the Gulf of Oman. Sturgeon, white salmon, whitefish, carp, bream, pike, and catfish predominate in the Caspian, and sardines, sole, tuna, bream, snapper, mackerel, swordfish, and shrimp predominate in the Persian Gulf.

The Caspian sturgeon was of particular importance because it produces the roe that is processed into caviar. Known as "gray pearls," Iranian caviar is said to be the finest in the world and commands a high price. The main importers of Iranian caviar were the Soviet Union and the West European countries. Increasing pollution in the Caspian Sea, however, posed a threat to the industry.

Forestry

Some of Iran's forest resources were nationalized under Mohammad Reza Shah's development plans, beginning in 1963. Since then, the state has gradually gained control over forest use. The plentiful commercial timber in the Alborz and Zagros mountains was diminished by illegal cutting that did not show up in official statistics; approximately 6.5 million cubic meters were cut in 1986 alone. Of an estimated 18 million hectares of forest lands, only about 3.2 million hectares near the Caspian Sea can be regarded as commercially productive.

Plentiful rainfall, a mild climate, and a long growing season have combined to create a dense forest of high-quality timber in the Caspian region. There is an extensive growth of temperate-zone hardwoods, including oak, beech, maple, Siberian elm, ash, walnut, ironwood, alder, basswood, and fig. About half of the Caspian forests consists of these trees; the remainder is low-grade scrub. The Zagros Mountains in the west and areas in Khorasan and Fars provinces abound in oak, walnut, and maple trees. Shiraz is renowned for its cypresses.

To curtail indiscriminate forest destruction, the government in 1967 moved to nationalize all forests and pastures. A forest service was established; by 1970 more than 3,000 forest rangers and guards were employed, and 1.3 million saplings had been planted on 526,315 hectares of land. The value of exported forest products was six times greater in 1973 than in 1984; the decrease in exports probably resulted from increased domestic and war-related consumption.

Foreign Trade

Imports

Overall trade contracted in 1986, with import restrictions matching falling export earnings. The trade statistics did not, however, reflect the flourishing black market for foreign goods. Gasoline was available on the black market for five times the official rate; food and other goods were available at similarly inflated prices. Rising prices and salaries (among civil servants, for example) compounded the rate of inflation, which ranged between 10 and 50 percent, depending on the kind of goods purchased.

Capital and consumer goods imports decreased after the 1979 Revolution, with capital goods falling from 30 percent of total imports in 1979 to 15 percent by 1982. Importation of luxury goods was restricted to conserve foreign currency and preserve the balance of payments. Food imports increased to more than US$2 billion

185

by FY 1983, despite the emphasis on agricultural self-sufficiency. Rice imports alone increased by 200,000 tons in 1986, despite increased rice production.

Food imports in early 1986 consumed as much as 20 percent of total foreign exchange. Iran had become one of the largest per capita purchasers of wheat in the world, buying 3.4 million tons annually. The nation spent about US$3 billion per year on food items such as wheat, rice, meat, vegetable oil, eggs, chicken, tea, and sugar. By December 1986, Iran's imports of meat and dairy products alone exceeded the value of the country's entire industrial output.

Between March and June 1986, imports declined to US$2.6 billion, a drop of 16 percent compared with the same period the previous year. Shrinking imports reflected a conscious government effort to contain the financial crisis by further restricting the entry of luxury goods into the country. Discretionary imports for private consumption were expected to be halved in FY 1987 to US$5 billion, from the FY 1986 low of US$8 to US$10 billion.

Iran resorted to barter agreements with some countries in 1986 and 1987, trading oil for goods such as tea from Sri Lanka, rice from Thailand, wheat from Argentina, and various foodstuffs from Turkey. Failure to pay its debts caused Iran to lose its contract with Peugeot-Talbot for automobile assembly kits. Although the contract was suspended officially in November 1986, no new kits had been shipped since January 1986, and Iran lost business worth US$190 million per year as production of the Peykan automobile ceased. Iran also lost its barter agreement with New Zealand after failing to pay cash debts for imported goods; thus, in 1987 Iran paid for 90,000 tons of imported lamb in cash rather than with oil, as it had for 135,000 tons of New Zealand lamb imported in 1986.

Non-Oil Exports

In 1985 the government announced its new goal of doubling non-oil exports in 1986. Although the value of non-oil exports increased 70 percent between March and June 1986, this increase shrank to 59 percent by August 1986. Because inflation had reduced the value of non-oil exports, the government abandoned its goal for non-oil exports.

Despite government encouragement, non-oil exports in 1985 accounted for only 10 percent of total exports. Industrial and mineral exports together accounted for 25 percent of the value of non-oil exports in 1985 but only 5 percent in 1986. The export of manufactured goods and cotton also declined appreciably as a result of the war. A further 25 percent of non-oil export income came from carpets and fruit. Carpet exports were the exception to the overall downturn in non-oil exports in 1985. Carpet exports more than tripled from 1985 to 1986, but as carpet output increased, prices on the international market fell.

The other key non-oil export was agricultural produce. Some agricultural exports increased in FY 1986, whereas industrial exports continued to decline. Official figures showed that agricultural exports were up in value 46 percent for the period March–August 1986, as compared with the same period during the preceding fiscal year. This figure is misleading, however, because there was a decline in the ratio of the value of agricultural exports to agricultural imports. In the mid-1980s, the agricultural sector operated at a subsistence level, growing food primarily to feed the general population and producing for export only the financially lucrative cash crops whose production varied according to seasonal fluctuations in rainfall. A halting though generally upward trend in the production and export of cash crops began just before the Revolution.

Fruit and vegetable exports increased in 1986 as a result of good weather, a big market in the Persian Gulf area for fresh produce, and incentives to grow and market cash crops, whose prices the government did not regulate. Fruit and vegetable exports accounted for 30 percent of the country's non-oil exports in the first half of FY 1987. Previously, fruit had not exceeded 5 percent of total non-oil exports.

Bumper crops of pistachios sold at the international market rate and bumper crops of fruit and vegetables were the only exceptions to a general decline in agricultural production. Production of pistachios was so competitive that the United States Department of Commerce imposed a 318-percent duty on imports of Iranian roasted pistachios in the fall of 1986, causing a decline in exports to the United States.

Through 1986, Iranian caviar exports in the 1980s fluctuated between US$20 million and US$40 million. In 1986 the exports were worth only about US$20 million. That year, Iran sought to recapture the Italian market (estimated at US$900,000 annually) from the Soviet Union. Iran had sold only US$100,000 worth of caviar (about 11 percent of the market) to Italy in 1985.

Trade Partners

Before 1979 Iran had relied on the industrial West for trade. Little changed in subsequent years except rhetoric. Although the government purportedly sought to develop trade relations with other

187

Islamic countries, figures showed that in 1985 approximately 64 percent of Iran's imports came from the West, 28 percent from developing countries, and 8 percent from Eastern Europe. These figures, although representing an absolute increase in trade with Third World countries, actually indicated only a small percentage increase in total trade. Economic necessity mandated that Iran trade with whatever country was willing, notwithstanding policy pronouncements regarding self-sufficiency and Third World communities of interest. Nearly all foreign trade occurred through government-controlled purchasing and distribution companies, which were charged with enforcing government trade policies and regulating the quantity and quality of imports.

Despite trade sanctions applied in 1980 by the United States, the European Economic Community, and Japan, Iranian imports from the West actually increased 13.5 percent from FY 1980 to FY 1981. West Germany remained Iran's primary supplier in 1985, followed by Japan, Britain, Italy, and Turkey (see table 7, Appendix).

As a result of United States trade restrictions following the Tehran embassy takeover in 1979, imports from the United States dropped dramatically. This lost market, coupled with the decline in oil revenues, forced the government to consider bartering Iranian oil for non-oil goods. It was estimated that total trade with new Islamic and Third World trade partners would increase from 20 percent in the mid-1980s to 35 percent in 1987 through barter.

Barter agreements became commonplace in 1984 to compensate for the fall in revenue from oil exports (see Balance of Payments, this ch.). These revenues were 15 percent less (or US$1.7 billion) than expected in FY 1984, with barter arrangements making up the difference. About one-quarter of 1984 oil exports resulted from barter or bilateral trade agreements. Barter became a point of contention between the Ministry of Oil, which opposed it, and the Ministry of Foreign Affairs, which supported barter as a key element of foreign policy. Bartering ceased in late 1985 as a result of disagreement between the ministries but resumed in 1986 because of economic necessity occasioned by depressed oil prices. Bartering with other countries, especially in Eastern Europe, mitigated the effects of the economy's structural problems but failed to solve them.

The United States resumed trade with Iran in FY 1981, with direct sales totaling US$300 million. United States exports to Iran fell to less than half that amount, however, in FY 1982. This led to Iran's renewal of the Regional Cooperation for Development pact with Pakistan and Turkey in October 1984, which by 1985 had greatly increased trade among these partners. By early 1987, trade among the three countries was worth over US$3 billion, as compared with US$100 million before the Revolution.

In 1986 the United States imported US$612 million worth of Iranian products, principally crude oil, caviar, rugs, furs, spices, and gems. Of those imports, crude oil represented US$508.8 million, pistachios and other nuts US$15 million, carpets US$5.5 million, and caviar about US$2 million. In the first five months of 1987, the United States imported US$418.5 million in Iranian goods. The increase was probably caused by fluctuations in petroleum spot prices and in the demand for oil in general.

In 1986 Iran acknowledged the role of the Soviet Union as a major future trade partner by announcing its plans to complete the electrification of the railroad between Tabriz and the Soviet city of Jolfa. Moreover, the construction of railroad lines—to be completed by 1989—linking other points in Iran with the Soviet Union and with Pakistan indicated the growing Iranian intent to deal with both countries as trade partners (see Transportation and Telecommunications, this ch.). In August 1987, Iran and the Soviet Union agreed to large-scale joint economic projects, including oil pipelines and a railroad to the Gulf. Despite the apparent intention on both sides to do business, overall Iranian-Soviet trade in FY 1986 was one-quarter that in FY 1985.

Balance of Payments

Oil revenues in the mid-1970s brought Iran a foreign exchange surplus. But when oil revenues fell sharply in 1978, an economic crisis resulted. Iran went from being a long-term lender in the 1970s to a short-term borrower in the 1980s, with the acquisition of foreign currency a perennial problem. The revolutionary government resorted to barter with several countries in the mid-1980s, but some customers soon insisted on receiving payment from Iran before shipment because of disagreements over the terms of payment. Problems arose when countries wanted to renegotiate barter contracts in 1986, to reflect the lower cost of oil, and Iran insisted on the original terms. Also, barter did not improve the foreign currency situation; to maintain a foreign exchange balance, Iran would have had to earn at least US$1 billion more than the sums received from civilian non-oil exports.

Another method used by the government to improve its balance of payments was the collection of funds owed to Iran by foreign suppliers and governments. The Iranian government estimated in 1986 that several countries, chiefly Egypt, the United States, and France, owed Iran US$5 to US$6 billion. Clearly, the continued costs of the war coupled with falling oil revenues afforded the economy little elasticity.

Iran had a US$5.4 billion balance of payments deficit during 1986, largely as a result of low oil prices and the disruption of oil shipments caused by Iraqi bombing. Oil prices fell from US$27 per barrel in November 1985 to US$12 in February 1986. Although prices rose in the fall of 1986, the average price of oil for the year was US$13 per barrel, half that in 1985. The estimated US$10 billion in export earnings in 1986 was the lowest since 1973.

As a result of its high balance of payments deficit and foreign exchange shortage, Iran reduced its imports and divested itself of foreign financial assets acquired by Mohammad Reza Shah. For example, in 1986 it sold 25.6 percent of its holdings, worth approximately US$150 million, in the West German engineering firm Deutsche Babcock. Iran's efforts to cope with its economic crisis by making barter agreements, repossessing funds, cutting imports, and divesting itself of foreign financial assets were superficial responses to deeper structural problems within the economy, such as the need for land and agricultural reforms and the redistribution of income.

The country's balance of payments looked bleak for the final years of the 1980s. The continuing war with Iraq, declining oil revenues, high unemployment, reduced consumer imports, severe inflation, a rising foreign debt, and a severe foreign currency shortage tested the economic policies of the revolutionary regime. The economy produced essential products and addressed in some measure the problems facing the national budget, a remarkable feat given the war, but failed to address basic structural issues.

*   *   *

Despite the disruptive influences of war on all aspects of the national life, a surprising number of good publications on the Iranian economy were readily available in the late 1980s. The Central Bank (Bank Markazi) of the Islamic Republic publishes reliable annual statistics on the state of the economy, the budget, finances, and balance of payments. A publication from Tehran called *Iran Press Digest* has a superb weekly update of economic and political events. *Iran Monitor,* a monthly publication based in Switzerland, provides an up-to-date account of international financial and trade issues. *Iran Times,* an independent weekly newspaper with sections in English and Persian, details current economic developments and statistics. Two other sources of consistently good coverage of Iran are the *Middle East Economic Digest (MEED),* published in London, and *Middle East Research and Information Project (MERIP) Reports,* published in Washington.

Eric Hooglund provides an understanding of land reform issues in *Land and Revolution in Iran, 1960–1980.* For concise reports on the economic situation in Iran, the following sources are helpful: Patrick Clawson's "Islamic Iran's Economic Policies and Prospects"; Sohrab Behdad's *Foreign Exchange Gap, Structural Constraints and the Political Economy of Exchange Rate Determination in Iran;* and Wolfgang Lautenschlager's "The Effects of an Overvalued Exchange Rate on the Iranian Economy, 1979–1984." (For further information and complete citations, see Bibliography.)

Chapter 4. Government and Politics

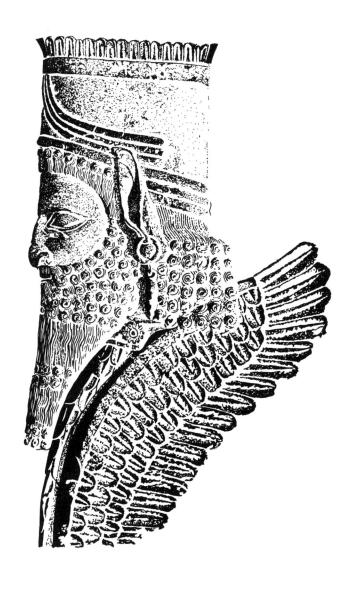

A bas-relief of a bearded sphinx, ca. 500 B.C., from Persepolis

THE IRANIAN ISLAMIC REVOLUTION of 1979 resulted in the replacement of the monarchy by the Islamic Republic of Iran. The inspiration for the new government came from Ayatollah Sayyid Ruhollah Musavi Khomeini, who first began formulating his concept of an Islamic government in the early 1970s, while in exile in the Shia Islam learning and pilgrimage center of An Najaf in Iraq. Khomeini's principal objective was that government should be entrusted to Islamic clergy (see Glossary) who had been appropriately trained in Islamic theology and jurisprudence. He referred to this ideal government as a *velayat-e faqih,* or the guardianship of the religious jurist. Khomeini did not, however, elaborate concrete ideas about the institutions and functions of this ideal Islamic government. The translation of his ideas into a structure of interrelated governmental institutions was undertaken by the special Assembly of Experts, which drafted the Constitution of the Islamic Republic during the summer and fall of 1979. Subsequently, this Constitution was ratified by popular vote in December 1979.

The political institutions established under the Constitution have been in the process of consolidation since 1980. These institutions have withstood serious challenges, such as the impeachment and removal from office of the first elected president and the assassination of the second one; the assassination of a prime minister, several members of the cabinet, and deputies of the parliament, or Majlis (see Glossary); an effort to overthrow the government by armed opposition; and a major foreign war. By 1987 the constitutional government's demonstrated ability to survive these numerous crises inspired confidence among the political elite.

At the top of the government structure is the *faqih* (see Glossary), the ultimate decision maker. The Constitution specifically names Khomeini as the *faqih* for life and provides a mechanism for choosing his successors. The role of the *faqih* has evolved into that of a policy guide and arbitrator among competitive views. Below the *faqih* a distinct separation of powers exists between the executive and legislative branches. The executive branch includes an elected president, who selects a prime minister and cabinet that must be approved by the elected legislative assembly, the Majlis. The judiciary is independent of both the executive and the Majlis.

Until 1987 the government was dominated by a single political party, the Islamic Republican Party (IRP). Other political parties were permitted as long as they accepted the Constitution and the

195

basic principles of *velayat-e faqih.* In practice, however, few other political parties have been permitted to operate legally since 1981. Most of the political parties that were formed in the immediate aftermath of the Revolution have disbanded, gone underground, or continued to operate in exile.

The Constitution stipulates that the government of the Republic derives its legitimacy from both God and the people. It is a theocracy in the sense that the rulers claim that they govern the Muslim people of Iran as the representatives of the divine being and the saintly Twelve Shia Imams (see Glossary). The people have the right to choose their own leaders, however, from among those who have demonstrated both religious expertise and moral rectitude. At the national level this is accomplished through parliamentary and presidential elections scheduled at four-year intervals. All citizens who have attained sixteen years of age are eligible to vote in these elections. There are also local elections for a variety of urban and rural positions.

Constitutional Framework

The government is based upon the Constitution that was approved in a national referendum in December 1979. This republican Constitution replaced the 1906 constitution, which, with its provisions for a shah to reign as head of state, was the earliest constitution in the Middle East. Soon after the Revolution, however, on March 30 and 31, 1979, the provisional government of Mehdi Bazargan asked all Iranians sixteen years of age and older to vote in a national referendum on the question of whether they approved of abolishing the monarchy and replacing it with an Islamic republic. Subsequently, the government announced that a 98-percent majority favored abrogating the old constitution and establishing such a republic. On the basis of this popular mandate, the provisional government prepared a draft constitution drawing upon some of the articles of the abolished 1906 constitution and the French constitution written under Charles de Gaulle in 1958. Ironically, the government draft did not allot any special political role to the clergy or even mention the concept of *velayat-e faqih.*

Although the provisional government initially had advocated a popularly elected assembly to complete the Constitution, Khomeini indicted that this task should be undertaken by experts. Accordingly the electorate was called upon to vote for an Assembly of Experts from a list of names approved by the government. The draft constitution was submitted to this seventy-three member assembly, which was dominated by Shia clergy. The Assembly of Experts convened in August 1979 to write the constitution in final form for approval by popular referendum. The clerical majority was generally dissatisfied with the essentially secular draft constitution and was determined to revise it to make it more Islamic. Produced after three months of deliberation, the final document, which was approved by a two-thirds majority of the Assembly of Experts, differed completely from the original draft. For example, it contained provisions for institutionalizing the office of supreme religious jurist, or *faqih,* and for establishing a theocratic government.

The first presidential elections took place in January 1980, and elections for the first Majlis were held in March and May of 1980. The Council of Guardians, a body that reviews all legislation to ensure that laws are in conformity with Islamic principles, was appointed during the summer of 1980. Presidential elections were held again in 1981 and 1985. The second Majlis was elected in 1984.

The Faqih

The preamble to the Constitution vests supreme authority in the *faqih.* According to Article 5, the *faqih* is the just and pious jurist who is recognized by the majority of the people at any period as best qualified to lead the nation. In both the preamble and Article 107 of the Constitution, Khomeini is recognized as the first *faqih.* Articles 108 to 112 specify the qualifications and duties of the *faqih.* The duties include appointing the jurists to the Council of Guardians; the chief judges of the judicial branch; the chief of staff of the armed forces; the commander of the Pasdaran (Pasdaran-e Enghelab-e Islami, or Islamic Revolutionary Guards Corps, or Revolutionary Guards); the personal representatives of the *faqih* to the Supreme Defense Council; and the commanders of the army, air force, and navy, following their nomination by the Supreme Defense Council. The *faqih* also is authorized to approve candidates for presidential elections. In addition, he is empowered to dismiss a president who has been impeached by the Majlis or found by the Supreme Court to be negligent in his duties (see fig. 9).

Articles 5 and 107 of the Constitution also provide procedures for succession to the position of *faqih.* After Khomeini, the office of *faqih* is to pass to an equally qualified jurist. If a single religious leader with appropriate qualifications cannot be recognized consensually, religious experts elected by the people are to choose from among themselves three to five equally distinguished jurists who then will constitute a collective *faqih,* or Leadership Council.

In accordance with Article 107, an eighty-three-member Assembly of Experts was elected in December 1982 to choose a successor

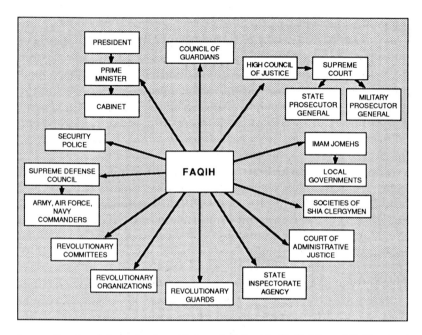

Source: Based on information from Shahrough Akhavi in N. Keddie and E. Hooglund (eds.), *The Iranian Revolution and the Islamic Republic,* Syracuse, New York, 1986.

Figure 9. Powers of the Faqih

to Khomeini. Even before the first meeting of the Assembly of Experts in the spring of 1983, some influential members of the clergy had been trying to promote Ayatollah Hosain Ali Montazeri (born 1923), a former student of Khomeini, as successor to the office of *faqih.* As early as the fall of 1981, Khomeini himself had indicated in a speech that he considered Montazeri the best qualified to be *faqih.* Hojjatoleslam Ali Akbar Hashemi-Rafsanjani, who as of late 1987 had been the speaker of the Majlis since its formation in 1980, also supported Montazeri's succession. Rafsanjani, in fact, nominated him at the first deliberations of the Assembly of Experts, as well as at subsequent conventions in 1984 and 1985. At the third meeting, Montazeri was designated "deputy" rather than "successor," but this put him in line to be Khomeini's successor. Since November 1985, the press and government radio and television broadcasts have referred to Montazeri as the *faqih*-designate.

The Presidency

The Constitution stipulates that the president is "the holder of the highest official power next to the office of *faqih.''* In effect, the president is the head of state of the Islamic Republic. Articles 113 to 132 of the Constitution pertain to the qualifications, powers, and responsibilities of the president. The president is elected for a four-year term on the basis of an absolute majority vote of the national electorate and may be reelected for one additional term. The president must be a Shia Muslim and a man ''of political and religious distinction.'' He is empowered to choose the prime minister, approve the nominations of ministers, sign laws into force, and veto decrees issued by the Council of Ministers, or cabinet.

Elected in January 1980, Abolhasan Bani Sadr was Iran's first president under the Constitution of 1979. His tenure of office was marked by intense rivalry with the IRP-dominated Majlis. Within one year of his election, relations between the president and his opponents in the Majlis had deteriorated so severely that the Majlis initiated impeachment proceedings against Bani Sadr. In June 1981, a majority of Majlis deputies voted that Bani Sadr had been negligent in his duties and requested that Khomeini dismiss him from office as specified under the Constitution.

Iran's second president, Mohammad Ali Rajai, was elected in July 1981 but served only a brief term before being assassinated in a bombing at the prime minister's office on August 30, 1981. The third president, Hojjatoleslam Ali Khamenehi, was elected in October 1981 and reelected to a second term in 1985. During his tenure, relations between the presidency and the Majlis have been relatively cooperative. Not only was Khamenehi an important religious figure but he also was secretary general of the IRP until its dissolution in 1987.

The Prime Minister and the Council of Ministers

The prime minister is chosen by the president and must be approved by the Majlis. According to Article 135 of the Constitution, the prime minister may remain in office as long as he retains the confidence of the Majlis, but he must submit a letter of resignation to the president upon losing a confidence vote. The prime minister is responsible for choosing the ministers who will form his government, known as the Council of Ministers (also known as the cabinet). In 1987 the Council of Ministers totaled twenty-five members. Each minister had to be approved by both the president and the Majlis. The prime minister and his cabinet establish government policies and execute laws.

Following each of his elections, President Khamenehi chose Mir-Hosain Musavi as prime minister. Musavi generally had consistent support in the Majlis, although a vocal minority of deputies opposed many of his economic policies. Policies pertaining to the nationalization of large industries and foreign trade and the expropriation of large-scale agricultural landholdings for redistribution among peasants were especially controversial in the years 1982 to 1987.

The Majlis

Articles 62 through 90 of the Constitution of 1979 invest legislative power in the Islamic Consultative Assembly, the parliament, or Majlis (see Glossary). Deputies are elected by direct, secret ballot once every four years. Each deputy represents a geographic constituency, and every person sixteen years of age and older from a given constituency votes for one representative. The Majlis cannot be dissolved: according to Article 63, "elections of each session should be held before the expiration of the previous session, so that the country may never remain without an assembly." Article 64 establishes the number of representatives at 270, but it also provides for adding one more deputy, at 10-year intervals, for each constituency population increase of 150,000. Five of the 270 seats are reserved for the non-Muslim religious minorities: one each for Assyrian Christians, Jews, and Zoroastrians, and two for Armenian Christians.

The Constitution permits the Majlis to draft its own regulations pertaining to the election of a speaker and other officers, the formation of committees, and the holding of hearings. When the first Majlis convened in the summer of 1980, the deputies voted to have annual elections for the position of speaker. Rafsanjani was elected as speaker of the first Majlis; he was reelected six times through the beginning of 1987. The speaker is assisted by deputy speakers and the chairmen of various committees.

The Majlis not only has the responsibility of approving the prime minister and cabinet members but also has the right to question any individual minister or anyone from the government as a whole about policies. Articles 88 and 89 require ministers to appear before the Majlis within ten days to respond to a request for interpellation. If the deputies are dissatisfied with the information obtained during such questioning, they may request the Majlis to schedule a confidence vote on the performance of a minister or the government.

Article 69 stipulates that Majlis sessions be open to the public, that regular deliberations may be broadcast over radio and television, and that minutes of all meetings be published. Since 1980 sessions of the Majlis have been broadcast regularly. The public airing of Majlis meetings has demonstrated that the assembly has been characterized by raucous debate. Economic policies, with the notable exception of oil policy, have been the most vigorously debated issues.

The Council of Guardians

The Constitution also provides for the Council of Guardians, which is charged with examining all legislation passed by the Majlis to ensure that it conforms to Islamic law. According to Article 91, the Council of Guardians consists of twelve members; six of them must be "just and pious" clergymen who are chosen by the *faqih* or the Leadership Council. The other six must be Muslim lawyers who are first selected by the High Council of Justice, then approved by a majority vote of the Majlis. The members of the Council of Guardians serve six-year terms, with half the members being changed every three years.

The responsibilities of the Council of Guardians are delineated in Articles 94 through 99. The members must review each law voted by the Majlis and determine, no later than ten days after the assembly has submitted a bill for consideration, whether or not it conforms with Islamic principles. If ten days are insufficient to study a particular piece of legislation, the Council of Guardians may request a ten-day extension. A majority of the clerical members of the Council of Guardians must agree that any given law does not violate religious precepts. If the Council of Guardians decides that a law contradicts Islam, the bill is returned to the Majlis for revision. If the Council of Guardians decides that a law conforms with Islam, that law is ratified.

During its first two years of operation, the Council of Guardians did not challenge Majlis bills and generally played a passive role in the political process. In May 1982, however, the Council of Guardians established its independent role by vetoing a law to nationalize all foreign trade. Since that time, the Council of Guardians has refused to ratify several pieces of legislation that would restrict property rights. In particular, the Council of Guardians has opposed the efforts of the Majlis to enact comprehensive land reform statutes.

The Judiciary

Article 156 of the Constitution provides for an independent judiciary. According to Articles 157 and 158, the highest judicial office is the High Council of Justice, which consists of five members who serve five-year, renewable terms. The High Council of Justice consists of the chief justice of the Supreme Court and the attorney general (also seen as State Prosecutor General), both of whom must be Shia *mujtahids* (members of the clergy whose demonstrated erudition in religious law has earned them the privilege of interpreting laws), and three other clergy chosen by religious jurists. The responsibilities of the High Council of Justice include establishing appropriate departments within the Ministry of Justice to deal with civil and criminal offenses, preparing draft bills related to the judiciary, and supervising the appointment of judges. Article 160 also stipulates that the minister of justice is to be chosen by the prime minister from among candidates who have been recommended by the High Council of Justice. The minister of justice is responsible for all courts throughout the country.

Article 161 provides for the Supreme Court, whose composition is based upon laws drafted by the High Council of Justice. The Supreme Court is an appellate court that reviews decisions of the lower courts to ensure their conformity with the laws of the country and to ensure uniformity in judicial policy. Article 162 stipulates that the chief justice of the Supreme Court must be a *mujtahid* with expertise in judicial matters. The *faqih,* in consultation with the justices of the Supreme Court, appoints the chief justice for a term of five years.

In 1980 Ayatollah Mohammad Beheshti was appointed by Khomeini as the first chief justice. Beheshti established judicial committees that were charged with drafting new civil and criminal codes derived from Shia Islamic laws. One of the most significant new codes was the Law of Qisas, which was submitted to and passed by the Majlis in 1982, one year after Beheshti's death in a bomb explosion (see The Rise and Fall of Bani Sadr, this ch.). The Law of Qisas provided that in cases of victims of violent crime, families could demand retribution, up to and including death. Other laws established penalties for various moral offenses, such as consumption of alcohol, failure to observe *hejab* (see Glossary), adultery, prostitution, and illicit sexual relations. Punishments prescribed in these laws included public floggings, amputations, and execution by stoning for adulterers.

The entire judicial system of the country has been desecularized. The attorney general, like the chief justice, must be a *mujtahid* and is appointed to office for a five-year term by the *faqih* (Article 162). The judges of all the courts must be knowledgeable in Shia jurisprudence; they must meet other qualifications determined by rules established by the High Council of Justice. Since there were insufficient numbers of qualified senior clergy to fill the judicial positions in the country, some former civil court judges who demonstrated their expertise in Islamic law and were willing to undergo religious training were permitted to retain their posts. In practice, however, the Islamization of the judiciary forced half of the former civil court judges out of their positions. To emphasize the independence of judges from the government, Article 170 stipulates that they are "duty bound to refrain from executing governmental decisions that are contrary to Islamic laws."

Local Government

As of 1987, Iran was divided into twenty-four provinces (*ostans*). Each province was subdivided into several counties (*shahrestans*). *Shahrestans* numbered 195, each of which was centered on the largest town within its boundaries. Most *shahrestans* took their names from those towns that served as county seats. All of the *shahrestans* consisted of two or more districts, or *bakhshs*. The 498 *bakhshs* were further subdivided into rural subdistricts (*dehestans*). Each *dehestan* consisted of several villages dispersed over an average area of 1,600 square kilometers.

The prerevolutionary provincial administrative structure was still employed in 1987. Thus, each province was headed by a governor general (*ostandar*), who was appointed by the minister of interior. Each county was headed by a governor (*farmandar*), also appointed by the minister of interior. Local officials, such as the chiefs of districts (*bakhshdars*), rural subdistricts (*dehyars*), and villages (*kadkhudas*—see Glossary), were appointed by the provincial governors general and county governors; these local officials served as representatives of the central government.

Prior to the Revolution, the governor general was the most powerful person in each province. Since 1979, however, the clerical *imam jomehs*, or prayer leaders, have exercised effective political power at the provincial level. The *imam jomeh* is the designated representative of the *faqih* in each county. Until 1987 each *imam jomeh* was appointed from among the senior clergy of the county. In June 1987, Khomeini approved guidelines for the election of *imam jomehs*. The *imam jomehs* have tended to work closely with the *komitehs* (revolutionary committees) and the Pasdaran, and in most counties these organizations are subordinate to the *imam jomehs*.

Political Dynamics

The Revolution replaced the old political elite, which had consisted of the Pahlavi family, wealthy families of the former Qajar dynasty, and wealthy industrialists and financiers, with a new political elite of Shia clergy and lay politicians of middle and lower middle class origin. The roots of most members of this new elite lay in the bazaar middle class (see Urban Society, ch. 2). Thus, the values of the new elite and the attitudes they professed were the ones most esteemed by the bazaar: respect for entrepreneurial skill, distrust of capitalist methods, and religious conservatism. Since the Revolution, they have striven to create a political order that incorporates their shared vision of an ideal society based upon Islamic principles.

Although the new political elite has been relatively united as to the overall goals envisaged for the Islamic Republic, its members have been deeply divided over various political, social, and economic policies deemed appropriate for achieving long-term objectives. These divisions have been manifested in political developments and struggles in the years since 1979. This period has been characterized by four phases, each dominated by distinct political issues. The first phase coincided with the provisional government of Prime Minister Bazargan, from February to November 1979. The next phase, which lasted until June 1981, was marked by the political rise and fall of Bani Sadr. During the third phase, which ended in December 1982, the government survived a major armed insurrection. During the next phase, which began in 1983, the political elite has been involved in the process of consolidating the theocratic regime, and that process was continuing in late 1987.

The Provisional Government

The government under the monarchy had been highly centralized. Although in theory the shah was a constitutional monarch, in practice he wielded extraordinary power as head of state, chief executive, and commander in chief of the armed forces. The shah was actively involved in day-to-day decision making and played a pivotal role as the most important formulator of national goals and priorities.

During the Revolution, the authority that had been concentrated in the shah and exercised through the bureaucracy based in Tehran was severely eroded; many governmental functions were usurped by several hundred *komitehs* that sprang up in urban neighborhoods, towns, and villages throughout the country. By the time the provisional government of Bazargan had acceded to power, these *komitehs*, usually attached to local mosques, were reluctant to surrender to the central government any of the wide-ranging powers they had assumed. Their determination to retain substantial power was supported by most members of the Revolutionary Council, a body formed by Khomeini in January 1979 to supervise the transition from monarchy to republic. The Revolutionary Council remained independent of the provisional government and undertook actions, or sanctioned those actions carried out by the revolutionary committees, that were in conflict with the policies pursued by the

The shah and his family, with eldest son, Reza Cyrus Pahlavi standing in rear. (Photo taken in the mid-1970s)

Bazargan cabinet. Inevitably, the provisional government, which wanted to reestablish the authority of the central government, would come into conflict with the *komitehs* and the proliferation of revolutionary organizations.

Bazargan's lack of essential backing from the Revolutionary Council, and ultimately from Khomeini, made it virtually impossible for his government to exercise effective control over arrests, trials, the appointment of officials, military-civilian relations, and property confiscations. Consequently, the various revolutionary organizations and the *komitehs* persistently challenged the authority of the provisional government throughout its brief tenure. Bazargan's apparent powerlessness even extended to the realm of foreign policy. When a group of college students overran the United States embassy in downtown Tehran, Bazargan and his cabinet were unable to prevent American personnel from being held as hostages. Acknowledging the impotence of his administration, Bazargan resigned after only nine months in office.

The issue of central versus local control that had plagued the Bazargan government continued to be a matter of political contention in 1987. Although the extreme diffusion of power that characterized the Bazargan government no longer prevailed in 1987, in comparison with the prerevolutionary situation, political power in Iran was relatively decentralized. This arrangement represented a balance between two vocal factions within the political elite. A procentralization faction has argued that the goals of an Islamic republic can best be achieved and maintained only if the institutions of government are strong. In contrast, a decentralization faction has insisted that bureaucratization is inherently destructive of long-term objectives and that the future of the Revolution can only be ensured through extensive popular participation in numerous revolutionary organizations.

The Rise and Fall of Bani Sadr

Bani Sadr was the first popularly elected president of the Islamic Republic. He assumed office with a decisive electoral vote—75 percent—and with the blessing of Khomeini. Within seventeen months, however, he had been impeached by the Majlis, and dismissed from office. Bani Sadr was destroyed, at least in part, by the same issue that had brought down Bazargan, that is, the efforts of the government to reestablish its political authority. Ironically, prior to his election as president, Bani Sadr had advocated decentralization of political power and had even helped to undermine the Bazargan government. As president, Bani Sadr became a convert to the principle that centralization of power was necessary;

soon, he was embroiled in a bitter political dispute with his former allies. The downfall of Bani Sadr, however, also involved a more fundamental issue, namely, the distribution of power among the new political institutions of the Republic. The fate of Bani Sadr demonstrated that the legislature was independent from and at least equal to the executive, the reverse situation of the Majlis under the Pahlavi shahs.

The conflict between Bani Sadr and the Majlis, which was dominated by the IRP, began when the assembly convened in June 1980. The first issue of controversy concerned the designation of a prime minister. Although the Constitution provides for the president to select the prime minister, it also stipulates that the prime minister must have the approval of the Majlis. After a protracted political struggle, the Majlis forced Bani Sadr to accept its own nominee, Rajai, as prime minister. The president, who had aspired to serve as a strong figure similar to de Gaulle when he was president of France, was unable to reconcile his differences with the prime minister, who preferred to formulate government policies in consultation with the Majlis. As Bani Sadr continued to lose influence over political developments to the Majlis, his own credibility as an effective leader was undermined.

The Majlis also frustrated Bani Sadr's attempts to establish the authority of the presidency in both domestic and foreign affairs. For example, the leaders of the IRP in the Majlis manipulated Bani Sadr's efforts to deal with Iran's international crises, the dispute with the United States over the hostages, and the war with Iraq that began in September 1980, in order to discredit him. When Bani Sadr tried to ally himself with the interests of the disaffected, secularized middle class, the IRP mobilized thousands of supporters, who were incited to assault persons and property derisively identified as "liberal," the euphemism used for any Iranian whose values were perceived to be Western. Bani Sadr attempted to defend his actions by writing editorials in his newspaper, *Enqelab-e Islami,* that criticized IRP policies and denounced the Majlis and other IRP-dominated institutions as being unconstitutional. Eventually, the leaders of the IRP convinced Khomeini that Bani Sadr was a danger to the Revolution. Accordingly, in June 1981 the Majlis initiated impeachment proceedings against the president and found him guilty of incompetence. Bani Sadr went into hiding even before Khomeini issued the decree dismissing him from office. At the end of July, he managed to flee the country in an airplane piloted by sympathetic air force personnel.

The Reign of Terror

The dismissal of Bani Sadr on June 21, 1981, brought to a head the underlying conflicts within the political elite and between its members and other groups contesting for power. In the final three months of Bani Sadr's presidency, political violence had intensified as organized gangs of *hezbollahis* (see Glossary) attacked individuals and organizations considered to be enemies of the Revolution. One of the main opposition parties, the Mojahedin (Mojahedin-e Khalq, or People's Struggle), rose up in a nation-wide armed rebellion (see Opposition Political Parties in Exile, this ch.). Although the Mojahedin's uprising was quickly contained, during the following eighteen months the country was in a virtual state of siege as the government used extraordinary measures to suppress not only the Mojahedin but also other opposition movements. The government's fears of the opposition's capabilities were exacerbated by several sensational acts of terrorism directed at regime officials. These included the bombing of the IRP headquarters on June 28, 1981, which killed at least seventy top leaders of the party, including Beheshti, the secretary general of the party and the chief justice of the Supreme Court; the bombing at the prime minister's office on August 30, which killed several more leaders including former prime minister Rajai, who had replaced Bani Sadr as president, and the cleric Mohammad Javad Bahonar, who was Rajai's prime minister; and the assassinations of several key officials in Tehran and important provincial cities.

The government responded to the Mojahedin challenge by carrying out mass arrests and executions. At the height of the confrontation, an average of 50 persons per day were executed; on several days during September 1981, the total number executed throughout the country exceeded 100. Although the government dramatized its resolve to crush the uprising by conducting many of these mass executions in public, officials showed little interest in recording the names and numbers of the condemned. Thus, no statistics exist for the total number executed. Nevertheless, by the end of 1982 an estimated 7,500 persons had been executed or killed in street battles with the Pasdaran. Approximately 90 percent of the deaths had been associated with the Mojahedin, and the rest with smaller political groups that had joined the Mojahedin in the attempt to overthrow the government by armed force.

The efforts to root out the Mojahedin were accompanied by a general assault on procedural rights. The Pasdaran and specially recruited gangs of *hezbollahis* patrolled urban neighborhoods, ostensibly looking for the safe houses in which supporters of the Mojahedin

*Voters cast their ballots in presidential election in January 1980
Copyright Lehtikuva/PHOTRI*

and other opposition groups were suspected of hiding. They invaded such homes and arrested occupants without warrants. Persons suspected of insufficient loyalty to the regime were harassed and often subjected to arbitrary arrest and expropriation of their property. Extensive purges were initiated within all government ministries, and thousands of employees who failed loyalty tests were dismissed. Complaints were voiced that government agents eavesdropped on telephone conversations and opened private mail to collect information to use against citizens. The courts generally failed to protect individuals against violations of due process during this period.

The reign of terror officially ended in December 1982 when Khomeini issued an eight-point decree that effectively instructed the courts to ensure that the civil and due process rights of citizens be safeguarded. The decree forbade forcible entry of homes and businesses, arrest and detention without judges' orders, property expropriation without court authorization, and all forms of government spying on private persons. Special councils were to be established to investigate all complaints about court violations of individual rights.

The Consolidation of Theocracy

By the time Khomeini issued his judicial decree, the armed opposition had been suppressed. Although isolated acts of terrorism continued to take place àfter December 1982, the political elite no longer perceived such incidents as threatening to the regime. Both religious and lay leaders remained generally intolerant of dissent, but a gradual decline was noted in government abuses of civil liberties in line with the provisions of the eight-point decree. As preoccupation with internal security abated, the leaders began to establish consensus on the procedures that they believed were necessary to ensure the continuity of the new political institutions. Accordingly, elections were held for the Assembly of Experts, which chose a successor to Khomeini, and regulations were promulgated for the smooth functioning of the ministerial bureaucracies. The politicians also were determined to restore relative normalcy to society, albeit within prescribed Islamic bounds. Thus, they permitted the universities, which had been closed in 1980, to reopen, and they tried to control the excesses of the *hezbollahis*.

The refocusing of political energies on consolidating the regime also brought into the open the debate among members of the political elite over government policies. Two main issues dominated this debate: the role of the revolutionary organizations that operated fairly autonomously of the central government; and government intervention in the economy. The government of Prime Minister Mir-Hosain Musavi, which was approved by the Majlis in October 1981 and won a second parliamentary mandate in October 1985, tried to restrain the revolutionary organizations and advocated broad regulatory economic control. The Majlis served as the principal arena in which these issues were debated. Opposition from the Majlis blocked some laws outright and forced the government to accept compromises that diluted the effects of other policies.

Political Parties

During the final years of the Pahlavi monarchy, only a single, government-sponsored political party, the Rastakhiz, operated legally. Nevertheless, several legally proscribed political parties continued to function clandestinely. These included parties that advocated peaceful political change and those that supported the armed overthrow of Mohammad Reza Shah Pahlavi. Among the former parties were the National Front, which actually was a coalition of democratically inclined political parties and other organizations that originally had been founded in 1949; the Nehzat-e Azadi-yi Iran, or the Iran Freedom Movement (IFM), established in 1961 by democratically inclined clergy and laymen; and the Tudeh Party, a Marxist party that had been founded in 1941. The two most important guerrilla organizations were the Islamic Mojahedin and the Marxist Fadayan (Cherikha-ye Fadayan-e Khalq, or People's

While adults pray, a boy holds up a picture
of Ayatollah Khomeini
Courtesy United Nations (John Isaac)

Guerrillas), both of which had been largely suppressed after carrying out several sensational terrorist actions in the early 1970s.

The overthrow of the Pahlavi monarchy allowed a full spectrum of Islamic, leftist, and secular ideas supporting the Revolution to flourish. With the exception of the monarchist Rastakhiz, which had dissolved, the prerevolutionary parties were reactivated, including the Mojahedin and Fadayan. In addition, several new parties were organized. These included secular parties, such as the National Democratic Front and the Radical Party; religious parties, such as the IRP and the Muslim Peoples' Republican Party; and leftist parties, such as the Paykar. All these parties operated openly and competitively until August 1979, when the Revolutionary Council forced the provisional government to introduce regulations to restrict the activities of most political parties.

The Domination of the Islamic Republican Party

Created in February 1979 by clergy who had been students of Khomeini before his exile from the country in 1964, the IRP emerged as the country's dominant political force. Core members included ayatollahs Beheshti, Abdol-Karim Musavi-Ardabili, and Mohammad Reza Mahdavi-Kani and hojjatoleslams Khamenehi, Rafsanjani, and Bahonar. All had been active in mobilizing large

211

crowds for the mass demonstrations during the Revolution. Following the overthrow of the shah, the IRP leaders continued to use their extensive contacts with religious leaders throughout the country to mobilize popular support. The IRP leaders perceived the secular, leftist, and more liberal Islamic parties as threats to their own political goals. As early as the summer of 1979, the IRP encouraged its supporters to attack political rallies and offices of these other parties.

Although Khomeini himself never became a member of the IRP, the party leaders exploited their close association with him to project a popular image of the IRP as the party following the line of the imam Khomeini. This implicit identification helped IRP candidates win a majority of seats in the elections for the Assembly of Experts that drafted the Constitution. During the 1980 elections for the first Majlis, IRP candidates and independents sympathetic with most IRP positions again won a majority of the seats. The party's effective control of the Majlis emboldened the IRP in its harassment of opponents. Throughout 1980 IRP-organized gangs of *hezbollahis* used intimidation tactics against supporters of other political parties, and consequently, most of the secular parties were cowed into silence as their leaders fled to foreign exile.

By 1981 the only political party that could seriously challenge the IRP was the Mojahedin. This Islamic organization had grown rapidly in two years from a few hundred supporters to a membership of 150,000, mostly educated young men and women in the cities, who were attracted by the Mojahedin's liberal, even radical, interpretations of traditional Shia concepts. The ideological conflict between the Mojahedin and the IRP was serious because the former rejected the IRP argument of a religious basis for the political principle of *velayat-e faqih*. In fact, in June 1980 Khomeini denounced the Mojahedin on account of the organization's insistence that laymen were as qualified as clergy to interpret religious doctrines. Although the Mojahedin closed most of its branch offices following this verbal assault, unlike the secular political parties it was not easily intimidated by IRP-organized political violence. On the contrary, Mojahedin members engaged in armed clashes with *hezbollahis*. Tensions between Mojahedin and IRP partisans intensified during the political conflict between Bani Sadr and the IRP leaders. The Mojahedin lent its support to the beleaguered president; after Bani Sadr was impeached, the organization rose in armed rebellion against the IRP-dominated government.

Several of the small leftist parties joined the Mojahedin uprising. These included the Paykar, a prerevolutionary Marxist splinter from the Mojahedin, and the Fadayan Minority. The latter had split from the main Fadayan (thereafter referred to as the Fadayan Majority) in 1980 after a majority of the party's Central Committee had voted to support the government. Both the Paykar and the Fadayan Minority shared the view of the Mojahedin that the IRP was "merely a group of fascist clerics blocking a true revolution." The Mojahedin had a much broader base of support than did either of its allies, but the combined strength of all the parties could not match the capabilities of the IRP in terms of mobilizing masses of committed supporters. Thus, the government eventually was able to break the back of the armed opposition. The Mojahedin survived largely because its leader, Masud Rajavi, escaped to France, where he reorganized the party while in exile.

Not all of the leftist parties supported the Mojahedin's call to arms. Significantly, both the Tudeh and the Fadayan Majority condemned the insurrection and proclaimed their loyalty to the constitutional process. Even though these parties were permitted to function within narrowly circumscribed limits, the IRP leaders remained deeply suspicious of them. Both parties were distrusted because of their espousal of Marxist ideas. In addition, a widespread perception prevailed that the Tudeh was subservient to the Soviet Union, an attitude derived from the Tudeh's historic practice of basing its own foreign policy stances upon the line of the Soviet Union. In the autumn of 1982, toleration for the Tudeh dissipated quickly once the party began to criticize the decision to take the Iran-Iraq War into Iraqi territory. In February 1983, the government simultaneously arrested thirty top leaders of the Tudeh and accused them of treason. The party was outlawed, its offices closed, and members rounded up. Subsequently, Tudeh leaders were presented on television, where they confessed to being spies for the Soviet Union.

After the spring of 1983, the only nonreligious political party that continued to operate with legal sanction was the IFM. Prominent members included the former prime minister, Bazargan, and the former foreign minister, Ibrahim Yazdi, both of whom were elected to the first Majlis in 1980. The IFM opposed most of the policies of the IRP. Whenever Bazargan or another IFM member dared to speak out against IRP excesses, however, gangs of *hezbollahis* ransacked party offices. Bazargan was subjected to verbal abuse and even physical assault. He was powerless to protect one of his closest associates from being tried and convicted of treason for actions performed as an aide in the provisional government. The IFM boycotted the 1984 Majlis elections and Bazargan was barred from being a candidate in the 1985 presidential elections.

213

In practice, the IFM has been intimidated into silence, and thus its role as a loyal opposition party has been largely symbolic.

The IRP's success in silencing or eliminating organized opposition was directed not only at political parties but also was extended to other independent organizations. Even religious associations were not exempt from being forcibly disbanded if they advocated policies that conflicted with IRP goals. Although it emerged as the dominant political party, the IRP leadership failed to institutionalize procedures for developing the IRP into a genuine mass party. IRP offices were set up throughout the country, but in practice these did not function to recruit members. Rather, the offices served as headquarters for local clergy who performed a variety of political roles distinct from purely party functions. At both the national and the local levels, the IRP's clerical leaders perceived themselves as responsible for enforcing uniform Islamic behavior and thought. Thus, they generally viewed the party as a means of achieving this goal and not as a means of articulating the political views of the masses. In actuality, therefore, the IRP remained essentially an elitist party.

The debate within the political elite on power distribution and economic policy also adversely affected the IRP. Intensified dissent over economic programs, beginning in 1986, virtually paralyzed the party. Consequently, President Khamenehi, who had become the IRP's secretary general in 1981 following the death of Beheshti and several other key party leaders, decided it would be politically expedient to disband the IRP. Khamenehi and Rafsanjani jointly signed a letter to Khomeini in June 1987, in which they notified him of the party's polarization and requested his consent to dissolve the party. The *faqih* agreed, and the political party that had played such an important role during the first eight years of the Republic ceased to exist.

Opposition Political Parties in Exile

Many of the opposition parties that were suppressed inside the country were reorganized abroad. In 1987 more than a dozen political parties were active among the Iranian exile communities in Western Europe, the United States, and Iraq. All of these parties belonged to one of four broad ideological groups: monarchists, democrats, Islamicists, and Marxists. With the notable exception of the Mojahedin and the ethnic Kurdish parties, the expatriate opposition parties eschewed the use of political violence to achieve their shared goal of overthrowing the regime in Tehran.

Monarchists

The several monarchist political parties supported the restoration of a royalist regime in Iran. With varying degrees of enthusiasm the monarchists contended that Reza Cyrus Pahlavi, the eldest son (born 1960) of the last shah, was the legitimate ruler of the country. The former crown prince proclaimed himself Shah Reza II in 1980 following his father's death. Subsequently, he announced that he wanted to reign as a constitutional monarch and have a role similar to the role of the king of Spain. The most active monarchist group has been the Paris-based National Resistance Movement of Iran under the leadership of Shapour Bakhtiar, the last royalist prime minister. The National Resistance Movement's official position was to restore the 1906 constitution as its original drafters intended, with a shah that reigns rather than rules. In 1983 Bakhtiar's group agreed to cooperate with another Paris-based party, the Iran Liberation Front, which was led by elder statesman and former royalist prime minister Ali Amini. In general, the monarchist parties have been weakened by personality conflicts among the several leaders. When Manuchehr Ganji, a former royalist cabinet officer, broke with Amini in 1986, many Iran Liberation Front followers joined him in forming a new rival party called the Banner of Kaveh, after the legendary pre-Islamic blacksmith hero who defeated an evil tyrant and restored the rule of ancient Iran to a just shah.

Democratic Parties

The democratic parties also consisted of several groups, all of which supported a republican form of government; some of them, such as the National Democratic Front and the Kurdish Democratic Party of Iran (KDP), also espoused varying forms of socialism. The National Front, under the nominal leadership of Karim Sanjabi, and the National Democratic Front of Hedayatollah Matin-Daftari were both headquartered in Paris. Neither the National Front nor the National Democratic Front has engaged in significant political activity since 1982, although the latter party joined the Mojahedin-dominated National Council of Resistance in that year and was still a member in 1987. In contrast, the KDP, which advocated political and cultural rights for the Kurdish ethnic minority within a federally organized government, has been fighting against the Islamic Republic since 1979. By the beginning of 1986, however, KDP forces had been driven out of Iranian Kordestan, although they continued to conduct sporadic hit-and-run operations against

215

units of the army and Pasdaran from bases in Iraqi and Turkish Kurdistan.

Islamic Groups

In 1987 the principal Islamic party in opposition to the government of Iran was the Mojahedin, which had been founded in 1965 by a group of religiously inspired young Shias. All were college graduates who believed that armed struggle was the only way to overthrow the shah. In the early 1970s, the Mojahedin engaged in armed confrontations with the military and carried out acts of terrorism, including the assassination of an American military adviser. The Mojahedin was crushed for the most part by 1975, but it reemerged in early 1979 and revitalized itself. Its interpretations of Islam, however, soon brought the organization into conflict with the IRP. During the summer of 1981, the Mojahedin unsuccessfully attempted an armed uprising against the government. More than 7,500 Mojahedin followers were killed during the conflict, and within one year the organization had once again been crushed (see The Domination of the Islamic Republican Party, this ch.).

Rajavi, the leader of the Mojahedin, managed to escape from Iran with Bani Sadr in July 1981. In France he reorganized the Mojahedin and tried to broaden its appeal by inviting all nonmonarchist parties to join the National Council of Resistance, which he and Bani Sadr established to coordinate opposition activities. Although most of the political parties refrained from cooperating with the Mojahedin, it nevertheless was most successful in recruiting new members and establishing a loyal following in United States and West European cities with sizable Iranian communities. From the perspective of the other political parties, one of the Mojahedin's most controversial positions was its public endorsement of direct contacts with Iraq, beginning in 1983. This was a contentious issue even within the National Council of Resistance and eventually led to Bani Sadr's break with Rajavi in 1984.

The Mojahedin maintained clandestine contact with sympathizers in Iran, and these underground cells regularly carried out isolated terrorist acts. For this reason, Tehran was more concerned about the Mojahedin than any other opposition group based abroad. The freedom of operation that the Mojahedin enjoyed in France became one of the issues that led to increasingly strained relations between the Iranian and French governments after 1982. When Paris actively sought to improve relations in late 1985, Prime Minister Musavi set restrictions on the Mojahedin as one of the conditions for normalizing relations. In June 1986, France pressured the

Mojahedin to curtail its activities. This move prompted Rajavi to accept an invitation from President Saddam Husayn of Iraq for the Mojahedin to establish its headquarters in Baghdad. Following the move to Iraq, the Mojahedin set up military training camps near the war front and periodically claimed that its forces had crossed into Iran and successfully fought battles against the Pasdaran. In June 1987, Rajavi announced the formation of the newly reorganized and expanded National Army of Liberation, open to non-Mojahedin members, to help overthrow the government of Iran.

Marxists

Like the Mojahedin, several Marxist political parties have maintained clandestine cells inside the country. Tudeh leaders, who managed to escape the government's mass arrests and forcible dissolution of their party in early 1983, reestablished the Tudeh in exile in the German Democratic Republic (East Germany). The Fadayan Majority, which later in 1983 suffered the same fate as the Tudeh, was decimated by government persecution; its surviving members eventually joined the Tudeh. The Komala (Komala-ye Shoreshgari-ye Zahmatkeshan-e Kordestan-e Iran, or Committee of the Revolutionary Toilers of Iranian Kordestan), a predominantly, but not exclusively, Kurdish party, had rejected as early as 1979 the Tudeh and Fadayan Majority policy of cooperation with the regime and continued to fight against central government forces up to the end of 1985, when it was forced to retreat to Iraqi Kurdistan. The Fadayan Minority had joined the Mojahedin uprising in 1981 and consequently lost most of its cadres in the ensuing confrontation with the regime. It has party offices in several West European cities and on university campuses in the United States. The Paykar, which also joined the Mojahedin's unsuccessful rebellion, was largely destroyed by 1982, although secret cells were believed still to exist in 1987.

Political Orientations

The Revolution of 1979 brought about a fundamental change in Iranian attitudes toward politics. Under the monarchy the political culture had been elitist in the sense that all major governmental decisions were made by the shah and his ministers. Most of the population acquiesced in this approach to politics. The fusion of traditional Shia Islamic ideals with political values during the Revolution resulted in the emergence of a populist political culture. The principal characteristics of this political culture are pervasive feelings that the government is obligated to ensure social justice and that every citizen should participate in politics. These feelings are acknowledged by the political leadership, which constantly expresses its concern for the welfare of the *mostazafin* (disinherited) and persistently praises the people's work in a host of political and religious associations.

The transformation of the political culture owed much to the charisma of Khomeini. He was determined not simply to overthrow the monarchy but also to replace it with a new society that derived its values from Islam. Khomeini believed that the long-term success of such an ideal Islamic government was dependent on the commitment and involvement of the masses. He envisaged the clergy as responsible for providing religious guidance, based on their expertise in Islamic law, to the people as they worked to create a new society in which religion and politics were fused. Khomeini's reputation for piety, learning, and personal integrity, as well as his forceful personality, have been important factors in the mobilization of thousands of committed followers to carry out the desecularization of the country's political institutions.

Mass political involvement has been both an objective and a characteristic of postrevolutionary Iran. Political participation, however, is not through political parties but through religious institutions. The mosque has become the single most important popular political institution. Participation in weekly congregational prayers, at which a political sermon is always delivered, is considered both a religious and a civic duty. For political aspirants, attendance at the weekly prayers is mandatory. Numerous religiopolitical associations are centered on the mosques. These organizations undertake a wide variety of activities, such as distributing ration coupons, investigating the religious credentials of aspirants for local offices, conducting classes in subjects ranging from the study of Arabic to superpower imperialism, and setting up teams to monitor shop prices and personal behavior. These organizations tend to be voluntary associations whose members devote several hours per week to their activities. Although most of these voluntary associations are for men, several are specifically for women.

Religious, rather than secular, organizations thus have the most important political roles. Factories, schools, and offices also have Islamic associations that undertake functions similar to those of the mosque voluntary associations. Although many secular groups exist, the majority of such associations as industrial and professional unions, university clubs, and mercantile organizations have acquired religious overtones. These private organizations generally have religious advisers who provide guidance to members on prayer ritual, Islamic law, and Shia history. Associations that try

A street vendor sells photographs of political leaders in the early 1980s
Courtesy United Nations (John Isaac)

to avoid mixing religion with business are suspected of being anti-Islamic and risk having their articles of incorporation revoked.

The Iranians who accept the dominant role of religion refer to themselves as *hezbollahis*. They tend to be fervent both in their profession of religious belief and in their loyalty to the Islamic Republic. Self-identified *hezbollahis* join the numerous mosque-related voluntary associations, the Pasdaran, and the personal staffs of the leading ayatollahs. Given their strong commitment to the regime, it was inevitable that *hezbollahis* would resent those whom they perceived as critical of the government. By 1987, however, it was still not possible, owing to the lack of field research in Iran from the time of the Revolution, to estimate what percent of the adult population considered themselves true *hezbollahis*, what percent was generally indifferent and simply acquiesced to regime policies, or what percent strongly disapproved of the government.

The Mass Media

The Constitution provides for freedom of the press as long as published material accords with Islamic principles. The publisher of every newspaper and periodical is required by law to have a valid publishing license. Any publication perceived as being anti-Islamic is not granted a publication license. In practice, the criteria for being anti-Islamic have been broadly interpreted to encompass all materials that include an antigovernment sentiment. In 1987 all the papers and magazines in circulation supported the basic political institutions of the Islamic Republic.

The major daily newspapers for the country are printed in Tehran. The leading newspapers include *Jumhori-yi Islami, Resalat, Kayhan, Abrar,* and *Etalaat.* The *Tehran Times* and *Kayhan International* are two English-language dailies in Tehran. While all these newspapers are considered to be appropriately Islamic, they do not endorse every program of the central government. For example, *Jumhori-yi Islami,* the official organ of the IRP before its dissolution in 1987, presents the official government line of prime minister Musavi. In contrast, *Resalat* is consistently critical of government policies, especially those related to the economy. The other newspapers criticize various aspects of governmental policies but do not have a consistent position.

No prior censorship of nonfiction exists, but any published book that is considered un-Islamic can be confiscated, and both the author and the publisher are liable for attempting to offend public morals or Islam. Private publishing companies thus tend to restrict their titles to subjects that will not arouse official ire. Numerous new books in history, science, geography, and classical poetry and literature have been published since 1987, including many manuscripts that had been banned under the shah. Although fiction is subject to prior censorship, numerous novels have been published.

All radio and television broadcasting is controlled by the government. Television and radio stations exist in Tehran and the major provincial cities. Stations in Azerbaijan and Kordestan are permitted to broadcast some programs in Azeri Turkish and Kurdish. Several of the banned opposition groups broadcast into Iran from stations in Iraq or the Caucasus republics of the Soviet Union. Both the British Broadcasting Company and the Voice of America broadcast Persian-language news and feature programs to FM radio channels in Iran.

Foreign Policy

Iran's foreign policy was dramatically reversed following the Revolution. After World War II, Iranian leaders considered their country to be part of the Western alliance system. They actively cultivated relations with the United States, both as a means of protecting their country from perceived political pressures emanating from the Soviet Union and as a matter of genuine ideological conviction.

The Revolution, which was laden with anti-American rhetoric, brought new leaders to power who disapproved of Iran's relationship with the United States. The new leaders were convinced that Washington had tried to maintain the shah in power, despite the mass demonstrations calling for his downfall, and were deeply suspicious of American intentions toward their Revolution. These leaders believed that the United States was plotting to restore the shah to power and were unresponsive to persistent efforts by American diplomats to persuade them that the United States had no ill intentions toward the new regime.

The more radical revolutionaries were determined to eradicate all traces of American influence from Iran. Fearing that the provisional government was seeking an accommodation with the United States, some of these radicals precipitated the seizure of the American embassy in November 1979. Subsequently, they exploited the protracted hostage crisis between Tehran and Washington to achieve their objective of terminating normal relations with the United States. The severing of ties with the United States was regarded not only as essential for expunging American influence from the country but also was considered a prerequisite for implementing their revolutionary foreign policy ideology. This new ideology consisted of two concepts: export of revolution and independence from both the East and the West. By the time the hostage

221

crisis was finally resolved in January 1981, these ideas were embraced by the entire political elite.

Concept of Export of Revolution

The concept of exporting the Islamic Revolution derives from a particular worldview that perceives Islamic revolution as the means whereby Muslims and non-Muslims can liberate themselves from the oppression of tyrants who serve the interests of international imperialism. Both the United States and the Soviet Union are perceived as the two principal imperialist powers that exploit Third World countries. A renewed commitment to Islam, as the experience of Iran in overthrowing the shah demonstrated, permits oppressed nations to defeat imperialism. According to this perspective, by following Iran's example any country can free itself from imperialist domination.

Although the political elite agrees upon the desirability of exporting revolution, no unanimity exists on the means of achieving this goal. At one end of the spectrum is the view that propaganda efforts to teach Muslims about the Iranian example is the way to export revolution. Material assistance of any form is not necessary because oppressed people demonstrate their readiness for Islamic revolution by rising against dictatorial governments. Those who subscribe to this line of reasoning argue that Iranians received no external assistance in their Revolution but were successful as a result of their commitment to Islam. Furthermore, they cite Khomeini's often stated dictum that Iran has no intention of interfering in the internal affairs of other countries. This view is compatible with the maintenance of normal diplomatic relations between Iran and other countries.

At the opposite end of the spectrum is the view of Iran as the vanguard of a world revolutionary movement to liberate Muslim countries specifically, and other Third World countries generally, from imperialist subjugation. This activist perspective contends that the effective export of revolution must not be limited to propaganda efforts but must also include both financial and military assistance. Advocates of this view also cite Khomeini to justify their position and frequently quote his statements on the inevitability of the spread of Islamic revolution throughout the world.

Although various viewpoints fall between these two perspectives, since 1979 the two extreme views have been in contention in the formulation of foreign policy. In general, those who advocate exporting revolution solely through education and example have dominated the Ministry of Foreign Affairs, while those who favor active assistance to nonstate revolutionary groups have not served in important government positions relating to foreign policy. Nevertheless, because the supporters of an activist approach include some prominent political leaders, they have been able to exercise influence over certain areas of foreign relations. This has been especially true with respect to policy toward Lebanon and, to a lesser degree, policy in the Persian Gulf (see Relations with Regional Powers, this ch.).

The earliest organization promoting the active export of revolution was Satja, established in the spring of 1979 by Mohammad Montazeri and his close associate, Mehdi Hashemi. Satja's contacts with numerous nonstate groups throughout the Arab Middle East soon brought the organization into direct conflict with both the IRP leadership and the provisional government. Ayatollah Hosain Ali Montazeri, the father of Mohammad Montazeri, rebuked his son publicly, saying his son had been suffering illusions since being tortured by the former shah's secret police. Satja was forced to disband, but Mohammad Montazeri and Hashemi then joined the Pasdaran, where they eventually set up within that organization the Liberation Movements Office. Mohammad Montazeri was subsequently killed in the June 1981 bombing of the IRP headquarters that claimed the lives of over seventy prominent politicians. Following that development, Hashemi emerged as the principal leader of those advocating both moral and material support for revolutionaries around the world.

Under Hashemi's direction, the Liberation Movements Office operated autonomously of the Ministry of Foreign Affairs and maintained contact with opposition movements in several countries. Inevitably, its goal of promoting revolution abroad conflicted with the government's objective of normalizing relations with at least some of the governments that the Liberation Movements Office was helping to overthrow. Control over the direction of foreign policy was eventually resolved in favor of the Ministry of Foreign Affairs. In 1984 the Liberation Movements Office was removed from the jurisdiction of the Pasdaran, and its functions were transferred to the Ministry of Foreign Affairs and Ministry of Information and Security. Dissatisfied with these arrangements, Hashemi resigned from his posts and went to Qom. There he obtained a position within the large bureaucracy of Ayatollah Montazeri, who supervised six seminaries, several charitable organizations, a publishing house, and numerous political offices. Having lost none of his zeal for exporting revolution, Hashemi succeeded in setting up the Office for Global Revolution, which, although nominally part of Montazeri's staff, actually operated independently. By 1986 Hashemi's activities had once again brought him into conflict with

Iran: A Country Study

the Ministry of Foreign Affairs. In October he and several of his
associates were arrested, and the Office for Global Revolution was
closed. During the summer of 1987, Hashemi and some of his colleagues were tried for "deviating from Islam"; Hashemi was found
guilty and subsequently executed.

Concept of Neither East nor West

During the Revolution, Khomeini and his associates condemned
both the United States and the Soviet Union as equally malevo-
lent forces in international politics. They believed the United States,
because of its close relationship with the regime of the shah, was
the superpower that posed the most immediate danger to their revolution. Thus, they referred to the United States as the "Great
Satan," a term that continued to be used in 1987. In contrast, they
regarded the Soviet Union, because it had not been as closely
involved with the shah, as the "Lesser Satan." The United States
represented the West, or capitalism, while the Soviet Union represented the East, or socialism. The revolutionaries embraced
Khomeini's view that these materialist ideologies were ploys to help
maintain imperialist domination of the Third World, and thus they
were inherently inimical to Islam. Consequently, a major foreign
policy goal from the time of the Revolution has been to preclude
all forms of political, economic, and cultural dependence on either
Western capitalism or Eastern socialism and to rely solely upon
Islam.

The most dramatic symbol of the revolutionary determination
to assert independence of both the East and the West was the hostage
crisis between Iran and the United States. Although the seizure
of the American embassy in Tehran in November 1979 initially
had been undertaken by nongovernmental groups to demonstrate
their anger at the admission of the shah into the United States,
this incident rapidly developed into a major international crisis when
Khomeini and the Revolutionary Council gave their ex post facto
sanction to it. The crisis lasted for 444 days, during which time
those political leaders who were most hostile to Western influences
used it to help achieve their aim of severing diplomatic and other
ties between Tehran and Washington.

After 1980 Iran adopted positions opposed to those of the United
States on a wide variety of international issues. Although officials
in both countries eventually approved of some secret contacts, most
notably those involving clandestine arms shipments to Iran from
Israel and the United States during 1985 and 1986, the bitterness
that the hostage crisis left on both sides made it difficult for either
country to consider normalizing relations as late as the end of 1987.

The West European allies of the United States were also viewed with suspicion. France, in particular, was singled out as a "mini-Satan" that collaborated with the United States in the oppression of Muslims. Although initially Iran's political elite were favorably disposed toward France because Paris had provided refuge to Khomeini when he was expelled from Iraq in 1978, relations between the two countries steadily deteriorated after 1980. Two issues were the source of the Iranian hostility: France's support of Iraq, especially its provision of weapons, and the fact that since 1981 France has been the headquarters for most of the expatriate opposition groups. France and Iran also had opposing perspectives on several international issues, most notably developments in Lebanon. In the spring of 1986, the French government initiated a policy of trying to reduce tensions with the Islamic Republic. As part of this effort, France pressured the Mojahedin to close its Paris headquarters and agreed to repay the Iranian government part of a US$1 billion loan that had been extended to a French nuclear energy consortium during the reign of the shah. France was unwilling, however, to accede to Iran's demand that it cease arms sales to Iraq. Consequently, relations between Paris and Tehran vacillated between correctness and tension.

This was dramatically illustrated in July 1987, when the two countries became involved in a major diplomatic confrontation. The Iranian embassy in Paris provided haven to an Iranian national who had been summoned to appear in court in connection with a series of terrorist bombings in the French capital. Although France broke diplomatic relations with Iran over this issue and a series of related incidents, both countries seemed determined to salvage their rapprochement policy. In December France agreed to expel more Iranian Mojahedin activists and to repay Iran a second installment on its outstanding loan, in return for Iranian mediation efforts in obtaining the release of French citizens being held as hostages in Lebanon. Diplomatic relations were restored as of the end of 1987.

Iran's postrevolutionary relations with the Soviet Union and its allies have been significantly less dramatic. Tehran has expressed its opposition to numerous Soviet international policies. For example, Iran severely criticized the Soviet Union for dispatching its troops into Afghanistan at the end of 1979 and took the lead several months later in denouncing Moscow at a conference of foreign ministers of Islamic countries. Soviet support for the Marxist-Leninist regime in Kabul continued to be a source of friction between the two countries in 1987. Soviet support of Iraq, especially the provision of weapons, has been another area of contention between Moscow and Tehran. Iran also has accused the Soviet Union of assisting Iranian opposition groups, especially the Tudeh. Nevertheless, Iran and the Soviet Union have maintained diplomatic relations, and the two countries have striven to keep their relations correct, if not always cordial.

Although Iran remained distrustful of the Soviet Union's international policies, it generally avoided injecting its anti-imperialist ideology into economic relations. Thus, trade with the Soviet Union became relatively important after 1979. This included not only direct trade between Iran and the Soviet Union but also transit trade from Iran through the Soviet Union to markets in Europe. Tensions over economic matters continued, however, particularly over the issue of natural gas shipments to the Caucasus republics via the pipeline that had been constructed before the Revolution. When in 1980 Moscow resisted Tehran's attempt to raise the price charged for this natural gas, the pipeline was closed. In the summer of 1986, the two countries worked out a new agreement but as of December 1987 natural gas shipments had not been resumed.

The Iran-Iraq War

One of the earliest focuses of Iran's interest in exporting revolution was the Persian Gulf area. The revolutionary leaders viewed the Arab countries of the Gulf, along with Iraq, as having tyrannical regimes subservient to one or the other of the superpowers. Throughout the first half of 1980, Radio Iran's increasingly strident verbal attacks on the ruling Baath (Arab Socialist Resurrection) Party of Iraq irritated that government, which feared the impact of Iranian rhetoric upon its own Shias, who constituted a majority of the population. Thus, one of the reasons that prompted Iraqi President Saddam Husayn to launch the invasion of Iran in the early autumn of 1980 was to silence propaganda about Islamic revolution. Baghdad believed that the postrevolutionary turmoil in Iran would permit a relatively quick victory and lead to a new regime in Tehran more willing to accommodate the interests of Iran's Arab neighbors. This hope proved to be a false one for Iraq.

From the point of view of foreign relations, Iran's war with Iraq had evolved through four phases by 1987. During the first phase, from the fall of 1980 until the summer of 1982, Iran was on the defensive, both on the battlefield and internationally. The country was preoccupied with the hostage crisis at the outbreak of the war, and most diplomats perceived its new government as generally ineffective. During the second phase, from 1982 to the end of 1984, the success of Iran's offensives alarmed the Arab states, which were concerned about containing the spread of Iran's Revolution. The third phase, 1985 to 1987, was characterized by Iranian efforts to win diplomatic support for its war aims. The fourth phase began in the spring of 1987 with the involvement of the United States in the Persian Gulf.

The Iraqi invasion and advance into Khuzestan during phase one surprised Iran. The Iraqis captured several villages and small towns in the provinces of Khuzestan and Ilam and, after brutal hand-to-hand combat, captured the strategic port city of Khorramshahr (see The Iran-Iraq War, ch. 5). The nearby city of Abadan, with its huge oil-refining complex, was besieged; Iraqi forces moved their offensive lines close to the large cities of Ahvaz and Dezful. Although the Iranians stemmed the Iraqi advance by the end of 1980, they failed to launch any successful counteroffensives. Consequently, Iraq occupied approximately one-third of Khuzestan Province, from which an estimated 1.5 million civilians had fled. Property damage to factories, homes, and infrastructure in the war zone was estimated in the billions of dollars.

Although the war had settled into a stalemate by the end of 1980, during the following eighteen months Iranian forces made gradual advances and eventually forced most of the Iraqi army to withdraw across the border. During this period, Iran's objectives were to end the war by having both sides withdraw to the common border as it had existed prior to the invasion. Baghdad wanted Tehran's consent to the revision of a 1975 treaty that had defined their common riparian border as the middle channel of the Shatt al Arab (which Iranians call the Arvand Rud). Baghdad's proclaimed reason for invading Iran, in fact, had been to rectify the border; Iraq claimed that the international border should be along the low water of the Iranian shore, as it had been prior to 1975. In international forums, Iran generally failed to win many supporters to its position.

The second phase of the war began in July 1982, when Iran made the fateful decision, following two months of military victories, to invade Iraqi territory. The change in Iran's strategic position also brought about a modification in stated war aims. Khomeini and other leaders began to say that a simple withdrawal of all forces to the pre-September 1980 borders was no longer sufficient. They now demanded, as a precondition for negotiations, that the aggressor be punished. Iran's leaders defined the new terms explicitly: the removal from office of Iraqi president Saddam Husayn and the payment of reparations to Iran for war damages in Khuzestan. The Iranian victories and intransigence on terms for peace coincided with the Israeli invasion of Lebanon; consequently, Iran decided to dispatch a contingent of its own Pasdaran to Lebanon to aid the Shia community there. These developments revived fears of Iranian-induced political instability, especially among the Arab rulers in the Persian Gulf. In 1983 Iraq acquired French-made Exocet missiles, which were used to launch attacks on Iranian oil facilities in the Persian Gulf. Iran retaliated by attacking tankers loaded with Arab oil, claiming that the profits of such oil helped to finance loans and grants to Iraq. Iraq responded by attacking ships loaded with Iranian oil, thus launching what became known as the tanker war.

By the beginning of 1985, the third phase of the war had begun. During this phase, Iran consciously sought to break out of its diplomatic isolation by making overtures to various countries in an effort to win international support for its war objectives. Iran's diplomatic efforts concentrated particularly on the countries of the Arab world. The Iranian initiatives led to significantly improved relations with such countries as Oman and Saudi Arabia.

Iraq responded to Iran's diplomatic initiatives by intensifying its attacks on Iran-related shipping in the Persian Gulf. Iranian retaliation increasingly focused on Kuwaiti shipping. By early 1987, Iran's actions prompted Kuwait to request protection for its shipping from both the Soviet Union and the United States. By the summer of 1987, most European and Arab governments were blaming Iran for the tensions in the Gulf, and Iran again found itself diplomatically isolated.

Relations with Regional Powers

The Persian Gulf States

Although the shah had been unpopular among the rulers of the six states on the Arab side of the Persian Gulf, the Revolution in Iran, nevertheless, was a shock to them. Iran under the shah had been the main guarantor of political stability in the region. Under the Republic, Iran was promising to be the primary promoter of revolution. All six countries—Bahrain, Kuwait, Oman, Qatar, Saudi Arabia, and the United Arab Emirates (UAE)—were ruled by hereditary monarchs who naturally feared the new rhetoric from Tehran. Indeed, during the first year following the Revolution, throughout the Gulf region numerous acts of political sabotage and violence occurred, claiming inspiration from the Iranian example. The most sensational of these was the assault by Muslim dissidents on the Grand Mosque in the holy city of Mecca, Saudi Arabia. Other clashes occurred between groups of local Shias and security forces in Saudi Arabia, Kuwait, and Bahrain.

The outbreak of war between Iran and Iraq further alarmed the Persian Gulf Arab states. In 1981 they joined together in a collective

*Foreign Minister Ali Akbar Velayati addressing
the United Nations General Assembly in 1982
Courtesy United Nations*

defense alliance known as the Gulf Cooperation Council (GCC). Although the GCC announced its neutrality with respect to the Iran-Iraq War, Iran perceived its formation as part of the Iraqi war effort and generally was hostile toward it. The GCC for its part suspected Iran of supporting antigovernment groups throughout the Persian Gulf. These concerns were heightened in December 1981, when authorities in Bahrain announced the discovery of a clandestine group that had plans to carry out sabotage and terrorist acts as part of an effort to overthrow the government; several of the plotters had links to Iranian clerics. In December 1983, a series of bombings occurred in Kuwait, including incidents at the American and French embassies; the Arab nationals who were captured and charged with these acts of terrorism were members of an Iraqi Shia movement, Ad Dawah, that was headquartered in Tehran. In May 1985, a suicide driver unsuccessfully tried to kill the ruler of Kuwait.

Despite GCC suspicions of Iranian involvement in subversive activities, until 1987 more cooperation than confrontation was found between Iran and the GCC members. In general, Iran avoided dealing with the GCC as an entity, preferring to ignore its existence and to treat each country separately. Iran's relations with the six component states varied from friendliness to hostility. For

229

example, Iran and the UAE maintained relatively cordial relations. The political ties between the two countries were reinforced by economic ties. An Iranian mercantile community in the UAE was concentrated in Dubayy, a city that emerged—following the destruction of Khorramshahr—as an important transit center where international goods destined for Iran were offloaded into smaller boats capable of entering small Iranian fishing towns that served as ports of entry despite their lack of docking facilities. In Bahrain, where the ruling family was Sunni Muslim and a majority of the population was Shia, lingering suspicions of Iranian intentions did not inhibit the government from improving diplomatic relations with Tehran. Because there were no outstanding issues between Iran and Qatar, relations between them were generally correct.

Iran's relations with the other three GCC members—Kuwait, Oman, and Saudi Arabia—have been more complex and, throughout the early and mid-1980s, have been characterized by alternating periods of tension and mutual accommodation. For example, immediately after the Revolution, Iranian propaganda singled out the sultan of Oman as an example of the kind of "un-Islamic tyrant" who should be overthrown. This hostility sprang from the revolutionaries' perception of the Omani ruler as having been a close friend of the shah. Iran's view had developed in the 1970s when the shah sent military assistance, including an Iranian military contingent, to help the sultan crush a long-term rebellion. More significant, however, the Iranian leaders regarded the sultan as subservient to the United States. They denounced his policies of supporting the Camp David Accords, providing facilities for American air crews who attempted the unsuccessful rescue of the hostages in April 1980, signing an agreement for American military use of the air base on Masirah Island, and discussing with the United States construction of an airfield on the Musandam Peninsula overlooking the Strait of Hormuz. Oman generally refrained from responding to Iranian charges and consequently avoided an escalation of the verbal barrages. Despite the many areas of friction, tensions between Iran and Oman gradually abated after 1981. The movement toward more correct diplomatic relations culminated in 1987 with a state visit of the Omani foreign minister to Iran.

Iran's relations with Saudi Arabia and Kuwait were strained because both of these countries provided major financial support to Iraq after the Iran-Iraq War began. In addition, Iran accused them of providing logistical assistance for Iraqi bombing raids on Iranian oil installations. For their part, Saudi Arabia and Kuwait believed that Iran supported subversive activities among their Shia minorities. They also resented Iranian attacks on their shipping.

Saudi Arabia annually confronted embarrassing incidents during the pilgrimage season when Iranians tried to stage political demonstrations. Nevertheless, both Saudi Arabia and Kuwait made efforts to seek a rapprochement with Iran in 1985 and 1986. The Saudi efforts were more successful and resulted in an exchange of visits of the Saudi and Iranian foreign ministers in 1985. The Saudis and Iranians also began to cooperate in some areas of mutual interest, such as international oil policy. In contrast, relations between Kuwait and Iran did not improve significantly. In the fall of 1986, Iran began to single out Kuwait's ships for retaliatory attacks, and this led to a worsening of diplomatic relations.

Political tensions between Tehran and Kuwait increased significantly after the United States agreed to reflag Kuwaiti oil tankers. Iran accused Kuwait and its neighbors, especially Saudi Arabia, of being mere puppets of the "Great Satan." During the pilgrimage to Mecca in the summer of 1987, Iran encouraged the pilgrims—150,000 of whom had come from Iran—to demonstrate against the United States and the corrupt rulers of the Gulf. More than 400 pilgrims, including at least 300 Iranians, were killed in a stampede in Mecca when Saudi security forces attempted to break up a demonstration.

Turkey, Pakistan, and Afghanistan

Relations with Turkey and Pakistan since the Revolution generally have been amicable and without any major issues. Before the Revolution, Iran had joined both countries in a defensive alliance (that included Britain with the United States as an observer), the Central Treaty Organization, and in an economic agreement, the Regional Cooperation for Development. Iran withdrew from both agreements after the Revolution. Nevertheless, Iran's economic ties with Pakistan and Turkey have expanded significantly. Both countries have become important trade partners of Iran. Turkey also has become the major transit route for goods traveling by truck and rail between Europe and Iran. The increased volume of trade with Turkey and Pakistan has been facilitated both by their location and by the ideology of "neither East nor West," which advocates reducing imports from the industrialized nations in favor of importing more from Muslim and Third World countries.

Although Iran maintained diplomatic relations with Afghanistan in 1987, Iran was critical of both the Marxist-Leninist government in Kabul and the presence of Soviet troops in the country. Although distrustful of the ideologies of most groups, Iran's leaders generally supported the cause of the Afghan resistance. Iran provided financial and limited military assistance to those Afghan resistance forces whose leaders had pledged loyalty to the Iranian vision of Islamic revolution. Iran also hosted about 2.3 million refugees who had fled Afghanistan.

Israel and the Non-Gulf Arab States

Prior to the Revolution, Iran and Israel had been de facto allies in the Middle East. One of the very first acts of the provisional government was to denounce that relationship and to turn over the former Israeli mission in Tehran to the Palestine Liberation Organization. All trade with Israel was banned, especially the sale of oil. Iranian leaders contended that Israel's existence was illegitimate, because it came about as a result of the destruction of Palestine. Therefore, Iran advocated eradicating Israel and reconstituting Palestine. Those Arabs who advocated compromise with Israel, such as Anwar as Sadat of Egypt, were excoriated as traitors. In general, Iran's relations with the Arab states have been based on perceptions of each state's relations with Israel. Thus, Iran has been hostile toward those states it regarded as willing to accept Israel's existence—Egypt, Jordan, Morocco, and Tunisia—and friendly toward those it regarded as sharing Iranian views—Algeria, Libya, and Syria. Despite its uncompromising position, however, Iran is known to have purchased weapons clandestinely from Israel as recently as 1985.

Syria has been revolutionary Iran's principal ally in the Middle East. This relationship involved both political and economic ties. The de facto alliance between the two countries emerged at the beginning of 1982. At that time, Iran supported the government of Hafiz al Assad against the Muslim Brotherhood, which had risen in rebellion against the secularizing policies of the ruling Baath Party. Iran's backing of the Syrian government was significant because the Muslim Brotherhood was the first Islamic political group to claim the Iranian Revolution as the primary inspiration for its rebellion. Soon after the Muslim Brotherhood had been crushed, Damascus shut down the pipeline through which Iraqi oil crossed Syria to reach Mediterranean ports. This action against another Arab state, which also was ruled by a Baath party, was an important gesture in support of the Iranian war effort. The action was also a hostile blow against Iraq because Iraqi Persian Gulf ports had been blockaded since the beginning of the war, and the only other exit route for its oil exports was through a smaller pipeline traversing Turkey. Iran had agreed to provide Syria 20,000 barrels of oil per day free of charge as compensation for the transit fees Syria would lose by closing the pipeline. Iran also agreed to sell Syria additional oil it required, at a heavily discounted price.

In 1987 this agreement was again renewed. Syria also provided Iran arms from its own stock of Soviet- and East European-made weapons.

Iran's Role in Lebanon

The Shia clergy in Iran have long had an interest in the Shia population of Lebanon. Clergy for the Lebanese Shia communities were trained in Iran before the Revolution, and intermarriage between clerical families in both countries had been occurring for several generations. Lebanon's most prominent Shia cleric, Imam Musa as Sadr, who mysteriously disappeared in 1978 while on a trip to Libya, was born in Iran into a clerical family with relatives in Lebanon, a fact that facilitated his acceptance in the latter country. Musa as Sadr was a political activist, like so many clerics of his generation trained in Qom and An Najaf, and he succeeded in politicizing the Lebanese Shias. Thus, it was natural that the Shia community of Lebanon should become one of the earliest to which Iranian advocates of exporting revolution turned their attention. Their analysis of the political situation in Lebanon in 1979 and 1980 convinced them that the country was ripe for achieving an Islamic revolution and that conditions were also favorable for eradicating Israel and recreating Palestine.

The main constraint on Iran's political involvement in Lebanon was Amal, the political organization established by Musa as Sadr. After Sadr's disappearance, Amal had fallen under the influence of secularized Shias who preferred the political integration of the Shia community within a pluralistic state and regarded the Iranian vision of Islamic revolution as inappropriate for Lebanon. The Israeli invasion of southern Lebanon in 1982, however, provided Iran an opportunity to circumvent Amal's domination of the Shias. Syria permitted a contingent of several hundred Pasdaran members to enter Lebanon, ostensibly to help fight against Israel. The Pasdaran established posts in the eastern Biqa Valley and from there proselytized on behalf of Islamic revolution among poor and uprooted Shia young people. The ideas of Islamic revolution appealed to many of the Shias who were recruited by new political groups such as Islamic Amal and the Hizballah, both of which opposed the comparative moderation of Amal. The support of the Pasdaran provided these groups with a direct link to Tehran, and this permitted Iran to become one of the foreign powers exerting influence in Lebanon. In 1987 an estimated 500 members of the Pasdaran were in Lebanon.

Iran and International Organizations

Iran is a charter member of the United Nations (UN). Although it belongs to all UN specialized agencies, the Republic has not participated as actively as the monarchy in the world organization. Iran criticized the UN for nonsupport during the Iran-United States crisis over the hostages. Iran also criticized the UN for failing to condemn Iraq as an "aggressor" following the Iraqi invasion of Iran in 1980.

As a major oil producer and exporter, Iran is a founding member of the Organization of Petroleum Exporting Countries (OPEC—see Glossary). Both under the monarchy and under the Republic the government has advocated that OPEC maintain high prices for the oil that members sell on the international market. Iran supported lower production quotas for members as a means of keeping international oil prices high. Between 1979 and 1985, Iran generally was regarded as uncooperative at the semi-annual OPEC ministerial conferences. Since 1985, however, Iran has worked with Saudi Arabia, the largest oil producer within OPEC, to draft production and pricing compromises acceptable to the whole OPEC membership.

*   *   *

The most detailed examination of the government of Iran during the first four years following the Revolution is Shaul Bakhash's *The Reign of the Ayatollahs.* Considerable detail about various policies pursued by the government can be found in Dilip Hiro's *Iran under the Ayatollahs.* A collection of essays that analyze the role of the clergy in politics, the postrevolutionary economy, the aspects of the "new" Islamic ideology, the opposition, and Iran's relations with the superpowers is found in *The Iranian Revolution and the Islamic Republic,* edited by Nikki Keddie and Eric Hooglund. *Revolutionary Iran* by Ruhollah Ramazani examines Iran's foreign policy in the Middle East since 1979. (For further information and complete citations, see Bibliography.)

Chapter 5. National Security

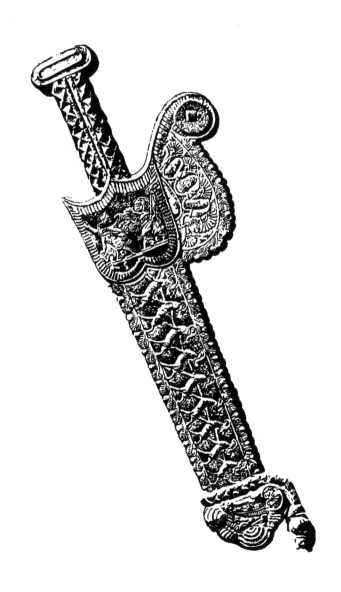

A sword and scabbard from a bas-relief at Persepolis, ca. 500 B.C.

DURING THE 1970s, imperial Iran developed one of the most impressive military forces in the Middle East, and it used those forces to assume a security role in the Persian Gulf after the British military withdrawal in 1971. The defense of the strategic Strait of Hormuz preoccupied the shah, as it did the other conservative monarchs in the area. Freedom of navigation in the Gulf was important for international shipping, and the shah was perceived, at least in certain quarters, as the undeclared "policeman of the West in the Gulf." When independent observers concluded that Iran's military buildup exceeded its defensive needs, the shah declared that his responsibilities extended beyond Iran and included the protection of the Gulf. Increasingly, the military played a pivotal role in promoting this policy and, in doing so, gained a privileged position in society. Under the Nixon Doctrine of 1969, according to which aiding local armed forces was considered preferable to direct United States military intervention, Washington played an important part in upgrading the Iranian military forces. The United States supplied Iran with sophisticated hardware and sent thousands of military advisers and technicians to help Iran absorb the technology.

By 1979 the United States military presence in Iran had drawn the wrath of Iranians. Ayatollah Sayyid Ruhollah Musavi Khomeini specifically identified the shah's pro-American policies as detrimental to Iranian interests and called on his supporters to oppose the United States presence. He cited special legal privileges granted United States personnel in Iran as an example of the shah's excessive identification of Iran's interests with those of Washington.

Following the Islamic Revolution of 1979, the armed forces underwent fundamental changes. The revolutionary government purged high-ranking officials as well as many mid-ranking officers identified with the Pahlavi regime and created a loyal military force, the Pasdaran (Pasdaran-e Enghelab-e Islami, or Islamic Revolutionary Guard Corps, or Revolutionary Guards), whose purpose was to defend the Revolution. When the Iran-Iraq War began, however, the revolutionary government had to acknowledge its need for the professional services of many of the purged officers to lead the armed forces in defending the country against Iraq. The army was unexpectedly successful in the war, even though, as of 1987, the regular armed forces continued to be regarded with considerable suspicion. Within the Iranian military there was competition between the regular and irregular armed forces. The Islamic clergy (see Glossary) continued to rely more heavily on the loyal Pasdaran to defend the regime. Moreover, most of the casualties were members of the Pasdaran and Basij volunteers who composed the irregular armed forces. In the late 1980s, in addition to defending the Revolution, Iran continued to follow certain national security policies that had remained constant during the previous four decades.

Armed Forces

Historical Background

The importance of the armed forces in Iran flows from Iran's long history of successive military empires. For over 2,500 years, starting with the conquests of the Achaemenid rulers of the sixth century B.C., Iran developed a strong military tradition. Drawing on a vast manpower pool in western Asia, the Achaemenid rulers raised an army of 360,000, from which they could send expeditions to Europe and Africa.

Iranian early military history boasts the epic performances of such great leaders as Cyrus the Great and Darius I. The last great Iranian military ruler was Nader Shah, whose army defeated the Mughals of India in 1739. Since then, however, nearly all efforts to conquer more territory or check encroaching empires have failed. During much of the nineteenth and early twentieth centuries, Iran was divided and occupied by British and Russian military forces. When their interests coincided in 1907, London and St. Petersburg entered into the Anglo-Russian Agreement, which formally divided Iran into two spheres of influence. During World War I, the weak and ineffective Qajar Dynasty, allegedly hindered by the effects of the Constitutional Revolution of 1905–1907, could not prevent increasing British and Russian military interventions, despite Iran's declaration of neutrality (see World War I, ch. 1).

In 1918 the Qajar armed forces consisted of four separate foreign-commanded military units. Several provincial and tribal forces could also be called on during an emergency, but their reliability was highly questionable. More often than not, provincial and tribal forces opposed the government's centralization efforts, particularly because Tehran was perceived to be under the dictate of foreign powers. Having foreign officers in commanding positions over Iranian troops added to these tribal and religious concerns. Loyal, disciplined, and well trained, the most effective government unit was the 8,000-man Persian Cossacks Brigade. Created in 1879 and commanded by Russian officers until the 1917 Bolshevik Revolution, after which its command passed into Iranian hands, the brigade represented the core of the new Iranian armed forces.

Swedish officers commanded the 8,400-man Gendarmerie (later the Imperial Gendarmerie and after 1979 the Islamic Iranian Gendarmerie), organized in 1911 as the first internal security force. The 6,000-man South Persia Rifles unit was financed by Britain and commanded by British officers from its inception in 1916. Its primary task was to combat tribal forces allegedly stirred up by German agents during World War I. The Qajar palace guard, the Nizam, commanded by a Swedish officer, was a force originally consisting of 2,000 men, although it deteriorated rapidly in numbers because of rivalries. Thus, during World War I the 24,400 troops in these four separate military units made up one of the weakest forces in Iranian history.

Upon signing the Treaty of Brest-Litovsk with Germany and Turkey on December 15, 1917, Russia put in motion its eventual withdrawal from Iran, preparing the way for an indigenous Iranian military. A hitherto little-known colonel, Reza Khan (later known as Reza Shah Pahlavi, founder of the Pahlavi dynasty), assumed leadership of the Persian Cossacks Brigade in November 1918, after the expulsion of its Russian commanders. In February 1921, Reza Khan and Sayyid Zia ad Din Tabatabai, a powerful civilian conspirator, entered Tehran at the head of 1,500 to 2,500 Persian Cossacks and overthrew the Qajar regime. Within a week, Tabatabai formed a new government and made Reza Khan the army chief. Recognizing the importance of a strong and unified army for the modern state, Reza Khan rapidly dissolved all "independent" military units and prepared to create a single national army for the first time in Iranian history.

Riding on a strong nationalist wave, Reza Khan was determined to create an indigenous officer corps for the new army, though an exception was made for a few Swedish officers serving in the Gendarmerie. Within a matter of months, officers drawn from the Persian Cossacks represented the majority. Nevertheless, Reza Khan recognized the need for Western military expertise and sent Iranian officers to European military academies, particularly St. Cyr in France, to acquire modern technical know-how. In doing so, he hoped the Iranian army would increase its professionalism without jeopardizing the country's still fragile social, political, and religious balance.

By 1925 the army had grown to a force of 40,000 troops, and Reza Khan, under the provisions of martial law, had gradually assumed control of the central government. His most significant political accomplishment came in 1925 when the parliament, or Majlis (see Glossary), enacted a universal military conscription law. In December 1925, Reza Khan became the commander in chief of the army; with the assistance of the Majlis, he assumed the title of His Imperial Majesty Reza Shah Pahlavi (see The Era of Reza Shah, 1921–41, ch. 1).

Reza Khan created the Iranian army, and the army made him shah. Under the shah, the powerful army was used not only against rebellious tribes but also against anti-Pahlavi demonstrations. Ostensibly created to defend the country from foreign aggression, the army became the enforcer of Reza Shah's internal security policies. The need for such a military arm of the central government was quite evident to Reza Shah, who allocated anywhere from 30 to 50 percent of total yearly national expenditures to the army. Not only did he purchase modern weapons in large quantities, but, in 1924 and 1927, respectively, he created an air force and a navy as branches of the army, an arrangement unchanged until 1955. With the introduction of these new services, the army established two military academies to meet the ever-rising demand for officers. The majority of the officers continued to be trained in Europe, however, and upon their return served either in the army or in key government posts in Tehran and the provinces. By 1941 the army had gained a privileged role in society. Loyal officers and troops were well paid and received numerous perquisites, making them Iran's third wealthiest class, after the shah's entourage and the powerful merchant and landowning families. Disloyalty to the shah, evidenced by several coup attempts, was punished harshly.

By 1941 the army stood at 125,000 troops—five times its original size—and was considered well trained and well equipped. Yet, when the army faced its first challenge, the shah was sorely disappointed; the Iranian army failed to repulse invading British and Soviet forces. London and Moscow had insisted that the shah expel Iran's large German population and allow shipments of war supplies to cross the country en route to the Soviet Union. Both of these conditions proved unacceptable to Reza Shah; he was sympathetic to Germany, and Iran had declared its neutrality in World War II. Iran's location was so strategically important to the Allied war effort, however, that London and Moscow chose to overlook Tehran's claim of neutrality. Against the Allied forces, the Iranian army was decimated in three short days, the fledgling air force and navy were totally destroyed, and conscripts deserted by the thousands. His institutional power base ruined, Reza Shah abdicated in favor of his young son, Mohammad Reza Shah Pahlavi.

In the absence of a broad political power base and with a shattered army, Mohammad Reza Shah faced an almost impossible task of rebuilding. There was no popular sympathy for the army in view of the widespread and largely accurate perception that it was a brutal tool used to uphold a dictatorial regime. The young shah, distancing Tehran from the European military, in 1942 invited the United States to send a military mission to advise in the reorganization effort. With American advice, emphasis was placed on quality rather than quantity; the small but more confident army was capable enough to participate in the 1946 campaign in Azarbaijan to put down a Soviet-inspired separatist rebellion (see World War II and the Azarbaijan Crisis, ch. 1).

Unlike its 1925 counterpart, the 1946 Majlis was suspicious of the shah's plans for a strong army. Many members of the parliament feared that the army would once again be used as a source of political power. To curtail the shah's potential domination of the country, they limited his military budgets.

Although determined to build an effective military establishment, the shah was forced to accept the ever-rising managerial control of the Majlis. Prime Minister Mohammad Mossadeq, backed by strong Majlis support, demanded and received the portfolio of minister of war in 1952. For the better part of a year, Mossadeq introduced changes in the high command, dismissing officers loyal to the shah and replacing them with pro-Mossadeq nationalists. With the assistance of British and United States intelligence, however, officers dismissed by Mossadeq staged the August 1953 coup d'état, which overthrew the prime minister and returned the shah to power (see Mossadeq and Oil Nationalization, ch. 1).

In a classic housecleaning, several hundred pro-Mossadeq officers were arrested, allegedly for membership in the communist Tudeh Party. Approximately two dozen were executed, largely to set an example and to demonstrate to the public that the shah was firmly in command. Within two years, the shah had consolidated his rule over the armed forces, as well as over the much-weakened Majlis. Separate commands were established for the army, air force, and navy; and all three branches of the military embarked on massive modernization programs, which flourished throughout the 1960s and 1970s.

Nonetheless, the shah's military was probably crippled as early as 1955. Mohammad Reza Shah, mistrustful of his subordinates as well as his close advisers, instituted an unparalleled system of control over all his officers. Not only did the monarch make all decisions pertaining to purchasing, promotions, and routine military affairs, but he also permitted little interaction among junior and senior officers. Even less was tolerated among senior officers. No meetings grouping all his top officers in the same room were ever held. Rather, the shah favored individual "audiences" with each service chief; he then delegated assignments and duties according to his overall plans. This approach proved effective for the shah, at least until his downfall in 1979. For the Iranian armed forces, it proved devastating.

As internal security agencies assumed the critical role of maintaining public order, the Imperial Iranian Armed Forces (IIAF) were charged with defending the country against foreign aggression. First among threats was the Soviet Union, which shares a 2,000-kilometer border with Iran. The shah feared that Moscow would try to gain access to warm-water port facilities, a Russian goal since Peter the Great, and seek to destabilize what the Soviets surely perceived to be a pro-Western, if not pro-American, regime. The majority of Iranian troops, therefore, were stationed in the north for the better part of the early 1960s. The resulting high level of tension between two mismatched neighboring forces was not a satisfactory arrangement for the politically and militarily astute monarch. Taking a pragmatic approach, the shah pursued economic cooperation to improve relations with the Soviet Union and thereby reduced military tensions along the border. Having softened Iran's Cold War rhetoric in relation to Moscow, the shah focused his attention on the Persian Gulf. When in 1971 Britain terminated its treaties of protection with the several small Arab shaykhdoms or amirates of the Arabian Peninsula, the shah's primary security concerns shifted to the border with Iraq.

When petroleum exports from the Gulf expanded rapidly in the 1970s and British withdrawal from the conservative shaykhdoms created a security vacuum, the Iranian military expanded its plans to include the defense of sea-lanes, especially the Strait of Hormuz, although navigation through the strait generally takes place entirely in Oman's territorial waters. Iran has always considered the forty-one-kilometer-wide strait vital to its oil exports and, since 1968, has made every effort to exert as much influence as possible there. The shah referred to the strait as Iran's "jugular vein," and the revolutionary regime has been similarly concerned with its security (see fig. 10).

In March 1975, Iran reached a geographic-political agreement with Iraq. This pact, called the Algiers Agreement, accomplished two important military objectives. First, because the existence of the agreement allowed Iran to terminate aid to the Kurdish rebels in Iraq, Iran could deploy more of its forces in areas other than the Iraqi border. Second, Baghdad's acceptance of Iran's boundary claim to a thalweg (the middle of the main navigable channel) in the Shatt al Arab settled a security issue, freeing the Iranian navy to shift its major facilities from Khorramshahr on the Iraqi border to Bandar-e Abbas near the strait and to upgrade its naval forces in the southern part of the Gulf.

Despite frequent public expressions of reserve, the weaker conservative Arab monarchies of the Persian Gulf supported the shah's military mission of guaranteeing freedom of navigation in and through the Gulf. They strongly objected, however, to Iran's military occupation in November 1971 of the islands of Abu Musa, belonging to Sharjah, and the Greater and Lesser Tunbs, belonging to Ras al Khaymah. These two members of the United Arab Emirates could offer no resistance to Tehran's swift military action, however. The Iranian navy used its Hovercraft to transport occupying troops, and it eventually installed military facilities on two of the islands. Despite its earlier agreement to respect Sharjah's claim to Abu Musa, Tehran justified the occupation of Abu Musa and the Tunbs on strategic grounds. Located near the strait between the deepest navigation lanes, the islands offered ideal bases from which to watch over shipping in the Gulf.

This action was only the precursor of other regional operations by which a strong Iranian military would deter foreign, especially Soviet or Soviet-inspired, incursions into the Gulf. Twice, during the 1970s, the shah provided military assistance—to Oman and Pakistan—to overcome internal rebellions. By doing so, he established Iran as the dominant regional military power.

The most significant combat operation involving Iranian (along with British and Jordanian) troops took place in Oman's Dhofar Province. Iran aided Sultan Qabus in fighting the Popular Front for the Liberation of Oman, which was supported by the People's Democratic Republic of Yemen (South Yemen) and the Soviet Union. Starting with an initial force of 300 in late 1972, the Iranian contingent grew in strength to 3,000 before its withdrawal in January 1977. The shah was proud that his forces had participated in the defeat of the guerrilla rebellion, even though the performance of Iranian troops in Oman was mixed. The air force received the most favorable reports from the battle zone. Reconnaissance flights provided valuable information, and helicopters proved effective in the rugged Dhofar region. Ground forces fared less well, suffering significant casualties, with 210 Iranian soldiers killed in 1976 alone. The high casualty rate was attributed to the overall lack of combat experience. Nearly 15,000 Iranian soldiers were rotated through Oman during the five-year period.

In 1976 Iranian counterinsurgency forces, relying on helicopter support, were deployed in Pakistan's Baluchistan Province to combat another separatist rebellion. This operation, albeit small and limited, was of considerable concern to Iran, which had a large

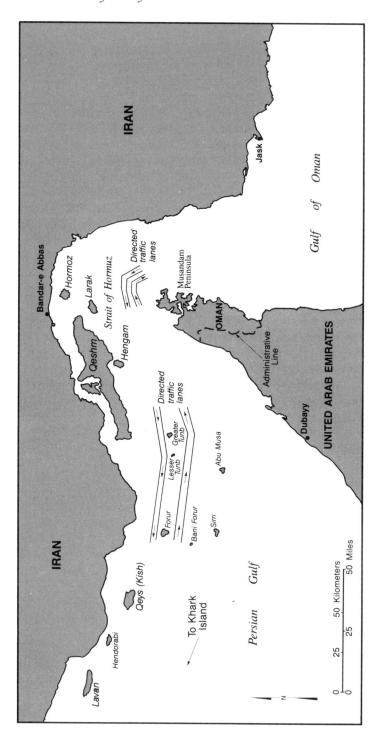

Figure 10. Strait of Hormuz and Vicinity

Baluch population of its own. The shah sought to buy insurance against a possible insurrection in Iran by helping Pakistan crush a Baluch uprising.

The shah continued to assist his allies in Oman and Pakistan after 1977. More important, Iran had served notice that it would engage its military to preserve the status quo in the Persian Gulf region, a status quo that was heavily tilted to its advantage. On more than one occasion, the shah stated that he would not refrain from maintaining the security of the Gulf, whether or not his troops were invited to intervene.

Iran had also come of age in the larger context of the Middle East. Between 1958 and 1978 Iran participated in war games conducted under the auspices of the Central Treaty Organization (CENTO), which grouped Turkey, Iran, Pakistan, and Britain (with the United States participating as an observer). Although CENTO declined in significance over the years, its military exercises, especially the yearly Midlink maritime maneuvers, provided useful training for the Iranian armed forces. The shah also participated in United Nations (UN) peacekeeping missions, sending a battalion to the UN buffer zone in the Golan Heights as part of the United Nations Disengagement Observer Force in 1977. The bulk of this force also served in southern Lebanon following the Israeli invasion of 1978. The Iranian contingent in the United Nations Interim Force in Lebanon was withdrawn in late 1978, however, following several desertions by Shia Muslim soldiers sympathetic to the local population.

On January 16, 1979, as the shah was preparing to leave Iran for the last time, he was still confident that his army could and would handle any internal disturbances. Still under the impression that the Soviet Union and Iraq were the greatest threats to his country, he left behind a United States-designed army prepared for external rather than domestic requirements.

The Revolutionary Period

Lack of leadership at the general staff level and below in the Imperial Iranian Armed Forces (IIAF) had literally frozen the military between December 1978 and February 1979. In the melee of the Revolution, mob scenes were frequent; on several occasions the army fired on demonstrators, killing and injuring many civilians, the most famous such encounter occurring at Jaleh Square in Tehran. In response to these incidents, army units of the IIAF, responsible for law and order in Tehran and other large cities, were attacked by mobs. Within days after the Revolution's success, several religious leaders, however, claimed that the armed forces had "joined the nation" or "returned to the nation" and cautioned against indiscriminate vengeance against the military.

The government took prompt steps to reconstitute the armed forces, weakened in both numbers and morale. Contrary to the general perception in 1979 and 1980, Khomeini did not seek the disintegration of the armed forces but rather wished to remold the shah's army into a loyal national Islamic force. Troops that had heeded Khomeini's appeal to disband were called back in March 1979. A new command group established in February 1979 was composed of nine officers with impeccable revolutionary credentials: they had all been imprisoned under the shah for different reasons. Khomeini relied on the advice of Colonel Nasrollah Tavakkoli, a retired Special Forces officer, to recruit ideologically compatible officers for the armed forces. General staff personnel were all called back to coordinate the nascent reorganization; division and brigade command positions were promptly filled by loyal and reliable officers. The Imperial Guard, the Javidan Guard, and the Military Household of the shah were the only organizations that were permanently disbanded.

The revolutionary government decided to formulate as clearly as possible the functions and roles of the armed forces, particularly in relation to internal security. In contrast to the shah's regime, it entrusted internal security functions to the newly established Pasdaran. Pasdaran clergy were also engaged to disseminate Islamic justice and were assigned to units of the armed forces to help communicate Khomeini's instructions and to provide religio-political indoctrination.

Much of this early cooperation was an extension of the military's existing support for the Revolution. For example, even though the head of the air force, General Amir Hosain Rabii, opposed the Revolution, many air force cadets and young *homafars* (skilled military technical personnel) supported it. Revolutionary groups that had played prominent roles in the seizure of power, however, were hostile to the military. These included the Mojahedin (Mojahedin-e Khalq, or People's Struggle), the Fadayan (Cherikha-ye Fadayan-e Khalq, or People's Guerrillas), and even the Tudeh, which called for a drastic purge of the military. The Mojahedin, especially, threatened the military's position because it had captured the Tehran arms factory and government arsenal depots and was thus armed. Moreover, the Mojahedin quickly organized into "councils" and recruited personnel in military posts throughout the country, seeing themselves as the military core of the new order. These councils were then turned into debating forums where conscripts could air past grievances against officers. The Tudeh, for its part, called on the government to return to active duty several hundred officers dismissed or imprisoned under the shah for their membership in the Tudeh.

The provisional government recognized the threat implicit in these demands. In the absence of a centralized command system, the military balance of power would eventually tilt toward the heavily armed guerrilla groups of the left. Hojjatoleslam Ali Khamenehi (who became president of Iran in 1981) and many of the leading ayatollahs were very suspicious of the leftist guerrillas. The members of the Revolutionary Council (a body formed by Khomeini in January 1979 to supervise the transition from monarchy to republic) would have preferred to balance the power of the leftist guerrillas with that of the Pasdaran, but the Pasdaran was in its formative stage and had neither the necessary strength nor the training.

The ultimate elimination of the Mojahedin, Fadayan, and Tudeh was a foregone conclusion in the ideological framework of an Islamic Iran. To this end, revolutionary leaders both defended and courted the military, hoping to maintain it as a countervailing force, loyal to themselves. In one of his frequent public pronouncements, Khomeini praised military service as "a sacred duty and worthy of great rewards before the Almighty" and solicited military support for his regime, declaring that "the great Iranian Revolution is more in need of defense and protection than at any other time." Prime Minister Mehdi Bazargan denounced guerrilla demands for a full-scale purge of the military.

In the end, the leadership decided in February 1979 that a purge of the armed forces would be undertaken, but on a limited scale, concentrating on "corrupt elements." The purge of the military started on February 15, 1979, when four general officers were executed. Two groups were purged, one consisting of those elements of the armed forces that had been closely identified with the shah and his repression of the revolutionary movement and the other including those that had committed actual crimes of violence, particularly murder and torture, against supporters of the Revolution. A total of 249 members of the armed forces, of whom 61 were SAVAK (Sazman-e Ettelaat va Amniyat-e Keshvar, the shah's internal security organization) agents, were tried, found guilty, and executed between February 19 and September 30, 1979. Significant as this figure is, it represented only a small percentage of military personnel.

Apart from the replacement of senior officers, various structural changes were introduced in the aftermath of the Revolution (see Command and Control; and Organization, Size, and Equipment, this ch.). But because of the lack of leadership at headquarters, command and control were at best tenuous. Local commanders exercised unprecedented autonomy, and integration of the regular armed forces with the Pasdaran was not even considered. Lack of coordination within the Pasdaran and between it and regular army personnel resulted in shortages for the Pasdaran of desperately needed supplies, ranging from daily rations to ammunition; such supplies usually found their way only to army depots.

In isolated areas, cooperation between the Pasdaran and the regular military eventually emerged. For example, in West Azarbaijan, prorevolutionary officers in the 64th Infantry Division in Urumiyeh (also cited as Urmia to which it has reverted after being known as Rezaiyeh under the Pahlavis) extended a helping hand to the Pasdaran in the latter's efforts to crush an uprising. The 64th Infantry Division's leading officers, including Colonel Qasem Ali Zahirnezhad and Colonel Ali Seyyed-Shirazi, were strong advocates of cooperation. They made proposals in which they argued that the Pasdaran and the regular military should be completely integrated at the operational level while maintaining separate administrations. They envisaged joint staffs at divisional and higher echelons, joint logistical systems, and joint procurement of equipment. By accepting logistical assistance from the military, the Pasdaran could become combat ready. From the regular armed forces' perspective, cooperation would turn members of the Pasdaran into professional soldiers. The process would also create a level of mutual dependence, thereby preventing antimilitary measures. Airings of proposals for similar cooperative measures received sympathy from some officers at the National Military Academy, where Commandant Colonel Musa Namju, expanding on Colonel Zahirnezhad's and Colonel Seyyed-Shirazi's earlier proposals, wrote several widely read documents. Little or no support came from Minister of Defense Mostofa Ali Chamran, who was more concerned with the impact that a full and rapid reorganization of the military might have on the Revolution.

Neglected for over a year, Iran's ground forces fared poorly during the first stages of the Iran-Iraq War (see The Iran-Iraq War, this ch.). Ironically, logistical shortcomings rather than desertions or combat defects were the problem. By the end of 1980, Iranian leaders finally recognized supply deficiencies and the more important command and control problems that were crippling the military. Colonel Namju resurrected the group proposals, and Chamran appointed Colonel Zahirnezhad and Colonel Seyyed-Shirazi to senior command and staff positions at the front.

In Tehran, President Abolhasan Bani Sadr attempted to gain control of the armed forces but failed for several reasons. Above all, Khomeini would not permit the Supreme Defense Council (SDC) to be dominated by any faction, and he was not prepared to make an exception for Bani Sadr. Prime Minister Mohammad Ali Rajai, Bazargan's successor, and his Islamic Republican Party (IRP) allies, concerned with the Revolution as much as the war, were adamant in their opposition to Bani Sadr's unilateral decisions. Bani Sadr was also weakened by his frequent interference in purely military affairs (in which his poor judgment in military matters became evident) as well as by competition with clergy members.

Despite the rift between Bani Sadr and the IRP, the SDC appointed him supreme commander over all regular and paramilitary units. His control of the military was tenuous, however, because by early 1981 IRP members were demanding representation at the senior levels of command. In addition, the front as an operational area was organized into subordinate field sectors and operational sectors, with little official liaison among the different service staffs. Moreover, the war effort was going poorly.

Bani Sadr's ouster from the presidency and Chamran's death at the front galvanized the Urumiyeh group to push for implementation of the reorganization proposals. Colonel Namju was the new defense minister, and reorganization of the command system received his full support. By September 1981, SDC approval was ensured and coordination with the Pasdaran initiated. Deputy Commander in Chief of the Pasdaran Kolahduz supervised the first operational integration of the regular military with the Pasdaran. Even the air force relented, and Brigadier General Javad Fakuri authorized additional close air support for ground forces. On September 24, 1981, a new command and control system was finalized at a Tehran meeting hosted by Pasdaran commander in chief Mohsen Rezai, who agreed to test the new proposals. An operation was launched to liberate Abadan and force the Iraqis to the west bank of the Karun River. Within four days, Iran's coordinated attack was successful, and the Iraqis retreated. For the first time since the outbreak of hostilities, a full-scale integration at the staff level produced positive results.

On September 29, 1981, several high-ranking military leaders, including Colonel Namju and Kolahduz, were killed in an airplane crash. Colonel Zahirnezhad, promoted to brigadier general, took over as chief of the Joint Staff of the armed forces, and Colonel Seyyed-Shirazi took Zahirnezhad's post as commander of armed forces. These appointments ensured the full implementation of the new command system.

Command and Control

According to Article 110 of the 1979 Constitution of the Islamic Republic of Iran, the *faqih* (see Glossary) is empowered to appoint and dismiss the chief of the Joint Staff, the commander in chief of the Pasdaran, two advisers to the SDC, and the commanders in chief of ground, naval, and air forces on the recommendation of the SDC. He is also authorized to supervise the activities of the SDC and to declare war and mobilize the armed forces on the recommendation of the SDC. As *faqih*, Khomeini, although maintaining the role of final arbiter, has delegated the post of commander in chief to the president of the Republic.

In addition to specifying the duties of the commander in chief, Article 110 establishes the composition of the SDC as follows: president of the country, prime minister, minister of defense, chief of the Joint Staff of the armed forces, commander in chief of the Pasdaran, and two advisers appointed by the *faqih*. Other senior officials may attend SDC meetings to deliberate national defense issues. In the past, the minister of foreign affairs, minister of interior, minister of the Pasdaran and his deputy, air force and navy commanders in chief, War Information Office director, and others have attended SDC meetings. The ground forces commander in chief, Colonel Seyyed-Shirazi, is a member of the SDC as a representative of the military arm for the *faqih*, whereas Majlis speaker Hojjatoleslam Ali Akbar Hashemi-Rafsanjani is representative of the political arm for the *faqih*.

Iran's strategic planning and the establishment of its military and defense policies are the responsibilities of the SDC, which has representatives at operational area and field headquarters to provide political and strategic guidance to field commanders. SDC representatives may also veto military decisions. But reports in 1987 indicated that SDC orders to regional representatives have been modified to limit the heavy casualty rates caused by their inappropriate advice. Inexperienced nonmilitary religious advisers have seen their interference in purely technical matters dramatically curtailed.

The Urumiyeh reorganization proposals recognized the administrative separation of the services as part of Iran's political reality. Consequently, as of 1987 there were two chains of command below the SDC, one administrative and the other operational. To some extent this dual chain of command existed because the revolutionary government had retained a modified version of the organizational structure of the IIAF, which was modeled on the United

States division of powers between the administrative functions of the service secretaries and the operational functions of the secretary of defense and chiefs of staff. In addition, the IRP leaders wanted to limit friction between the regular military and the Pasdaran. According to Speaker Hashemi-Rafsanjani, the service commanders in chief, the minister of defense, and the minister of the Pasdaran were removed from the operational chain to avoid further friction between the two groups.

In 1987 the Ministry of Defense continued to handle administrative matters for the regular armed forces. The chain of command flowed from senior unit commanders (division, wing, and fleet) to intermediate-echelon service commanders and to service commanders in chief and their staffs. Similarly, the Ministry of the Pasdaran handled the administrative affairs of the Pasdaran. The chain of command flowed from senior unit commanders (operational brigades in the case of combat units) to the ministry staff officers. In the case of internal security units, the chain of command went from local commanders to provincial commanders (who were colonels) and then to provincial general commanders (who were generals).

The Joint Staff of the armed forces, composed of officers assigned from the various services, the Pasdaran, the National Police, and the Gendarmerie, was responsible for all operational matters. Its primary tasks included military planning and coordination and operational control over the regular services, combat units of the Pasdaran, and units of the Gendarmerie and National Police assigned to the war front. Joint Staff members were also empowered to integrate fully the regular and paramilitary forces in operational planning. The components of the armed forces Joint Staff were modeled on the United States joint and combined staff system.

Staff members of J1—Personnel and Administration—conducted planning and liaison duties with their counterparts at the ministries of defense, interior, and the Pasdaran. They also supervised budgeting and financial accountability and the preparation of operational budgets for Majlis approval for all the armed services.

Personnel of J2—Intelligence and Security—carried out operational control for intelligence planning, intelligence operations, intelligence training, counterintelligence, and security for all elements of the armed forces. They also handled liaison with the *komitehs* (revolutionary committees) for internal security matters and with SAVAMA for foreign intelligence (see SAVAMA, this ch.).

Staff members of J3—Operations and Training—conducted training, operational planning, operations, and communications. The operational planning and operations sections were further

divided into eleven subsections for planning and coordination of
the services, including: the Iranian Islamic Ground Forces (IIGF),
IIGF Aviation, IIGF Chemical Troops, IIGF Artillery Troops,
IIGF Engineer Troops, Iranian Islamic Air Force (IIArF), Iranian
Islamic Navy (IIN), IIN Aviation, the Pasdaran, the Gendarmerie,
and the National Police.

Personnel of J4—Logistics and Support—coordinated and
provided liaison for the services. Primary responsibility for logistics and supply rested with the services through the ministries of
defense, interior, and the Pasdaran; collection and coordination
of supplies and coordination of transportation to the war front,
however, remained under the control of J4.

Staff members of J5—Liaison—handled liaison and coordination with nonmilitary organizations and with those military organizations not covered by Joint Staff-level arrangements. Organizations
covered by J5 included the Ministry of Defense, Ministry of Interior, Ministry of the Pasdaran, Office of the Prime Minister, Council of Ministers' Secretariat, SDC, Majlis (particularly the Defense
and Foreign Affairs Committee), the Foundation for Popular
Mobilization, the Foundation for the Disinherited, the Foundation for Martyrs (Bonyad-e Shahid), the Foundation for War Victims, and the Crusade for Reconstruction (Jihad-e Sazandegi or
Jihad).

The office of the staff judge advocate provided legal counsel to
the Joint Staff and facilitated liaison with the revolutionary prosecutor general and the military tribunal system of the armed forces.
The Political-Ideological Directorate (P-ID) staff members operated the political-ideological bureaus of the Joint Staff components
and the political-ideological directorates and bureaus of the operational commands. This office also developed and disseminated
political-ideological training materials, in close cooperation with
the Foundation for the Propagation of Islam and the Islamic associations of the services. Finally, P-ID members conducted liaison
duties between the Joint Staff and the Islamic Revolutionary Court
of the Armed Forces.

Members of the Inspectorate General handled oversight functions over the staff components and liaison with the inspectors
general of the operational commands. Special Office for Procure-
ments staff members controlled and coordinated procurement of
military equipment and supplies from foreign sources through the
Ministry of Defense, the Ministry of the Pasdaran, the Ministry
of Commerce and Foreign Trade, and the Central Bank of Iran.

In general, operational area commands were subordinate to the
Joint Staff, and each armed force component was subordinate to

Members of the shah's Imperial Iranian Armed Forces

the operational area command in accordance with its own command structure. In 1987 there was only the Western Operational Area Command, which was responsible for the war with Iraq. Established to provide more effective control of wartime operations, this area may have been the precursor of the planned Northern, Southern, and Eastern Operational Area Commands.

The Western Operational Area Command was similar in structure to the armed forces Joint Staff except that it was also the lowest operational echelon at which naval forces were integrated into combined-services operations and planning. Although operational area command Joint Staff members exercised operational control over all troops within their area, they were subject to several constraints. Generally speaking, Pasdaran, Gendarmerie, and National Police units operating in an internal security mission, particularly against insurgents, were detached from the operational area command and subordinated to the senior Pasdaran commander in the province in which they were engaged. Air and naval units continued to be partially controlled by their service commanders and responded to the Western Operational Area Command Joint Staff through specialized liaison staffs. The commander of the operational area was further burdened by the presence at his headquarters of an SDC representative and a personal representative of Khomeini. Both of these influential individuals could effectively take any matter over the commander's head to higher authority. In 1987 the SDC representative in the Western Operational Area Command was also the Pasdaran commander for the operational area command, a situation that further complicated the command and control system.

Below the Operational Area Command were four field headquarters (FHQ), code-named FHQ Karbala, FHQ Hamzeh Seyyed ash Shohada, FHQ Ramadah, and FHQ An Najaf. The FHQs were organized on the model of the Western Operational Area Command except that they did not have naval integration. Subordinate to each FHQ were from three to eight operational sectors. Each operational sector did not necessarily have its own air support unit.

Additional echelons consisting of a commander and staff drawn from the Joint Staff of the participating FHQs could be created during major offensives. The purpose of these echelons was to overcome logistical shortcomings, concentrate and deploy forces as needed, and combine the services, particularly the naval forces, in offensive operations.

The reorganization of the command-and-control system could largely be attributed to the Urumiyeh proposals. The war with Iraq naturally increased the level of integration, particularly between regular military officers commanding Pasdaran units and Pasdaran officers commanding regular military units. Logistical problems also came under increasing scrutiny because of the war. The military's weak infrastructure required the centralization of logistics and supply. The sophisticated computer inventory and accounting systems of the ground, air, and naval logistical commands had been sabotaged during the Revolution, and the country lost valuable time while bringing these systems back into service.

Improvements in logistical support proved quite rewarding, revealing, for example, that Iran possessed twice as many critical spare parts for its aircraft as were previously believed to exist. Nevertheless, the Iranian armed forces faced a logistical dilemma in deploying supplies to troops at the front; lack of maintenance skills translated into a decreased repair and salvage capacity, creating serious bottlenecks. Vehicles in need of repair had to be transported to repair centers hundreds of kilometers from the front, along stretches of poorly maintained roads and railroads. Under such circumstances cannibalization of damaged equipment for spare parts, particularly for sophisticated equipment, became the norm. Without a solution in sight, Iranian authorities relied on the "down time" between major offensives to resupply units before resuming offensive operations. This practice further prolonged the war, because multiphased operations could not be launched and sustained.

Organization, Size, and Equipment

As *faqih*, Khomeini is constitutionally designated supreme commander of the armed forces. He has delegated his powers to the president, who may in turn delegate authority as required. Important decisions regarding defense policies are made by the SDC, which combines senior members of the armed services with senior members of the government.

Army

In 1979, the year of the shah's departure, the army experienced a 60-percent desertion from its ranks. By 1986 the regular army was estimated to have a strength of 305,000 troops (see table 8, Appendix). In the fervor of the Revolution and in the light of numerous changes affecting conscripts and reservists, the army underwent a structural reorganization. Under the shah, the army had been deployed in 6 divisions and 4 specialized combat regiments supported by more than 500 helicopters and 14 Hovercraft. An 85-percent readiness rate was usually credited to the force, although some outside observers doubted this claim. Following the Revolution the army was renamed the Islamic Iranian Ground Forces (IIGF) and in 1987 was organized as follows: three mechanized divisions, each with three brigades, each of which in turn was composed of three armored and six mechanized battalions; seven infantry divisions; one airborne brigade; one Special Forces division composed of four brigades; one Air Support Command; and some independent armored brigades including infantry and a "coastal force." There was also in reserve the Qods battalion, composed of ex-servicemen.

After the mid-1970s, military manpower was unevenly deployed. Nearly 80 percent of Iran's ground forces were deployed along the Iraqi border, although official sources maintained that the military was capable of rapid redeployment. Although air force transports were used extensively, redeployment was slow after the start of the war. The Mashhad division headquarters, in the eastern part of the country, has remained important because of Soviet military operations in Afghanistan and resulting Afghan migration into Iran (see Refugees, ch. 2).

In the past, Iran purchased army equipment from many countries, including the United States, Britain, France, the Federal Republic of Germany (West Germany), Italy, and the Soviet Union. By late 1987, Iran had diversified its acquisitions, obtaining arms from a number of suppliers. Among them were the Democratic People's Republic of Korea (North Korea), China, Brazil, and

Israel. The diversity of the weapons purchased from these countries greatly complicated training and supply procedures, but, faced with a war of attrition and a continuous shortage of armaments, Iran was willing to purchase from all available sources (see Foreign Influences in Weapons, Training, and Support Systems, this ch.).

The IIGF operated almost 1,000 medium tanks in 1986 (see table 9, Appendix). Although a large number were British-made Chieftains and American-made M-60s, an undetermined number of Soviet-made T-54 and T-55s, T-59s, T-62s, and T-72s were also part of the inventory, all captured from the Iraqis or acquired from North Korea and China. There was also a complement of fifty British-made Scorpion light tanks. Several hundred Urutu and Cascavel armored fighting vehicles from Brazil joined American-made M-113s and Soviet-made BTR-50s and BTR-60s. An undetermined number of Soviet-made Scud surface-to-surface missiles were acquired from a third country, believed to be Libya. And in November 1986, the United States revealed that it had supplied the Iranian military with Hawk surface-to-air missiles and TOW antitank missiles via Israel.

The army's aviation unit, whose main operational facilities were located at Esfahan, was largely equipped with United States aircraft, although some helicopters were of Italian manufacture. In 1986 army aviation operated some 65 light fixed-wing aircraft, but its strength lay in its estimated 320 combat helicopters, down from 720 in 1980.

Navy

The Iranian navy has always been the smallest of the three services, having about 14,500 personnel in 1986, down from 30,000 in 1979. Throughout the 1970s, the role of the navy had expanded as Iran recognized the need to defend the region's vital sea-lanes (see table 10, Appendix). In 1977 the bulk of the fleet was shifted from Khorramshahr to the newly completed base at Bandar-e Abbas, the new naval headquarters. Bushehr was the other main base; smaller facilities were located at Khorramshahr, Khark Island, and Bandar-e Khomeini (formerly known as Bandar-e Shahpur). Bandar-e Anzelli (formerly known as Bandar-e Pahlavi) was the major training base and home of the small Caspian fleet, which consisted of a few patrol boats and a minesweeper. The naval base at Bandar-e Beheshti (formerly known as Chah Bahar) on the Gulf of Oman had been under construction since the late 1970s and in late 1987 still was not completed. Smaller facilities were located near the Strait of Hormuz.

The Navy's airborne component, including an antisubmarine
warfare (ASW) and minesweeping helicopter squadron and a transport battalion, continued to operate in 1986 despite wartime losses.
Of six P–3F Orion antisubmarine aircraft, perhaps two remained
operational, and of twenty SH–3D ASW helicopters, possibly only
ten were airworthy. Despite overall losses, the navy increased the
number of its marine battalions from two to three between 1979
and 1986.

Entirely of foreign origin, Iran's naval fleet has suffered major
losses since the beginning of the war, when it was made up of
American- and British-made destroyers and frigates, and some sixty
smaller vessels and one of the largest Hovercraft fleets in the world.
The Hovercraft had been expressly chosen to operate in the shal-
low waters of the Persian Gulf and proved useful in the 1971 occupation of Abu Musa and the Tunbs. After the cancellation of foreign
orders in 1979, the rapid matériel advance of the navy was halted.
For example, the shah's government had ordered six Spruance-
class destroyers equipped for antiaircraft operations and three diesel-
powered Tang-class submarines from the United States. Washington canceled the sale of these vessels, selling the submarines to Turkey and absorbing the destroyers into the United States Navy. In
1979 Khomeini also canceled an order for six type-209 submarines
from West Germany.

What naval vessels remained in 1987 suffered from two major
problems—lack of maintenance and lack of spare parts. After the
departure of British-United States maintenance teams, the Iranian
navy conducted only limited repairs, despite the availability of a
completed Fleet Maintenance Unit at Bandar-e Abbas; consequently, several ships were laid up. Lack of spare parts also plagued
the navy more than other services, because Western naval equipment was less widely available on world arms markets than other
equipment.

Iran's ambitious plans for escort and patrol capabilities in the
Persian Gulf and the Indian Ocean may not be realized until the
Bandar-e Beheshti naval facility is completed. The country's interest in navigation through the Strait of Hormuz has not diminished,
as the contemplated deployment of Chinese-made Silkworm HY–2
surface-to-surface missiles on Larak Island in 1987 clearly indicated.
This development underscored Iran's interest in Gulf waters and
the navy's role, along with that of Pasdaran units, in protecting
them or in denying them to others.

Air Force

The shah's air force had more than 450 modern combat aircraft, including top-of-the-line F-14 Tomcat fighters and about 5,000 well-trained pilots. By 1979 the air force, numbering close to 100,000 personnel, was by far the most advanced of the three services and among the most impressive air forces in the developing world. Reliable information on the air force after the Revolution was difficult to obtain, but it seems that by 1987 a fairly large number of aircraft had been cannibalized for spare parts.

Before the Revolution, the air force was organized into fifteen squadrons with fighter and fighter-bomber capabilities and one reconnaissance squadron. In addition, one tanker squadron, and four medium and one light transport squadron provided impressive logistical backup. By 1986 desertions and depletions led to a reorganization of the air force into eight squadrons with fighter and fighter-bomber capabilities and one reconnaissance squadron. This reduced force was supported by two joint tanker-transport squadrons and five light transport squadrons. Some seventy-six helicopters and five surface-to-air missile (SAM) squadrons supplemented this capability.

Air force headquarters was located at Doshan Tapeh Air Base, near Tehran. Iran's largest air base, Mehrabad, outside Tehran, was also the country's major civil airport. Other major operational air bases were at Tabriz, Bandar-e Abbas, Hamadan (Shahroki Air Base), Dezful (Vahdati Air Base), Shiraz, and Bushehr. Since 1980 air bases at Ahvaz, Esfahan (Khatami Air Base), and Bandar-e Beheshti have also become operational.

Throughout the 1970s, Iran purchased sophisticated aircraft for the air force. The acquisition of 77 F-14A Tomcat fighters added to 166 F-5 fighters and 190 F-4 Phantom fighter-bombers, gave Iran a strong defensive and a potential offensive capability. Before the end of his reign, the shah placed orders for F-16 fighters and even contemplated the sharing of development costs for the United States Navy's new F-18 fighter. Both of these combat aircraft have been dropped from the revolutionary regime's military acquisitions list, however.

When the Iran-Iraq War started in 1980, Iran's F-14s, equipped with Phoenix missiles, capable of identifying and destroying six targets simultaneously from a range of eighty kilometers or more, inflicted heavy casualties on the Iraqi air force, which was forced to disperse its aircraft to Jordan and Oman. The capability of the F-14s and F-4s was enhanced by the earlier acquisition of a squadron of Boeing 707 tankers, thereby extending their combat radius to 2,500 kilometers with in-flight refueling.

By 1987, however, the air force faced an acute shortage of spare parts and replacement equipment. Perhaps 35 of the 190 Phantoms were serviceable in 1986 (see table 11, Appendix). One F-4 had been shot down by Saudi F-15s, and two pilots had defected to Iraq with their F-4s in 1984. The number of F-5s dwindled from 166 to perhaps 45, and the F-14 Tomcats from 77 to perhaps 10. The latter were hardest hit because maintenance posed special difficulties after the United States embargo on military sales.

China and North Korea with their "independent" policies on arms sales, were the only countries willing to sell Iran combat airplanes. Iran had acquired two Chinese-made Shenyang J-6 trainers in 1986. Unconfirmed reports in 1987 indicated that Iran was receiving Shenyang F-6s (Chinese-built MiG-19SFs), and that Iranian pilots were receiving training in North Korea. The reconnaissance squadron has also struggled to perform its duties with limited equipment. Once flying close to thirty-four aircraft, by late 1987 it may have been reduced to eight, having converted five Tomcats to serve in a noncombat role. It was not clear whether these five airplanes were in addition to the ten in the interceptor squadrons. Given the technical sophistication of reconnaissance aircraft, it was almost impossible to acquire from non-Western sources new ones capable of performing to Iranian standards. The only substantial acquisition was the purchase of forty-six Pilatus PC-7s from Switzerland. Iran requested three Kawasaki C-1 transports and a 3D air defense radar system from Japan, but this transaction did not appear to have materialized by 1987. Reports also indicated that Iran had placed with Argentina an order for thirty Hughes 500D helicopters.

From its inception, the air force also assumed responsibility for air defense. The existing early warning systems, built in the 1950s under the auspices of CENTO, were upgraded in the 1970s with a modern air defense radar network. To complement the ground radar component and provide a blanket coverage of the Gulf region, the United States agreed to sell Iran seven Boeing 707 airborne warning and control system (AWACS) aircraft in late 1977. Because of the Revolution, Washington canceled the AWACS sale, claiming that this sensitive equipment might be compromised. Finally, the air force's three SAM battalions and eight improved Hawk battalions were reorganized in the mid-1980s (in a project involving more than 1,800 missiles) into five squadrons that also contained Rapiers and Tigercats. Washington's sale of Hawk spare parts and missiles in 1985 and 1986 may have enhanced this capability.

The air force's primary maintenance facility was located at Mehrabad Air Base. The nearby Iran Aircraft Industries, in addition to providing main overhaul backup for the maintenance unit, has been active in manufacturing spare parts.

Source and Quality of Manpower

Armed forces manpower increased substantially throughout the 1970s as the shah implemented Iran's "guardian" role in the Gulf. Following the outbreak of the Revolution, there was a sharp drop in the number of military personnel, which in 1982 stood at 235,000, including the Pasdaran but excluding reserves. In contrast, total military personnel, including the Pasdaran but excluding reserves, stood at 704,500 in 1986. In addition to active-duty personnel, some 400,000 veterans, organized in reserve units after the outbreak of the war, were subject to recall to duty. Two-thirds of army personnel were conscripts; in the air force and navy, the majority were volunteers.

The National Military Academy was the largest single source of commissioned officers in the 1970s, but since 1980 a significant number of commissions have been awarded for wartime heroism and leadership at the front. Although air force and navy officers had attended military academies or participated in cadet programs in the United States, Britain, or Italy before 1979, few foreign contacts have been recorded since the Revolution. In the few instances in which contact was established, it was with Asian states, namely China and North Korea. Unlike the army, the air force and navy have experienced high attrition, and it must be assumed that operations have been streamlined to be effective with fewer personnel.

Class differences in the armed forces remained virtually undisturbed by the Revolution. Commissioned officers came from upper class families, career noncommissioned and warrant officers from the urban middle class, and conscripts from lower class backgrounds. By 1986, an increasing segment of the officer corps came from the educated middle class, and a significant number of lower middle-class personnel were commissioned by Khomeini for leadership on the battlefield.

Iran's 1986 population of approximately 48.2 million (including approximately 2.6 million refugees) gave the armed forces a large pool from which to fill its manpower needs, despite the existence of rival irregular forces. Of about 8 million males between the ages of eighteen and forty-five, nearly 6 million were considered physically and mentally fit for military service. Revolutionary leaders have repeatedly declared that Iran could establish an army of 20 million to defend the country against foreign aggression. Since the beginning of 1986, women have also been encouraged to receive military training, and women were actually serving in special Pasdaran units as of late 1987. The decision to encourage women to join in the military effort may indicate an increasing demand for personnel or an effort to gain increased popular support for the Revolution. It could also mean that conscription was not replacing war losses or retirements.

Compulsory conscription has been in effect since 1926, when Reza Shah's Military Service Act was passed by the Majlis. All males must register at age nineteen and begin their military service at age twenty-one; the law, however, is of limited significance in view of government pressures for volunteer enlistments in military units at an earlier age. According to the act, the total period of service is twenty-five years, divided as follows: two years of active military service, six years in standby military service for draftees, then eight years in first-stage reserve and nine years in second-stage reserve. In 1984 the Majlis passed the new Military Act. It amended conscription laws to reduce the high number of draft dodgers. Newspapers have carried reports of people caught trying to buy their way out of military service, at an unofficial figure of about US$8,000 for forged exemption documents. Under the prerevolutionary law, temporary or permanent exemptions were provided for the physically disabled, hardship cases, convicted felons, students, and certain professions. Draft evaders were subject to arrest, trial before a military court, and imprisonment for a maximum of two years *after* serving the required two years of active duty. Few draft dodgers, if any, were sent to jail; the normal procedure was to fine them the equivalent of US$75 (1986 exchange rate). Under the 1984 law, draft evaders were subject to restrictions for a period of up to ten years. They could be prevented from holding a driver's license, running for elective office, registering property ownership, being put on the government payroll, or receiving a passport, in addition to being forced to pay fines and/or receive jail sentences. Exemptions were given only to solve family problems. Moreover, all exemptions, except for physical disabilities, were only for five years. Those seeking relief for medical reasons had to serve but were not sent on combat duty. Under the amended law, men of draft age were subject to conscription, whether in war or peace, for a minimum period of two years and could be recalled as needed.

In the past, a consistent weakness of the armed forces had been the high illiteracy rate among conscripts and volunteers. This reflected the country-wide illiteracy rate, which stood at 60 percent in 1979. Compounding this dilemma, many conscripts came from those areas where Persian was not spoken. Thus, the military first had to teach the conscripts Persian by instituting extensive literacy training programs.

By 1986 the country's overall literacy rate was estimated at 50 percent, a dramatic improvement. This gain was also reflected in the regular armed forces. Of the three services, the air force fared best in this respect, as it had always done. Yet even the air force, which had developed training facilities for support personnel and *homafars,* was short of its real requirements. With the 1979 withdrawal of foreign military and civilian advisers, particularly from the United States and Pakistan, the operation, maintenance, and logistical functioning of armed forces' equipment was hampered by a critical shortage of skilled manpower. As purchases from non-Western countries increased, Iran came to rely on Chinese, Syrian, Bulgarian (unconfirmed), and North Korean instructors and those from the German Democratic Republic (East Germany), among others.

In 1987 the impressive progress of the regular armed forces was counterbalanced by manpower shortages. Without the support of large numbers of irregular forces and volunteers, it was difficult to foresee how this shortage might be overcome.

Foreign Influences in Weapons, Training, and Support Systems

Foreign influence on the regular armed forces has historically been massive, vital, and controversial. Around the turn of the century, before Reza Shah unified the military, officers from Sweden, Britain, and Russia commanded various Iranian units (see Historical Background, this ch.). These officers were unpopular because they were perceived as occupiers rather than as advisers, and the seeds of xenophobia were planted. Aware of these sentiments, Reza Shah tried to minimize direct foreign military influence, although an exception was made for Swedish officers serving with the Gendarmerie. Between the two world wars, a large number of Iranian officers attended military academies in France and Germany, where they received command and technical training. In a further effort to counter the influence of both Britain and Russia (by that time, the Soviet Union) in Iranian affairs, Reza Shah attempted to establish closer ties with Germany, a relationship that would be controversial during World War II. After 1945 the United States gradually became more influential and had a significant impact on the Pahlavi dynasty's leadership and the military.

With the establishment during World War II of a small United States military mission to the Gendarmerie (known as GENMISH) in 1943, Washington initiated a modest military advisory program. In 1947 the United States and Tehran reached a more comprehensive agreement that established the United States Army Mission Headquarters (ARMISH). Its purpose was to provide the

Ministry of War and the Iranian army with advisory and technical assistance to enhance their efficiency. As a result, the first Iranian officers began training in the United States, and they were followed by many more over the next three decades. The United States initiated its military assistance grant program to Iran in 1950 (the bilateral defense agreement between Iran and the United States was not concluded until 1959) and established a Military Assistance Advisory Group (MAAG) to administer the program. In 1962 the two missions were consolidated into a single military organization, ARMISH-MAAG, which remained active in Iran until the Islamic revolutionary regime came to power in 1979. Between 1973 and 1979, the United States also provided military support in the form of technical assistance field teams (TAFTs), through which civilian experts instructed Iranians on specific equipment on a short-term basis. Although the GENMISH program ended in 1973, United States military assistance to Iran rose rapidly in the six years before the Revolution.

United States military assistance to Iran between 1947 and 1969 exceeded US$1.4 billion, mostly in the form of grant aid before 1965 and of Foreign Military Sales credits during the late 1960s. The financial assistance programs were terminated after 1969, when it was determined that Iran, by then an important oil exporter, could assume its own military costs. Thereafter, Iran paid cash for its arms purchases and covered the expenses of United States military personnel serving in the ARMISH-MAAG and TAFT programs. Even so, in terms of personnel the United States military mission in Iran in 1978 was the largest in the world. Department of Defense personnel in Iran totaled over 1,500 in 1978, admittedly a small number compared with the 45,000 United States citizens, mostly military and civilian technicians and their dependents, living in Iran. Almost all of these individuals were evacuated by early 1979 as the ARMISH-MAAG program came to an abrupt end. Ended also was the International Military Education and Training (IMET) Program, under which over 11,000 Iranian military personnel had received specialized instruction in the United States.

Washington broke its diplomatic ties with Tehran in April 1980, closing an important chapter with a former CENTO ally whose security it had guaranteed since 1959. The relationship had evolved dramatically from the early 1950s, when Iran depended on the United States for security assistance, to the mid-1970s, when the government-to-government Foreign Military Sales program dominated other issues. Arms transfers increased significantly after the 1974 oil price rise, accelerating at a dizzying pace until 1979. From fiscal year (FY—see Glossary) 1950 through FY 1979, United States arms sales to Iran totaled approximately US$11.2 billion, of which US$10.7 billion were actually delivered.

The transfer of such large volumes of arms and the presence of thousands of United States advisers had an unmistakable influence on the Iranian armed forces. The preponderance of American weapons led to a dependence on the United States for support systems and for spare parts. Technical advisers were indispensable for weapons operations and maintenance.

After the Revolution, Iranians continued to buy arms from the United States using Israeli, European, and Latin American intermediaries to place orders, despite the official United States embargo. Israeli sales, for example, were recorded as early as 1979. On several occasions, attempted arms sales to Iran have been thwarted by law enforcement operations or broker-initiated leaks. One operation set up by the United States Department of Justice foiled the shipment of more than US$2 billion of United States weapons to Iran from Israel and other foreign countries. The matériel included 18 F–4 fighter-bombers, 46 Skyhawk fighter-bombers, and nearly 4,000 missiles. But while the Department of Justice was attempting to prevent arms sales to Iran, senior officials in the administration of President Ronald Reagan admitted that 2,008 TOW missiles and 235 parts kits for Hawk missiles had been sent to Iran via Israel. These were intended to be an incentive for the release of American hostages held by pro-Iranian militiamen in Lebanon. Unverified reports in 1987 indicated that Iranian officials claimed that throughout 1986 the Reagan administration had sold Iran ammunition and parts for F–4s, F–5s, and F–14s. In addition, Tehran reportedly purchased United States-made equipment from international arms dealers and captured United States weapons from Vietnam.

Despite official denials, it is believed that Israel has been a supplier of weapons and spare parts for Iran's American-made arsenal. Reports indicate that an initial order for 250 retread tires for F–4 Phantom jets was delivered in 1979 for about US$27 million. Since that time, unverified reports have alleged that Israel agreed to sell Iran Sidewinder air-to-air missiles, radar equipment, mortar and machine gun ammunition, field telephones, M–60 tank engines and artillery shells, and spare parts for C–130 transport planes.

By 1986 Iran's largest arms suppliers were reportedly China and North Korea. China, for example, is believed to have supplied Iran with military equipment in sales funneled through North Korea. According to an unconfirmed report in the *Washington Post,* one particular deal in the spring of 1983 netted Beijing close to US$1.3 billion for fighters, T–59 tanks, 130mm artillery, and light arms.

China also delivered a number of Silkworm HY–2 surface-to-surface missiles, presumably for use in defending the Strait of Hormuz. As of early 1987, China denied all reported sales, possibly to enhance its diminishing position in the Arab world. North Korea agreed to sell arms and medical supplies to Iran as early as the summer of 1980. Using military cargo versions of the Boeing 747, Tehran ferried ammunition, medical supplies, and other equipment that it purchased from the North Korean government. According to unverified estimates, total sales by 1986 may have reached US$3 billion.

Other countries directly or indirectly involved over the years in supplying weapons to Iran have included Syria (transferring some Soviet-made weapons), France, Italy, Libya (Scud missiles), Brazil, Algeria, Switzerland, Argentina, and the Soviet Union. Direct foreign influence, however, was minimal because most purchases were arranged in international arms markets. Moreover, the influence of the major arms suppliers was balanced by other international relationships. Many of the above-mentioned West European states in 1987 had arms embargoes against shipments to Iran, but nevertheless some matériel slipped through. Also, West European states often wished to keep communication channels open, no matter how difficult political relations might have become. For example, despite strong protests from the United States, the British government in 1985 transferred to Iran a fleet-refueling ship and two landing ships without their armament. The British also allowed the repair of two Iranian BH-7 Hovercraft. In 1982 Tehran began negotiations with Bonn for the sale of submarines. Iran also approached the Netherlands and, in 1985, purchased two landing craft, each sixty-five meters long and having a capacity exceeding 1,000 tons. The influence of the Asian arms-supplying countries was further minimized because purchases were made in cash upon delivery with no strings attached. Finally, foreign influence was less pronounced in 1987 than at any time since 1925 because a defiant Tehran espoused ''independent'' foreign and military policies, based on a strong sense of Islamic and nationalistic values.

Domestic Arms Production

In 1963 Iran placed all military factories under the Military Industries Organization (MIO) of the Ministry of War. Over the next fifteen years, military plants produced small arms ammunition, batteries, tires, copper products, explosives, and mortar rounds and fuses. They also produced rifles and machine guns under West German license. In addition, helicopters, jeeps, trucks, and trailers were assembled from imported kits. Iran was on its way to manufacturing rocket launchers, rockets, gun barrels, and grenades, when the Revolution halted all military activities. The MIO, plagued by the upheavals of the time, was unable to operate without foreign specialists and technicians; by 1981 it had lost much of its management ability and control over its industrial facilities.

The outbreak of hostilities with Iraq and the Western arms embargo served as catalysts for reorganizing, reinvigorating, and expanding defense industries. In late 1981, the revolutionary government brought together the country's military industrial units and placed them under the Defense Industries Organization (DIO), which would supervise production activities. In 1987 the DIO was governed by a mixed civilian-military board of directors and a managing director responsible for the actual management and planning activities. Although the DIO director was accountable to the deputy minister of defense for logistics, Iran's president, in his capacity as the chairman of the SDC, had ultimate responsibility for all DIO operations.

By 1986 a large number of infantry rifles, machine guns, and mortars and some small-arms ammunition were being manufactured locally. On several occasions, clerics delivering their Friday sermons in Tehran claimed that Iran was engaged in a full-scale military production program, and the Iranian press regularly reported the successful production of new items ranging from washers to helicopter fuselage parts. For example, the professional military displayed, at the Permanent Industrial Exhibition in Tehran, a collection of hermetic sealing cylinders for Chieftain tanks and artillery flame-deflectors with artillery pads. They also displayed Katyusha gauges, personnel carrier shafts, gears, gun pulleys, carriages for 50mm caliber guns, 155mm shells, bases for night-vision telescopic rifles, parts for G–3 rifles, various firing pins, and flash suppressors for 130mm guns.

In 1987 the military took pride in being able to repair various transmitters, receivers, and helicopter engines. A number of unverified reports also alluded to the repair of the testing equipment of F–14 hydraulic pressure transmitters and generators. Similarly, Iran claimed to have manufactured an undisclosed number of Oghab rockets, probably patterned on the Soviet-made Scud-B surface-to-surface missiles the Iranians received from Libya. In mid-1984 the navy claimed to have successfully repaired the gas turbines of several vessels in Bandar-e Abbas. Moreover, Pasdaran units reportedly repaired Soviet- and Polish-made T–54, T–55, T–62, and T–72 tanks, captured from the Iraqis in 1982, at their armor repair center.

Troops of the Pasdaran in Qasr-e Shirin
Copyright Lehtikuva/PHOTRI

The monopoly of the regular armed forces over domestic arms production and repair industries ended in 1983 when the SDC authorized the Pasdaran to establish its own military industries. This new policy was in line with the Pasdaran's growing political and military weight. Beginning in 1984, the first Pasdaran armaments factory manufactured 120mm mortars, antipersonnel grenades, various antichemical-warfare equipment, antitank rockets, and rocket-propelled grenades.

Special and Irregular Armed Forces

A primacy of state interest over revolutionary ideology was reflected in the Khomeini regime's treatment of the military. Reports to the contrary notwithstanding, the Khomeini regime never eliminated imperial Iran's regular armed forces. Certainly, key military personnel identified with the deposed shah were arrested, tried, and executed. But the purges were limited to high-profile military and political figures and had a clear purpose: to eliminate Pahlavi loyalists. As a means of countering the threat posed by either the leftist guerrillas or the officers suspected of continued loyalty to the shah, however, Khomeini created the Pasdaran, designated as the guardians of the Revolution. The Constitution of the new republic entrusts the defense of Iran's territorial integrity and political independence to the military, while it gives the Pasdaran the responsibility of preserving the Revolution itself.

Soon after Khomeini's return to Tehran, the Bazargan interim administration established the Pasdaran under a decree issued by Khomeini on May 5, 1979. The Pasdaran was intended to protect the Revolution and to assist the ruling clerics in the day-to-day enforcement of the new government's Islamic codes and morality. There were other, perhaps more important, reasons for establishing the Pasdaran. The Revolution needed to rely on a force of its own rather than borrowing the previous regime's tainted units. As one of the first revolutionary institutions, the Pasdaran helped legitimize the Revolution and gave the new regime an armed basis of support. Moreover, the establishment of the Pasdaran served notice to both the population and the regular armed forces that the Khomeini regime was quickly developing its own enforcement body. Thus, the Pasdaran, along with its political counterpart, Crusade for Reconstruction, brought a new order to Iran. In time, the Pasdaran would rival the police and the judiciary in terms of its functions. It would even challenge the performance of the regular armed forces on the battlefield.

Since 1979 the Pasdaran has undergone fundamental changes in mission and function. Some of these changes reflected the control of the IRP (until its abolition in 1987) over both the Pasdaran and the Crusade for Reconstruction. Others reflected the IRP's exclusive reliance on the Pasdaran to carry out certain sensitive missions. Still others reflected personal ambitions of Pasdaran leaders. The Pasdaran, with its own separate ministry, has evolved into one of the most powerful organizations in Iran. Not only did it function as an intelligence organization, both within and outside the country, but it also exerted considerable influence on government policies. In addition to its initial political strength, in the course of several years the Pasdaran also became a powerful military instrument for defending the Revolution and Islamic Iran.

Organization and Functions

According to a classified report captured and released by the students who occupied the United States embassy in Tehran, initially the Pasdaran was planned as an organization that would be directly subordinate to the ruling clerics of the Revolution. According to this report, the Revolutionary Council in 1979 was composed of 12 members and the Pasdaran of 30,000 members, divided as follows: Central Council of Saltanatabad, Tehran, 4,000 members; Provincial Command, 20,000; other commands for border checkpoints and key areas, 3,000; and a training center at Aliabad, 3,000.

The commander of the Pasdaran was Ayatollah Lahuti and its chiefs of staff were Hojjatoleslams Hashemi-Rafsanjani and Gholam Ali Afrouz.

From this modest beginning, the Pasdaran became a formidable force. According to the International Institute for Strategic Studies, in 1986 the Pasdaran consisted of 350,000 personnel organized in battalion-size units that operated either independently or with units of the regular armed forces. In 1986 the Pasdaran acquired small naval and air elements, and it has claimed responsibility for hit-and-run raids on shipping in the Persian Gulf. Darting out from bases on a chain of small islands in Swedish-built speedboats equipped with machine guns and rocket-propelled grenades, the Pasdaran has established a naval zone in northern Gulf waters. Hosain Alai, the Pasdaran naval commander, announced on April 27, 1987, that the Pasdaran was in "full control" of certain portions of Gulf waters and would continue to operate from Farsi Island, between Iran and Saudi Arabia, as well as from Sirri, Abu Musa, and Larak islands. At that time 200 Pasdaran pilots reportedly were in training in East Germany.

According to the Muslim Student Followers of the Iman's Line, the Pasdaran, under the guidance of such clerics as Lahuti and Hashemi-Rafsanjani, was also "to act as the eyes and ears of the Islamic Revolution" and "as a special task force of the Imam (see Glossary) Khomeini to crush any counterrevolutionary activities within the government or any political usurper against [the] Islamic Government." Over the years the IRP's leadership used the Pasdaran to eliminate opposition figures and to enhance its own position. Pasdaran units worked with and were subordinate to clergy leaders not just at the national level, but throughout the country as well.

Operations

An early operations commander of the Pasdaran was Abbas Zamani (Abu Sharif), a former teacher from Tehran. A graduate of the College of Education (Islamic Law Section), Zamani received guerrilla training in Lebanon. As early as 1970, when he first traveled to Beirut, he established contacts in Lebanon with the Palestine Liberation Organization (PLO) and various guerrilla groups there. Unverified reports have claimed that the Pasdaran has received organizational and training assistance from the PLO, but no Palestinians were known to have visited the Aliabad or other Pasdaran training grounds. Khomeini and his supporters in Iran, as well as many other Iranians, have continued to support the Palestinians, however. For example, PLO leader Yasir Arafat was one of the first world leaders to visit Tehran after the Revolution; he opened a diplomatic office in what formerly had been the Israeli mission.

The Pasdaran has been quite active in Lebanon. By the summer of 1982, shortly after the second Israeli invasion of Lebanon, the Pasdaran had nearly 1,000 personnel deployed in the predominantly Shia Biqa Valley. From its headquarters near Baalbek, the Pasdaran has provided consistent support to Islamic Amal, a breakaway faction of the mainstream Amal organization that contemplated the establishment of an Islamic state in Lebanon. The secular Baathist Syrian regime has found the Pasdaran presence in Lebanon alternately helpful and threatening. In 1987 the Pasdaran's alleged involvement in anti-American terrorism in Lebanon remained difficult to confirm.

By September 1980, the Pasdaran was capable of deploying forces at the front. Initially, the forces were sent to conduct operations against Kurdish rebels, but before long they were deployed alongside regular armed forces units to conduct conventional military operations. Despite differences, the Pasdaran and the regular armed forces have cooperated on military matters.

The Pasdaran was also given the mandate of organizing a large people's militia, the Basij, in 1980. In a 1985 Iranian News Agency report, Hojjatoleslam Rahmani, head of the Basij forces of the Pasdaran, was quoted as stating that there were close to 3 million volunteers in the paramilitary force receiving training in some 11,000 centers. It is from Basij ranks that volunteers have been drawn to launch "human wave" attacks against the Iraqis, particularly around Basra. More recently, the Pasdaran, on Khomeini's instructions, has initiated the training of women to serve the Revolution.

Role in National Security

From the beginning of the new Islamic regime, the Pasdaran functioned as a corps of the faithful. Its role in national security evolved from securing the regime and eliminating opposition forces to becoming a branch of the military establishment. The Pasdaran's most problematic role, however, has been in intelligence.

Although little is known about the Ministry of the Pasdaran, its intelligence-gathering operations, and its relationship with SAVAMA, several reports have speculated that the Pasdaran has maintained an intelligence branch to spy on the regime's adversaries and to participate in their arrests and trials (see SAVAMA, this ch.). Khomeini implied Pasdaran involvement in intelligence when he congratulated the Pasdaran on the arrest of Iranian communist Tudeh leaders. Observers also believed that the Pasdaran had contacts with underground movements in the Gulf region. Given their importance in domestic politics, it would have been possible for Pasdaran members to be assigned to Iranian diplomatic missions, where, in the course of routine intelligence activities, they could monitor dissidents. Observers believed that Pasdaran influence might be particularly important in Kuwait, Bahrain, and the United Arab Emirates.

Under the command of Mohsen Rezai, the Pasdaran became large enough to match the strength of the regular military. Its power base remained strong in 1987, with the continuing support of Khomeini and other religious authorities. Having eliminated armed leftist groups such as the Mojahedin and the Fadayan, the Pasdaran had fulfilled all IRP expectations. With the abolition of the IRP in 1987, however, observers were uncertain whether the Pasdaran would continue to enjoy unlimited support from high-ranking clerics. Staunchly religious, nationalistic, and battle-trained since 1980, the Pasdaran had emerged as a critical force in determining Iran's national security strategy. In a post-Khomeini era, the Pasdaran could wield enormous power to approve or disapprove governmental changes. In contrast to the Pasdaran, which had a primary responsibility for upholding the Revolution, the major concern of the Iranian military was the prosecution of the war with Iraq.

The Iran-Iraq War

As of June 1987, the major events of the war could generally be divided into six overlapping phases: the original Iraqi offensive, Iranian mobilization and resistance, the Iranian counteroffensive, the war of attrition, Iraqi internationalization of the war, and the surge in superpower involvement. In addition, there was the tanker war in the Persian Gulf, which extended over several of these phases.

The Original Iraqi Offensive

Baghdad originally planned a quick victory over Tehran. On September 22, 1980, Iraqi fighter aircraft attacked ten air bases in Iran. Their aim was to destroy the Iranian air force on the ground—a lesson learned from the Arab-Israeli June 1967 War. They succeeded in destroying runways and fuel and ammunition depots, but much of Iran's aircraft inventory was left intact. Simultaneously, six Iraqi army divisions entered Iran on three fronts in an initially successful surprise attack. On the northern front, an Iraqi mountain infantry division captured Qasr-e Shirin, a border town in Bakhtaran (formerly known as Kermanshahan) Province, and occupied territory thirty kilometers eastward to the base of the Zagros Mountains. This area was strategically significant because the main Baghdad-Tehran highway traversed it. On the central front, Iraqi forces captured Mehran, on the western plain of the Zagros Mountains in Ilam Province, and pushed eastward to the mountain base. Mehran occupied an important position on the major north-south road, close to the border on the Iranian side. The main thrust of the attack, however, was in the south. Iraqi armored units easily crossed the Shatt al Arab waterway and entered the Iranian province of Khuzestan. While some divisions headed toward Khorramshahr and Abadan, others moved toward Ahvaz, the provincial capital and site of an air base. Supported by heavy artillery fire, the troops made a rapid and significant advance— almost eighty kilometers in the first few days. In the battle for Dezful in Khuzestan, where a major air base is located, the local Iranian army commander requested air support in order to avoid a defeat. President Bani Sadr, therefore, authorized the release from jail of many pilots, some of whom were suspected of still being loyal to the shah. With the increased use of the Iranian air force, the Iraqi progress was somewhat curtailed (see fig. 11).

The last major Iraqi territorial gain took place in early November 1980. On November 3, Iraqi forces reached Abadan but were repulsed by a Pasdaran unit. Even though they surrounded Abadan on three sides and occupied a portion of the city, the Iraqis could not overcome the stiff resistance; sections of the city still under Iranian control were resupplied by boat at night. On November 10, Iraq captured Khorramshahr after a bloody house-to-house fight. The price of this victory was high for both sides, approximately 6,000 casualties for Iraq and even more for Iran.

Iranian Mobilization and Resistance

Iran may have prevented a quick Iraqi victory by a rapid mobilization of volunteers and deployment of loyal Pasdaran forces to the front. Besides enlisting the Iranian pilots, the new revolutionary regime also recalled veterans of the old imperial army, although many experienced officers, most of whom had been trained in the United States, had been purged. Furthermore, the Pasdaran and Basij (what Khomeini called the "Army of Twenty Million" or People's Militia) recruited at least 100,000 volunteers. Approximately 200,000 soldiers were sent to the front by the end of November 1980. They were ideologically committed troops (some members even carried their own shrouds to the front in the expectation of martyrdom) that fought bravely despite inadequate armor support. For example, on November 7 commando units played a significant role, with the navy and air force, in an assault on Iraqi oil export terminals at Mina al Bakr and Al Faw. Iran hoped to diminish Iraq's financial resources by reducing its oil revenues. Iran also attacked the northern pipeline in the early days of the war and successfully closed Basra's access to the Persian Gulf.

Iran's resistance at the outset of the Iraqi invasion was unexpectedly strong, but it was neither well organized nor equally successful on all fronts. Iraq easily advanced in the northern and central sections and crushed the Pasdaran's scattered resistance there. Iraqi troops, however, faced untiring resistance in Khuzestan. President Saddam Husayn of Iraq may have thought that the ethnic Arab minority of Khuzestan would join the Iraqis against Tehran. Instead, many allied with Iran's regular and irregular armed forces and fought in the battles at Dezful, Khorramshahr, and Abadan. Soon after capturing Khorramshahr, the Iraqi troops lost their initiative and began to dig in along their line of advance.

The Iranian Counteroffensive

Iran had created the SDC in 1980 to undertake what the Iranians called Jang-e Tahmili, or the imposed war. Iran launched a counteroffensive in January 1981. Both the volunteers and the regular armed forces were eager to fight, the latter seeing an opportunity to regain prestige lost because of their association with the shah's regime. Iran's first major counterattack failed, however, for political and military reasons. President Bani Sadr was engaged in a power struggle with key religious figures and eager to gain political support among the armed forces by direct involvement in military operations. Lacking military expertise, he initiated a premature attack by three regular armored regiments without the assistance of the Pasdaran units. He also failed to take into account that the ground near Susangerd, muddied by the preceding rainy season, would make resupply difficult. As a result of his tactical decision making, the Iranian forces were surrounded on three sides. In a long exchange of fire, many Iranian armored vehicles were destroyed or had to be abandoned because they were either stuck in the mud or needed minor repairs. Fortunately for Iran, however, the Iraqi forces failed to follow up with another attack.

After Bani Sadr was ousted as president and commander in chief, Iran gained its first major victory, when, as a result of Khomeini's initiative, the army and Pasdaran suppressed their rivalry and cooperated to force Baghdad to lift its long siege of Abadan in September 1981. Iranian forces also defeated Iraq in the Qasr-e Shirin area in December 1981 and January 1982. The Iraqi armed forces

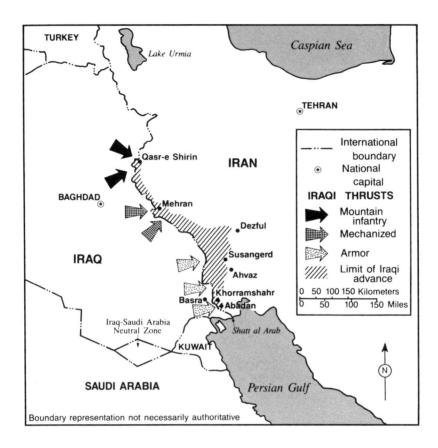

Figure 11. Initial Iraqi Attack on Iran, September–November 1980

were hampered by their unwillingness to sustain a high casualty rate and therefore refused to initiate a new offensive.

In March 1982, Tehran launched a major offensive called "Undeniable Victory." Its forces broke the Iraqi line near Susangerd, separating Iraqi units in northern and southern Khuzestan. Within a week, they succeeded in destroying a large part of three Iraqi divisions. This operation, another combined effort of the army, Pasdaran, and Basij, was a turning point in the war because the strategic initiative shifted from Iraq to Iran. In May 1982, Iranian units finally regained Khorramshahr, but with high casualties. After this victory, the Iranians maintained the pressure on the remaining Iraqi forces, and President Saddam Husayn announced that the Iraqi units would withdraw from Iranian territory.

The War of Attrition

The "war of attrition" began after the Iranian high command passed from regular military leaders to clergy in mid-1982. Although Basra was within range of Iranian artillery, the clergy used "human-wave" attacks by the Pasdaran and Basij against the city's defenses, apparently waiting for a coup to topple Saddam Husayn. All such assaults faced Iraqi artillery fire and received heavy casualties.

Throughout 1983 both sides demonstrated their ability to absorb and to inflict severe losses. Iraq, in particular, proved adroit at constructing defensive strong points and flooding lowland areas to stymie the Iranian thrusts, hampering the advance of mechanized units. Both sides also experienced difficulties in effectively utilizing their armor. Rather than maneuver their armor, they tended to dig in tanks and use them as artillery pieces. Furthermore, both sides failed to master tank gunsights and fire controls, making themselves vulnerable to antitank weapons.

Internationalization of the War

Beginning in 1984, Baghdad's inability to end the war on the ground led to new military and diplomatic strategies. Iraq tried to force Iran to the negotiating table by various means. First, President Saddam Husayn sought to increase the war's manpower and economic cost to Iran. For this purpose, Iraq purchased new weapons, mainly from the Soviet Union and France. Iraq also completed the construction of what came to be known as "killing zones" (which consisted primarily of artificially flooded areas near Basra) to stop Iranian units. In addition, according to *Jane's Defence Weekly* and other sources, Baghdad used chemical weapons against Iranian troop concentrations and launched attacks on many economic centers. Despite Iraqi determination to halt further Iranian progress, Iranian units in March 1984 captured parts of the Majnun Islands, whose oil fields had economic as well as strategic value.

Second, Iraq turned to diplomatic and political means. In April 1984, Saddam Husayn proposed to meet Khomeini personally in a neutral location to discuss peace negotiations. But Tehran rejected this offer and restated its refusal to negotiate with Saddam Husayn.

Third, Iraq sought to involve the superpowers as a means of ending the war. The Iraqis believed this objective could be achieved by attacking Iranian shipping. Initially, Baghdad used borrowed French Super Etendard aircraft armed with Exocets. In 1984 Iraq returned these airplanes to France and purchased approximately thirty Mirage F-1 fighters equipped with Exocet missiles. Iraq launched a new series of attacks on shipping on February 1, 1984 (see The Tanker War, this ch.)

Gradual Superpower Involvement

In early 1987, both superpowers indicated their interest in the security of the region. Soviet deputy foreign minister Vladimir Petrovsky made a Middle East tour expressing his country's concern over the effects of the Iran-Iraq War. In May 1987, United States assistant secretary of state Richard Murphy also toured the Gulf emphasizing to friendly Arab states the United States commitment in the region, a commitment which had become suspect as a result of Washington's transfer of arms to the Iranians, officially as an incentive for them to assist in freeing American hostages held in Lebanon. In another diplomatic effort, both superpowers supported the UN Security Council resolutions seeking an end to the war (see Foreign Policy, ch. 4).

The war appeared to be entering a new phase in which the superpowers were becoming more involved. For instance, the Soviet Union, which had ended military supplies to both Iran and Iraq in 1980, resumed large-scale arms shipments to Iraq in 1982 after Iran had launched its offensive into Iraqi territory. Subsequently, despite its professed neutrality, the Soviet Union became the major supplier of sophisticated arms to Iraq. In 1985 the United States began clandestine direct and indirect negotiations with Iranian officials that resulted in several arms shipments to Iran.

Iranian military gains inside Iraq after 1984 were a major reason for increased superpower involvement in the war. In February 1986, Iranian units captured the port of Al Faw, which had oil facilities and was one of Iraq's major oil-exporting ports before the war.

By late 1986, rumors of a final Iranian offensive against Basra proliferated. On January 8, Operation Karbala Five began, with Iranian units pushing westward between Fish Lake and the Shatt al Arab. They captured the town of Duayji and inflicted 20,000 casualties on Iraq, but at the cost of 65,000 Iranian casualties. In this intensive operation, Baghdad also lost forty-five airplanes. Attempting to capture Basra, Tehran launched several attacks, some of them well-disguised diversion assaults such as Operation Karbala Six and Operation Karbala Seven. Iran finally aborted Operation Karbala Five on February 26.

In late May 1987, just when the war seemed to have reached a complete stalemate on the southern front, reports from Iran indicated that the conflict was intensifying on Iraq's northern front.

This assault, Operation Karbala Ten, was a joint effort by Iranian units and Iraqi Kurdish rebels. They surrounded the garrison at Mawat, endangering Iraq's oil fields near Kirkuk and the northern oil pipeline to Turkey.

By late spring of 1987, the superpowers became more directly involved because they feared that the fall of Basra might lead to a pro-Iranian Islamic republic in largely Shia-populated southern Iraq. They were also concerned about the intensified tanker war. During the first four months of 1987, Iran attacked twenty ships and Iraq assaulted fifteen. Kuwaiti ships were favorite targets because Iran strongly objected to Kuwait's close relationship with the Baghdad regime. Kuwait turned to the superpowers, partly to protect oil exports but largely to seek an end to the war through superpower intervention. Moscow leased three tankers to Kuwait, and by June the United States had reflagged half of Kuwait's fleet of twenty-two tankers.

Finally, direct attacks on the superpowers' ships drew them into the conflict. On May 6, for the first time, a Soviet freighter was attacked in the southern Gulf region, hit by rockets from Iranian gunboats. Ten days later, a Soviet tanker was damaged by a mine allegedly placed by Iranians near the Kuwait coast. More shocking to the United States was the May 17 accidental Iraqi air attack on the U.S.S *Stark* in which thirty-seven sailors died. The attack highlighted the danger to international shipping in the Gulf.

The Tanker War

The tanker war seemed likely to precipitate a major international incident for two reasons. First, some 70 percent of Japanese, 50 percent of West European, and 7 percent of American oil imports came from the Persian Gulf in the early 1980s. Second, the assault on tankers involved neutral shipping as well as ships of the belligerent states.

The tanker war had two phases. The relatively obscure first phase began in 1981, and the well-publicized second phase began in 1984. As early as May 1981, Baghdad had unilaterally declared a war zone and had officially warned all ships heading to or returning from Iranian ports in the northern zone of the Gulf to stay away or, if they entered, to proceed at their own risk. The main targets in this phase were the ports of Bandar-e Khomeini and Bandar-e Mashur; very few ships were hit outside this zone. Despite the proximity of these ports to Iraq, the Iraqi navy did not play an important role in the operations. Instead, Baghdad used Super Frelon helicopters equipped with Exocet missiles or Mirage F–1s and MiG-23s to hit its targets.

In March 1984, the tanker war entered its second phase when an Iraqi Super Etendard fired an Exocet missile at a Greek tanker south of Khark Island. Until the March assault, Iran had not intentionally attacked civilian ships in the Gulf. The new wave of Iraqi assaults, however, led Iran to reciprocate. In April 1984, Tehran launched its first attack against civilian commercial shipping by shelling an Indian freighter. Most observers considered that Iraqi attacks, however, outnumbered Iranian assaults by three to one.

Iran's retaliatory attacks were largely ineffective because a limited number of aircraft equipped with long-range antiship missiles and ships with long-range surface-to-surface missiles were deployed. Moreover, despite repeated Iranian threats to close the Strait of Hormuz, Iran itself depended on the sea-lanes for vital oil exports. Nonetheless, by late 1987 Iran's mine-laying activities and attacks on ships had drawn a large fleet of Western naval vessels to the Gulf to ensure that the sea-lanes were kept open.

Role of the Air Force

Despite Iraqi success in causing major damage to exposed Iranian ammunition and fuel dumps in the early days of the war, the Iranian air force prevailed initially in the air war. One reason was that Iranian airplanes could carry two or three times more bombs or rockets than their Iraqi counterparts. Moreover, Iranian pilots demonstrated considerable expertise. For example, the Iranian air force attacked Baghdad and key Iraqi air bases as early as the first few weeks of the war, seeking to destroy supply and support systems. The attack on Iraq's oil field complex and air base at Al Walid, the base for T-22 and Il-28 bombers, was a well-coordinated assault. The targets were more than 800 kilometers from Iran's closest air base at Urumiyeh, so the F-4s had to refuel in midair for the mission.

Iran's air force relied on F-4s and F-5s for assaults and a few F-14s for reconnaissance. Although Iran used its Maverick missiles effectively against ground targets, lack of airplane spare parts forced Iran to substitute helicopters for close air support. Helicopters served not only as gunships and troop carriers but also as emergency supply transports. In the mountainous area near Mehran, helicopters proved advantageous in finding and destroying targets and maneuvering against antiaircraft guns or man-portable missiles. During Operation Karbala Five and Operation Karbala Six, the Iranians reportedly engaged in large-scale helicopter-borne operations on the southern and central fronts, respectively. Chinooks and smaller Bell helicopters, such as the Bell 214A, were escorted by Sea Cobra choppers.

In confronting the Iraqi air defense, Iran soon discovered that a low-flying group of two, three, or four F–4s could hit targets almost anywhere in Iraq. Iranian pilots overcame Iraqi SA–2 and SA–3 antiaircraft missiles, using American tactics developed in Vietnam; they were less successful against Iraqi SA–6s. Iran's Western-made air defense system seemed more effective than Iraq's Soviet-made counterpart. Nevertheless, Iran experienced difficulty in operating and maintaining Hawk, Rapier, and Tigercat missiles and instead used antiaircraft guns and man-portable missiles.

As the war continued, however, Iran was increasingly short of spare parts for damaged airplanes and had lost a large number of airplanes in combat. As a result, by late 1987 Iran had become less able to mount an effective defense against the resupplied Iraqi air force, let alone stage aerial counterattacks.

Role of the Navy

In late 1987, an accurate estimate of Iranian naval capability was difficult. In the November 1980 offensive against Iraqi ports and oil facilities, Iran lost at least two corvettes and two missile boats. Nevertheless, the Iranian navy was able to supply Abadan by night (with food and arms for the armed forces and the remaining civilians) until late 1981, when Iranian forces regained the city.

Lacking parts and qualified personnel, few Iranian ships were deployed outside limited coastal areas, where their main functions were patrol and search missions. The Iranian navy stopped and searched hundreds of ships suspected of carrying military equipment destined for Iraq. Beginning in 1984, some Iranian military elements such as the Pasdaran also assaulted ships in the Persian Gulf. In May 1987, reliable sources reported that a Soviet ship was assaulted by a Pasdaran unit speedboat; such Pasdaran raids were largely ineffective, however, because of the weapons used— machine guns and rocket-propelled grenades.

Armed Forces and Society

Status in National Life

Since 1979 Iran has witnessed political and military changes with long-lasting domestic repercussions. The shah relied on the country's considerable military strength to implement his policy goals. When his rule was replaced by a theocratic regime with a new domestic agenda, political power presumably rested in the hands of Khomeini and a group of cautious clerics bound by deeply conservative religious values. In the turmoil of the Revolution, the regular armed forces lost their preeminent position in society primarily because of their close identification with the shah.

The military was paralyzed by fast-moving events and incapable of effective action, and its downfall was accelerated when a number of key senior officers fled the country, fearing reprisals from the revolutionary regime. The public trials and executions of high-ranking military officers further tainted the military's image. On February 15, 1979, three days after the official declaration of the republic, a secret Islamic revolutionary court in Tehran handed down death sentences on four generals. Five days later the regime ordered the execution of four more generals. Other military officers were executed for the Islamic crimes of "causing corruption on earth" and "fighting Allah," according to an interpretation of *shariat* (see Glossary). The new regime considered these officers as Pahlavi holdovers, lacking proper Islamic credentials and therefore potential instigators of military coups. When protests were voiced about summary executions, Ayatollah Mohammad Reza Mahdavi-Kani, the cleric in charge of the *komitehs,* replied, "We must purify society in order to renew it." The resulting leadership vacuum in the military took several years to fill.

Mobilized to fight a foreign enemy, the armed forces by 1981 were gradually developing autonomy and an esprit de corps, despite their acrimonious infighting with the Pasdaran, whose independent military power acted as a check on any possible coup attempts by the armed forces. The Khomeini regime, aware of its dependence on the armed forces, adopted a new strategy aimed at assimilating the military into the Revolution by promoting loyal officers and propagating Islamic values. Leaders recognized that as long as the country was at war with Iraq and was experiencing internal political turmoil, they would need a loyal army on the battlefield as well as the loyal Pasdaran on the homefront. Despite the need for military support, however, the revolutionary regime continued to exercise tight control over the armed forces and to regard them with some suspicion.

Political rivalries notwithstanding, the regular armed forces' professionalism and impressive performance in the war stood as clear alternatives to the early "human-wave" tactics of the Pasdaran and Basij, which cost hundreds of thousands of lives and achieved little. The armed forces' respectable military performance also helped exonerate them from the role they had played during the Pahlavi period. Since September 1980, the military has demonstrated that it could and would defend the country and the legitimate government.

The Defense Burden

Military expenditures under the shah were high and unpopular. Even after the 1974 rise in the price of petroleum, a dispropor-
tionately high percentage of the government's annual budget was
devoted to military expenditures. Iran's military establishment
occupied a special place, and the civilian population, particularly
in the rural areas, disapproved of its privileged status. Despite the
nation-building activities in which the armed forces were engaged
(especially in the area of education), Iranian society in general never
fully shared the shah's commitment to a buildup that drained the
treasury of scarce resources.

Since 1980 the armed forces' budget has been prepared by the
Ministry of Defense (formerly the Ministry of War under the shah)
in consultation with the SDC. The latter is also consulted by the
Ministry of the Pasdaran in preparing its budget. In turn, the prime
minister, who is also a member of the SDC, submits the completed
package to the Majlis for debate, approval, and appropriation.

In the absence of official data, the precise levels of military
expenditures are difficult to determine. Figures collected and ana-
lyzed by the Stockholm International Peace Research Institute for
the 1976–83 period indicate a reduction in defense expenditures
from the equivalent of US\$14.6 billion in 1976 to US\$5.2 billion
in 1983. Not surprisingly, the sharpest decline occurred in 1979,
when the revolutionary regime either canceled or postponed contracted purchases. The most notable cancellations were the navy's
six Spruance-class destroyers and three Tang-class submarines. The
air force also canceled big-ticket items, including 160 F–16 fighters and 7 Boeing E3A–AWACS aircraft. Admittedly, some cancellations were caused by economic difficulties during the shah's
last years in power. With a reduction in Iran's oil revenues during the 1977–78 period, the shah reluctantly agreed to scale down
ambitious construction projects, such as the naval facility at Chah
Bahar (now Bandar-e Beheshti) on the Gulf of Oman and the military industrial complex at Esfahan.

Nevertheless, the revolutionary government abandoned many
military projects, not only because most were contracted with
American corporations such as Northrop and Boeing, but also
because the new regime's priorities were different. The Khomeini
government claimed to represent the oppressed masses and
promised to provide for their needs. To this end the government
chose to reallocate massive defense expenditures in other directions.

This trend was rapidly reversed, however, with the revolutionary government's first war budget in 1981. Because published

figures are lacking, reliable estimates of Iran's defense expenditures are difficult to make. For example, according to the International Institute for Strategic Studies, defense expenditures in FY 1981–82 may have been somewhere between US$4.4 and US$13.3 billion; if so, the latter figure would represent 41.6 percent of Iran's total budget. By 1987 all defense expenditures, including those of the Pasdaran and Basij and payments to the families of war martyrs, may have totaled US$100 billion.

Iran's prerevolutionary defense budgets were high by the standards of developing countries, and large expenditures for its armed forces continued through the early 1980s. Despite the outbreak of the war, Iran's gross national product (GNP—see Glossary) climbed from an estimated US$107 billion in 1979 to US$158 billion in 1984. Military expenditures climbed similarly from an estimated US$8.8 billion in 1979 to US$11.3 billion in 1984. The United States Arms Control and Disarmament Agency's statistics indicated that military expenditures as a percentage of GNP increased from 6.6 percent to 7.2 percent between 1980 and 1984. More significantly, according to some estimates, military expenditures represented 19.7 percent of central government expenditures in 1980 and 29.9 percent in 1984. By all accounts, the impact of these large military expenditures on Iranian society has been considerable.

The World Bank (see Glossary) estimated that with almost one-third of the annual budget allocated to the war effort, other sectors of the economy, including education, health, and housing, experienced sharp declines. Iran's revolutionary government, however, rechanneled some of its military disbursements to the nonmilitary population. For example, veterans, disabled veterans, and widows continued to receive financial support from the government. In rural areas, ad hoc procurement mechanisms were rapidly put in place to feed and clothe the swelling volunteer ranks. These activities created employment opportunities that channeled government monies to the civilian population.

Ingenious as these steps were, the burden of defense expenditures left some of Tehran's revolutionary promises unfulfilled. Khomeini had criticized the shah's regime for squandering Iran's assets by pouring a large percentage of oil revenues into the military and denying basic services to the majority of the population, but in some cases Khomeini was obliged to do the same thing. It was true that after 1980, economic conditions improved proportionately faster for the lower classes than for any other group (see War Costs, ch. 3). Still, the revolutionary regime was exacting great sacrifices from those who could least afford it.

The Impact of Casualties on Society

Iran's population, based on the preliminary results of the October 1986 census, was slightly more than 48 million, including approximately 2.6 million refugees from Afghanistan and Iraq. The population was expected, according to United States Bureau of Census projections, to increase to nearly 56 million in 1990 and 76 million in the year 2000. In 1986 the 18 to 30-year-old and 31 to 45-year-old male populations stood at about 5.2 and 3.5 million, respectively. In the absence of reliable information on Iran's war casualties, the significance of these figures was difficult to assess. Estimates of war-related deaths ranged between 180,000 and 300,000. Loss of life was especially high among the 18- to 30-year-old male population; a generation of young and potentially productive citizens had been reduced significantly, and the survivors had been physically and mentally scarred by the war.

Casualties also affected Iran's attempts at industrial recovery. The campaign to resuscitate steel, petrochemical, and other plants faced critical manpower shortages, raising criticisms from the more conservative elements in the regime. The manpower shortages were exacerbated by the 1982 military campaigns that had mobilized up to 1 million volunteers on more than one occasion.

Coupled with the deteriorating economic situation, the high human cost of the abortive Iranian thrusts into Iraq in 1982 to 1984 generated war-weariness and discontent even among the regime's staunchest supporters, the urban and lower classes. The number of recruits dropped because of disenchantment stemming from political divisions, which sometimes produced conflicts that turned violent in the streets of major cities. The Khomeini regime, relying on the total devotion of the Pasdaran and the Basij, appealed to national and religious feelings to rekindle morale. In a series of rulings issued in the autumn of 1982, Khomeini declared that parental permission was unnecessary for those going to the front, that volunteering for military duty was a religious obligation, and that serving in the armed forces took priority over all other forms of work or study. The government mounted a simultaneous effort to quell demonstrations by political groups like the Mojahedin and the Tudeh (see Internal Security, this ch.). The demise of left-wing guerrilla organizations, however, did not reduce opposition to the war. New elements calling for a settlement of the conflict with Iraq emerged. Because of this opposition, former Prime Minister Bazargan urged a negotiated end to the war, realizing that Iran might fall victim to its own political rigidity. For the revolutionary regime, however, the war remained a legitimizing tool, despite its high cost.

Treatment of Veterans and Widows

In 1980 the Khomeini government established two special foundations to care for those affected by war. The Foundation for Martyrs and the Foundation for War Refugees (Bonyad-e Jang-zadegan) provided welfare and services to veterans and survivors. It also established the Foundation for War Victims (veterans) and the Foundation for the Disinherited (Bonyad-e Mostazafin), which looked after orphans.

With more than 1 million people killed or maimed by the war, the cost of financing compensations and pensions mounted rapidly. War-related expenses included the costs of the Pasdaran and the Basij, compensations and pensions to the war disabled and the families of the dead, the funding of the Foundation for War Victims and the War Reconstruction Fund. Despite these mounting costs, the government was generous to the survivors of the dead. A regular soldier's family reportedly received compensation of US$24,000 and full salary as a pension; additionally, the equivalent of US$60 monthly was deposited in the bank account of each of his minor children until they reached eighteen. The government assisted the family in renting, buying, or building a house. Less generous amounts were paid to the families of the Pasdaran and the Basij who died on the front. Disabled soldiers reportedly received US$30 monthly, and the seriously injured were cared for in veterans' hospitals.

In an official Iranian publication, *Summary Report: An Estimate of the Economic Damages of the Imposed War of Iraq Against Iran,* the damages caused to the Iranian economy up to March 1983 were cited as equivalent to US$135.8 billion, including the loss of oil revenue (US$35 billion) and agricultural output (US$23 billion). A dozen cities and 1,200 villages were reported destroyed and another 19 cities partially damaged. The war had created no fewer than 1.5 million Iranian refugees by early 1983. In 1987 more recent documentation cited the war's costs at approximately US$300 billion.

Internal Security

The Islamic Revolution destroyed the structures on which the shah's internal security policies depended. Mohammad Reza Shah had not tolerated dissent, had reacted strongly when challenged, and had relied on an elaborate internal security police force to enforce his absolute authority. Over the years, Khomeini had vigorously condemned the shah's secret police operations and continually called on Iranians to rise against a perceived tyrannical ruler.

Iraqi forces severely damaged the port
of Khorramshahr in October 1980
Copyright Lehtikuva/PHOTRI

By the late 1970s, the shah's internal security organizations were in disgrace because of their abuses. In early 1979, the revolutionary regime dismantled existing security organizations and called on loyal citizens to protect the Revolution. Yet, like the shah, the revolutionary regime faced clear opposition to its authority.

Internal Security in the 1970s

The Pahlavi regime identified the Fadayan, the Tudeh, and several ethnic groups as opponents to the shah's rule. To meet their rising challenge, the shah relied on security forces whose agents infiltrated many underground organizations. By early 1970, a sophisticated intelligence-gathering system was in place, reporting all currents of political dissent directly to the monarch.

In 1971 opposition forces took the initiative by launching a terrorist campaign against the regime. At the time, this was perceived as a nuisance and an embarrassment to the shah, because the monarchy was not "threatened." Nevertheless, opposition to the shah grew stronger when the monarch authorized unrelenting punishment of those accused of security violations. Hundreds of young Iranians were arrested, tried, and sentenced. Many were tortured and some executed for their unwavering opposition. In 1976 opposition forces clashed with the police in a series of gun

285

battles that took place in the streets of Tehran. With heightened visibility, terrorist groups mounted successful attacks on police posts, further threatening the regime's hold on internal security. By 1978 organized opposition to the monarchy reached a high point with ideologically incompatible groups joining in efforts to overthrow the shah. Leftist guerrillas joined student and religious organizations in calling for political change.

The two most important leftist guerrilla groups operating in Iran in 1979 were the Mojahedin and the Fadayan (see Antiregime Opposition Groups, this ch.). After its initial formation in 1965 as a discussion group of religiously inspired university graduates, the Mojahedin had splintered several times. The graduates who composed the Mojahedin were thoroughly disillusioned with the shah's regime and advocated armed struggle. In the course of the 1970s the Mojahedin gradually gained notoriety. The Mojahedin and the Fadayan conducted a systematic assassination campaign from 1971 to 1976 against Iranian security officials and United States military and defense-related personnel stationed in Tehran. The shah was also a target, as evidenced by periodic uncoverings of assassination plots. This wave of violence was met by an equally strong and determined campaign of arrests and executions. Iranian students abroad also became part of a cycle of action and counteraction: in the United States and Western Europe, students who protested against the shah were kept under surveillance so that punitive action could later be taken against them. In addition, the Mojahedin and the Fadayan conducted a propaganda campaign in support of "the Iranian armed struggle" and against the shah, SAVAK, and what was termed "institutionalized repression in Iran" (see SAVAK, this ch.).

Within Iran's borders, stiff government security measures notwithstanding, organized opposition was never eliminated. Although the shah had declared illegal all opposition political parties, labor unions, peasant organizations, and university student groups, antigovernment sentiments remained high, especially among the clerical community. By late 1977, student demonstrations increased in frequency, with a vocal minority calling on Iranians to "raise their voices against absolute rule." These protests, timed to call President Jimmy Carter's attention to the human rights situation in Iran, resulted in the arrest of hundreds of demonstrators, many of whom were allegedly tortured by SAVAK forces.

In January 1978, conservative religious students demonstrated in the holy city of Qom to protest an article in the progovernment newspaper *Etalaat* that they considered slandered Ayatollah Khomeini, who was then living in exile in An Najaf in Iraq.

Religious leaders were also outraged at what they perceived to be the shah's violations of sacred Islamic laws in such areas as the role of women in society and the imposition of a secular legal system that usurped clerical authority. Attempts by the police to disperse demonstrators resulted in several deaths.

The religious leadership called for a general strike across the country for February 18, to highlight the forty-day mourning period for those killed in Qom. Far more serious disturbances erupted on that day in the city of Tabriz, precipitating the worst riots since 1963. After several days of widespread arson directed at banks, movie theaters, and hotels in Tabriz, the army moved in to restore order. Nonviolent protests occurred in Tehran and other major cities. According to the government 12 persons were killed in Tabriz and 250 persons arrested. In reality, the casualty figure was much higher and the arrests more numerous. Ironically, the deaths presented the next opportunity for confrontation. When demonstrators, commemorating the forty-day mourning period, defiantly marched through streets of many cities, the armed forces reacted as expected. To protect themselves and restore order, they opened fire, killing and injuring more civilians. The result was a sequence of events in which the opposition, led by influential clerics, conducted "religious commemorations," and the government interpreted them as challenges to law and order. With neither side relenting, the cycle of violence spread.

Observers of these tragic events pointed out that the reemergence of large-scale protest demonstrations was only made possible because of the shah's more liberal policies toward the nonviolent expression of dissent. Indeed, the shah confirmed on several occasions his commitment to more "liberal" political reforms, but at the same time he warned that the dissident movement was "completely illegal" and that he would "not let it get out of hand." Illegal or not, mass protest demonstrations did get out of control when the shah openly chastised the clerics for "destroying the country." The shah could not end these demonstrations, which gathered more support throughout 1978. Workers from the oil industry, heeding the call of the religious authorities, slowly paralyzed Iran's economic sector. It became only a matter of time before the shah lost control over Iran's internal security.

Law Enforcement Agencies

Intensely concerned with matters of internal security in the post-1953 environment, the shah authorized the development of one of the most extensive systems of law enforcement agencies in the developing world. The Gendarmerie—the rural police—and the National Police gained in numbers and responsibilities. The secret police organization, SAVAK, gained special notoriety for its excessive zeal in "maintaining" internal security. But as in the regular armed forces, the shah's management style virtually eliminated all coordination among these agencies. A favorite approach was to shuffle army personnel back and forth between their ordinary duties and temporary positions in internal security agencies, in order to minimize the possibility of any organized coups against the throne. Added to this list of institutional shortcomings was agencies' all-important public image, cloaked in mystery and fear. Iranians in and out of the country came to perceive these agencies as "arms" of the shah's absolute power and resented them deeply.

SAVAK

Formed under the guidance of United States and Israeli intelligence officers in 1957, SAVAK developed into an effective secret agency. General Teymur Bakhtiar was appointed its first director, only to be dismissed in 1961, allegedly for organizing a coup; he was assassinated in 1970 under mysterious circumstances, probably on the shah's direct order. His successor, General Hosain Pakravan, was dismissed in 1966, allegedly for having failed to crush the clerical opposition in the early 1960s. The shah turned to his childhood friend and classmate, General Nematollah Nassiri, to rebuild SAVAK and properly "serve" the monarch. Mansur Rafizadeh, the SAVAK director in the United States throughout the 1970s, claimed that General Nassiri's telephone was tapped by SAVAK agents reporting directly to the shah, an example of the level of mistrust pervading the government on the eve of the Revolution.

In 1987 accurate information concerning SAVAK remained publicly unavailable. A flurry of pamphlets issued by the revolutionary regime after 1979 indicated that SAVAK had been a full-scale intelligence agency with more than 15,000 full-time personnel and thousands of part-time informants. SAVAK was attached to the Office of the Prime Minister, and its director assumed the title of deputy to the prime minister for national security affairs. Although officially a civilian agency, SAVAK had close ties to the military; many of its officers served simultaneously in branches of the armed forces. Another childhood friend and close confidant of the shah, Major General Hosain Fardust, was deputy director of SAVAK until the early 1970s, when the shah promoted him to the directorship of the Special Intelligence Bureau, which operated inside Niavaran Palace, independently of SAVAK.

Founded to round up members of the outlawed Tudeh, SAVAK expanded its activities to include gathering intelligence and neutralizing the regime's opponents. An elaborate system was created to monitor all facets of political life. For example, a censorship office was established to monitor journalists, literary figures, and academics throughout the country; it took appropriate measures against those who fell out of line. Universities, labor unions, and peasant organizations, among others, were all subjected to intense surveillance by SAVAK agents and paid informants. The agency was also active abroad, especially in monitoring Iranian students who publicly opposed Pahlavi rule.

Over the years, SAVAK became a law unto itself, having legal authority to arrest and detain suspected persons indefinitely. SAVAK operated its own prisons in Tehran (the Komiteh and Evin facilities) and, many suspected, throughout the country as well. Many of these activities were carried out without any institutional checks. Thus, it came as no surprise when, in 1979, SAVAK was singled out as a primary target for reprisals, its headquarters overrun, and prominent leaders tried and executed by *komiteh* representatives. High-ranking SAVAK agents were purged between 1979 and 1981; there were 61 SAVAK officials among 248 military personnel executed between February and September 1979. The organization was officially dissolved by Khomeini shortly after he came to power in 1979.

SAVAMA

Little information existed in 1987 on SAVAK's successor agency, SAVAMA. According to General Robert E. Huyser, President Jimmy Carter's last special envoy to imperial Iran, SAVAMA's first director was Major General Fardust, who was arrested in December 1985 for being a "Soviet informer." But after this major arrest the revolutionary government's keen desire to gain an upper hand over leftist guerrilla organizations may have influenced certain IRP leaders to relax their previously unrelenting pursuit of military intelligence personnel. Key religious leaders, including Majlis speaker Hashemi-Rafsanjani, insisted on recalling former agents to help the regime eliminate domestic opposition. Consequently, some intelligence officers and low-ranking SAVAK and army intelligence officials were asked to return to government service because of their specialized knowledge of the Iranian left. Others had acquired in-depth knowledge of Iraq's Baath Party and proved to be invaluable in helping decision makers.

Although it is impossible to verify, in 1987 observers speculated that some of SAVAK's intelligence-gathering operations were turned over to SAVAMA. It remained to be determined whether these newly authorized operations proved effective and whether there was coordination with other branches of government, including the powerful Pasdaran.

Gendarmerie and National Police

The Gendarmerie, numbering nearly 74,000 in 1979, was subordinate to the Ministry of Interior. Its law enforcement responsibilities extended to all rural areas and to small towns and villages of fewer than 5,000 inhabitants. The International Institute for Strategic Studies estimated its manpower at 70,000 in 1986.

The National Police operated with approximately 200,000 men in 1979, a figure that has not fluctuated much since. Like the Gendarmerie, the National Police was under the Ministry of Interior, and its responsibilities included all cities with more than 5,000 in population—a total of 53 percent of the population. In addition, the National Police was responsible for passport and immigration procedures, issuance and control of citizens' identification cards, driver and vehicle licensing and registration, and railroad and airport policing. Some of these duties were absorbed into the Ministry of the Pasdaran during the early years of the Revolution, and cooperation between these two branches seemed extensive.

Since 1979 both these paramilitary organizations have undergone complete reorganizations. IRP leaders quickly appointed Gendarmerie and police officers loyal to the Revolution to revive and reorganize the two bodies under the Republic. Between 1979 and 1983, no fewer than seven officers were given top National Police portfolios. Colonel Khalil Samimi, appointed in 1983 by the influential Hojjatoleslam Nategh-e Nuri, then minister of interior, was credited with reorganizing the National Police according to the IRP's Islamic guidelines. The Gendarmerie followed a similar path. Seven appointments were made between 1979 and 1986, leading to a full reorganization. In addition to Brigadier General Ahmad Mohagheghi, the commander in the early republican period who was executed in late summer of 1980, five colonels were purged. Colonel Ali Kuchekzadeh played a major role in reorganizing and strengthening the Gendarmerie after its near collapse in the early revolutionary period. The commander in 1987, Colonel Mohammad Sohrabi, had served in that position since February 1985 and was the first top officer to have risen from the ranks.

As of 1987, the National Police and the Gendarmerie reflected the ideology of the state. Despite their valuable internal security operations, the roles of both bodies were restricted by the rising influence of the Pasdaran and the Basij.

Antiregime Opposition Groups

The Khomeini regime has faced severe challenges from several opposition groups, including royalists, National Front bureaucrats, intellectuals and professionals, communists, guerrilla organizations, Kurdish rebels, and distinguished *mujtahids* (Shia clerics whose demonstrated erudition in religious law has earned them the privilege to interpret law). Of these, the royalists and the National Front leaders have operated mainly from foreign bases or underground cells. The communists were purged in 1983 when the Tudeh's leadership was almost entirely arrested. The main guerrilla group, the Mojahedin, claimed to have made strides in organizing a war of attrition against the regime. But because it has operated since July 1986 primarily from Baghdad, thus giving the impression of collaboration with Iraq, the Mojahedin's effectiveness and credibility may have been lessened by the war. The Kurds have been fighting the regime since their 1979 rebellion, even though Tehran has kept them off balance by using Pasdaran forces. Finally, National Front politicians have openly displayed their differing views, mostly in West European capitals, although the group led by former Prime Minister Bazargan was the only domestic "opposition" party tolerated by the regime.

Mojahedin

In the early 1970s, founders of the Mojahedin movement decided to organize operations against the shah's government. Initial demands made by Mojahedin leaders, most of whom were executed between 1972 and 1975, covered such points as the cancellation of all security agreements with the United States; expropriation of multinational corporations; nationalization of agricultural and urban land, banks, and large industries; administration of the army and other institutions by people's councils; creation of a "people's army"; regional autonomy for Iran's ethnic minorities; and various measures to benefit workers and peasants. Unlike other anti-shah organizations, the Mojahedin channeled its efforts into gaining supporters and developing an effective party network. The members were ideologically inspired by a combination of Shia philosophy and Marxist sociology and attacked the shah and his perceived abuses. By 1979 the membership of the Mojahedin had reached a record high of 25,000, and it had hundreds of thousands of supporters. The movement frequently mobilized these masses against the shah.

The organization fell out of favor immediately after the Revolution, however, when its new leader, Masud Rajavi, boycotted the referendum on the new Constitution and advocated the total separation of the religious establishment and the state. Khomeini considered this a calculated and direct challenge to the IRP and the revolutionary regime. Rumors spread that the Mojahedin organization was a pawn of foreign powers, especially the United States. In response, the Mojahedin launched its own anti-Khomeini campaign by calling on the government to purify the Revolution.

President Bani Sadr supported the Mojahedin. When he lost the support of Khomeini, Bani Sadr sought refuge with Mojahedin leaders and was smuggled out of Iran, along with Rajavi and other senior representatives. In July 1981, the two leaders announced the formation of the National Council of Resistance (NCR) and launched a campaign to overthrow the Khomeini regime. From its headquarters in France, the NCR recruited additional support both within and outside Iran and welcomed ethnic minority leaders to its ranks. Its published charter was almost identical to the program of the Mojahedin. Partly to satisfy its diverse constituency and partly to distinguish itself from the Khomeini regime, the NCR offered a new agenda that reflected special concern for the interests of the lower middle class. In its attempt to gain the support of minor civil servants, shopkeepers, artisans, and small merchants, it adopted a slightly more moderate position than the one the Khomeini government had espoused concerning private property. The charter also promised to respect individual liberties, "except for persons identified with the shah's or Khomeini's regime," and guaranteed special rights for ethnic minorities, particularly the Kurds.

A score of other promises were made, including the return of land to farmers who would, however, be encouraged to consolidate their holdings in collective farms; the increase of available housing, education, and health services; the guarantee of equality for women; and the establishment of a "democratic army" in which the rank and file would be consulted on decisions and selections of officers. Yet, these promises could not be implemented because the NCR was not in power. The organization had to operate inside Iran, and the process strained the leadership's unity; disagreements over goals eventually led to the dissolution of the NCR. By March 1984, Bani Sadr and Kurdish leaders withdrew from the coalition. The French government asked Rajavi to leave France in July 1986. The Mojahedin set up their headquarters in Baghdad, whence they continued to launch military and propaganda offensives against the Khomeini regime.

In June 1987, Rajavi announced the formation of the Iranian National Army of Liberation, open to non-Mojahedin members,

*A unit of the Iranian National Army of Liberation celebrates
a victory over Iranian forces in Khuzestan Province*
Courtesy Iran Liberation

that would escalate attacks. Subsequently, Mojahedin sources claimed to have set up military training camps near the war front and to have launched numerous attacks against Pasdaran outposts. The Mojahedin has also been active in Western Europe and the United States; it has organized numerous rallies, distributed anti-Khomeini literature, and recruited Iranians living abroad (see Opposition Political Parties in Exile, ch. 4).

Fadayan

Among the armed leftist guerrilla groups operating in Iran in 1987, the Fadayan was the most active. The Fadayan was established when smaller groups operating in Tabriz, Mashhad, and Tehran merged in 1970. Its founders were university students and graduates who saw violence as the only means to oppose the shah. As Iran's economic situation deteriorated in the mid-1970s, the Fadayan recruited workers from large manufacturing industries and the oil sector. Recruitment expanded to include such national and ethnic movements as those of Kurdish, Turkoman, Baluch, and Arab minorities. The Fadayan opposed both imperial and republican regimes but did participate fully in the Revolution, taking over various military barracks and police stations in Tehran, Tabriz, Hamadan, Abadan, and Shiraz in 1979.

In early June 1980, the Fadayan split into two factions: the Fadayan "Minority" and the Fadayan " Majority." The "Minority" faction, which was actually the larger of the two, has consistently opposed the Republic and considered Khomeini "reactionary." It vehemently condemned the Tudeh's cooperation with Khomeini prior to 1983. It also rejected the armed activities of the Mojahedin and advocated instead the expansion of underground cells. The "Minority" faction refused to join the NCR because of Bani Sadr's past association with the Khomeini regime. Subsequently, the "Minority" faction, along with a number of smaller leftist groups, established a new organization known as the Organization of Revolutionary Workers of Iran.

The Fadayan "Majority" faction moved closer to the views held by the Tudeh and supported Khomeini because of his anti-imperialist stance. This support of Khomeini changed in early 1983 when Khomeini turned against the Tudeh. In late 1987, the "Majority" faction was a satellite of the Tudeh (see Opposition Political Parties in Exile, ch. 4).

The falling out of the Fadayan with the Islamic government within the first year of the Revolution was attributed to the ideological rift that emerged between the Fadayan's leftist-secular agenda and the religious and ideological views of the clerical leadership. Khomeini's *velayat-e faqih* (see Glossary) was a powerful concept that swept aside all leftist arguments; the Khomeini view of the Revolution was appealing precisely because of its religious aspects, which were easily assimilated by the Iranian population.

Paykar

The Paykar (Struggle) Organization was formed in 1979 from a Mojahedin splinter group that advocated the total separation of the religious establishment and the state. It considered Khomeini's policies backward and damaging to Iran's long-term socioeconomic development. The Paykar, perceived by other leftist groups as a dogmatic movement, called for an end to the Iran-Iraq War, viewing it as a diversionary tactic "waged by two reactionary and unpopular regimes." In 1982, when several Paykar leaders were arrested, the organization ceased to function overtly, but in 1987 it was still suspected of operating underground cells in major Iranian cities.

The Role of Minorities in Internal Security

Ethnic cooperation has been a consistent national security problem for successive regimes throughout the twentieth century, and, after the 1979 Revolution, the Khomeini government faced one of its earliest challenges from Kurdish, Baluch, and Turkoman tribal members. The Turkoman and Baluch rebellions, which attempted to achieve greater autonomy, were quickly ended. The revolutionary regime went out of its way to accommodate opposition because it did not want any instability to develop on the border with neighboring Afghanistan. Tehran wanted at all costs to prevent foreign powers from exploiting ethnic discontent in southwestern Iran. By emphasizing shared religious and cultural values, the revolutionary government persuaded some tribal members to accept the central authority of Tehran, while it sought to co-opt others, such as the Turkomans and Baluchs, by providing special economic incentives.

A more pressing ethnic challenge to the regime came from Kurdish rebels in the northwest, who had long struggled for independence. In several 1979 meetings, Khomeini warned key Kurdish leaders that any attempts at dismantling Iran would be met with the harshest response, and he sent Pasdaran units to the north, underlining the seriousness of the government's intention. Despite these warnings, in the spring of 1979, seizing on the turmoil of the Revolution, the Kurdish Democratic Party of Iran, the Komala (Komala-ye Shureshgari-ye Zahmat Keshan-e Kordestan-e Iran, or Komala, or Committee of the Revolutionary Toilers of Iranian Kordestan) and the Kurdish branch of the Fadayan mounted a rebellion that the revolutionary regime crushed rather easily.

The confrontation between Tehran and the Kurds lessened sharply when the Iran-Iraq War broke out. Contrary to assumptions, Iraqi Kurds and their Iranian brothers did not cooperate to exploit weaknesses on both sides. Past divisions within the Kurdish communities effectively prevented joint pursuit of the long-cherished goal of an independent state. Not surprisingly, neither Baghdad nor Tehran was displeased by this outcome. Rather, both sides insisted on organizing special loyalist Kurdish military units to participate in the war and to demonstrate allegiance to their respective states.

In contrast to the Kurds, the Arab population of Khuzestan stood firmly behind the revolutionary government. Iranian Arabs rejected Saddam Husayn's call to "liberate Arabistan" from Persian rule and overwhelmingly opted to remain loyal to their country. Since 1980 Khuzestan has witnessed some of the bloodiest battles in the twentieth century, but its Arab inhabitants have not wavered in their allegiance.

Iran regards ethnic minority challenges with apprehension. It has taken every precaution, for example, to resist Iraqi- or Soviet-sponsored efforts to persuade the Kurdish minority to secede from

Iran. Much as the Pahlavi regime before it had done, the revolutionary government considered the unity of Iran vital to its national security. The commitment to defend the entire country, with all its ethnic groups, remained an uncompromised objective, and sensitive, pragmatic, and political steps have been taken since 1979 to strengthen national unity. Despite the commitment of the Khomeini regime to the revival of the Islamic community (*ummah*), it, no less than the shah's regime, sought to preserve Iran's territorial integrity as an aspect of national security.

Of all the issues facing revolutionary Iran since 1979, none was more serious than alleged human rights violations. Although the trend was toward greater adherence to constitutional guarantees, particularly after December 1982, when Khomeini issued several orders restricting arbitrary arrest and detention, Iran's human rights record showed serious abuses. Procedural safeguards were lacking for defendants tried in revolutionary courts, which handled virtually all political cases. In evaluating the hundreds of executions ordered each year, separating cases of executions for actual crimes from executions based purely on the defendant's beliefs, statements, or associations, was difficult, given the regime's practice of cloaking the latter category with trumped-up charges from the former category. Reliable statistics were not available in 1987 on the number killed for political or religious reasons under the Khomeini regime, but the number of persons executed each year for political reasons was high.

Amnesty International's 1986 annual report recorded an estimated 6,500 executions in Iran between February 1979 and the end of 1985; the report noted, however, that "Amnesty International believed the true figures were much higher, as former prisoners and relatives of prisoners consistently testified that large numbers of political prisoners were executed in secret." These killings were largely conducted by the government's own organizations, including the Pasdaran and the SAVAMA.

Political opposition to the revolutionary regime was punished in ways other than execution. Iranians listed as "killed while resisting arrest," but actually alive and in jail, were too numerous to count, according to Amnesty International. Torture in Iran's prisons was rampant and covered a wide range of inhuman practices, particularly in Tehran's notorious Evin Prison. Mock executions, along with blindfolding and solitary confinement, were favorite methods of torture, according to witness reports assembled by Amnesty International. Beatings of all kinds were common, and prisoners were regularly beaten on the soles of their feet until they could no longer walk. Individuals also suffered damaged kidneys as a result of being kicked and beaten.

The revolutionary prosecutors continued to revise Iran's civil code to conform more closely with their interpretation of Islamic law. In January 1985, for example, Tehran announced the inauguration of a new machine for surgical amputation of the hands of convicted thieves. As interpreted in Iran, this punishment consisted of amputation of the four fingers of the right hand. There were subsequent announcements of the occasional use of this device to administer justice. Death by stoning was allegedly reinstituted as a punishment for certain morality crimes, at least in remote areas of the country. There were many reports of floggings, both as a means of torture and as a formal punishment for sexual offenses.

Although the Constitution guarantees many basic human rights, including rights related to due process (e.g., the right to be informed in writing of charges immediately after arrest, the right to legal counsel, the right to trial by jury in political cases), the revolutionary court system ignored these provisions in practice for "security reasons." When there was a formal accusation, the charge was usually subversion, antiregime activities, or treason. Political arrests were made by members of the Pasdaran or, less commonly, by *komiteh* members. Members of the National Police and Gendarmerie were not normally involved in arrests made on political or moral charges. In political cases, warrants for arrests were seldom used. Consequently, there was no judicial determination of whether these detentions were in conformity with Iranian law. Detainees were frequently held for long periods without charge and in some cases were tortured. For political crimes, no access to a lawyer was permitted; such cases were heard, if at all, by the revolutionary judiciary, and bail was not permitted.

Religious opposition as well as political opposition has met with severe punishment. For example, Iran's largest non-Muslim minority, the Bahais, have suffered persecution. Charges against Bahais were vague, but penalties were severe. As of December 1986, 767 Bahais had been imprisoned and approximately 200 Bahais had been executed or had died following torture (see Non-Muslim Minorities, ch. 2).

Between 1979 and 1982, these abuses of human rights were all defended as necessary to safeguard the Revolution. Tehran launched a systematic attack on its opponents in order to protect its own interpretations of revolutionary norms. Since then, many revolutionary leaders have adopted a more relaxed mood without jeopardizing perceived internal security requirements. It remained to be seen in late 1987 whether the revolutionary regime would be able to maintain the internal security it felt it needed without returning to the drastic measures characteristic of the early period of the Revolution.

*   *   *

An early, albeit cursory, introduction to the Iranian armed forces after the 1979 Revolution is William F. Hickman's *Ravaged and Reborn*. Gregory F. Rose's "The Post-Revolutionary Purge of Iran's Armed Forces: A Revisionist Assessment" and "Soldiers of Islam: The Iranian Armed Forces since the Revolution" provide detailed information on the purges of the military and the ensuing reorganization. Nikola B. Schahgaldian's *The Iranian Military under the Islamic Republic* is the most complete source on the Pasdaran and Basij forces. The best source of current data on the size, budget, and equipment inventory of the armed forces is the annual *The Military Balance,* published by the International Institute for Strategic Studies. Historical background material is presented most completely in J.C. Hurewitz's *Middle East Politics.* On the postrevolutionary period, Dilip Hiro's *Iran under the Ayatollahs* and Ruhollah K. Ramazani's *Revolutionary Iran* are indispensable. For the Iran-Iraq War, Jasim M. Abdulghani's *Iraq and Iran* provides comprehensive coverage of events leading up to the war. The writings of Anthony H. Cordesman on the war itself are very valuable, as is the excellent account in Efraim Karsh's "The Iran-Iraq War: A Military Analysis." (For further information and complete citations, see Bibliography.)

Appendix

Table 1. Metric Conversion Coefficients and Factors

When you know	Multiply by	To find
Millimeters	0.04	inches
Centimeters	0.39	inches
Meters	3.3	feet
Kilometers	0.62	miles
Hectares (10,000 m²)	2.47	acres
Square kilometers	0.39	square miles
Cubic meters	35.3	cubic feet
Liters	0.26	gallons
Kilograms	2.2	pounds
Metric tons	0.98	long tons
....	1.1	short tons
....	2,204	pounds
Degrees Celsius	9	degrees Fahrenheit
(Centigrade)	divide by 5 and add 32	

Table 2. Major Cities, Census Years 1976 and 1986

City	1976	1986*
Tehran	4,496,000	6,022,000
Mashhad	670,000	1,419,000
Isfahan	671,000	928,000
Tabriz	598,000	808,000
Shiraz	416,000	800,000
Ahvaz	329,000	396,000
Kermanshah (Bakhtaran after 1979)	290,000	389,000
Qom	246,000	338,000
Rasht	187,000	259 000
Karaj	138,000	252,000
Abadan	296,000	250,000
Qazvin	139,000	244,000
Urumiyeh	163,000	219,000
Hamadan	155,000	207,000
Kerman	140,000	202,000

*Preliminary.

Table 3. Ethnic and Linguistic Groups, 1986
(exclusive of refugees)

Ethnic Group	Language	Population [1]	Percentage
Persians	Persian	23,100,000	51.0
Azarbaijanis	Turkic	11,500,000	25.2
Kurds	Kurdish	4,000,000	8.8
Gilakis and Mazandaranis	Persian dialects	3,450,000	7.5
Baluchis	Baluchi	600,000	1.3
Lurs	Luri	550,000	1.2
Arabs	Arabic	530,000	1.2
Fars Turks [2]	Turkic dialects	250,000	0.5
Qashqais	Turkish	250,000	0.5
Turkomans	-do-	250,000	0.5
Bakhtiaris	Luri	250,000	0.5
Armenians	Armenian	250,000	0.5
Assyrians	Assyrian	32,000	--[3]
Other	Persian and Turkic dialects, English, French, German, Georgian, Russian	600,000	1.3
TOTAL		45,612,000	100.0

[1] Estimated; rounded off to nearest 10,000.
[2] Includes Abivardis, Afshars, Baharlus, Inanlus, detribalized Qashqais, and other Turkic-speaking groups.
[3] 0.007 percent.

Source: Based on information from Patricia Higgins, "Minority-State Relations in Contemporary Iran," in Ali Banuazizi and Myron Weiner, eds., *The State, Religion, and Ethnic Politics,* Syracuse, 1986, 178.

Table 4. Non-Muslim Religious Minorities, 1986

Religious Minority	Language	Population*
Bahais	Persian, Turkish	350,000
Armenian Christians	Armenian	250,000
Jews	Persian, Kurdish	50,000
Assyrian Christians	Assyrian	32,000
Zoroastrians	Persian	32,000

*Estimated.

Table 5. Oil Production and Exports, 1980–85
(in millions of barrels per day)

	1980	1981	1982	1983	1984	1985
Production	1.47	1.32	2.39	2.44	2.03	2.19
Exports	0.80	0.71	1.62	1.72	1.52	1.57

Source: Based on information from George Jaffé and Keith McLachlan, *Iran and Iraq: The Next Five Years,* Special Report No. 1083, Economist Intelligence Unit, London, 1987, 12.

Table 6. Estimated Production of Major Crops
1981, 1982, and 1983
(in thousands of tons)

	1981–82	1982–83	1983–84
Barley	1,700	1,903	2,034
Cotton (lint)	275	358	300
Legumes	290	296	290
Oil Seeds*	105	138	188
Onions	675	965	736
Pistachios	122	95	84
Potatoes	1,540	1,814	1,740
Rice	1,624	1,605	1,215
Sugar beets	3,231	4,321	3,648
Sugar cane	1,677	1,810	2,053
Wheat	6,610	6,660	5,956

*Sunflower seeds and soybeans.

Source: Based on information from *The Middle East and North Africa, 1987,* London: Europa Publications, 1986, 416.

Table 7. Major Trading Partners, 1985
(in percentages)

Destination of exports from Iran		Sources of imports to Iran	
Japan	15.9	West Germany	16.3
Italy	9.4	Japan	13.4
Turkey	8.8	Britain	6.7
Singapore	7.1	Italy	6.0
Syria	6.5	Turkey	5.9
Spain	5.6	Soviet Union	4.5
Netherlands	5.5	Singapore	3.9
France	5.0	Spain	2.8
United States	4.8	Argentina	2.8
Romania	4.4	Netherlands	2.7
West Germany	4.0	Kuwait	2.0
Other	23.0	Other	33.0
TOTAL	100.0	TOTAL	100.0

Source: Based on information from Economist Intelligence Unit, *Iran: Country Report, 1987*, No. 1, London, 1987, 2.

Table 8. Armed Forces Manpower
Selected Years, 1977-86

Type and Description	1977	1979	1982	1984	1986
Armed forces					
Reserves	300,000	300,000	400,000	350,000	350,000
Army	220,000	285,000[1]	150,000[2]	250,000[2]	305,000[2]
Navy	22,000	30,000	10,000	20,000	14,500
Air force	100,000	100,000	35,000	35,000	35,500
Total armed forces	642,000	715,000	595,000	655,000	704,500
Paramilitary forces					
Gendarmerie	70,000	74,000	5,000	5,000	70,000
Pasdaran	–	30,000	40,000	250,000	350,000
Basij	–	n.a.	n.a.	2,500,000	3,000,000
Mojahedin	–	n.a.	30,000	n.a.	n.a.
Total paramilitary forces	70,000	104,000	75,000	2,755,000	3,420,000
Forces abroad					
Oman	1,000	5,000[3]	–	–	–
Syria (UNDOF)	383[4]	–	–	–	–
Lebanon	–	–	n.a.	650	1,000
Total forces abroad	1,383	5,000	–	650	1,000

n.a.—not available.

[1] Sixty percent of the army is reported to have deserted in 1979 after the Revolution began. Figures given are for prerevolutionary period.

[2] Conscripts made up 100,000 personnel for 1982 and 1984. The number was estimated at 200,000 for 1986.

[3] The Oman contingent had grown to 5,000 by 1979, when it was brought home.

[4] Some of the United Nations Disengagement Observer Force (UNDOF) soldiers also served in United Nations Interim Force in Lebanon, from which they were also withdrawn in 1979.

Table 9. Major Army Weapons, 1986

Type and Description	Number in Inventory
Tanks (medium)	
T-54,T-55, T-59, T-62, T-72,	
Chieftain Mk3/5, M-47/-48, M-60A1	1,000
Tanks (light)	
Scorpion	50
Armored vehicles	
EE-9 Cascavel	130
BMP-1	180
BTR-50/-60	500
M-113	250
EE-11 Urutu	300
Guns, howitzers (including self-propelled), mortars, and surface-to-surface missiles (SSM)	
105mm, 130mm, 155mm, 175mm, 203mm	600
81mm, 120mm	3,000
SSM: Scud	n.a.
Recoilless rifles	
57mm, 75mm, M-40A/C 106mm	n.a.
Antiaircraft guns (including self-propelled) and surface-to-air missiles (SAM)	
25mm, 57mm	1,500
SAM: Hawk/Improved Hawk, SA-7, RBS-70	n.a.
Antitank weapons	
ENTAC, SS-11/-12, M-47 Dragon, BGM-71A TOW	n.a.
Fixed-wing aircraft	
Cessna (185, 310, O-2A)	56
Fokker F-27	2
Rockwell Shrike Commander	5
Dassault Mystère-Falcon	2
Helicopters	
AH-1J Cobra (attack)	n.a.
Bell 214A	270
AB-205A	35
CH-47C Chinook	n.a.

n.a.—not available.

Source: Based on information from International Institute for Strategic Studies, *The Military Balance, 1986–1987,* London, 1986, 96.

Table 10. Major Naval Weapons, 1986

Type and Description	Number in Inventory
Destroyers	
With surface-to-air missiles (SAM)	1
US Sumner-class	2
Submarines, Type-1200	6*
Frigates, with surface-to-surface missiles (SSM) and SAM	4
Corvettes, US PF-103	2
Fast patrol boats	
Kaman (La Combattante II) with 7 Harpoon SSM	8
Patrol boats	7
Minesweepers (US MSC 292/268 coastal)	2
Landing ships and craft	8
Logistical support ships	4
Hovercraft, Wellington BH-7	2
Fixed-wing aircraft	
Orion P-3F	2
Shrike Commander	4
Fokker F-27	4
Dassault Mystère-Falcon 20	1
Helicopters	
Sikorsky SH-3D	10
Sikorsky RH-53D	2
AB-212	7

*On order; delivery pending end of Iran-Iraq War.

Source: Based on information from International Institute for Strategic Studies, *The Military Balance, 1986–1987,* London, 1986, 96–97.

Table 11. Air Force Weapons, 1986

Type and Description	Number in Inventory
Fighter-bombers, with air-to-air missiles (AAM) and air-to-surface missiles (ASM)	
F–4D/E Phantom	35
Fighters	
F–5E/F Tiger	45
Fighters-interceptors	
F–14A Tomcat	10
Reconnaissance	
RF–4E	3
F–14A	5
Tankers-transports	
Boeing 707	10
Boeing 747	7
Transports	
C–130E/H Hercules	26
Fokker F–27	9
Aero Commander 690	2
Dassault Mystère-Falcon 20	4
Trainers	
Bonanza F–33 A/C	26
Shooting Star T–33A	7
Pilatus PC–7	46
Shenyang J–6	2
Helicopters	
AB–206A Jet Ranger	10
AB–212	5
Bell 214C	39
CH–47 Chinook	10
Sikorsky S–55 (HH–34F)	10
Sikorsky S–61A4	2
Surface-to-air missiles	
Rapier	n.a.
Tigercat	25
Hawk (improved?)	1,000
Air-to-air missiles	
Phoenix	n.a.
AIM–9 Sidewinder	n.a.
AIM–7 Sparrow	n.a.
Air-to-surface missiles	
AS–12 Maverick	n.a.

Source: Based on information from International Institute for Strategic Studies, *The Military Balance, 1986–1987,* London, 1986, 97.

Bibliography

Chapter 1

Abrahamian, Ervand. *Iran Between Two Revolutions.* Princeton: Princeton University Press, 1982.

Afkhami, Gholam R. *The Iranian Revolution: Thanatos on a National Scale.* Washington: Middle East Institute, 1985.

Akhavi, Shahrough. *Religion and Politics in Contemporary Iran: Clergy-State Relations in the Pahlavi Period.* Albany: State University of New York Press, 1980.

Alexander, Yonah, and Allan Nanes (eds.). *The United States and Iran: A Documentary History.* Frederick, Maryland: University Publications of America, 1980.

Algar, Hamid. *Religion and State in Iran in 1785–1906: The Role of the Ulama in the Qajar Period.* Berkeley and Los Angeles: University of California Press, 1969.

Amirsadeghi, Hossein. *Twentieth Century Iran.* London: Heinemann, 1977.

Amnesty International. *Iran: Documents Sent by Amnesty International to the Government of the Islamic Republic of Iran.* London: 1987.

Arberry, A.J. *The Legacy of Persia.* Oxford: Oxford University Press, 1953.

Arfa, Hassan. *Under Five Shahs.* London: John Murray, 1964.

Arjomand, Said Amir (ed.). *From Nationalism to Revolutionary Islam: Essays on Social Movements in the Contemporary Near and Middle East.* Albany: State University of New York Press, 1984.

_____. *The Shadow of God and the Hidden Imam.* Chicago: University of Chicago Press, 1984.

Avery, Peter. *Modern Iran.* New York: Praeger, 1965.

Bakhash, Shaul. *Iran: Monarchy, Bureaucracy, and Reform under the Qajars, 1858–1896.* London: Ithaca Press, 1978.

_____. *The Reign of the Ayatollahs: Iran and the Islamic Revolution.* (2d ed.) New York: Basic Books, 1984.

Bakhtiar, Chapour. *Ma fidelité.* Paris: Albin Michel, 1982.

Bamdad, Badr ol-Muluk. *From Darkness into Light: Women's Emancipation in Iran.* (Ed. and trans., F.R.C. Bagley.) Hicksville, New York: Exposition Press, 1977.

Banani, Amin. *The Modernization of Iran, 1921–1941.* Stanford: Stanford University Press, 1961.

Bani-Sadr, Abol Hassan. *L'espérance trahie.* Paris: Papyrus, 1982.

Bartol'd, Vasilii Vladimirovich. *Turkestan down to the Mongol Invasion.* London: Luzac, 1968.

Bashiriyeh, Hossein. *The State and Revolution in Iran, 1962-1982.* New York: St. Martin's Press, 1984.

Bayat, Mangol. *Mysticism and Dissent: Socioreligious Thought in Qajar Iran.* Syracuse: Syracuse University Press, 1982.

Bayne, E.A. *Persian Kingship in Transition.* New York: American Universities Field Staff, 1968.

Beck, Lois. *The Qashqa'i of Iran.* New Haven: Yale University Press, 1986.

Bellan, L. L. *Chah Abbas I: sa vie, son histoire.* Paris: 1932.

Bharier, Julian. *Economic Development in Iran, 1900-1970.* New York: Oxford University Press, 1971.

Bill, James A. "Iran: Is the Shah Pushing It Too Fast?" *Christian Science Monitor,* November 9, 1977, 16-17.

_____. *Iran: The Politics of Groups, Classes, and Modernization.* Columbus, Ohio: Merril, 1972.

Binder, Leonard. *Iran: Political Development in a Changing Society.* Berkeley and Los Angeles: University of California Press, 1962.

Bosworth, C.E. *The Ghaznavids: Their Empire in Afghanistan and Eastern Iran, 994-1040.* Edinburgh: Edinburgh University Press, 1963.

_____. *The Medieval History of Iran, Afghanistan, and Central Asia.* London: Variorum Reprints, 1977.

Bosworth, C.E. (ed.). *Iran and Islam.* Edinburgh: Edinburgh University Press, 1971.

Bosworth, Edmund, and Carole Hillenbrand (eds.). *Qajar Iran: Political, Social, and Cultural Change, 1800-1925.* Edinburgh: Edinburgh University Press, 1983.

Browne, E.G. *A Literary History of Persia.* 4 vols. Cambridge: Cambridge University Press, 1925-28.

_____. *The Persian Revolution of 1905-1909.* London: Cambridge University Press, 1910.

Burrell, R.M. "Iranian Foreign Policy During the Last Decade," *Asian Affairs* [London], 61, February 1974, 7-15.

Busse, Heribert (ed. and trans.). *History of Persia under Qajar Rule.* (Translated from the Persian of Hasan-e Fasai's Farsnameh-ye Naseri). New York: Columbia University Press, 1972.

The Cambridge History of Iran. 6 vols. Cambridge: Cambridge University Press, 1968-86.

Christopher, Warren (ed.). *American Hostages in Iran.* New Haven: Yale University Press, 1985.

Chubin, Shahram, and Sepehr Zabih. *The Foreign Relations of Iran: A Developing State in a Zone of Great-Power Conflict.* Berkeley and Los Angeles: University of California Press, 1974.

Cole, Juan R.I., and Nikki R. Keddie (eds.). *Shi'ism and Social Protest.* New Haven: Yale University Press, 1986.

Cottam, Richard W. *Nationalism in Iran.* Pittsburgh: University of Pittsburgh Press, 1964.

Curzon, George. *Persia and the Persian Question.* 2 vols. London: Frank Cass, 1966.

Eagleton, William. *The Kurdish Republic of 1946.* London: Oxford University Press, 1963.

Elgood, Cyril. *Safavid Medical Practice.* London: Luzac, 1970.

Elwell-Sutton, L.P. *Modern Iran.* New York: Gordon Press, 1976.

_____. *Persian Oil: A Study in Power Politics.* London: Lawrence and Wishart, 1955.

Eskelund, Karl. *Behind the Peacock Throne.* New York: Alvin Redman, 1965.

Fesharaki, Fereidun. *Development of the Iranian Oil Industry: International and Domestic Aspects.* (Praeger Special Studies in International Economics and Developments.) New York: Praeger, 1976.

Fischer, Michael M.J. *Iran: From Religious Dispute to Revolution.* Cambridge: Harvard University Press, 1980.

Frye, Richard Nelson. *The Golden Age of Persia.* London: Weidenfeld and Nicolson, 1975.

_____. *The Heritage of Persia.* London: Weidenfeld and Nicolson, 1962.

_____. *Persia.* (3d ed.) London: Allen and Unwin, 1969.

Garthwaite, Gene. *Khans and Shahs: The Bakhtiyari in Iran.* Cambridge: Cambridge University Press, 1983.

Ghirshman, R. *Iran: From the Earliest Times to the Islamic Conquest.* London: Pelican, 1954.

Goodell, Grace. *The Elemental Structures of Political Life: Rural Development in Pahlavi Iran.* Oxford: Oxford University Press, 1986.

Graham, Robert. *Iran: The Illusion of Power.* London: Croom Helm, 1978.

Greaves, Louise Rose. *Persia and the Defence of India, 1884–1892.* London: University of London, Athalone Press, 1959.

Hairi, Abdul Hadi. *Shi'ism and Constitutionalism in Iran.* Leiden: E.J. Brill, 1977.

Halliday, Fred. *Iran: Dictatorship and Development.* Harmondsworth, New York: Penguin Books, 1979.

Heikal, Mohamed. *The Return of the Ayatollah.* London: André Deutsch, 1981.

Hodgson, Marshall G.S. *The Venture of Islam.* Chicago: University of Chicago Press, 1974.

Holod, Renata (ed.). *Studies on Isfahan: Proceedings of the Isfahan Colloquium.* (Iranian Studies, 7.) Boston: Society for Iranian Studies, 1974.

Hoveyda, Ferydoun. *The Fall of the Shah.* London: Weidenfeld and Nicolson, 1979.

Huot, Jean Louis. *Persia.* (2 Vols.) Cleveland: World Publishing, 1965–1967.

Huyser, Robert E. *Mission to Tehran.* New York: Harper and Row, 1986.

Ismael, Tareq Y. *Iraq and Iran: Roots of Conflict.* Syracuse: Syracuse University Press, 1982.

Issawi, Charles. *The Economic History of Iran, 1800–1914.* Chicago: University of Chicago Press, 1971.

Jacqz, J. (ed.). *Iran: Past, Present, and Future.* New York: Aspen Institute, 1976.

Katouzian, Homa. *The Political Economy of Modern Iran: Despotism and Pseudo-Modernism, 1926–1979.* New York: New York University Press, 1981.

Kazemi, Farhad. *Poverty and Revolution in Iran: The Migrant Poor, Urban Marginality, and Politics.* New York: New York University Press, 1980.

Kazemzadeh, Firuz. *Russia and Britain in Persia, 1864–1914.* New Haven: Yale University Press, 1968.

Keddie, Nikki R. *Iran: Religion, Politics, and Society.* London: Frank Cass, 1980.

_____. *An Islamic Response to Imperialism: Political and Religious Writings of Sayyid Jamal ad-Din "al-Afghani."* Berkeley and Los Angeles: University of California Press, 1968.

_____. *Religion and Politics in Iran: Shi'ism from Political Quietism to Revolution.* New Haven: Yale University Press, 1983.

_____. *Religion and Rebellion in Iran: The Iranian Tobacco Protest of 1891–1892.* London: Frank Cass, 1966.

_____. *Roots of Revolution: An Interpretive History of Modern Iran.* New Haven: Yale University Press, 1981.

_____. *Sayyid Jamal ad-Din "al-Afghani": A Political Biography.* Berkeley and Los Angeles: University of California Press, 1972.

Kedouri, Elie, and Sylvia Haim (eds.). *Towards a Modern Iran: Studies in Thought, Politics, and Society.* London: Frank Cass, 1980.

Kelly, J.B. *Britain and the Persian Gulf.* Oxford: Oxford University Press, 1968.

Keyuani, M. "Artisans and Guild Life in the Later Safavid Period: Contributions to the Socio-Economic History of Persia," *Islamkundliche Untersuchungen* [Berlin], 65, 1982.

Khomeini, Ruhollah. *Islam and Revolution: Writings and Declarations of Imam Khomeini.* (Trans. and annotated by Hamid Algar.) Berkeley: Mizan Press, 1981.

Kuniholm, Bruce R. *The Origins of the Cold War in the Middle East: Great Power Conflict and Diplomacy in Iran, Turkey, and Greece.* Princeton: Princeton University Press, 1980.

Ladjevardi, Habib. *Labor Unions and Autocracy in Iran.* Syracuse: Syracuse University Press, 1985.

Laing, Margaret. *The Shah.* London: Sidwick and Jackson, 1977.

Lambton, Ann K.S. *Landlord and Peasant in Persia: A Study of Land Tenure and Land Revenue Administration.* London: Oxford University Press, 1969.

————. *State and Government in Medieval Islam: An Introduction to the Study of the Islamic Political Theory of the Jurists.* Oxford: Oxford University Press, 1981.

Ledeen, Michael, and William Lewis. *Debacle: The American Failure in Iran.* New York: Random House, 1981.

Lenczowski, George. *Russia and the West in Iran, 1918–48.* Ithaca: Cornell University Press, 1949.

Lenczowski, George (ed.). *Iran under the Pahlavis.* Stanford: Hoover Institution Press, 1978.

Lockhart, Laurence. *The Fall of the Safavid Dynasty and the Afghan Occupation of Persia.* Cambridge: Cambridge University Press, 1958.

————. *Nadir Shah: A Critical Study Based Mainly on Contemporary Sources.* London: Luzac, 1938.

McDaniel, R. *The Shuster Mission and the Persian Constitutional Revolution.* Minneapolis: Bibliotheca Islamica, 1974.

Malcolm, Sir John. *A History of Persia.* 2 vols. London: John Murray, 1815.

Mazzaoui, Michel. *The Origins of the Safavids: Shi'ism, Sufism, and the Gulat.* Wiesbaden, West Germany: F. Steiner, 1972.

Millspaugh, Arthur. *The American Task in Persia.* New York: Arno Press, 1973.

Minorsky, Vladimir. *The Turks, Iran, and the Caucasus in the Middle Ages.* London: Variorum Prints, 1978.

Minorsky, Vladimir (ed. and trans.). *Tadhkirat al-Muluk: A Manual of Safavid Administration.* London: Luzac, 1943.

Mottahedeh, Roy P. *Loyalty and Leadership in an Early Islamic Society.* Princeton: Princeton University Press, 1980.

————. *The Mantle of the Prophet: Religion and Politics in Iran.* New York: Simon and Schuster, 1985.

Munshi, Iskandar. *The History of Shah Abbas the Great.* 2 vols. (Trans., R.M. Savory.) Boulder, Colorado: Westview Press, 1978.

Nashat, Guity. *The Origins of Modern Reform in Iran, 1870–80.* Urbana: University of Illinois Press, 1982.

Oberling, Pierre. *The Qashqa'i: Nomads of Fars.* The Hague: Mouton, 1974.

Olmstead, A.T. *History of the Persian Empire: Achaemenid Period.* Chicago: University of Chicago Press, 1948.

Pahlavi, Ashraf. *Faces in a Mirror: Memoirs from Exile.* Englewood Cliffs, New Jersey: Prentice-Hall, 1980.

Pahlavi, Mohammad Reza Shah. *Answer to History.* New York: Stein and Day, 1980.

_____. *Mission for My Country.* London: Hutchinson, 1961.

Parsons, Anthony. *The Pride and the Fall: Iran, 1974–1979.* London: Jonathan Cape, 1984.

Perry, John R. *Karim Khan Zand: A History of Iran, 1747–1779.* Chicago: University of Chicago Press, 1979.

Ramazani, Ruhollah K. *The Foreign Policy of Iran, 1500–1941: A Developing Nation in World Affairs.* Charlottesville: University Press of Virginia, 1966.

_____. *Iran's Foreign Policy, 1941–1973: A Study of Foreign Policy in Modernizing Nations.* Charlottesville: University Press of Virginia, 1975.

_____. *The Persian Gulf: Iran's Role.* Charlottesville: University Press of Virginia, 1972.

_____. *Revolutionary Iran: Challenge and Response in the Middle East.* Baltimore: Johns Hopkins University Press, 1986.

Roosevelt, Kermit. *Countercoup: The Struggle for the Control of Iran.* New York: McGraw-Hill, 1979.

Rubin, Barry. *Paved with Good Intentions: The American Experience and Iran.* Oxford: Oxford University Press, 1982.

Sachednia, A.A. *The Idea of the Mahdi in Twelver Shi'ism.* Albany: State University of New York Press, 1981.

Saikal, Amin. *The Rise and Fall of the Shah.* Princeton: Princeton University Press, 1980.

Savory, Roger. *Iran under the Safavids.* Cambridge: Cambridge University Press, 1980.

Shuster, W. Morgan. *The Strangling of Persia.* New York: Century Company, 1912, Reprint Greenwood Press, 1968.

Sick, Gary. *All Fall Down: America's Tragic Encounter with Iran.* New York: Random House, 1985.

Spuler, Bertold. *Die Mongolen in Iran.* Leiden: E.J. Brill, 1985.

Stempel, John D. *Inside the Iranian Revolution.* Bloomington: Indiana University Press, 1981.

Upton, Joseph M. *The History of Modern Iran: An Interpretation.* Cambridge: Harvard University Press, 1960.

Wilber, Donald. *Iran: Past and Present.* (rev. ed.) Princeton: Princeton University Press, 1981.

_____. *Riza Shah Pahlavi, 1878-1944.* Hicksville, New York: Exposition Press, 1975.

Wilson, Arnold. *The Persian Gulf.* London: Allen and Unwin, 1928.

Woods, John. *The Aqquyunlu: Clan, Confederation, Empire.* Minneapolis: Bibliotheca Islamica, 1976.

Wright, Denis. *The English Amongst the Persians.* London: Heinemann, 1977.

_____. *The Persians Amongst the English.* London: I.B. Tauris, 1985.

Yeselson, Abraham. *United States-Persian Diplomatic Relations, 1883-1921.* New Brunswick, New Jersey: Rutgers University Press, 1956.

Zonis, Marvin. *The Political Elite of Iran.* Princeton: Princeton University Press, 1971.

Chapter 2

Abrahamian, Ervand. *Iran Between Two Revolutions.* Princeton: Princeton University Press, 1982.

Akhavi, Shahrough. *Religion and Politics in Contemporary Iran: Clergy-State Relations in the Pahlavi Period.* Albany: State University of New York Press, 1980.

Arasteh, Reza. *Education and Social Awakening in Iran.* Leiden: E.J. Brill, 1962.

Arjomand, Said, Eric Hooglund, and William Royce. *The Iranian Islamic Clergy: Governmental Politics and Theocracy.* Washington: Middle East Institute, 1984.

Ashraf, Ahmad. "Bazaar and Mosque in Iran's Revolution." Pages 16-18 in *MERIP Reports,* No. 113. Washington: Middle East Research and Information Project, March-April 1983.

Bakhash, Shaul. *The Reign of the Ayatollahs: Iran and the Islamic Revolution.* New York: Basic Books, 1984.

Bashiriyeh, Hossein. *The State and Revolution in Iran, 1962-1982.* London: Croom Helm, 1984.

Bayat, Assef. "Workers' Control after the Revolution." Pages 19-23 in *MERIP Reports,* No. 113. Washington: Middle East Research and Information Project, March-April 1983.

Beck, Lois. *The Qashqa'i of Iran.* New Haven: Yale University Press, 1986.

Chesnoff, Richard Z. "Paris: The Iranian Exiles," *New York Times Magazine,* February 12, 1984, 23.

Fassih, Ismail. *Sorraya in a Coma.* London: Zed Press, 1985.

Ferdows, Adele. "Shariati and Khomeini on Women." Pages 127-38 in Nikki R. Keddie and Eric Hooglund (eds.), *The Iranian*

Revolution and the Islamic Republic. Syracuse: Syracuse University Press, 1986.

Ferdows, Emad. "The Reconstruction Crusade and Class Conflict in Iran." Pages 11–15 in *MERIP Reports,* No. 113. Washington: Middle East Research and Information Project, March–April 1983.

Fischer, Michael M.J. *Iran: From Religious Dispute to Revolution.* Cambridge: Harvard University Press, 1980.

_____. "Islam and the Revolt of the Petite Bourgeoisie," *Daedalus,* 111, No. 1, Winter 1982, 101–25.

Fisher, W.B. "Physical Geography." Pages 3–110 in W.B. Fisher (ed.), *The Cambridge History of Iran,* 1. Cambridge: Cambridge University Press, 1968.

Good, Mary-Jo Delvecchio. "The Changing Status and Composition of an Iranian Provincial Elite." Pages 269–88 in Michael Bonine and Nikki R. Keddie (eds.), *Modern Iran: The Dialectics of Continuity and Change.* Albany: State University of New York Press, 1981.

Haeri, Shahla. "Power of Ambiguity: Cultural Improvisations on the Theme of Temporary Marriage," *Iranian Studies,* 19, No. 2, Spring 1986, 123–54.

Halliday, Fred. *Iran: Dictatorship and Development.* New York: Penguin Books, 1979.

Higgins, Patricia. "Minority-State Relations in Contemporary Iran." Pages 167–97 in Ali Banuazizi and Myron Weiner (eds.), *The State, Religion, and Ethnic Politics: Afghanistan, Iran, and Pakistan.* Syracuse: Syracuse University Press, 1986.

Hiro, Dilip. *Iran under the Ayatollahs.* London: Routledge and Kegan Paul, 1985.

Hooglund, Eric. "Iran, 1980–1985: Political and Economic Trends." Pages 17–31 in Nikki R. Keddie and Eric Hooglund (eds.), *The Iranian Revolution and the Islamic Republic.* Syracuse: Syracuse University Press, 1986.

_____. *Land and Revolution in Iran, 1960–1980.* Austin: University of Texas Press, 1982.

_____. "Reza Shah Pahlavi." Pages 175–76 in Ainslie Embree (ed.), *Encyclopedia of Asian History,* III.

_____. "Rural Participation in the Revolution." Pages 3–6 in *MERIP Reports,* No. 87. Washington: Middle East Research and Information Project, May 1980.

_____. "The Search For Iran's 'Moderates'." Pages 5–6 in *MERIP Reports,* No. 144. Washington: Middle East Research and Information Project, January–February 1987.

_____. "Social Origins of the Revolutionary Clergy." Pages 74–83 in Nikki R. Keddie and Eric Hooglund (eds.), *The Iranian Revolution and the Islamic Republic.* Syracuse: Syracuse University Press, 1986.

Iran. *Statistical Yearbook.* Tehran: Center for Statistical Studies, 1364 [1985–86].

Kazemi, Farhad. *Poverty and Revolution in Iran: The Migrant Poor, Urban Marginality, and Politics.* New York: New York University Press, 1980.

Keddie, Nikki R. "The Minorities Question in Iran." Pages 85–108 in Shirin Tahir-Kheli and Shaheen Ayubi (eds.), *The Iran-Iraq War: New Weapons, Old Conflicts.* New York: Praeger, 1983.

_____. *Roots of Revolution: An Interpretive History of Modern Iran.* New Haven: Yale University Press, 1981.

Keddie, Nikki R., and Eric Hooglund (eds.). *The Iranian Revolution and the Islamic Republic.* Syracuse: Syracuse University Press, 1986.

Ladjevardi, Habib. *Labor Unions and Autocracy in Iran.* Syracuse: Syracuse University Press, 1985.

Loeffler, Reinhold. "Economic Changes in a Rural Area since 1979." Pages 93–108 in Nikki R. Keddie and Eric Hooglund (eds.), *The Iranian Revolution and the Islamic Republic.* Syracuse: Syracuse University Press, 1986.

_____. "The National Integration of Boir Ahmad," *Iranian Studies,* 24, No. 4, 1982, 689–711.

Momen, Moojan. *An Introduction to Shi'i Islam.* New Haven: Yale University Press, 1985.

Najmabadi, Afsaneh. "Mystifications of the Past and Illusions of the Future." Pages 147–61 in Nikki R. Keddie and Eric Hooglund (eds.), *The Iranian Revolution and the Islamic Republic.* Syracuse: Syracuse University Press, 1986.

Smith, Terrence. "Iran: Five Years of Fanaticism," *New York Times Magazine,* February 12, 1984, 21–22.

Sunderland, E. "Pastoralism, Nomadism, and the Social Anthropology of Iran." Pages 611–83 in W.B. Fisher (ed.), *The Cambridge History of Iran,* I. Cambridge: Cambridge University Press, 1968.

(Various issues of the following publications were also used in the preparation of this chapter: Foreign Broadcast Information Service, *Daily Report: Middle East and Africa* and *Daily Report: Near East and South Asia;* and *Iran Times.*)

Chapter 3

Abrahamian, Ervand. *Iran Between Two Revolutions.* Princeton: Princeton University Press, 1982.

Alnasrawi, Abbas. "Dependency Status and Economic Development of Arab States," *Journal of Asian and African Studies,* 21, Nos. 1–2, 1986, 17–31.

_____. "Economic Consequences of the Iran-Iraq War," *Third World Quarterly* [London], 1986, 869–95.

_____. *OPEC in a Changing World Economy.* Baltimore: Johns Hopkins University Press, 1985.

Amuzegar, Jahangir. *Iran: An Economic Profile.* Washington: Middle East Institute, 1977.

Bakhash, Shaul. *The Reign of the Ayatollahs: Iran and the Islamic Revolution.* New York: Basic Books, 1984.

Bamberger, Robert, and Clyde Mark. *Distribution of Oil from the Persian Gulf: Near-Term US Vulnerability.* Washington: Library of Congress Congressional Research Service, October 1, 1986.

Behdad, Sohrab. *Foreign Exchange Gap, Structural Constraints, and the Political Economy of Exchange Rate Determination in Iran.* Granville, Ohio: Denison University, forthcoming.

Central Bank of the Islamic Republic of Iran. *Economic Report and Balance Sheet, 1362* [1984]. Tehran: 1984.

Clawson, Patrick. "Islamic Iran's Economic Policies and Prospects." (rev. ed.) (Paper presented to Council on Foreign Relations, November 1986.) Washington: February 1987.

Cottam, Richard. "The Iranian Revolution." Pages 55–87 in Juan R.I. Cole and Nikki R. Keddie (eds.), *Shi'ism and Social Protest.* New Haven: Yale University Press, 1986.

Economist Intelligence Unit. *Iran: Country Profile, 1986.* London: 1986

_____. *Iran: Country Profile, 1987.* London: 1987.

_____. *Iran: Country Report, 1986,* Nos. 1–4, London: 1986.

_____. *Iran: Country Report, 1987,* No. 1, London: 1987.

Ferdows, Emad. "The Reconstruction Crusade and Class Conflict in Iran." Pages 11–15 in *MERIP Reports,* No. 113. Washington: Middle East Research and Information Project, March–April 1983.

Fisher, W.B. "Iran." Pages 404–30 in *The Middle East and North Africa, 1987.* (33d ed.) London: Europa, 1986.

Halliday, Fred. "Iranian Foreign Policy since 1979: Internationalism and Nationalism in the Islamic Revolution." Pages 88–107 in Juan R.I. Cole and Nikki R. Keddie (eds.), *Shi'ism and Social Protest.* New Haven: Yale University Press, 1986.

_____. "Year IV of the Islamic Republic." Pages 3-8 in *MERIP Reports,* No. 113. Washington: Middle East Research and Information Project, March–April 1983.

Hooglund, Eric. *Land and Revolution in Iran, 1960-1980.* Austin: University of Texas Press, 1982.

Hooglund, Eric, and Nikki Keddie (eds.). *The Iranian Revolution and the Islamic Republic.* Syracuse: Syracuse University Press, 1986.

"An Initial Glance at the 1366 [1987-88] Budget Bill," *Iran Press Digest* [Tehran], March 17, 1987, 2-6.

International Road Federation. *World Road Statistics, 1981-85.* Geneva: 1986.

International Road Transport Unit. *World Transport Data.* Geneva: 1985.

Iran: A Special Report. London: Middle East Economic Digest, February 1977.

Jaffé, George and Keith McLachlan. *Iran and Iraq: The Next Five Years.* Economist Intelligence Unit Special Report No. 1083. London: 1987.

Jakubiak, Henry, and M. Taher Dajani. "Oil Income and Financial Policies in Iran and Saudi Arabia," *Finance and Development.* Washington: International Monetary Fund, 1986.

Johns, Richard, and Michael Field. "Oil in the Middle East and North Africa." Pages 96-142 in *The Middle East and North Africa, 1987.* (33d ed.) London: Europa, 1986.

Kazemi, Farhad. *Poverty and Revolution in Iran: The Migrant Poor, Urban Marginality, and Politics.* New York: New York University Press, 1980.

Keddie, Nikki R. "Oil Economic Policy and Social Conflict in Iran," *Race and Class,* 21, No. 1, 1979, 13-29.

Kielmas, Maria. "Iran Restores the Soviet Connection," *Middle East* [London], November 1986, 23.

Lautenschlager, Wolfgang. "The Effects of an Overvalued Exchange Rate on the Iranian Economy, 1979-1984," *International Journal of Middle East Studies,* 18, 1986, 31-52.

McCaslin, John C. (ed.). *International Petroleum Encyclopedia.* Tulsa: Penn Well, 1986.

The Middle East and North Africa, 1987. London: Europa, 1986.

Nyrop, Richard F. (ed.). *Iran: A Country Study.* Washington: GPO for The American University, 1978.

Rosen, Barry M. (ed.). *Iran since the Revolution: Internal Dynamics, Regional Conflict, and the Superpowers.* New York: Columbia University Press, 1985.

Sarkis, Nicolas (ed.). *Arab Oil and Gas Directory, 1982.* Paris: Arab Petroleum Research Center, 1982.

Sciolino, Elaine. "Iran Allows Pragmatism to Dictate Its Shopping List," *New York Times,* April 26, 1987, A3.

Tibi, Bassam. "The Iranian Revolution and the Arabs: The Quest for Islamic Identity and the Search for an Islamic System of Government," *Arab Studies Quarterly,* 8, No. 1, Winter 1986, 29-44.

_____. "The Renewed Role of Islam in the Political and Social Development of the Middle East," *Middle East Journal,* 37, No. 1, Winter 1983, 3-13.

United Nations. Food and Agriculture Organization. *Yearbook of Fishery Statistics, 1984.* 58. Rome: 1984.

_____. *Yearbook of Forest Products, 1973-1984.* Rome: 1986.

United States. Central Intelligence Agency. *Economic and Energy Indicators.* Washington: January 1986-March 1987.

_____. *Handbook of Economic Statistics, 1986.* Washington: 1986.

United States. Department of Agriculture. *Middle East and North Africa: Situation and Outlook Report.* Washington: GPO, April 1986.

_____. *World Indices of Agriculture and Food Production, 1976-85,* No. 744. Washington: GPO, July 1986.

United States. Department of the Interior. Bureau of Mines. *Mineral Industries of the Middle East.* Washington: April 1986.

Welt, Leo. "The Middle East's Changing Economy," *Management Review,* 76, February 1987, 63-65.

World Bank. *World Development Report, 1986.* Oxford: Oxford University Press, 1986.

_____. *World Tables, 1986.* Baltimore: 1986.

(Various issues of the following publications were also used in the preparation of this chapter: British Broadcasting Corporation, *Summary of World Broadcasts* [Reading, United Kingdom]; *Christian Science Monitor; Daily News* [Tehran]; Economist Intelligence Unit, *Country Report: Iran* [London]; Foreign Broadcast Information Service, *Daily Report: Middle East and Africa; Foreign Report* [London]; International Monetary Fund, *Direction of Trade Statistics* and *International Financial Statistics; Iran Monitor* [Geneva, Switzerland]; *Iran Times;* Joint Publications Research Service, *Near East/South Asia Report; Middle East* [London]; *Middle East Economic Digest (MEED)* [London]; *Middle East Economic Survey* [Limassol, Cyprus]; *Middle East Research and Information Project (MERIP) Reports; MEMO* [Limassol, Cyprus]; *News Review on West Asia* [New Delhi]; *Oil and Gas Journal;* and *Taxes and Investment in the Middle East* [Amsterdam].)

Chapter 4

Abdulghani, Jasim M. *Iraq and Iran: The Years of Crisis.* Baltimore: Johns Hopkins University Press, 1984.

Abrahamian, Ervand. *Iran Between Two Revolutions.* Princeton: Princeton University Press, 1982.

Akhavi, Shahrough. "Clerical Politics in Iran since 1979." Pages 57–73 in Nikki R. Keddie and Eric Hooglund (eds.), *The Iranian Revolution and the Islamic Republic.* Syracuse: Syracuse University Press, 1986.

_____. "Elite Factionalism in the Islamic Republic of Iran," *Middle East Journal,* 41, No. 2, Spring 1987, 181–201.

Alaolmolki, Nozar. "The New Iranian Left," *Middle East Journal,* 41, No. 2, Spring 1987, 218–33.

Atkin, Muriel. "The Islamic Republic and the Soviet Union." Pages 191–208 in Nikki R. Keddie and Eric Hooglund (eds.), *The Iranian Revolution and the Islamic Republic.* Syracuse: Syracuse University Press, 1986.

Bakhash, Shaul. "Islam and Social Justice in Iran." Pages 95–115 in Martin Kramer (ed.), *Shi'ism, Resistance, and Revolution.* Boulder, Colorado: Westview Press, 1987.

_____. *The Reign of the Ayatollahs: Iran and the Islamic Revolution.* New York: Basic Books, 1984.

Bashiriyeh, Hossein. *The State and Revolution in Iran, 1962–1982.* London: Croom Helm, 1984.

Benard, Cheryl, and Zalmay Khalilzad. *"The Government of God": Iran's Islamic Republic.* New York: Columbia University Press, 1984.

Bulliet, Richard. "Time, Perceptions, and Conflict Resolution." Pages 65–81 in Shirin Tahir-Kheli and Shaheen Ayubi (eds.), *The Iran-Iraq War: New Weapons, Old Conflicts.* New York: Praeger, 1983.

Chesnoff, Richard Z. "Paris: The Iranian Exiles," *New York Times Magazine,* February 12, 1984, 22–23.

Chubin, Shahram. "The Islamic Republic's Foreign Policy in the Gulf." Pages 159–71 in Martin Kramer (ed.), *Shi'ism, Resistance, and Revolution.* Boulder, Colorado: Westview Press, 1987.

Cobban, Helena. "The Growing Shi'i Power in Lebanon and Its Implications for the Future." Pages 137–55 in Juan Cole and Nikki R. Keddie (eds.), *Shi'ism and Social Protest.* New Haven: Yale University Press, 1986.

"Constitution of the Islamic Republic of Iran," *Middle East Journal,* 34, No. 2, Spring 1980, 184–204.

Cottam, Richard. "Iran and Soviet-American Relations." Pages 227–40 in Nikki R. Keddie and Eric Hooglund (eds.), *The Iranian Revolution and the Islamic Republic.* Syracuse: Syracuse University Press, 1986.

———. "Iran's Perception of the Superpowers." Pages 133–47 in Barry Rosen (ed.), *Iran since the Revolution: Internal Dynamics, Regional Conflicts, and the Superpowers.* New York: Columbia University Press for Brooklyn College, 1985.

Ferdows, Adele. "Shariati and Khomeini on Women." Pages 127–38 in Nikki R. Keddie and Eric Hooglund (eds.), *The Iranian Revolution and the Islamic Republic.* Syracuse: Syracuse University Press, 1986.

Halliday, Fred. "Year IV of the Islamic Republic." Pages 3–8 in *MERIP Reports,* No. 113. Washington: Middle East Research and Information Project, March–April 1983.

Hiro, Dilip. *Iran under the Ayatollahs.* London: Routledge and Kegan Paul, 1985.

Hooglund, Eric. "Iran and the Gulf War." Pages 12–18 in *MERIP Reports,* No. 148. Washington: Middle East Research and Information Project, September–October 1987.

———. "Iran, 1980–1985: Political and Economic Trends." Pages 17–31 in Nikki R. Keddie and Eric Hooglund (eds.), *The Iranian Revolution and the Islamic Republic.* Syracuse: Syracuse University Press, 1986.

———. "The Search for Iran's 'Moderates'." Pages 5–6 in *MERIP Reports,* No. 144. Washington: Middle East Research and Information Project, January–February 1987.

———. "Social Origins of the Revolutionary Clergy." Pages 74–83 in Nikki R. Keddie and Eric Hooglund (eds.), *The Iranian Revolution and the Islamic Republic.* Syracuse: Syracuse University Press, 1986.

Karimi, Setareh. "Economic Policies and Structural Changes since the Revolution." Pages 32–54 in Nikki R. Keddie and Eric Hooglund (eds.), *The Iranian Revolution and the Islamic Republic.* Syracuse: Syracuse University Press, 1986.

Khalilzad, Zalmay. "The Iranian Revolution and the Afghan Resistance." Pages 257–73 in Martin Kramer (ed.), *Shi'ism, Resistance, and Revolution.* Boulder, Colorado: Westview Press, 1987.

Kostiner, Joseph. "Shi'i Unrest in the Gulf." Pages 173–86 in Martin Kramer (ed.), *Shi'ism, Resistance, and Revolution.* Boulder, Colorado: Westview Press, 1987.

Loeffler, Reinhold. "Economic Changes in a Rural Area since 1979." Pages 93–108 in Nikki R. Keddie and Eric Hooglund (eds.), *The Iranian Revolution and the Islamic Republic.* Syracuse: Syracuse University Press, 1986.

Mottahedeh, Roy P. "Iran's Foreign Devils," *Foreign Policy,* No. 38, 1980, 19–34.

Norton, Augustus R. "The Origins and Resurgence of Amal."
   Pages 203-18 in Martin Kramer (ed.), *Shi'ism, Resistance, and
   Revolution.* Boulder, Colorado: Westview Press, 1987.
_____. "Shi'ism and Social Protest in Lebanon." Pages 156-78
   in Juan R.I. Cole and Nikkie R. Keddie (eds.), *Shi'ism and Social
   Protest.* New Haven: Yale University Press, 1986.
Ramazani, Ruhollah K. *Revolutionary Iran: Challenge and Response
   in the Middle East.* Baltimore: Johns Hopkins University Press,
   1986.
Sick, Gary. *All Fall Down: America's Tragic Encounter with Iran.* New
   York: Random House, 1985.
_____. "Iran's Quest for Superpower Status," *Foreign Affairs,* 65,
   No. 4, Spring 1987, 697-715.

(Various issues of the following publications were also used in
the preparation of this chapter: Foreign Broadcast Information Service, *Daily Report: Middle East and Africa; Daily Report: Near East and
South Asia; Iran Times; New York Times;* and *Washington Post.*)

Chapter 5

Abdulghani, Jasim M. *Iraq and Iran: The Years of Crisis.* Baltimore:
   Johns Hopkins University Press, 1984.
Afshar, Haleh. "The Army." Pages 175-98 in Haleh Afshar (ed.),
   Iran: A Revolution in Turmoil. Albany: State University of New
   York Press, 1985.
Akhavi, Shahrough. "Elite Factionalism in the Islamic Republic
   of Iran," *Middle East Journal,* 41, No. 2, Spring 1987, 181-201.
Alaolmolki, Nozar. "The New Iranian Left," *Middle East Jour-
   nal,* 41, No. 2, Spring 1987, 218-33.
Amnesty International. *Amnesty International Report, 1986.* London:
   1986.
Amnesty International. *Law and Human Rights in the Islamic Repub-
   lic of Iran.* London: Amnesty International Secretariat, 1980.
Arjomand, Said Amir (ed.). *From Nationalism to Revolutionary Islam:
   Essays on Social Movements in the Contemporary Near and Middle East.*
   Albany: State University of New York Press, 1984.
El-Azhary, M.S. (ed.). *The Iran-Iraq War: An Historical, Economic,
   and Political Analysis.* New York: St. Martin's Press, 1984.
Bakhash, Shaul. *The Reign of the Ayatollahs: Iran and the Islamic Revo-
   lution.* New York: Basic Books, 1984.
Ball, George W. *Error and Betrayal in Lebanon.* Washington: Foun-
   dation for Middle East Peace, 1984.

Benard, Cheryl, and Zalmay Khalilzad. *"The Government of God":
Iran's Islamic Republic.* New York: Columbia University Press,
1984.

Bill, James A. "Power and Religion in Revolutionary Iran," *Middle
East Journal,* 36, No. 1, Winter 1982, 22–47.

Bradley, C. Paul. *Recent United States Policy in the Persian Gulf.* Gran-
tham, New Hampshire: Thompson and Rutter, 1982.

Bussert, Jim. "Iran-Iraq War Turns Strategic," *Defense Electronics,*
16, September 1984, 136–46.

Canby, Steven L. "The Iranian Military: Political Symbolism
Versus Military Usefulness." Pages 100–130 in Hossein Amirsadeghi (ed.), *The Security of the Persian Gulf.* New York: St. Martin's Press, 1981.

Chubin, Shahram. "Hedging in the Gulf: Soviets Arm Both
Sides," *International Defense Review,* 20, No. 6, June 1987, 731–35.
_____. "Leftist Forces in Iran," *Problems of Communism,* July-
August 1980, 1–25.

Cordesman, Anthony H. *The Gulf and the Search for Strategic Stability:
Saudi Arabia, the Military Balance in the Gulf, and Trends in the Arab-
Israeli Military Balance.* Boulder, Colorado: Westview Press, 1984.
_____. "The Iran-Iraq War in 1984: An Escalating Threat to the
Gulf and the West," *Armed Forces Journal,* 121, March 1984, 22–24.
_____. "The Iraq-Iran War: Attrition Now, Chaos Later," *Armed
Forces Journal,* 120, May 1983, 36–43.

Daly, Thomas M. "The Enduring Gulf War," *United States Naval
Institute Proceedings,* 111, No. 5, May 1985, 148–61.

Danziger, Raphael. "The Persian Gulf Tanker War," *United States
Naval Institute Proceedings,* 111, No. 5, May 1985, 160–67.

Darius, Robert G., John W. Amos, and Ralph H. Magnus. *Gulf
Security into the 1980s: Perceptual and Strategic Dimensions.* Stanford:
Hoover Institution Press, 1984.

Dekmejian, R. Hrair. *Islam in Revolution.* Syracuse: Syracuse University Press, 1985.

Dowdy, William L., and Russell Troods (eds.). *The Indian Ocean:
Perspectives on a Strategic Area.* Durham, North Carolina: Duke
University Press, 1985.

Evans, David, and Richard Campany. "Iran-Iraq: Bloody Tomor-
rows," *United States Naval Institute Proceedings,* 111, No. 1, January 1985, 33–43.

Fischer, Michael M.J. *Iran: From Religious Dispute to Revolution.* Cambridge: Harvard University Press, 1980.

Hammond, Thomas T. *Red Flag over Afghanistan: The Communist
Coup, the Soviet Invasion, and the Consequences.* Boulder, Colorado:
Westview Press, 1984.

Heller, Mark (ed.). *The Middle East Military Balance, 1985.* Tel Aviv: Jaffee Center for Strategic Studies, Tel Aviv University, 1985.

Hickman, William F. *Ravaged and Reborn: The Iranian Army, 1982.* Washington: Brookings Institution, 1982.

Hiro, Dilip. *Iran under the Ayatollahs.* London: Routledge and Kegan Paul, 1985.

Hunter, Shireen. "After the Ayatollah," *Foreign Policy,* No. 66, Spring 1987, 77–97.

Hurewitz, J.C. *Middle East Politics: The Military Dimension.* New York: Praeger, 1969.

Huyser, Robert E. *Mission to Tehran.* New York: Harper and Row, 1986.

International Institute for Strategic Studies. *The Military Balance, 1978-1979.* London: 1978.

_____. *The Military Balance, 1981-1982.* London: 1981.

_____. *The Military Balance, 1982-1983.* London: 1982.

_____. *The Military Balance, 1983-1984.* London: 1983.

_____. *The Military Balance, 1984-1985.* London: 1984.

_____. *The Military Balance, 1985-1986.* London: 1985.

_____. *The Military Balance, 1986-1987.* London: 1986.

Iran. *Summary Report: An Estimate of the Economic Damages of the Imposed War of Iraq Against Iran.* Tehran: Islamic Republic of Iran, Ministry of Foreign Affairs, March 1983.

Ismael, Tareq Y. *Iraq and Iran: Roots of Conflict.* Syracuse: Syracuse University Press, 1982.

Karsh, Efraim. "The Iran-Iraq War: A Military Analysis," *Adelphi Papers,* No. 220, Spring 1987.

Keddie, Nikki R. *Roots of Revolution: An Interpretive History of Modern Iran.* New Haven: Yale University Press, 1981.

Khalilzad, Zalmay. "Islamic Iran: Soviet Dilemma," *Problems of Communism,* January–February 1984, 1–20.

Kurth, James R. "American Perceptions of the Israeli-Palestinian Conflict and the Iranian-Iraqi War," *Naval War College Review,* 38, No. 1, January–February 1985, 75–86.

Malik, Hafeez (ed.). *International Security in Southwest Asia.* New York: Praeger, 1984.

Martin, Douglas. *The Persecution of the Baha'is in Iran, 1844–1984.* Ottawa: Association for Baha'i Studies, 1984.

Martin, Lenore G. *The Unstable Gulf.* Lexington, Massachusetts: D.C. Heath, 1984.

Modarres, Morteza. *Tarikh-e Ravabet-e Iran va Iraq: Siyasi, Farhangi, Eghtesadi.* (Iran and Iraq: A History of Political, Cultural, and Economic Relations.) Tehran: Ketan Foroshi Foroghi, 1351 [1973].

Mottale, Morris Mehrdad. *The Arms Buildup in the Persian Gulf.* Lanham, Maryland: University Press of America, 1986.

O'Ballance, Edgar. "The Iraqi-Iranian War: The First Round," *Parameters,* 11, 54–59.

_____. "The Kurdish Factor in the Gulf War," *Military Review,* 61, No. 6, June 1981, 13–20.

Olson, William J. (ed.). *US Strategic Interests in the Gulf Region.* Boulder, Colorado: Westview Press, 1987.

Perron, Ronald A. "The Iranian Islamic Revolutionary Guard Corps," *Middle East Insight,* 4, No. 21, June–July 1985, 35–39.

Rafizadeh, Mansur. *Witness: From the Shah to the Secret Arms Deal: An Insider's Account of U.S. Involvement in Iran.* New York: W. Morrow, 1987.

Rajaee, Farhang. *Islamic Values and World View: Khomeyni on Man, the State and International Politics.* Lanham, Maryland: University Press of America, 1983.

Ramazani, Ruhollah K. *The Foreign Policy of Iran, 1500–1941: A Developing Nation in World Affairs.* Charlottesville: University Press of Virginia, 1966.

_____. "The Iran-Iraq War: Underlying Conflicts," *Middle East Insight,* 3, No. 5, July–August 1984, 8–11.

_____. *Iran's Foreign Policy, 1941–1973: A Study of Foreign Policy in Modernizing Nations.* Charlottesville: University Press of Virginia, 1975.

_____. "Iran's Islamic Revolution and the Persian Gulf," *Current History,* 84, January 1985, 5–8.

_____. *The Persian Gulf and the Strait of Hormuz.* Alpen aan den Rijn, The Netherlands: Sijthoff and Noordhoff, 1979.

_____. *The Persian Gulf: Iran's Role.* Charlottesville: University Press of Virginia, 1972.

_____. *Revolutionary Iran: Challenge and Response in the Middle East.* Baltimore: Johns Hopkins University Press, 1986.

_____. *The United States and Iran: The Patterns of Influence,* New York: Praeger, 1982.

Renfrew, Nita M. "Who Started the War?" *Foreign Policy,* No. 66, Spring 1987, 98–108.

Rose, Gregory F. "The Iranian Islamic Armed Forces: An Assessment." (Paper prepared for Office of Assistant Chief of Staff, G2/DSEC, 4th Infantry Division [Mechanized], Fort Carson, Colorado, September 1983.)

_____. "The Post-Revolutionary Purge of Iran's Armed Forces: A Revisionist Assessment," *Iranian Studies,* 17, Nos. 2–3, Spring-Summer 1984, 153–94.

_____. "Soldiers of Islam: The Iranian Armed Forces since the Revolution." (Paper prepared for Office of Assistant Chief of Staff, G2/DSEC, 4th Infantry Division [Mechanized], Fort Carson, Colorado, 1984.)

Rubinstein, Alvin Z. *The Great Game: Rivalry in the Persian Gulf and South Asia.* New York: Praeger, 1983.

_____. "Perspectives on the Iran-Iraq War," *Orbis,* 29, No. 3, Fall 1985, 597–608.

Schahgaldian, Nikola B. *The Iranian Military under the Islamic Republic.* (R–3473–USDP.) Santa Monica: Rand, March 1987.

Sick, Gary. *All Fall Down: America's Tragic Encounter with Iran.* New York: Random House, 1985.

Sreberny-Mohammadi, Annabelle, and Ali Mohammadi. "Post-Revolutionary Iranian Exiles: A Study in Impotence," *Third World Quarterly,* 9, No. 1, January 1987, 108–29.

Stempel, John D. *Inside the Iranian Revolution.* Bloomington: Indiana University Press, 1981.

Taheri, Amir. *The Spirit of Allah: Khomeini and the Islamic Revolution.* Bethesda, Maryland: Adler and Adler, 1986.

Tahir-Kheli, Shirin, and Shaheen Ayubi (eds.). *The Iran-Iraq War: New Weapons, Old Conflicts.* New York: Praeger, 1983.

United States. Arms Control and Disarmament Agency. *World Military Expenditures and Arms Transfers, 1986.* Washington: GPO, April, 1987.

Vlahos, Michael. "Middle Eastern, North African, and South Asian Navies," *United States Naval Institute Proceedings,* 111, No. 3, March 1985, 52–57.

_____. "Middle Eastern, North African, and South Asian Navies," *United States Naval Institute Proceedings,* 112, No. 3, March 1986, 53–58.

World Armaments and Disarmament: SIPRI Yearbook. Cambridge: MIT Press, for Stockholm International Peace Research Institute, 1976.

World Armaments and Disarmament: SIPRI Yearbook. Cambridge: MIT Press, for Stockholm International Peace Research Institute, 1977.

World Armaments and Disarmament: SIPRI Yearbook. Cambridge: MIT Press, for Stockholm International Peace Research Institute, 1978.

World Armaments and Disarmament: SIPRI Yearbook. Cambridge: MIT Press, for Stockholm International Peace Research Institute, 1979.

World Armaments and Disarmament: SIPRI Yearbook. Cambridge: MIT Press, for Stockholm International Peace Research Institute, 1980.

World Armaments and Disarmament: SIPRI Yearbook. Cambridge: MIT Press, for Stockholm International Peace Research Institute, 1981.

World Armaments and Disarmament: SIPRI Yearbook. Cambridge: MIT Press, for Stockholm International Peace Research Institute, 1982.

World Armaments and Disarmament: SIPRI Yearbook. Cambridge: MIT Press, for Stockholm International Peace Research Institute, 1983.

World Bank. *World Development Report, 1986.* Oxford: Oxford University Press, 1986.

Wright. Robin. *Sacred Rage: The Wrath of Militant Islam.* New York: Simon and Schuster, 1985.

Yodfat, Aryeh Y. *The Soviet Union and the Arabian Peninsula: Soviet Policy Towards the Persian Gulf and Arabia.* New York: St. Martin's Press, 1983.

(Various issues of the following publications were also used in the preparation of this chapter: *BBC Summary of World Broadcasts* [Reading, United Kingdom]; *Jane's Defence Weekly; Middle East* [London]; *Middle East Economic Digest (MEED)* [London]; *United Nations Chronicle;* and *Washington Post.*)

Glossary

barrels per day—Production of crude oil and petroleum products is frequently measured in barrels per day, often abbreviated bpd or bd. A barrel is a volume measure of forty-two United States gallons. Conversion of barrels to tons depends on the density of the specific product. About 7.3 barrels of average crude oil weigh one ton. Heavy crude would be about seven barrels per ton. Light products, such as gasoline and kerosene, average close to eight barrels per ton.

beg—A tribal leader; term is used by some Turkic-speaking tribes.

development plan—Iran's development plans have been of varying length and had various names. The plans and their dates under Mohammad Reza Shah were as follows: First Development Plan—September 21, 1948, to September 20, 1955; Second Development Plan—September 21, 1955, to September 20, 1962; Third Development Plan—September 21, 1962, to March 20, 1968; Fourth Development Plan—March 21, 1968, to March 20, 1973; and Fifth Development Plan—March 21, 1973, to March 20, 1978. The Sixth Development Plan, beginning March 21, 1978, was never completed because of the 1979 Revolution. The First Development Plan of the Islamic Republic ran from March 21, 1983, through March 20, 1988.

faqih—An expert in religious jurisprudence, specifically a Shia (*q.v.*) cleric whose mastery of the Quran, the traditions of the Prophet and the Twelve Imams, and the codices of Shia Islamic law permit him to render binding interpretations of religious laws and regulations.

fiscal year (FY)—Corresponds to the Iranian calendar year, which begins March 21 and ends March 20.

gross domestic product (GDP)—The total value of goods and services produced within a country's borders during a fixed period, usually one year. Obtained by adding the value contributed by each sector of the economy in the form of compensation of employees, profits, and depreciation (consumption of capital). Subsistence production is included and consists of the imputed value of production by the farm family for its own use and the imputed rental value of owner-occupied dwellings.

gross national product (GNP)—Gross domestic product (*q.v.*) plus the income received from abroad by residents, less payments remitted abroad to nonresidents.

hadith—Tradition based on the precedent of Muhammad's words that serves as one of the sources of Islamic Law (*shariat, q.v.*).

hejab—Modesty in attire; defined by the Shia clergy to mean that women and girls must cover all their hair and flesh except for hands and face when in public. It is not necessary to wear a *chador* (a cloth serving as a cloak) to conform with *hejab*, although the two terms often are equated.

hezbollahi—Literally, a follower of the party of God. *Hezbollahis* originally were followers of a particular religious figure who eventually came to constitute an unofficial political party. They were not an irregular or paramilitary group.

imam—Among Twelver Shias the principal meaning is a designation of one of the twelve legitimate successors of the Prophet Muhammad. Also used by both Shias (*q.v.*) and Sunnis (*q.v.*) to designate a congregational prayer leader or cleric.

International Monetary Fund (IMF)—Established along with the World Bank (*q.v.*) in 1945, the IMF is a specialized agency affiliated with the United Nations and is responsible for stabilizing international exchange rates and payments. The main business of the IMF is the provision of loans to its members (including industrialized and developing countries) when they experience balance of payments difficulties. These loans frequently carry conditions that require substantial internal economic adjustments by the recipients, most of which are developing countries.

Islamic clergy—The religious leaders of Shia (*q.v.*) Islam, which group includes numerous mullahs (*q.v.*), who in general possess only rudimentary religious education; *mujtahids*, a relatively small body of religious scholars, the majority of whom are accorded the title of *hojjatoleslam;* and a small number of the most learned and pious of the *mujtahids*, who are given the title of *ayatollah.*

jihad—The struggle to establish the law of God on earth, often interpreted to mean holy war.

kadkhuda—The village headman in rural Iran; also used as the title for leaders of some tribal clans.

madraseh—A religious college or seminary that trains men in Islamic jurisprudence.

mahriyeh—An agreed upon amount of money and/or property that a groom provides his bride as specified in the marriage contract.

Majlis—the term is used in two senses: the legislative body of imperial Iran, which included both a senate—composed of members appointed by the shah and elected members—and an elected lower house of representatives; and, the lower house alone. The Senate provided for in the constitution did not come into existence until 1950; the Senate was dissolved under Mossadeq but was revived later. Khomeini's revolutionary Constitution of 1979 eliminated the Senate, leaving only the lower house, or Majlis, in existence.

maktab—Primary school operated by Shia clergy.

mostazafin—Literally, the disinherited; originally a religious term for the poor, which has become popularized.

mullah—Generic term for a member of the Islamic clergy; usually refers to a preacher or other low-ranking cleric who has not earned the right to interpret religious laws.

muta—A temporary marriage, the duration of which is stipulated by contract. Only Twelver Shias (*q.v.*) recognize *muta* marriages.

Organization of Petroleum Exporting Countries (OPEC)—Coordinates petroleum policies of thirteen major producing countries. In early 1987 members included Algeria, Ecuador, Gabon, Indonesia, Iran, Iraq, Kuwait, Libya, Nigeria, Qatar, Saudi Arabia, the United Arab Emirates, and Venezuela.

rial—Iranian currency. Average official rate in 1987 was 71.46 rials to US$1. Official exchange rate, as of December 19, 1984, is determined daily based on Special Drawing Right (*q.v.*) rial rate and applies to all foreign exchange transactions. In practice, the unofficial black market rate is as much as ten times the official exchange rate.

shariat (sharia in Arabic)—Islamic canon law. Among Shias (*q.v.*) the *shariat* includes the Quran and the authenticated sayings of the Prophet (hadith) and the Twelve Imams.

shaykh—Leader or chief. Term is used by Iranian Arabs for tribal chiefs and by Lurs and Kurds for religious leaders.

Shia (or Shiite)—A member of the smaller of the two great divisions of Islam. The Shias supported the claims of Ali and his line to presumptive right to the caliphate and leadership of the world Muslim community, and on this issue they divided from the Sunnis (*q.v.*) in the first great schism of Islam. Later schisms have produced further divisions among the Shias.

Special Drawing Right (SDR)—A standardized monetary unit used by the International Monetary Fund (*q.v.*). It is standardized against all currencies using it instead of the home country's currency and is drawn from a pool of contributions by member countries.

Sunni—A member of the larger of the two great divisions of Islam. The Sunnis, who rejected the claim of Ali's line, believe that they are the true followers of the sunna, the guide to proper behavior composed of the Quran and the hadith (*q.v.*).

topping plant—A plant that removes only the lightest commodity from crude oil.

velayat-e faqih—The guardianship of the religious jurist. Concept elaborated by Ayatollah Khomeini to justify political rule by the clergy.

White Revolution—Term used by Mohammad Reza Shah Pahlavi to designate the program of economic and social reforms he initiated in 1963.

World Bank—Informal name used to designate a group of three affiliated international institutions: the International Bank for Reconstruction and Development (IBRD), the International Development Association (IDA), and the International Finance Corporation (IFC). The IBRD, established in 1945, has the primary purpose of providing loans to developing countries for productive projects. The IDA, a legally separate loan fund but administered by the staff of the IBRD, was set up in 1960 to furnish credits to the poorest developing countries on much easier terms than those of conventional IBRD loans. The IFC, founded in 1956, supplements the activities of the IBRD through loans and assistance specifically designed to encourage the growth of productive private enterprises in the less developed countries. The president and certain senior officers of the IBRD hold the same positions in the IFC. The three institutions are owned by the governments of the countries that subscribe their capital. To participate in the World Bank group, member states must first belong to the International Monetary Fund (IMF—*q.v.*).

Index

Abadan refinery, 154, 164, 165
Abbasids, 14
Abu Bakr, 11
Abu Musa: occupation by Iran of, 39, 243, 257
Achaemenid Empire, xxv, 3, 6-9, 238
Ad Dawah, 229
administrative divisions, xviii-xix
Afghanistan: relations of Iran with, 231-32; rule of Iran by, 19-20
Afghan refugees in Iran, 82, 83, 157-58
agriculture, xvii; emphasis under Khomeini regime on, 147, 178; emloyment under Khomeini in, 156, 182; land under cultivation for, 178-79, 181-84
Ahl-e Haqq sect, 125-26
AIOC. See Anglo-Iranian Oil Company (AIOC)
air force: before and after Revolution, 257-59; role in Iran-Iraq War, 278-79
airports, xviii, 177
Alai, Hosain, 269
Alam, Asadollah, 33, 34
Alexander the Great, 3, 9
Algeria, 232
Algiers Agreement (1975), 39, 60, 242-43
Amal. See Islamic Amal
Ahmad Shah, 25
Amini, Ali: leader of exiled Iranian Liberation Front, 215; as prime minister, 32-33
Amnesty International, 42-43, 63, 296
Amuzegar, Jamshid, 43, 44, 146-47
Anglo-Iranian Oil Company (AIOC): concession agreements of, 162-63; dispute with Iran over nationalization of, 29-30, 163; renamed the Consortium, 163; revenues from, 141
Anglo-Persian Agreement (1919), 24
Anglo-Persian Oil Company, 162
Anglo-Russian Agreement (1907), 23-24, 238
Arabic language, 13, 94-96
Arabs: conquest of Iran by, 11, 13; in Khuzestan, 52, 95-96, 295
Arafat, Yasir, 270
Aramaic language, 7
Ardeshir, 9-10

armed forces (see also air force; army; navy), class differences in, 260; control by revolutionary regime of, 280; expenditures for, 281-82; foreign influences on, 262-65; ground forces in Iran-Iraq War, 248; history and importance of, 238-45; Joint Staff of, 251; manpower for, 260-62; organization under Khomeini regime, 250-62; purge of, 247-48
Armenians in Iran, 96-97, 127-28
ARMISH. See United States Army Mission Headquarters (ARMISH)
ARMISH-MAAG, 263
arms production, domestic: regulated after Revolution by DIO, 266; regulated by Pasdaran, 267; regulation of domestic factories by MIO, 265-66
arms suppliers, 38, 40, 232, 263-65, 276
army (see also Islamic Iranian Ground Forces (IIGF)), 255-56
Arsacids or Parthians, 9-10
Artaxerxes I, 7
Assembly of Experts: to consider draft Constitution, 54, 195, 196-97; to determine Khomeini successor, xxvii, 67
Assyrians in Iran, 94-96, 127-28
Atomic Energy Organization of Iran, 175
Azarbaijan Democratic Party, 28-29
Azarbaijani language and people in Iran, 91-92
Azarbaijan rebellion (1946), 241
Azhari, Golam-Reza, 45

Baath Party, 226
Baghdad Pact (see also Central Treaty Organization (CENTO)), 31
Bahais: non-Muslim religious groups, 126-27; persecution of, 297
Bahonar, Hojjatoleslam Mohammad Javad, 208, 211
Bahrain: becomes independent state, 39; relations with Iran, 228-30
Bakhtiar, Shahpour: as exiled leader of National Resistance Movement, 48, 215; government of, 46-48
Bakhtiar, Teymur, 288

333

Progressive Center. *See* Iran Novin (New Iran) Party; Hasan Ali Mansur

Prophet Muhammad, 11, 116, 118

prosthetics manufacture, 169

provisional government, 204, 206

public health, 133-34

Qajar dynasty, xxvi, 4, 20-22; armed forces of, 238-39; nomads under, 108

qanat system: destruction in Mongol invasion of, 15; importance for agriculture of, 179

Qashqais, 92-94

Qotbzadeh, Sadeq, 49, 58, 61, 64

Rabii, Amir Hosain, 246

Rafsenjani, Ali Akbar, *See* Hashemi-Rafsanjani, Hojjatoleslam Ali Akbar.

Rahmani, Hojjatoleslam, 270

railroad facilities, xviii, 175, 177, 189

Rajai, Mohammad Ali: death of, 63; as president of Islamic Republic, 199, 208, 249; as prime minister under Bani Sadr, 207-8

Rajavi, Masud: escapes to France, 62; forms Iranian National Army of Liberation, 292-93; leader of Mojahedin, 213, 216; loses favor with Khomeini, 291-92

Rastakhiz Party, 44, 210, 211

RCD. *See* Regional Cooperation for Development (RCD)

Reagan, Ronald, xxxi, 59

reconstruction (*see also* Crusade for Reconstruction), xxxii

refugees: from Afghanistan, 82-83, 157-58; to cities, xxix; from Iraq, 83

Regional Cooperation for Development (RCD), 38, 188-89

religion (*see also* Christians; Muslims; Shia Islam; Sunni Islam), xvi

religious groups: anti-government demonstrations by, 43-45; and institutions, 118-23; leaders of anti-shah groups, 286-87; in opposition to political organizations, 53; opposition to secular reforms, 26, 33-34, 38

religious hierarchy, 25, 123

Reuter, Baron Julius de: business dealings in Iran of, 22

revolution, Iran. *See* Constitutional Revolution; Islamic Revolution

Revolutionary Council: Bani Sadr as chairman of, 49, 55-56; power of, 49-53, 58; during provisional government, 204, 206, 247; during Revolution, 204

revolutionary courts, 50-51; failure of Bani Sadr to control, 57; incorporated into court system, 67

Revolutionary Guards. *See* Pasdaran

revolutionary organizations: legitimization of, 66-67; terror and repression by, 60-65, 208-9

Reza Cyrus Pahlavi (Shah Reza II), 37, 215

Rezai, Mohsen, 271

Reza Khan. *See* Reza Shah Pahlavi (Reza Khan)

Reza Shah Pahlavi (Reza Khan): centralized economic planning under, 141-42; modernization under, xxvi, 139, 177; oil policy of, 141; reforms of, 4-5, 25-27, 108, 139-40, 142-45; as Reza Khan seizes power, xxv, 24-25; role in creating armed forces, 239-40

roads, xvii, 177

Rome, 10

rural society, 104-7

Russia: effect of wars with, 20-21; interference with Iran by, 20-24

Sadr, Musa as, 233

Safavid empire, xxvi, 4, 16

Saffarids, 14

Samanids, 14

sanitation, 134

Sassanids, xxv, 3, 10-11

Satja, 223

satrapy system, 7

Saudi Arabia: relations of Iran with, 39-40, 228, 230-31; support of Iraq in Iran-Iraq War, xxx

SAVAK: dissolution, 289; officers executed, 247; under reign of Mohammad Reza Shah Pahlavi, xxvi, 32, 288-89

SAVAMA: relation with Pasdaran, 270; successor to SAVAK, 289-90

schools: after Islamic Revolution, 131; evolution of system of, 129-32; medical, 133; nationalization of, 42, 130; under Reza Shah Pahlavi, 25; run by clergy, 119-20, 129-30

Scythians, 5-6
SDC. *See* Supreme Defense Council (SDC)
secret police. *See* SAVAK
secular law, 26
security, internal, 285-90
segregation by sex, 112-13
Seleucids, 9
self-reliance program, 139, 140, 178, 182-83
Seljuk Turks, 3, 14-15
Semitic languages in Iran, 94-96
sexes. *See* segregation; women
shah. *See* Mohammad Reza Shah Pahlavi; Reza Shah Pahlavi
Shah Abbas, 18-19
Shahpur I, 10
Shariatmadari: arrest and trial of, 64-65; political opposition of, 49, 54
Sharif-Emami, Jafar, 44, 45
Shia Islam (*see also* jihad), among Arabs in Iran, 95; as Azarbaijani and Qashqai religion, 92; beliefs of, 114-18; clergy as political leaders, 73-74, 99; clergy's position in society, 97; constitution establishes domination by clergy of, 54, 73; form of temporary marriage in, 112; origin of, 13-14; under Safavid empire, 4, 16, 18, 115; unorthodox sects in, 124-26
Shia population in Lebanon, 233
shrines, 122-23
silica, 170
Sirri Island, 154-55, 161
social structure, 97-114
society in Iran, 97-115
South Persia Rifles, 24, 239
Soviet Union: arms shipments to Iraq by, 276; occupation of Iran by, 27; officers in Iran, 262; relations of Iran with, 225-26, 31-32, 38; trade with, 189
Status of Forces bill, 35
Strait of Hormuz, 237, 242, 257, 278
Sufism, xxvi, 124-25
sugar, 183-84
Sullivan, William, 48
Sumerian influence, 5
Sunni Islam, 18, 126; among Iranian Arabs, 95-96; beliefs of, 115-16; religion of Baluchis, 88
Supreme Defense Council (SDC), 250
Susiana. *See* Elamites; Khuzestan Province

Sweden, 262
Syria, 232-33

TAFT. *See* technical assistance field team (TAFT)
Tahirids, 14
Tajiks, 90
Tamerlane (Timur the Lame), xxv, 4, 16
tanker war, 228, 277-79
Tavakkoli, Nasrollah, 246
tax system. *See* fiscal policy
technical assistance field team (TAFT), 263
Tehran Conference, 27-28
telecommunications, xviii, 177-78
terrorism, 208-9
theocracy under Islamic Republic, xxvii, 209-10
topography, 75-76
tourism, 177
trade. *See* foreign trade
trading partners. *See* barter agreements
Trans-Persian Railway: construction of, 139; effect of expansion of, 142
transportation system, 142, 164-65, 175-77
Treaty of Brest-Litovsk (1917), 239
Treaty of Gulistan (1812), 20
Treaty of Paris (1857), 21
Treaty of Qasr-e Shirin (1639), 18
Treaty of Turkmanchay (1828), 20
tribal confederations, 108-9
Trucial States federation, 39
Truman, Harry S, 30
Tudeh Party, 40, 210, 213, 246-47; collaboration with Soviet Union of, 28-29; in exile, 217; Khomeini against, 66; opposition to shah of, 285-86
Tunbs, Greater and Lesser: occupation by Iran of, 39, 243, 257
Tunisia, 232
Turkey, 38, 231
Turkic-speaking groups (*see also* Seljuk Turks), 91-94
Turkomans, 52, 295
Twelvers. *See* Shia Islam

UAE. *See* United Arab Emirates (UAE)
Umayyad dynasty, xxv, 13-14
underground groups: for armed action, 41
unemployment, 156, 157

Published Country Studies

(Area Handbook Series)

550-65	Afghanistan		550-153	Ghana
550-98	Albania		550-87	Greece
550-44	Algeria		550-78	Guatemala
550-59	Angola		550-174	Guinea
550-73	Argentina		550-82	Guyana
550-169	Australia		550-151	Honduras
550-176	Austria		550-165	Hungary
550-175	Bangladesh		550-21	India
550-170	Belgium		550-154	Indian Ocean
550-66	Bolivia		550-39	Indonesia
550-20	Brazil		550-68	Iran
550-168	Bulgaria		550-31	Iraq
550-61	Burma		550-25	Israel
550-37	Burundi/Rwanda		550-182	Italy
550-50	Cambodia		550-30	Japan
550-166	Cameroon		550-34	Jordan
550-159	Chad		550-56	Kenya
550-77	Chile		550-81	Korea, North
550-60	China		550-41	Korea, South
550-26	Colombia		550-58	Laos
550-33	Commonwealth Caribbean, Islands of the		550-24	Lebanon
550-91	Congo		550-38	Liberia
550-90	Costa Rica		550-85	Libya
550-69	Côte d'Ivoire (Ivory Coast)		550-172	Malawi
550-152	Cuba		550-45	Malaysia
550-22	Cyprus		550-161	Mauritania
550-158	Czechoslovakia		550-79	Mexico
550-36	Dominican Republic/Haiti		550-76	Mongolia
550-52	Ecuador		550-49	Morocco
550-43	Egypt		550-64	Mozambique
550-150	El Salvador		550-88	Nicaragua
550-28	Ethiopia		550-157	Nigeria
550-167	Finland		550-94	Oceania
550-155	Germany, East		550-48	Pakistan
550-173	Germany, Fed. Rep. of		550-46	Panama

550-156	Paraguay	550-89	Tunisia
550-185	Persian Gulf States	550-80	Turkey
550-42	Peru	550-74	Uganda
550-72	Philippines	550-97	Uruguay
550-162	Poland	550-71	Venezuela
550-181	Portugal	550-32	Vietnam
550-160	Romania	550-183	Yemens, The
550-51	Saudi Arabia	550-99	Yugloslavia
550-70	Senegal	550-67	Zaire
550-180	Sierra Leone	550-75	Zambia
550-184	Singapore	550-171	Zimbabwe
550-86	Somalia		
550-93	South Africa		
550-95	Soviet Union		
550-179	Spain		
500-96	Sri Lanka		
550-27	Sudan		
550-47	Syria		
550-62	Tanzania		
550-53	Thailand		

☆U.S. GOVERNMENT PRINTING OFFICE: 1989 242-444 00011

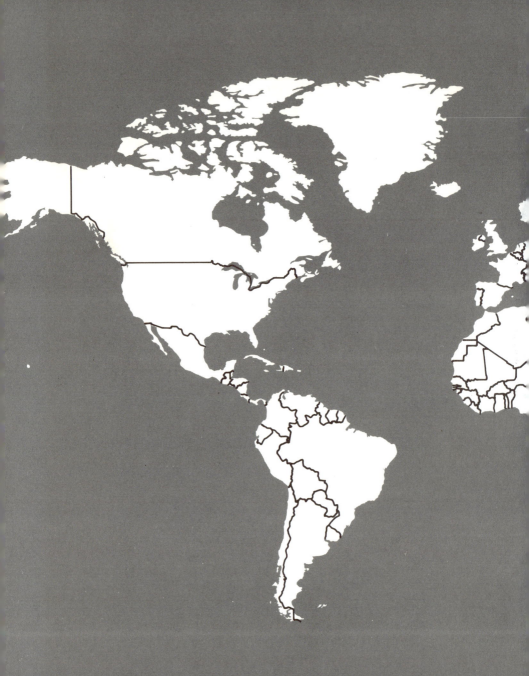